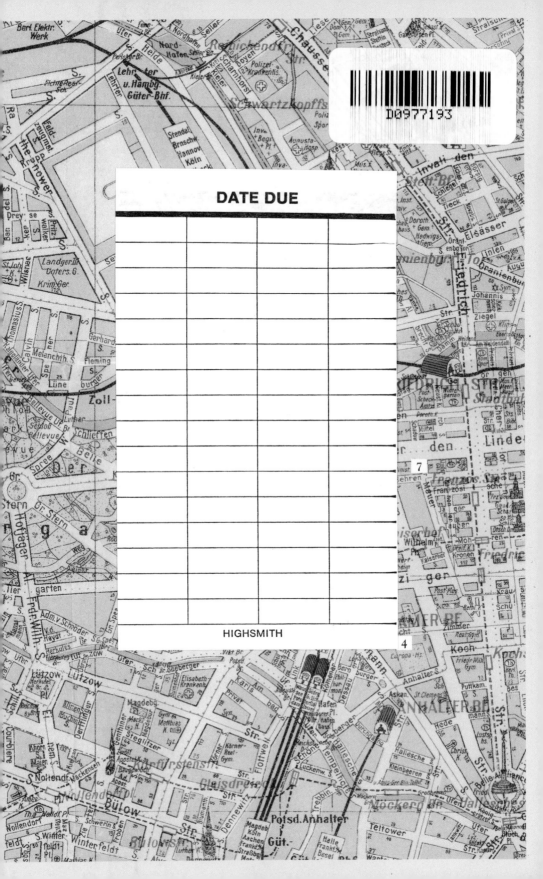

DATE DUE

IN THE GARDEN OF BEASTS

Also by Erik Larson

Thunderstruck

The Devil in the White City

Isaac's Storm

Lethal Passage

The Naked Consumer

LOVE, TERROR,
AND AN AMERICAN FAMILY IN
HITLER'S BERLIN

CROWN
NEW YORK

IN THE GARDEN OF BEASTS

ERIK LARSON

Copyright © 2011 by Erik Larson

Published in the United States by Crown Publishers, an imprint of the Crown Publishing Group, a division of Random House, Inc., New York.

www.crownpublishing.com

CROWN and the Crown colophon are registered trademarks of Random House, Inc.

Endpapers © Pharus-Plan, Berlin
Photo credits appear on page 435.

Library of Congress Cataloging-in-Publication Data
Larson, Erik.
    In the garden of beasts : love, terror, and an American family in Hitler's Berlin / by Erik Larson.—1st ed.
       p.   cm.
    Includes bibliographical references.
    1. Dodd, William Edward, 1869–1940. 2. Diplomats—United States—Biography. 3. Historians—United States—Biography. 4. Germany—Social conditions—1933–1945. 5. National socialism—Germany. I. Title.
    E748.D6L37 2011
    943.086—dc22

                             2010045402

ISBN 978-0-307-40884-6
eISBN 978-0-307-88795-5

PRINTED IN THE UNITED STATES OF AMERICA

Book design by Elina Nudelman
Jacket design by Whitney Cookman
Jacket photograph © The Art Archive/Marc Charmet

10   9   8

To the girls, and the
next twenty-five

(and in memory of Molly, a good dog)

CONTENTS

In the middle of the journey of our life I came to myself in a dark wood where the straight way was lost.

—DANTE ALIGHIERI,
The Divine Comedy: Canto I
(Carlyle-Wicksteed Translation, 1932)

Das Vorspiel

prelude; overture; prologue; preliminary match; foreplay; performance; practical (exam); audition; das ist erst das ~ *that is just for starters*

—Collins German Unabridged Dictionary
(seventh edition, 2007)

Once, at the dawn of a very dark time, an American father and daughter found themselves suddenly transported from their snug home in Chicago to the heart of Hitler's Berlin. They remained there for four and a half years, but it is their first year that is the subject of the story to follow, for it coincided with Hitler's ascent from chancellor to absolute tyrant, when everything hung in the balance and nothing was certain. That first year formed a kind of prologue in which all the themes of the greater epic of war and murder soon to come were laid down.

I have always wondered what it would have been like for an outsider to have witnessed firsthand the gathering dark of Hitler's rule. How did the city look, what did one hear, see, and smell, and how did diplomats and other visitors interpret the events occurring around them? Hindsight tells us that during that fragile time the course of history could so easily have been changed. Why, then, did no one change it? Why did it take so long to recognize the real danger posed by Hitler and his regime?

Like most people, I acquired my initial sense of the era from books and photographs that left me with the impression that the world of then had no color, only gradients of gray and black. My two main protagonists, however, encountered the flesh-and-blood reality, while also managing the routine obligations of daily life. Every morning they moved through a city hung with immense banners of red, white, and black; they sat at the same outdoor cafés as did the lean, black-suited members of Hitler's SS, and now and then they caught sight of Hitler himself, a smallish man in a large, open Mercedes. But they also walked each day past homes with balconies lush with red geraniums; they shopped in the city's vast department stores, held tea parties, and breathed deep the spring fragrances of the Tiergarten, Berlin's main park. They knew Goebbels and Göring as social acquaintances with whom they dined, danced, and joked—until, as their first year reached its end, an event occurred that proved to be one of the most significant in revealing the true character of Hitler and that laid the keystone for the decade to come. For both father and daughter it changed everything.

This is a work of nonfiction. As always, any material between quotation marks comes from a letter, diary, memoir, or other historical document. I made no effort in these pages to write another grand history of the age. My objective was more intimate: to reveal that past world through the experience and perceptions of my two primary subjects, father and daughter, who upon arrival in Berlin embarked on a journey of discovery, transformation, and, ultimately, deepest heartbreak.

There are no heroes here, at least not of the *Schindler's List* variety, but there are glimmers of heroism and people who behave with unexpected grace. Always there is nuance, albeit sometimes of a disturbing nature. That's the trouble with nonfiction. One has to put aside what we all know—*now*—to be true, and try instead to accompany my two innocents through the world as they experienced it.

These were complicated people moving through a complicated time, before the monsters declared their true nature.

—Erik Larson
Seattle

1933

The Man Behind
the Curtain

It was common for American expatriates to visit the U.S. consulate in Berlin, but not in the condition exhibited by the man who arrived there on Thursday, June 29, 1933. He was Joseph Schachno, thirty-one years old, a physician from New York who until recently had been practicing medicine in a suburb of Berlin. Now he stood naked in one of the curtained examination rooms on the first floor of the consulate where on more routine days a public-health surgeon would examine visa applicants seeking to immigrate to the United States. The skin had been flayed from much of his body.

Two consular officials arrived and entered the examination room. One was George S. Messersmith, America's consul general for Germany since 1930 (no relation to Wilhelm "Willy" Messerschmitt, the German aircraft engineer). As the senior Foreign Service man in Berlin, Messersmith oversaw the ten American consulates located in cities throughout Germany. Beside him stood his vice consul, Raymond Geist. As a rule Geist was cool and unflappable, an ideal subaltern, but Messersmith registered the fact that Geist looked pale and deeply shaken.

Both men were appalled by Schachno's condition. "From the neck down to his heels he was a mass of raw flesh," Messersmith saw. "He had been beaten with whips and in every possible way until his flesh was literally raw and bleeding. I took one look and got as quickly as I could to one of the basins where the [public health surgeon] washed his hands."

The beating, Messersmith learned, had occurred nine days earlier, yet the wounds were still vivid. "From the shoulder blades to his knees, after nine days there were still stripes showing that he had been beaten from both sides. His buttocks were practically raw and large areas thereof still without any skin over them. The flesh had at places been practically reduced to a pulp."

If this was nine days later, Messersmith wondered, what had the wounds been like immediately after the beating had been delivered?

The story emerged:

On the night of June 21, Schachno had been visited at his home by a squad of uniformed men responding to an anonymous denunciation of him as a potential enemy of the state. The men searched the place, and although they found nothing, they took him to their headquarters. Schachno was ordered to undress and immediately subjected to a severe and prolonged beating by two men with a whip. Afterward, he was released. He somehow made his way to his home, and then he and his wife fled to central Berlin, to the residence of his wife's mother. He lay in bed for a week. As soon as he felt able, he went to the consulate.

Messersmith ordered him taken to a hospital and that day issued him a new U.S. passport. Soon afterward, Schachno and his wife fled to Sweden and then to America.

There had been beatings and arrests of American citizens ever since Hitler's appointment as chancellor in January, but nothing as severe as this—though thousands of native Germans had experienced equally severe treatment, and often far worse. For Messersmith it was yet another indicator of the reality of life under Hitler. He understood that all this violence represented more than a passing spasm of atrocity. Something fundamental had changed in Germany.

He understood it, but he was convinced that few others in America did. He was growing increasingly disturbed by the difficulty of persuading the world of the true magnitude of Hitler's threat. It was utterly clear to him that Hitler was in fact secretly and aggressively girding Germany for a war of conquest. "I wish it were really possible to make our people at home understand," he wrote in a June 1933 dispatch to the State Department, "for I feel that they should understand it, how definitely this martial spirit is being developed in Germany. If this Government remains in power for another year and carries on in the same measure in this direction, it will go far towards making Germany a danger to world peace for years to come."

He added: "With few exceptions, the men who are running this Government are of a mentality that you and I cannot understand. Some of them are psychopathic cases and would ordinarily be receiving treatment somewhere."

But Germany still did not have a U.S. ambassador in residence. The former ambassador, Frederic M. Sackett, had left in March, upon the inauguration of Franklin D. Roosevelt as America's new president. (Inauguration day in 1933 took place on March 4.) For nearly four months the post had been vacant, and the new appointee was not expected to arrive for another three weeks. Messersmith had no firsthand knowledge of the man, only what he had heard from his many contacts in the State Department. What he did know was that the new ambassador would be entering a cauldron of brutality, corruption, and zealotry and would need to be a man of forceful character capable of projecting American interest and power, for power was all that Hitler and his men understood.

And yet the new man was said to be an unassuming sort who had vowed to lead a modest life in Berlin as a gesture to his fellow Americans left destitute by the Depression. Incredibly, the new ambassador was even shipping his own car to Berlin—a beat-up old Chevrolet—to underscore his frugality. This in a city where Hitler's men drove about town in giant black touring cars each nearly the size of a city bus.

PART I

Into the Wood

The Dodds arrive in Hamburg.

CHAPTER 1

Means of Escape

The telephone call that forever changed the lives of the Dodd family of Chicago came at noon on Thursday, June 8, 1933, as William E. Dodd sat at his desk at the University of Chicago.

Now chairman of the history department, Dodd had been a professor at the university since 1909, recognized nationally for his work on the American South and for a biography of Woodrow Wilson. He was sixty-four years old, trim, five feet eight inches tall, with blue-gray eyes and light brown hair. Though his face at rest tended to impart severity, he in fact had a sense of humor that was lively, dry, and easily ignited. He had a wife, Martha, known universally as Mattie, and two children, both in their twenties. His daughter, also named Martha, was twenty-four years old; his son, William Jr.—Bill—was twenty-eight.

By all counts they were a happy family and a close one. Not rich by any means, but well off, despite the economic depression then gripping the nation. They lived in a large house at 5757 Blackstone Avenue in Chicago's Hyde Park neighborhood, a few blocks from the university. Dodd also owned—and every summer tended—a small farm in Round Hill, Virginia, which, according to a county survey, had 386.6 acres, "more or less," and was where Dodd, a Jeffersonian democrat of the first stripe, felt most at home, moving among his twenty-one Guernsey heifers; his four geldings, Bill, Coley, Mandy, and Prince; his Farmall tractor; and his horse-drawn Syracuse plows. He made coffee in a Maxwell House can atop his old wood-burning stove. His wife was not as fond of the place and was more than happy to let him spend time there by himself while the rest of the family remained behind in Chicago. Dodd named the farm Stoneleigh, because of all the rocks strewn across its expanse, and spoke of it the way other men spoke of first loves. "The fruit is so beautiful, almost flawless, red and luscious, as we look at it, the trees still bending under the weight of their burden," he wrote one fine night during the apple harvest. "It all appeals to me."

Though generally not given to cliché, Dodd described the telephone call as a "sudden surprise out of a clear sky." This was, however, something of an exaggeration. Over the preceding several months there had been talk among his friends that one day a call like this might come. It was the precise nature of the call that startled Dodd, and troubled him.

FOR SOME TIME NOW, Dodd had been unhappy in his position at the university. Though he loved teaching history, he loved writing it more, and for years he had been working on what he expected would be the definitive recounting of early southern history, a four-volume series that he called *The Rise and Fall of the Old South*, but time and again he had found his progress stymied by the routine demands of his job. Only the first volume was near completion, and he was of an age when he feared he would be buried alongside the unfinished remainder. He had negotiated a reduced schedule with his department, but as is so often the case with such artificial ententes, it did not work in the manner he had hoped. Staff departures and financial pressures within the university associated with the Depression had left him working just as hard as ever, dealing with university officials, preparing lectures, and confronting the engulfing needs of graduate students. In a letter to the university's Department of Buildings and Grounds dated October 31, 1932, he pleaded for heat in his office on Sundays so he could have at least one day to devote to uninterrupted writing. To a friend he described his position as "embarrassing."

Adding to his dissatisfaction was his belief that he should have been further along in his career than he was. What had kept him from advancing at a faster clip, he complained to his wife, was the fact that he had not grown up in a life of privilege and instead had been compelled to work hard for all that he achieved, unlike others in his field who had advanced more quickly. And indeed, he had reached his position in life the hard way. Born on October 21, 1869, at his parents' home in the tiny hamlet of Clayton, North Carolina, Dodd entered the bottom stratum of white southern society, which still adhered to the class conventions of the antebellum era. His father, John D. Dodd, was a barely literate subsistence farmer; his mother, Evelyn Creech, was descended from a more exalted strain of North Carolina stock and deemed to have married down. The couple raised cotton on land given to them by Evelyn's father and barely made a living. In the years after the Civil War, as cotton production soared and prices sank, the family fell steadily into debt to the town's general store, owned by a relative of Evelyn's who was one of Clayton's three men of privilege—"hard men," Dodd called them: ". . . traders and aristocratic masters of their dependents!"

Dodd was one of seven children and spent his youth working the family's land. Although he saw the work as honorable, he did not wish to spend the rest of his life farming and recognized that the only way a man of his lowly background could avoid this fate was by gaining an education. He fought his way upward, at times focusing so closely on his studies that other students dubbed him "Monk Dodd." In February 1891 he entered Virginia Agricultural and Mechanical College (later Virginia Tech). There too he was a sober, focused presence. Other students indulged in such pranks as painting the college president's cow and staging fake duels so as to convince freshmen that they had killed their adversaries. Dodd only studied. He got his bachelor's degree in 1895 and his master's in 1897, when he was twenty-six years old.

At the encouragement of a revered faculty member, and with a loan from a kindly great-uncle, Dodd in June 1897 set off for Germany and the University of Leipzig to begin studies toward a doctorate. He brought his bicycle. He chose to focus his dissertation on Thomas Jefferson, despite the obvious difficulty of acquiring eighteenth-century American documents in Germany. Dodd did his necessary classwork and found archives of relevant materials in London and Berlin. He also did a lot of traveling, often on his bicycle, and time after time was struck by the atmosphere of militarism that pervaded Germany. At one point one of his favorite professors led a discussion on the question "How helpless would the United States be if invaded by a great German army?" All this Prussian bellicosity made Dodd uneasy. He wrote, "There was too much war spirit everywhere."

Dodd returned to North Carolina in late autumn 1899 and after months of search at last got an instructor's position at Randolph-Macon College in Ashland, Virginia. He also renewed a friendship with a young woman named Martha Johns, the daughter of a well-off landowner who lived near Dodd's hometown. The friendship blossomed into romance and on Christmas Eve 1901, they married.

At Randolph-Macon, Dodd promptly got himself into hot water. In 1902 he published an article in the *Nation* in which he attacked a successful campaign by the Grand Camp of Confederate Veterans to have Virginia ban a history textbook that the veterans deemed an affront to southern honor. Dodd charged that the veterans believed the only valid histories were those that held that the South "was altogether right in seceding from the Union."

The backlash was immediate. An attorney prominent in the veterans' movement launched a drive to have Dodd fired from Randolph-Macon. The school gave Dodd its full support. A year later he attacked the veterans again, this time in a speech before the American Historical Society in which he decried their efforts to "put out of the schools any and all books which do not come up to their standard of local patriotism." He railed that "to remain silent is out of the question for a strong and honest man."

Dodd's stature as a historian grew, and so too did his family. His son was born in 1905, his daughter in 1908. Recognizing that an increase in salary would come in handy and that pressure from his southern foes was unlikely to abate, Dodd put his name in the running for an opening at the University of Chicago. He got the job, and in the frigid January of 1909, when he was thirty-nine years old, he and his family made their way to Chicago, where he would remain for the next quarter century. In October 1912, feeling the pull of his heritage and a need to establish his own credibility as a true Jeffersonian democrat, he bought his farm. The grueling work that had so worn on him during his boyhood now became for him both a soul-saving diversion and a romantic harking back to America's past.

Dodd also discovered in himself an abiding interest in the political life, triggered in earnest when in August 1916 he found himself in the Oval Office of the White House for a meeting with President Woodrow Wilson. The encounter, according to one biographer, "profoundly altered his life."

Dodd had grown deeply uneasy about signs that America was sliding toward intervention in the Great War then being fought in Europe. His experience in Leipzig had left him no doubt that Germany alone was responsible for starting the war, in satisfaction of the yearnings of Germany's industrialists and aristocrats, the Junkers, whom he likened to the southern aristocracy before the Civil War. Now he saw the emergence of a similar hubris on the part of America's own industrial and military elites. When an army general tried to include the University of Chicago in a national campaign to ready the nation for war, Dodd bridled and took his complaint directly to the commander in chief.

Dodd wanted only ten minutes of Wilson's time but got far more and found himself as thoroughly charmed as if he'd been the recipient of a potion in a fairy tale. He came to believe that Wilson was correct in advocating U.S. intervention in the war. For Dodd, Wilson became the modern embodiment of Jefferson. Over the next seven years, he and Wilson became friends; Dodd wrote Wilson's biography. Upon Wilson's death on February 3, 1924, Dodd fell into deep mourning.

At length he came to see Franklin Roosevelt as Wilson's equal and threw himself behind Roosevelt's 1932 campaign, speaking and writing on his behalf whenever an opportunity arose. If he had hopes of becoming a member of Roosevelt's inner circle, however, Dodd soon found himself disappointed, consigned to the increasingly dissatisfying duties of an academic chair.

NOW HE WAS sixty-four years old, and the way he would leave his mark on the world would be with his history of the old South, which also happened to be the one thing that every force in the universe seemed aligned to defeat, including the university's policy of not heating buildings on Sundays.

More and more he considered leaving the university for some position that would allow him time to write, "before it is too late." The idea occurred to him that an ideal job might be an undemanding post within the State Department, perhaps as an ambassador in Brussels or The Hague. He believed that he was sufficiently prominent to be considered for such a position, though he tended to see himself as far more influential in national affairs than in fact he was. He had written often to advise Roosevelt on economic and political matters, both before and immediately after Roosevelt's victory. It surely galled Dodd that soon after the election he received from the White House a form letter stating that while the president wanted every letter to his office answered promptly, he could not himself reply to all of them in a timely manner and thus had asked his secretary to do so in his stead.

Dodd did, however, have several good friends who were close to Roosevelt, including the new secretary of commerce, Daniel Roper. Dodd's son and daughter were to Roper like nephew and niece, sufficiently close that Dodd had no compunction about dispatching his son as intermediary to ask Roper whether the new administration might see fit to appoint Dodd as minister to Belgium or the Netherlands. "These are posts where the government must have somebody, yet the work is not heavy," Dodd told his son. He confided that he was motivated mainly by his need to complete his *Old South*. "I am not desirous of any appointment from Roosevelt but I am very anxious not to be defeated in a life-long purpose."

In short, Dodd wanted a sinecure, a job that was not too demanding yet that would provide stature and a living wage and, most important, leave him plenty of time to write—this despite his recognition that serving as a diplomat was not something to which his character was well suited. "As to high diplomacy (London, Paris, Berlin) I am not the kind," he wrote to his wife early in 1933. "I am distressed that this is so on your account. I simply am not the sly, two-faced type so necessary to 'lie abroad for the country.' If I were, I might go to Berlin and bend the knee to Hitler—and relearn German." But, he added, "why waste time writing about such a subject? Who would care to live in Berlin the next four years?"

Whether because of his son's conversation with Roper or the play of other forces, Dodd's name soon was in the wind. On March 15, 1933, during a sojourn at his Virginia farm, he went to Washington to meet with Roosevelt's new secretary of state, Cordell Hull, whom he had met on a number of previous occasions. Hull was tall and silver haired, with a cleft chin and strong jaw. Outwardly, he seemed the physical embodiment of all that a secretary of state should be, but those who knew him better understood that when angered he had a most unstatesmanlike penchant for releasing torrents of profanity and that he suffered a speech impediment that turned his *r*'s to *w*'s in the manner of the cartoon character Elmer Fudd—a trait that Roosevelt now and then made fun of privately, as when he once spoke of Hull's "twade tweaties." Hull, as usual, had four or five red pencils in his shirt pocket, his favored tools of state. He raised the possibility of Dodd receiving an appointment to Holland or Belgium, exactly what Dodd had hoped for. But now, suddenly forced to imagine the day-to-day reality of what such a life would entail, Dodd balked. "After considerable study of the situation," he wrote in his little pocket diary, "I told Hull I could not take such a position."

But his name remained in circulation.

And now, on that Thursday in June, his telephone began to ring. As he held the receiver to his ear, he heard a voice he recognized immediately.

CHAPTER 2

That Vacancy in Berlin

No one wanted the job. What had seemed one of the least challenging tasks facing Franklin D. Roosevelt as newly elected president had, by June 1933, become one of the most intransigent. As ambassadorial posts went, Berlin should have been a plum—not London or Paris, surely, but still one of the great capitals of Europe, and at the center of a country going through revolutionary change under the leadership of its newly appointed chancellor, Adolf Hitler. Depending on one's point of view, Germany was experiencing a great revival or a savage darkening. Upon Hitler's ascent, the country had undergone a brutal spasm of state-condoned violence. Hitler's brown-shirted paramilitary army, the Sturmabteilung, or SA—the Storm Troopers—had gone wild, arresting, beating, and in some cases murdering communists, socialists, and Jews. Storm Troopers established impromptu prisons and torture stations in basements, sheds, and other structures. Berlin alone had fifty of these so-called bunkers. Tens of thousands of people were arrested and placed in "protective custody"—*Schutzhaft*—a risible euphemism. An estimated five hundred to seven hundred prisoners died in custody; others endured "mock drownings and hangings," according to a police affidavit. One prison near Tempelhof Airport became especially notorious: Columbia House, not to be confused with a sleekly modern new building at the heart of Berlin called Columbus House. The upheaval prompted one Jewish leader, Rabbi Stephen S. Wise of New York, to tell a friend, "the frontiers of civilization have been crossed."

Roosevelt made his first attempt to fill the Berlin post on March 9,

1933, less than a week after taking office and just as the violence in Germany reached a peak of ferocity. He offered it to James M. Cox, who in 1920 had been a candidate for president with Roosevelt as his running mate.

In a letter laced with flattery, Roosevelt wrote, "It is not only because of my affection for you but also because I think you are singularly fitted to this key place, that I want much to send your name to the Senate as American Ambassador to Germany. I hope much that you will accept after talking it over with your delightful wife, who, by the way, would be perfect as the wife of the Ambassador. Do send me a telegram saying yes."

Cox said no: the demands of his various business interests, including several newspapers, compelled him to decline. He made no mention of the violence wracking Germany.

Roosevelt set the matter aside to confront the nation's worsening economic crisis, the Great Depression, which by that spring had put a third of the nation's nonagricultural labor force out of work and had cut the gross national product in half; he did not return to the problem until at least a month later, when he offered the job to Newton Baker, who had been secretary of war under Woodrow Wilson and was now a partner in a Cleveland law firm. Baker also declined. So did a third man, Owen D. Young, a prominent businessman. Next Roosevelt tried Edward J. Flynn, a key figure in the Democratic Party and a major supporter. Flynn talked it over with his wife "and we agreed that, because of the age of our small children, such an appointment would be impossible."

At one point Roosevelt joked to a member of the Warburg family, "You know, Jimmy, it would serve that fellow Hitler right if I sent a Jew to Berlin as my ambassador. How would you like the job?"

Now, with the advent of June, a deadline pressed. Roosevelt was engaged in an all-consuming fight to pass his National Industrial Recovery Act, a centerpiece of his New Deal, in the face of fervent opposition by a core group of powerful Republicans. Early in the month, with Congress just days away from its summer adjournment, the bill seemed on the verge of passage but was still under assault by Republicans and some Democrats, who launched salvos of proposed amendments and forced the Senate into marathon sessions. Roosevelt feared that the longer the battle dragged on, the more likely the bill was to fail or be severely weakened, in part because any extension of the congressional session meant risking the wrath of legislators intent on leaving Washington for summer vacation. Everyone was growing cranky. A late-spring heat wave had driven temperatures to record levels throughout the nation at a cost of over a hundred lives. Washington steamed; men stank. A three-column headline on the front page of the *New York Times* read, "ROOSEVELT TRIMS PROGRAM TO HASTEN END OF SESSION; SEES HIS POLICIES MENACED."

Herein lay a conflict: Congress was required to confirm and fund new ambassadors. The sooner Congress adjourned, the greater the pressure on Roosevelt to choose a new man for Berlin. Thus, he now found himself compelled to consider candidates outside the bounds of the usual patronage choices, including the presidents of at least three colleges and an ardent pacifist named Harry Emerson Fosdick, the Baptist pastor of Riverside Church in Manhattan. None of these seemed ideal, however; none was offered the job.

On Wednesday, June 7, with the congressional adjournment just days away, Roosevelt met with several close advisers and mentioned his frustration at not being able to find a new ambassador. One of those in attendance was Commerce Secretary Roper, whom Roosevelt now and then referred to as "Uncle Dan."

Roper thought a moment and threw out a fresh name, that of a longtime friend: "How about William E. Dodd?"

"Not a bad idea," Roosevelt said, although whether he truly thought so at that instant was by no means clear. Ever affable, Roosevelt was prone to promise things he did not necessarily intend to deliver.

Roosevelt said, "I'll consider it."

DODD WAS ANYTHING BUT the typical candidate for a diplomatic post. He wasn't rich. He wasn't politically influential. He wasn't one of Roosevelt's friends. But he did speak German and was said to know the country well. One potential problem was his past allegiance to Woodrow Wilson, whose belief in engaging other nations on the world stage was anathema to the growing camp of Americans who insisted that the United States avoid entangling itself in the affairs of foreign nations. These "isolationists," led by William Borah of Idaho and Hiram Johnson of California, had become increasingly noisy and powerful. Polls showed that 95 percent of Americans wanted the United States to avoid involvement in any foreign war. Although Roosevelt himself favored international engagement, he kept his views on the subject veiled so as not to impede the advance of his domestic agenda. Dodd, however, seemed unlikely to spark the isolationists' passions. He was a historian of sober temperament, and his firsthand understanding of Germany had obvious value.

Berlin, moreover, was not yet the supercharged outpost it would become within the year. There existed at this time a widespread perception that Hitler's government could not possibly endure. Germany's military power was limited—its army, the Reichswehr, had only one hundred thousand men, no match for the military forces of neighboring France, let alone the combined might of France, England, Poland, and the Soviet Union. And Hitler himself had begun to seem like a more temperate actor than might have been predicted given the violence that had swept Germany earlier in the year. On May 10, 1933, the Nazi Party burned unwelcome books—Einstein, Freud, the brothers Mann, and many others—in great pyres throughout Germany, but seven days later Hitler declared himself committed to peace and went so far as to pledge complete disarmament if other countries followed suit. The world swooned with relief. Against the broader backdrop of the challenges facing Roosevelt—global depression, another year of crippling drought—Germany seemed more an irritant than anything else. What Roosevelt and Secretary Hull considered the most pressing German problem was the $1.2 billion that Germany owed to American creditors, a debt that Hitler's regime seemed increasingly unwilling to pay.

No one appeared to give much thought to the kind of personality a man might need in order to deal effectively with Hitler's government. Secretary Roper believed "that Dodd would be astute in handling diplomatic duties and, when conferences grew tense, he would turn the tide by quoting Jefferson."

ROOSEVELT DID TAKE Roper's suggestion seriously.

Time was running out, and there were far more pressing matters to be dealt with as the nation sank ever more deeply into economic despair.

The next day, June 8, Roosevelt ordered a long-distance call placed to Chicago.

He kept it brief. He told Dodd: "I want to know if you will render the government a distinct service. I want you to go to Germany as ambassador."

He added, "I want an American liberal in Germany as a standing example."

It was hot in the Oval Office, hot in Dodd's office. The temperature in Chicago was well into the nineties.

Dodd told Roosevelt he needed time to think and to talk with his wife.

Roosevelt gave him two hours.

FIRST DODD SPOKE with university officials, who urged him to accept. Next he walked home, quickly, through the intensifying heat.

He had deep misgivings. His *Old South* was his priority. Serving as ambassador to Hitler's Germany would leave him no more time to write, and probably far less, than did his obligations at the university.

His wife, Mattie, understood, but she knew his need for recognition and his sense that by this time in his life he should have achieved more than he had. Dodd in turn felt that he owed something to her. She had stood by him all these years for what he saw as little reward. "There is no place suitable to my kind of mentality," he had told her earlier that year in a letter from the farm, "and I regret it much for your sake and that of the children." The letter continued, "I know it must be distressing to such a true and devoted wife to have so inept a husband at [a] critical moment of history which he has so long foreseen, one who can not fit himself to high position and thus reap some of the returns of a life of toilsome study. It happens to be your misfortune."

After a brisk bout of discussion and marital soul-searching, Dodd and his wife agreed he should accept Roosevelt's offer. What made the decision a little easier was Roosevelt's concession that if the University of Chicago "insists," Dodd could return to Chicago within a year. But right now, Roosevelt said, he needed Dodd in Berlin.

At two thirty, half an hour late, his misgivings temporarily suppressed, Dodd called the White House and informed Roosevelt's secretary that he would accept the job. Two days later Roosevelt placed Dodd's appointment before the Senate, which confirmed him that day, requiring neither Dodd's presence nor the kind of interminable hearing that one day would become commonplace for key nominations. The appointment attracted little comment in the press. The *New York Times* placed a brief report on page twelve of its Sunday, June 11, newspaper.

Secretary Hull, on his way to an important economic conference in London, never had a voice in the matter. Even had he been present when Dodd's name first came up, he likely would have had little say, for one emerging characteristic of Roosevelt's governing style was to make direct appointments within agencies without involving their superiors, a trait that annoyed Hull no end. He would claim later, however, that he had no objection to Dodd's appointment, save for what he saw as Dodd's tendency to "get out of bounds in his excess enthusiasm and impetuosity and run off on tangents every now and then like our friend William Jennings Bryan. Hence I had some reservations about sending a good friend, able and intelligent though he was, to a ticklish spot such as I knew Berlin was and would continue to be."

Later, Edward Flynn, one of the candidates who had turned down the job, would claim falsely that Roosevelt had phoned Dodd in error—that he had meant instead to offer the ambassadorship to a former Yale law professor named Walter F. Dodd. Rumor of such a mistake gave rise to a nickname, "Telephone Book Dodd."

+ + +

NEXT DODD INVITED his two grown children, Martha and Bill, promising the experience of a lifetime. He also saw in this adventure an opportunity to have his family together one last time. His *Old South* was important to him, but family and home were his great love and need. One cold December night when Dodd was alone on his farm, Christmas near, his daughter and wife in Paris, where Martha was spending a year of study, Bill away as well, Dodd sat down to write a letter to his daughter. He was in a gloomy mood that night. That he now had two grown children seemed an impossibility; soon, he knew, they would be venturing off on their own and their future connection to him and his wife would grow inevitably more tenuous. He saw his own life as nearly expended, his *Old South* anything but complete.

He wrote: "My dear child, if you will not take offense at the term? You are to me so precious, your happiness through this troubled life so near to my heart that I never cease to think of you as a buoyant, growing child; yet I know your years and admire your thought and maturity. I no longer have a child." He mused upon "the roads ahead of us. Yours just beginning, mine so far advanced that I begin to count the shadows that fall about me, the friends that have departed, other friends none too secure of their tenure! It's May and almost December." Home, he wrote, "has been the joy of my life." But now everyone was scattered to the far corners of the world. "I can not endure the thought of our lives all going in different directions—and so few years remaining."

With Roosevelt's offer, an opportunity had arisen that could bring them all together again, if only for a while.

The Choice

Given the nation's economic crisis, Dodd's invitation was not one to be accepted frivolously. Martha and Bill were lucky to have jobs—Martha's as assistant literary editor of the *Chicago Tribune*, Bill's as a teacher of history and a scholar in training—though thus far Bill had pursued his career in a lackluster manner that dismayed and worried his father. In a series of letters to his wife in April 1933, Dodd poured out his worries about Bill. "William is a fine teacher, but he dreads hard work of all kinds." He was too distractible, Dodd wrote, especially if an automobile was anywhere near. "It would never do for us to have a car in Chicago if we wish to help him forward his studies," Dodd wrote. "The existence of a car with wheels is too great a temptation."

Martha had fared much better in her work, to Dodd's delight, but he worried about the tumult in her personal life. Though he loved both his children deeply, Martha was his great pride. (Her very first word, according to family papers, was "Daddy.") She was five feet three inches tall, blonde, with blue eyes and a large smile. She had a romantic imagination and a flirtatious manner, and these had inflamed the passions of many men, both young and not so young.

In April 1930, when she was only twenty-one years old, she became engaged to an English professor at Ohio State University named Royall Henderson Snow. By June the engagement had been canceled. She had a brief affair with a novelist, W. L. River, whose *Death of a Young Man* had been published several years earlier. He called her Motsie and pledged himself to her in letters composed of stupendously long run-on sentences, in one case seventy-four lines of single-spaced typewriting. At the time this passed for experimental prose. "I want nothing from life except you," he wrote. "I want to be with you forever, to work and write for you, to live wherever you want to live, to love nothing, nobody but you, to love you with the passion of earth but also with the above earthly elements of more eternal, spiritual love. . . ."

He did not, however, get his wish. Martha fell in love with a different man, a Chicagoan named James Burnham, who wrote of "kisses soft, light like a petal brushing." They became engaged. Martha seemed ready this time to go through with it, until one evening every assumption she had made as to her impending marriage became upended. Her parents had invited a number of guests to a gathering at the family house on Blackstone Avenue, among them George Bassett Roberts, a veteran of the Great War and now vice president of a bank in New York City. His friends called him simply Bassett. He lived in Larchmont, a suburb north of the city, with his parents. He was tall, full lipped, and handsome. An admiring newspaper columnist, writing about his promotion, observed, "His face is smooth-shaven. His voice is soft. His speech inclined to slowness. . . . There is nothing about him to suggest the old-fashioned hard-shell banker or the dry-as-dust statistician."

At first, as he stood among the other guests, Martha did not think him terribly compelling, but later in the evening she came across him standing apart and alone. She was "stricken," she wrote. "It was pain and sweetness like an arrow in flight, as I saw you anew and away from the rest, in the hallway of our home. This sounds perfectly ridiculous, but truly it was like that, the only time I knew love at first sight."

Bassett was similarly moved, and they launched a long-distance romance full of energy and passion. In a letter on September 19, 1931, he wrote, "What fun it was in the swimming pool that afternoon, and how cute you were with me after I had taken my bathing suit off!" And a few lines later, "Ye gods, what a woman, what a woman!" As Martha put it, he "deflowered" her. He called her "honeybunch" and "honeybuncha mia."

But he confounded her. He did not behave in the manner she had grown to expect from men. "Never before or since have I loved and been loved so much and not had proposals of marriage within a short time!" she wrote to him years later. "So I was deeply wounded and I think there was wormwood embittering my tree of love!" She was the first to want marriage, but he was uncertain. She maneuvered. She maintained her engagement to Burnham, which of course made Bassett jealous. "Either you love me, or you don't love me," he wrote from Larchmont, "and if you do, and are in your senses, you cannot marry another."

At length they wore each other down and did marry, in March 1932, but it was a measure of their lingering uncertainty that they resolved to keep the marriage a secret even from their friends. "I desperately loved and tried to 'get' you for a long time, but afterwards, maybe with the exhaustion of the effort, the love itself became exhausted," Martha wrote. And then, the day after their wedding, Bassett made a fatal mistake. It was bad enough that he had to leave for New York and his job at the bank, but worse was his failure that day to send her flowers—a "trivial" error, as she later assessed it, but emblematic of something deeper. Soon afterward Bassett traveled to Geneva to attend an international conference on gold, and in so doing committed another such error, failing to call her before his departure to "show some nervousness about our marriage and impending geographical separation."

They spent the first year of their marriage apart, with periodic come-togethers in New York and Chicago, but this physical separation amplified the pressures on their relationship. She acknowledged later that she should have gone to live with him in New York and turned the Geneva trip into a honeymoon, as Bassett had suggested. But even then Bassett had seemed uncertain. In one telephone call he wondered aloud whether their marriage might have been a mistake. "That was IT for me," Martha wrote. By then she had begun "flirting"—her word—with other men and had begun an affair with Carl Sandburg, a longtime friend of her parents whom she had known since she was fifteen years old. He sent her drafts of poems on tiny, odd-shaped slips of thin paper and two locks of his blond hair, tied with black coat-button thread. In one note he proclaimed, "I love you past telling I love you with Shenandoah shouts and dim blue rain whispers." Martha dropped just enough hints to torment Bassett. As she told him later, "I was busy healing my wounds and hurting you with Sandburg and others."

All these forces coalesced one day on the lawn of the Dodd house on Blackstone Avenue. "Do you know really why our marriage didn't turn out?" she wrote. "Because I was too immature and young, even at 23, to want to leave my family! My heart broke when my father said to me, while fussing with something on our front lawn, shortly after you married me, 'So my dear little girl wants to leave her old father.'"

And now, in the midst of all this personal turmoil, her father came to her with an invitation to join him in Berlin, and suddenly she confronted a choice: Bassett and the bank and ultimately, inevitably, a house in Larchmont, kids, a lawn—or her father and Berlin and who knew what?

Her father's invitation was irresistible. She told Bassett later, "I had to choose between him and 'adventure,' and you. I couldn't help making the choice I did."

CHAPTER 4

Dread

The following week Dodd took a train to Washington, where, on Friday, June 16, he met Roosevelt for lunch, which was served on two trays at the president's desk.

Roosevelt, smiling and cheerful, launched with obvious relish into a story about a recent visit to Washington by the head of Germany's Reichsbank, Hjalmar Schacht—full name Hjalmar Horace Greeley Schacht—who held the power to determine whether Germany would repay its debts to American creditors. Roosevelt explained how he had instructed Secretary Hull to deploy gamesmanship to defuse Schacht's legendary arrogance. Schacht was to be brought to Hull's office and made to stand in front of the secretary's desk. Hull was to act as if Schacht weren't there and "to pretend to be deeply engaged in looking for certain papers, leaving Schacht standing and unobserved for three minutes," as Dodd recalled the story. At last, Hull was to find what he'd been searching for—a stern note from Roosevelt condemning any attempt by Germany to default. Only then was Hull to stand and greet Schacht, while simultaneously handing him the note. The purpose of this routine, Roosevelt told Dodd, "was to take a little of the arrogance out of the German's bearing." Roosevelt seemed to think the plan had worked extremely well.

Roosevelt now brought the conversation around to what he expected of Dodd. First he raised the matter of Germany's debt, and here he expressed ambivalence. He acknowledged that American bankers had made what he called "exorbitant profits" lending money to German businesses and cities and selling associated bonds to U.S.

citizens. "But our people are entitled to repayment, and while it is altogether beyond governmental responsibility, I want you to do all you can to prevent a moratorium"—a German suspension of payment. "It would tend to retard recovery."

The president turned next to what everyone seemed to be calling the Jewish "problem" or "question."

FOR ROOSEVELT, THIS WAS treacherous ground. Though appalled by Nazi treatment of Jews and aware of the violence that had convulsed Germany earlier in the year, he refrained from issuing any direct statement of condemnation. Some Jewish leaders, like Rabbi Wise, Judge Irving Lehman, and Lewis L. Strauss, a partner at Kuhn, Loeb & Company, wanted Roosevelt to speak out; others, like Felix Warburg and Judge Joseph Proskauer, favored the quieter approach of urging the president to ease the entry of Jews into America. Roosevelt's reluctance on both fronts was maddening. By November 1933, Wise would describe Roosevelt as "immovable, incurable and even inaccessible excepting to those of his Jewish friends whom he can safely trust not to trouble him with any Jewish problems." Wrote Felix Warburg, "So far all the vague promises have not materialized into any action." Even Roosevelt's good friend Felix Frankfurter, a Harvard law professor whom he later named to the Supreme Court, found himself unable to move the president to action, much to his frustration. But Roosevelt understood that the political costs of any public condemnation of Nazi persecution or any obvious effort to ease the entry of Jews into America were likely to be immense, because American political discourse had framed the Jewish problem as an immigration problem. Germany's persecution of Jews raised the specter of a vast influx of Jewish refugees at a time when America was reeling from the Depression. The isolationists added another dimension to the debate by insisting, as did Hitler's government, that Nazi oppression of Germany's Jews was a domestic German affair and thus none of America's business.

Even America's Jews were deeply divided on how to approach the problem. On one side stood the American Jewish Congress, which called for all manner of protest, including marches and a boycott of German goods. One of its most visible leaders was Rabbi Wise, its honorary president, who in 1933 was growing increasingly frustrated with Roosevelt's failure to speak out. During a trip to Washington when he sought in vain to meet with the president, Rabbi Wise wrote to his wife, "If he refuse [sic] to see me, I shall return and let loose an avalanche of demands for action by Jewry. I have other things up my sleeve. Perhaps it will be better, for I shall be free to speak as I have never spoken before. And, God helping me, I will fight."

On the other side stood Jewish groups aligned with the American Jewish Committee, headed by Judge Proskauer, which counseled a quieter path, fearing that noisy protests and boycotts would only make things worse for Jews still in Germany. One who shared this point of view was Leo Wormser, a Jewish attorney in Chicago. In a letter to Dodd, Wormser wrote that "we in Chicago . . . have been steadfastly opposing the program of Mr. Samuel Untermeyer and Dr. Stephen Wise to further an organized Jewish boycott against German goods." Such a boycott, he explained, could stimulate more intense persecution of Germany's Jews, "and we know that, as to many of them, it could be still worse than it now is." He stated also that a boycott would "hamper efforts of friends in Germany to bring about a more conciliatory attitude through an appeal to reason and to self interest," and could impair Germany's ability to pay its bond debt to American holders. He feared the repercussions of an act that would be identified solely with Jews. He told Dodd, "We feel that the boycott if directed and publicized by Jews, will befog the issue which should not be 'will Jews endure,' but 'will liberty endure.'" As Ron Chernow wrote in The Warburgs, "A fatal division sapped 'international Jewry' even as the Nazi press claimed that it operated with a single, implacable will."

Where both factions did agree, however, was on the certainty that any campaign that explicitly and publicly sought to boost Jewish immigration to America could only lead to disaster. In early June 1933 Rabbi Wise wrote to Felix Frankfurter, at this point a Harvard law professor, that if debate over immigration reached the floor of the House it could "lead to an explosion against us." Indeed, anti-immigration sentiment in America would remain strong into 1938, when a *Fortune* poll reported that some two-thirds of those surveyed favored keeping refugees out of the country.

Within the Roosevelt administration itself there was deep division on the subject. Secretary of Labor Frances Perkins, the first woman in American history to hold a cabinet position, was energetic in trying to get the administration to do something to make it easier for Jews to gain entry to America. Her department oversaw immigration practices and policy but had no role in deciding who actually received or was denied a visa. That fell to the State Department and its foreign consuls, and they took a decidedly different view of things. Indeed, some of the department's most senior officers harbored an outright dislike of Jews.

One of these was William Phillips, undersecretary of state, the second-highest-ranking man in the department after Secretary Hull. Phillips's wife and Eleanor Roosevelt were childhood friends; it was FDR, not Hull, who had chosen Phillips to be undersecretary. In his diary Phillips described a business acquaintance as "my little Jewish friend from Boston." Phillips loved visiting Atlantic City, but in another diary entry he wrote, "The place is infested with Jews. In fact, the whole beach scene on Saturday afternoon and Sunday was an extraordinary sight—very little sand to be seen, the whole beach covered by slightly clothed Jews and Jewesses."

Another key official, Wilbur J. Carr, an assistant secretary of state who had overall charge of the consular service, called Jews "kikes." In a memorandum on Russian and Polish immigrants he wrote, "They are filthy, Un-American and often dangerous in their habits." After a trip to Detroit, he described the city as being full of "dust, smoke, dirt, Jews." He too complained of the Jewish presence in Atlantic City. He and his wife spent three days there one February, and for each of the days he made an entry in his diary that disparaged Jews. "In all our day's journey along the Boardwalk we saw but few Gentiles," he wrote on the first day. "Jews everywhere, and of the commonest kind." He and his wife dined that night in the Claridge Hotel and found its dining room full of Jews, "and few presented a good appearance. Only two others beside myself in dinner jacket.

Very careless atmosphere in dining room." The next night the Carrs
went to dinner at a different hotel, the Marlborough-Blenheim, and
found it far more refined. "I like it," Carr wrote. "How different from
the Jewish atmosphere of the Claridge."

An official of the American Jewish Committee described Carr as
"an anti-Semite and a trickster, who talks beautifully and contrives
to do nothing for us."

Both Carr and Phillips favored strict adherence to a provision in
the nation's immigration laws that barred entry to all would-be immigrants considered "likely to become a public charge," the notorious "LPC clause." A component of the Immigration Act of 1917, it
had been reinstated by the Hoover administration in 1930 to discourage immigration at a time when unemployment was soaring.
Consular officials possessed great power over who got to come to
America because they were the ones who decided which visa applicants could be excluded under the LPC clause. Immigration law
also required that applicants provide a police affidavit attesting to
their good character, along with duplicate copies of birth certificates
and other government records. "It seems quite preposterous," one
Jewish memoirist wrote, "to have to go to your enemy and ask for a
character reference."

Jewish activists charged that America's consulates abroad had
been instructed quietly to grant only a fraction of the visas allowed
for each country, a charge that proved to have merit. The Labor
Department's own solicitor, Charles E. Wyzanski, discovered in 1933
that consuls had been given informal oral instructions to limit the
number of immigration visas they approved to 10 percent of the total
allowed by each nation's quota. Jewish leaders contended, further,
that the act of acquiring police records had become not merely difficult, but dangerous—"an almost insuperable obstacle," as Judge
Proskauer stated in a letter to Undersecretary Phillips.

Phillips took offense at Proskauer's depiction of consuls as obstacles. "The consul," Phillips replied, gently chiding, "is only
concerned with determining in a helpful and considerate manner
whether applicants for visas have met the requirements of law."

One result, according to Proskauer and other Jewish leaders, was that Jews simply did not apply for immigration to the United States. Indeed, the number of Germans who applied for visas was a tiny fraction of the twenty-six thousand allowed under the annual quota set for the country. This disparity gave officials within the State Department a powerful statistical argument for opposing reform: how could there be a problem if so few Jews applied in the first place? It was an argument that Roosevelt, as early as April 1933, appeared to accept. He also knew that any effort to liberalize immigration rules might well prompt Congress to respond with drastic reductions of existing quotas.

By the time of his lunch with Dodd, Roosevelt was acutely aware of the sensitivities at play.

"The German authorities are treating the Jews shamefully and the Jews in this country are greatly excited," Roosevelt told him. "But this is also not a governmental affair. We can do nothing except for American citizens who happen to be made victims. We must protect them, and whatever we can do to moderate the general persecution by unofficial and personal influence ought to be done."

THE CONVERSATION TURNED to practicalities. Dodd insisted he would live within his designated salary of $17,500, a lot of money during the Depression but a skimpy sum for an ambassador who would have to entertain European diplomats and Nazi officials. It was a point of principle for Dodd: he did not think an ambassador should live extravagantly while the rest of the nation suffered. For him, however, it also happened to be a moot point, since he lacked the independent wealth that so many other ambassadors possessed and thus could not have lived extravagantly even if he had wanted to.

"You are quite right," Roosevelt told him. "Aside from two or three general dinners and entertainments, you need not indulge in any expensive social affairs. Try to give fair attention to Americans in Berlin and occasional dinners to Germans who are interested in American relations. I think you can manage to live within your income and not sacrifice any essential parts of the service."

After some additional conversation about trade tariffs and arms reductions, the lunch came to an end.

It was two o'clock. Dodd left the White House and walked to the State Department, where he planned to meet with various officials and to read dispatches filed from Berlin, namely the lengthy reports written by Consul General George S. Messersmith. The reports were disconcerting.

Hitler had been chancellor for six months, having received the appointment through a political deal, but he did not yet possess absolute power. Germany's eighty-five-year-old president, Field Marshal Paul von Beneckendorff und von Hindenburg, still held the constitutional authority to appoint and remove chancellors and their cabinets and, equally important, commanded the loyalty of the regular army, the Reichswehr. By contrast to Hindenburg, Hitler and his deputies were surprisingly young—Hitler only forty-four, Hermann Göring forty, and Joseph Goebbels thirty-six.

It was one thing to read newspaper stories about Hitler's erratic behavior and his government's brutality toward Jews, communists, and other opponents, for throughout America there was a widely held belief that such reports must be exaggerated, that surely no modern state could behave in such a manner. Here at the State Department, however, Dodd read dispatch after dispatch in which Messersmith described Germany's rapid descent from democratic republic to brutal dictatorship. Messersmith spared no detail—his tendency to write long had early on saddled him with the nickname "Forty-Page George." He wrote of the widespread violence that had occurred in the several months that immediately followed Hitler's appointment and of the increasing control the government exerted over all aspects of German society. On March 31, three U.S. citizens had been kidnapped and dragged to one of the Storm Troopers' beating stations, where they had been stripped of their clothing and left to spend the night in the cold. Come morning, they had been beaten until they lost consciousness, then discarded on the street. A correspondent for United Press International had disappeared but after inquiries by Messersmith had been released unharmed. Hitler's government had declared a one-day boycott of all Jewish businesses in Germany—stores, law firms, doctors' offices. And there were the book burnings, the firings of Jews from businesses, the seemingly endless marches of Storm Troopers, and the suppression of Germany's once-vibrant free press, which according to Messersmith had been placed under government control to a degree greater than "has probably ever existed in any country. The press censorship may be considered an absolute."

In one of his latest dispatches, however, Messersmith took a markedly more positive tone, which Dodd doubtless found heartening. With uncharacteristic optimism Messersmith now reported seeing signs that Germany was growing more stable and attributed this to the growing confidence of Hitler, Göring, and Goebbels. "Responsibility has already changed the primary leaders of the Party very considerably," he wrote. "There is every evidence that they are becoming constantly more moderate."

Dodd, however, never got the chance to read a letter that Messersmith wrote soon afterward in which he retracted this cheerier assessment. Marked "Personal & Confidential," he sent it to Undersecretary Phillips. The letter, dated June 26, 1933, reached Phillips just as the Dodds were about to leave for Berlin.

"I have tried to point out in my dispatches that the higher leaders of the party are growing more moderate, while the intermediary leaders and the masses are just as radical as ever, and that the question is whether the higher leaders will be able to impose their moderate will on the masses," Messersmith wrote. "It begins to look pretty definitely that they will not be able to do so, but that the pressure from the bottom is becoming stronger all the time." Göring and Goebbels in particular no longer seemed so moderate, he wrote. "Dr. Goebbels is daily preaching that the revolution has just begun and what has so far been done is just an overture."

Priests were being arrested. A former president of Lower Silesia, whom Messersmith knew personally, had been placed in a concentration camp. He sensed a rising "hysteria" among midlevel leaders of the Nazi Party, expressed as a belief "that the only safety lies in getting everybody in jail." The nation was quietly but aggressively readying itself for war, deploying propaganda to conjure the perception "that the whole world is against Germany and that it lies defenseless before the world." Hitler's vows of peaceful intent were illusory, meant only to buy time for Germany to rearm, Messersmith warned. "What they most want to do, however, definitely is to make Germany the most capable instrument of war that there has ever existed."

WHILE IN WASHINGTON, Dodd attended a reception thrown for him by the German embassy, and there he met Wilbur Carr for the first time. Later, Carr jotted a quick description of Dodd in his diary: "Pleasing, interesting person with fine sense of humor and simple modesty."

Dodd also paid a call on the State Department's chief of Western European affairs, Jay Pierrepont Moffat, who shared Carr's and Phillips's distaste for Jews as well as their hard-line attitude toward immigration. Moffat recorded his own impression of the new ambassador: "He is extremely sure of his opinion, expresses himself forcibly and didactically and tends to dramatize the points he makes. The only fly in the ointment is that he is going to try and run the Embassy with a family of four persons on his salary, and how he is going to do it in Berlin, where prices are high, is something beyond me."

What neither Carr nor Moffat expressed in these entries was the surprise and displeasure they and many of their peers had felt at Dodd's appointment. Theirs was an elite realm to which only men of a certain pedigree could expect ready admission. Many had gone to the same prep schools, mainly St. Paul's and Groton, and from there to Harvard, Yale, and Princeton. Undersecretary Phillips grew up in Boston's Back Bay neighborhood in a giant Victorian pile of a house. He was independently wealthy from the age of twenty-one and later in life became a regent of Harvard College. Most of his peers in the State Department also had money and while abroad spent heavily from their own funds with no expectation of reimbursement. One such official, Hugh Wilson, in praise of his fellow diplomats wrote, "They have all felt that they belonged to a pretty good club. That feeling has fostered a healthy esprit de corps."

By the club's standards, Dodd was about as poor a fit as could be imagined.

HE RETURNED TO CHICAGO to pack and attend various good-bye functions, after which he and his wife and Martha and Bill all set out by train for Virginia and a last stay at the Round Hill farm. His eighty-six-year-old father, John, lived relatively near, in North Carolina, but Dodd, despite his wish that his own children remain close at hand, did not at first plan to visit him, given that Roosevelt wanted his new ambassador in Berlin as soon as possible. Dodd had written to his father to tell him of his appointment and that he would not have a chance to visit before his departure. He enclosed a little money and wrote, "I am sorry to be so far away all my life." His father immediately replied how proud he was that Dodd had received "this great honor from D.C.," but added that tincture of vinegar that only parents seem to know how to apply—that little something that causes guilt to flare and plans to change. The elder Dodd wrote, "If I never see you any more while I live it will be alright I shall be proud of you to the last hours I live."

Dodd changed his plans. On July 1, a Saturday, he and his wife boarded a sleeper car bound for North Carolina. During their visit with Dodd's father, they made time for a tour of local landmarks. Dodd and his wife touched old ground, as if saying good-bye for the last time. They visited the family cemetery, where Dodd stood before the grave of his mother, who had died in 1909. As he walked the grass he came upon the plots of ancestors caught up in the Civil War, including two who surrendered with General Robert E. Lee at Appomattox. It was a visit filled with reminders of "family misfortune" and the precariousness of life. "A rather sorrowful day," he wrote.

He and his wife returned to Virginia and the farm, then proceeded by train to New York. Martha and Bill drove the family's Chevrolet, intending to drop it off at the wharf for transit to Berlin.

DODD WOULD HAVE PREFERRED to spend the next couple of days with his family, but the department had insisted that once he got to New York he attend a number of meetings with bank executives on the issue of Germany's debt—a subject in which Dodd had little interest—and with Jewish leaders. Dodd feared that both the American and German press could twist these meetings to taint the appearance of objectivity that he hoped to present in Berlin. He complied, however, and the result was a day of encounters that evoked the serial visits of ghosts in Dickens's A *Christmas Carol*. A letter from a prominent Jewish relief activist told Dodd that he would be visited on the night of Monday, July 3, by two groups of men, the first to arrive by eight thirty, the second at nine o'clock. The meetings were to take place at the Century Club, Dodd's base while in New York.

First, however, Dodd met the bankers, and did so at the offices of the National City Bank of New York, which years later would be called Citibank. Dodd was startled to learn that National City Bank and Chase National Bank held over one hundred million dollars in German bonds, which Germany at this point was proposing to pay back at a rate of thirty cents on the dollar. "There was much talk but no agreement other than that I should do all I possibly could to prevent Germany's defaulting openly," Dodd wrote. He had little sympathy for the bankers. The prospect of high interest rates on German bonds had blinded them to the all-too-obvious risk that a war-crushed, politically volatile country might default.

That evening the Jewish leaders arrived as scheduled, among them Felix M. Warburg, a leading financier who tended to favor the quieter tactics of the American Jewish Committee, and Rabbi Wise of the noisier American Jewish Congress. Dodd wrote in his diary: "For an hour and a half the discussion went on: The Germans are killing Jews all the time; they are being persecuted to the point where suicide is common (the Warburg family is reported to have had cases of this kind); and all Jewish property is being confiscated."

During this meeting, Warburg appears to have mentioned the suicide of two elderly relatives, Moritz and Käthie Oppenheim, in Frankfurt some three weeks earlier. Warburg wrote later, "No doubt the Hitler Regime made life for them a plague and they were yearning for the end of their days."

Dodd's visitors urged him to press Roosevelt for official intervention, but he demurred. "I insisted that the government could not intervene officially but assured the members of the conference that I would exert all possible personal influence against unjust treatment of German Jews and of course protest against maltreatment of American Jews."

Afterward, Dodd caught an 11:00 p.m. train to Boston and, upon his arrival early the next morning, July 4, was driven by chauffeured car to the home of Colonel Edward M. House, a friend who was a close adviser to Roosevelt, for a meeting over breakfast.

In the course of a wide-ranging conversation, Dodd learned for the first time how far he had been from being Roosevelt's first choice. The news was humbling. Dodd noted in his diary that it tamped any inclination on his part to be "over-egotistical" about his appointment.

When the conversation turned to Germany's persecution of Jews, Colonel House urged Dodd to do all he could "to ameliorate Jewish sufferings" but added a caveat: "the Jews should not be allowed to dominate economic or intellectual life in Berlin as they have done for a long time."

In this, Colonel House expressed a sentiment pervasive in America, that Germany's Jews were at least partly responsible for their own troubles. Dodd encountered a more rabid form of it later that same day after returning to New York, when he and his family went to dinner at the Park Avenue apartment of Charles R. Crane, seventy-five, a philanthropist whose family had grown wealthy selling plumbing supplies. Crane was an Arabist said to be influential in certain Middle Eastern and Balkan nations and was a generous supporter of Dodd's department at the University of Chicago, where he had endowed a chair for the study of Russian history and institutions.

Dodd already knew that Crane was no friend of Jews. When Crane earlier had written to congratulate Dodd on his appointment, he had offered some advice: "The Jews, after winning the war, galloping along at a swift pace, getting Russia, England and Palestine, being caught in the act of trying to seize Germany, too, and meeting their first real rebuff have gone plumb crazy and are deluging the world—particularly easy America—with anti-German propaganda—I strongly advise you to resist every social invitation."

Dodd partly embraced Crane's notion that the Jews shared responsibility for their plight. He wrote to Crane later, after arriving in Berlin, that while he did not "approve of the ruthlessness that is being applied to the Jews here," he did think the Germans had a valid grievance. "When I have occasion to speak unofficially to eminent Germans, I have said very frankly that they had a very serious problem but that they did not seem to know how to solve it," he wrote. "The Jews had held a great many more of the key positions in Germany than their numbers or their talents entitled them to."

Over dinner, Dodd heard Crane express great admiration for Hitler and learned as well that Crane himself had no objection to how the Nazis were treating Germany's Jews.

As the Dodds left that evening, Crane gave the ambassador one more bit of advice: "Let Hitler have his way."

AT ELEVEN O'CLOCK the next morning, July 5, 1933, the Dodds took a taxi to the wharf and boarded their ship, the *Washington*, bound for Hamburg. They ran into Eleanor Roosevelt just after she had bid bon voyage to son Franklin Jr., who was sailing to Europe to begin a sojourn abroad.

A dozen or so reporters also swarmed aboard and cornered Dodd on deck as he stood with his wife and Bill. At that moment Martha was elsewhere on the ship. The reporters threw out questions and prodded the Dodds to pose as if waving good-bye. With reluctance they did so, Dodd wrote, "and unaware of the similarity of the Hitler salute, then unknown to us, we raised our hands."

The resulting photographs caused a minor outcry, for they seemed to capture Dodd, his wife, and son in mid-*Heil*.

Dodd's misgivings flared. By this point he had begun to dread leaving Chicago and his old life. As the ship eased from its moorage the family experienced what Martha described later as "a disproportionate amount of sadness and foreboding."

Martha wept.

CHAPTER 5

First Night

Martha continued to cry off and on for the better part of the next two days—"copiously and sentimentally," as she put it. Not out of anxiety, for she had given little thought to what life in Hitler's Germany might really be like. Rather she wept for all she was leaving behind, the people and places, her friends and job, the familiar comfort of the house on Blackstone Avenue, her lovely Carl, all of which composed the "inestimably precious" life she had led in Chicago. If she needed a reminder of what she stood to lose, the seating at her going-away party provided it. She sat between Sandburg and another close friend, Thornton Wilder.

Gradually her sorrow eased. The seas were calm, the days bright. She and Roosevelt's son chummed around and danced and drank champagne. They examined each other's passports—his identifying him succinctly as "son of the President of the United States," hers a tad more pretentious: "daughter of William E. Dodd, Ambassador Extraordinary and Plenipotentiary of the United States to Germany." Her father required that she and her brother come to his stateroom, number A-10, for at least an hour a day and listen to him read aloud in German so that they would gain a sense of how the language sounded. He seemed unusually solemn, and Martha sensed an unaccustomed nervousness.

For her, however, the prospect of the adventure ahead soon pushed aside her anxiety. She knew little of international politics and by her own admission did not appreciate the gravity of what was occurring in Germany. She saw Hitler as "a clown who looked like Charlie

Chaplin." Like many others in America at this time and elsewhere in the world, she could not imagine him lasting very long or being taken seriously. She was ambivalent about the Jewish situation. As a student at the University of Chicago she had experienced a "subtle and undercurrent propaganda among the undergraduates" that promulgated hostility toward Jews. Martha found "that even many of the college professors resented the brilliance of Jewish colleagues and students." As for herself: "I was slightly anti-Semitic in this sense: I accepted the attitude that Jews were not as physically attractive as Gentiles and were less socially desirable." She also found herself absorbing a view that Jews, while generally brilliant, were rich and pushy. In this she reflected the attitude of a surprising proportion of other Americans, as captured in the 1930s by practitioners of the then-emerging art of public-opinion polling. One poll found that 41 percent of those contacted believed Jews had "too much power in the United States"; another found that one-fifth wanted to "drive Jews out of the United States." (A poll taken decades in the future, in 2009, would find that the total of Americans who believed Jews had too much power had shrunk to 13 percent.)

A classmate described Martha as Scarlett O'Hara and "an enchantress—luscious and blonde, with luminous blue eyes and pale, translucent skin." She considered herself a writer and hoped eventually to make a career of writing short stories and novels. Sandburg urged her forward. "The personality is all there in you," he wrote. "Time, solitude, toil are the main oldtime simple requisites for you; you've got just about everything else for the doing of whatever you want to do as a writer." Shortly after the family's departure for Berlin, Sandburg instructed her to keep notes on everything and anything and to "give way to every beckoning to write short things impressions sudden lyric sentences you have a gift for outpouring." Above all, he urged, "find out what this man Hitler is made of, what makes his brain go round, what his bones and blood are made of."

Thornton Wilder also offered some parting advice. He warned Martha to avoid writing for newspapers, because such "hackwork" would destroy the concentration she would need for serious writing. He did recommend that she keep a diary of "what things looked

like—the rumors, and opinions of people during a political time."
In the future, he wrote, such a diary would be "of liveliest interest to
you and—oh my God—to me." Some of Martha's friends believed
she was romantically involved with him as well, though in fact his
affinities lay elsewhere. Martha kept a picture of him in a locket.

ON DODD'S SECOND DAY at sea, as he strolled the deck of the *Washington*, he spotted a familiar face, Rabbi Wise, one of the Jewish
leaders he had met in New York three days earlier. Over the week's
voyage that followed, they spoke together about Germany "half a
dozen or more" times, Wise reported to a fellow Jewish leader, Julian
W. Mack, a federal appellate judge. "He was most friendly and cordial, and indeed confidential."

Dodd, true to character, spoke at length about American history
and at one point told Rabbi Wise, "One cannot write the whole
truth about Jefferson and Washington—people are not ready and
must be prepared for it."

This startled Wise, who called it "the only disturbing note of the
week." He explained: "If people must be prepared for the truth about
Jefferson and Washington, what will [Dodd] do with the truth when
he learns it about Hitler, in view of his official post?!"

Wise continued, "Whenever I suggested that the greatest service
he could render his own country and Germany would be to tell the
truth to the chancellor, to make clear to him how public opinion, including Christian opinion and political opinion, had turned against
Germany . . . he answered again and again: 'I cannot tell until I talk
to Hitler: if I find I can do so, I will talk very frankly to him and tell
him everything.'"

Their many talks aboard ship drew Wise to conclude "that W.E.D.
feels himself deputized to cultivate American liberalism in Germany." He quoted Dodd's last remark: "'It will be pretty serious if I
fail—serious for liberalism and all the things for which the President
stands, for which I, too, stand.'"

By this point, indeed, Dodd had come to envision his ambassadorial role as more than that of mere observer and reporter. He believed

that through reason and example he ought to be able to exercise a moderating influence over Hitler and his government and, at the same time, help nudge America from its isolationist course toward more international engagement. The best approach, he believed, was to be as sympathetic and nonjudgmental as possible and try to understand Germany's perception that it had been wronged by the world. To an extent, Dodd agreed. In his diary he wrote that the Treaty of Versailles, so loathed by Hitler, was "unfair at many points, like all treaties which end wars." His daughter, Martha, in a memoir, put it more strongly, stating that Dodd had "deplored" the treaty.

Ever a student of history, Dodd had come to believe in the inherent rationality of men and that reason and persuasion would prevail, particularly with regard to halting Nazi persecution of Jews.

He told a friend, Assistant Secretary of State R. Walton Moore, that he would rather resign than "simply to remain a protocol and social figurehead."

THE DODDS REACHED GERMANY on Thursday, July 13, 1933. Dodd had assumed erroneously that all arrangements for the family's arrival were in place, but after a slow and tedious passage up the Elbe they disembarked in Hamburg to find that no one from the embassy had booked a train, let alone the customary private railcar, to take them to Berlin. An official, George Gordon, counselor of embassy, met them at the dock and hastily secured compartments on an old, conventional train, a far cry from the famous "Flying Hamburger," which made the run to Berlin in just over two hours. The family Chevrolet posed another problem. Bill Jr. had planned to drive it to Berlin but had failed to fill out the advance paperwork needed to get it off the ship and onto Germany's roads. Once this was resolved, Bill set off. Meanwhile, Dodd fielded questions from a group of reporters that included a writer for a Jewish newspaper, the *Hamburger Israelitisches Familienblatt*, which subsequently published an article implying that Dodd's primary mission was to stop Nazi persecution of Jews—exactly the kind of distortion Dodd had hoped to avoid.

As the afternoon progressed, the Dodds developed a dislike for

Counselor Gordon. He was second in command of the embassy and oversaw a cadre of first and second secretaries, stenographers, file and code clerks, and assorted other employees, about two dozen in all. He was stiff and arrogant and dressed like an aristocrat from the prior century. He carried a walking stick. His mustache was curled, his complexion ruddy and inflamed, a marker of what one official called his "very choleric temperament." He spoke in a manner that Martha described as "clipped, polite, and definitely condescending." He made no attempt to hide his disdain for the family's simple appearance or his displeasure at the fact that they arrived alone, without a battalion of valets, maids, and chauffeurs. The previous ambassador, Sackett, had been much more Gordon's kind of man, rich, with ten servants at his Berlin residence. Martha sensed that to Gordon her family represented a class of human being "the like of which he had not permitted himself to mingle with for perhaps most of his adult life."

Martha and her mother rode in one compartment, among bouquets of flowers given to them in welcome at the dock. Mrs. Dodd—Mattie—was uneasy and downhearted, anticipating "the duties and change in life-patterns" that lay ahead, Martha recalled. Martha rested her head on her mother's shoulder and soon fell asleep.

Dodd and Gordon sat together in a separate compartment discussing embassy matters and German politics. Gordon warned Dodd that his frugality and his resolve to live only within his State Department income would prove a barrier to establishing a relationship with Hitler's government. Dodd was no longer a mere professor, Gordon reminded him. He was an important diplomat up against an arrogant regime that respected only strength. Dodd's approach to daily life would have to change.

The train raced through pretty towns and forested glens bladed with afternoon light and in about three hours reached greater Berlin. At last it steamed into Berlin's Lehrter Bahnhof, at a bend in the Spree where the river flowed through the heart of the city. One of Berlin's five major rail portals, the station rose above its surroundings like a cathedral, with a barrel-vaulted ceiling and banks of arched windows.

On the platform, the Dodds encountered a crowd of Americans and Germans waiting to meet them, including officials from the German foreign office and reporters armed with cameras and flash apparatus known then as "flashlights." An energetic-seeming man, midsized, about five feet six inches tall—"a dry, drawling, peppery man," as historian and diplomat George Kennan later described him—stepped forward and introduced himself. This was George Messersmith, consul general, the Foreign Service officer whose lengthy dispatches Dodd had read while in Washington. Martha and her father liked him immediately, judging him to be a man of principle and candor and a likely friend, though this appraisal was destined for significant revision.

Messersmith returned this initial goodwill. "I liked Dodd from the outset," Messersmith wrote. "He was a very simple man in his manner and in his approach." He noted, however, that Dodd "gave the impression of being rather fragile."

In the crowd of greeters the Dodds also encountered two women who over the next several years would play important roles in the family's life, one a German, the other an American from Wisconsin who was married to a member of one of Germany's loftiest scholarly dynasties.

The German woman was Bella Fromm—"Auntie Voss," society columnist for a highly respected newspaper, the *Vossische Zeitung*, one of two hundred newspapers then still operating in Berlin and, unlike most of them, still capable of independent reportage. Fromm was full figured and handsome, with striking eyes—onyx under black gull-wing brows, her pupils partially curtained by upper lids in a manner that conveyed both intellect and skepticism. She was trusted by virtually all members of the city's diplomatic community as well as by senior members of the Nazi Party, no small achievement considering that she was Jewish. She claimed to have a source high in Hitler's government who gave her advance warning of future Reich actions. She was a close friend of Messersmith's; her daughter, Gonny, called him "uncle."

Fromm in her diary recorded her initial observations of the Dodds. Martha, she wrote, seemed "a perfect example of the intelligent young American female." As for the ambassador, he "looks like a scholar. His dry humor attracted me. He is observant and precise. He learned to love Germany when he was a student in Leipzig, he said, and will dedicate his strength to build a sincere friendship between his country and Germany."

She added: "I hope he and the President of the United States will not be too disappointed in their efforts."

The second woman, the American, was Mildred Fish Harnack, a representative of the American Women's Club in Berlin. She was Fromm's physical opposite in every way—slender, blonde, ethereal, reserved. Martha and Mildred liked each other at once. Mildred wrote later that Martha "is clear and capable and has a real desire to understand the world. Therefore our interests touch." She sensed that she had found a soul mate, "a woman who is seriously interested in writing. It's a hindrance to be lonely and isolated in one's work. Ideas stimulate ideas, and the love of writing is contagious."

Martha in turn was impressed by Mildred. "I was drawn to her immediately," she wrote. Mildred exhibited an appealing combination of strength and delicacy. "She was slow to speak and express opinions; she listened quietly, her large grey blue eyes serious . . . weighing, evaluating, trying to understand."

COUNSELOR GORDON PLACED MARTHA in a car with a young protocol secretary assigned to accompany her to the hotel where the Dodds were to live until they could find a suitable house to lease. Her parents traveled separately with Gordon, Messersmith, and Messersmith's wife. Martha's car proceeded south over the Spree into the city.

She found long, straight boulevards that evoked the rigid grid of Chicago, but the similarity ended there. Unlike the skyscraper-forested landscape she had walked through every workday in Chicago, here most buildings were rather short, typically five stories or so, and these amplified the low, flat feel of the city. Most looked to be very old, but a few were jarringly new, with walls of glass, flat roofs, and curved facades, the offspring of Walter Gropius, Bruno Taut, and Erich Mendelsohn, all condemned by the Nazis as decadent, communist, and, inevitably, Jewish. The city was full of color and energy. There were double-decked omnibuses, S-Bahn trains, and brightly colored trams whose catenaries fired off brilliant blue sparks. Low-slung automobiles thrummed past, most painted black, but others red, cream, and deep blue, many of unfamiliar design: the adorable Opel 4/16 PS, the Horch with its lethal arrow-in-bow hood ornament, and the ubiquitous Mercedes, black, low, edged with chrome. Joseph Goebbels himself was moved to capture in prose the energy of the city as exhibited in one of its most popular shopping avenues, the Kurfürstendamm, albeit in an essay meant not to praise but to condemn, calling the street "the abscess" of the city. "The bells on the streetcars ring, buses clatter by honking their horns, stuffed full with people and more people; taxis and fancy private automobiles hum over the glassy asphalt," he wrote. "The fragrance of heavy perfume floats by. Harlots smile from the artful pastels of fashionable women's faces; so-called men stroll to and fro, monocles glinting; fake and precious stones sparkle." Berlin was, he wrote, a "stone desert" filled with sin and corruption and inhabited by a populace "borne to the grave with a smile."

The young protocol officer pointed out various landmarks. Martha asked question after question, oblivious to the fact that she was trying the officer's patience. Early in their drive, they came to an open plaza dominated by an immense building of Silesian sandstone, with two-hundred-foot towers at each of its four corners, built in what one of Karl Baedeker's famous guidebooks described as "florid Italian Renaissance style." This was the Reichstagsgebäude, in which Germany's legislative body, the Reichstag, had convened until the building was set afire four months earlier. A young Dutchman— a lapsed communist named Marinus van der Lubbe—was arrested and charged with the arson, along with four other suspects named as accomplices, though a widely endorsed rumor held that the Nazi regime itself had orchestrated the fire to stir fears of a Bolshevik uprising and thereby gain popular support for the suspension of civil liberties and the destruction of the Communist Party in Germany. The upcoming trial was the talk of Berlin.

But Martha was perplexed. Contrary to what news reports had led her to expect, the building seemed intact. The towers still stood and the facades appeared unmarked. "Oh, I thought it was burned down!" she exclaimed as the car passed the building. "It looks all right to me. Tell me what happened."

After this and several other outbursts that Martha conceded were imprudent, the protocol officer leaned toward her and hissed, "Sssh! Young lady, you must learn to be seen and not heard. You mustn't say so much and ask so many questions. This isn't America and you can't say all the things you think."

She stayed quiet for the rest of the drive.

UPON REACHING THEIR HOTEL, the Esplanade, on the well-shaded and lovely Bellevuestrasse, Martha and her parents were shown the accommodations that Messersmith himself had arranged.

Dodd was appalled, Martha enchanted.

The hotel was one of Berlin's finest, with gigantic chandeliers and fireplaces and two glass-roofed courtyards, one of which—the Palm Courtyard—was famous for its tea dances and as the place where Berliners had gotten their first opportunity to dance the Charleston. Greta Garbo had once been a guest, as had Charlie Chaplin. Messersmith had booked the Imperial Suite, a collection of rooms that included a large double-bedded room with private bath, two single bedrooms also with private baths, one drawing room, and one conference room, all arrayed along the even-numbered side of a hall, from room 116 through room 124. Two reception rooms had walls covered with satin brocade. The suite was suffused with a spring-like scent imparted by flowers sent by well-wishers, so many flowers, Martha recalled, "that there was scarcely space to move in—orchids and rare scented lilies, flowers of all colors and descriptions." Upon entering the suite, she wrote, "we gasped at its magnificence."

But such opulence abraded every principle of the Jeffersonian ideal that Dodd had embraced throughout his life. Dodd had made it known before his arrival that he wanted "modest quarters in a modest hotel," Messersmith wrote. While Messersmith understood

Dodd's desire to live "most inconspicuously and modestly," he also knew "that the German officials and German people would not understand it."

There was another factor. U.S. diplomats and State Department officials had always stayed at the Esplanade. To do otherwise would have constituted an egregious breach of protocol and tradition.

THE FAMILY SETTLED IN. Bill Jr. and the Chevrolet were not expected to arrive for a while yet. Dodd retired to a bedroom with a book. Martha found it all hard to grasp. Cards from well-wishers continued to arrive, accompanied by still more flowers. She and her mother sat in awe of the luxury around them, "wondering desperately how all this was to be paid for without mortgaging our souls."

Later that evening the family rallied and went down to the hotel restaurant for dinner, where Dodd dusted off his decades-old German and in his dry manner tried to joke with the waiters. He was, Martha wrote, "in magnificent humor." The waiters, more accustomed to the imperious behavior of world dignitaries and Nazi officials, were unsure how to respond and adopted a level of politeness that Martha found almost obsequious. The food was good, she judged, but heavy, classically German, and demanded an after-dinner walk.

Outside, the Dodds turned left and walked along Bellevuestrasse through the shadows of trees and the penumbrae of streetlamps. The dim lighting evoked for Martha the somnolence of rural American towns very late at night. She saw no soldiers, no police. The night was soft and lovely; "everything," she wrote, "was peaceful, romantic, strange, nostalgic."

They continued on to the end of the street and crossed a small square into the Tiergarten, Berlin's equivalent of Central Park. The name, in literal translation, meant "animal garden" or "garden of the beasts," which harked back to its deeper past, when it was a hunting preserve for royalty. Now it was 630 acres of trees, walkways, riding paths and statuary that spread west from the Brandenburg Gate to the wealthy residential and shopping district of Charlottenburg. The Spree ran along its northern boundary; the city's famous zoo stood at its southwest corner. At night the park was especially alluring. "In the Tiergarten," a British diplomat wrote, "the little lamps flicker among the little trees, and the grass is starred with the fireflies of a thousand cigarettes."

The Dodds entered the Siegesallee—Avenue of Victory—lined with ninety-six statues and busts of past Prussian leaders, among them Frederick the Great, various lesser Fredericks, and such once-bright stars as Albert the Bear, Henry the Child, and Otho the Lazy. Berliners called them *Puppen*—dolls. Dodd held forth on the history of each, revealing the detailed knowledge of Germany he had acquired in Leipzig three decades earlier. Martha could tell that his sense of foreboding had dissipated. "I am sure this was one of the happiest evenings we spent in Germany," she wrote. "All of us were full of joy and peace."

Her father had loved Germany ever since his tenure in Leipzig, when each day a young woman brought fresh violets for his room. Now on this first night, as they walked along the Avenue of Victory, Martha too felt a rush of affection for the country. The city, the overall atmosphere, was nothing like what news reports back home had led her to expect. "I felt the press had badly maligned the country and I wanted to proclaim the warmth and friendliness of the people, the soft summer night with its fragrance of trees and flowers, the serenity of the streets."

This was July 13, 1933.

PART II

House Hunting in the Third Reich

Ambassador Dodd at his desk

CHAPTER 6

Seduction

In her first few days in Berlin, Martha fell ill with a cold. As she lay convalescing at the Esplanade she received a visitor, an American woman named Sigrid Schultz, who for the preceding fourteen years had been a correspondent in Berlin for Martha's former employer, the *Chicago Tribune*, and was now its correspondent in chief for Central Europe. Schultz was forty years old, five foot three—the same height as Martha—with blond hair and blue eyes. "A little pudgy," as Martha put it, with "an abundance of golden hair." Despite her size and cherub's gleam, Schultz was known to fellow correspondents and Nazi officials alike as being tenacious, outspoken, and utterly fearless. She made every diplomat's invitation list and was a regular at parties thrown by Goebbels, Göring, and other Nazi leaders. Göring took a perverse delight in calling her "the dragon from Chicago."

Schultz and Martha chatted at first about innocuous things, but soon the conversation turned to the rapid transformation of Berlin during the six months since Hitler had become chancellor. Schultz told stories of violence against Jews, communists, and anyone the Nazis saw as unsympathetic to their revolution. In some cases the victims had been American citizens.

Martha countered that Germany was in the midst of a historic rebirth. Those incidents that did occur surely were only inadvertent expressions of the wild enthusiasm that had gripped the country. In the few days since her arrival Martha had seen nothing at all to corroborate Schultz's tales.

But Schultz pressed on with stories of beatings and capricious imprisonments in the "wild" camps—ad hoc prisons that had sprung up throughout the country under the control of Nazi paramilitary forces—and in more formal prisons, known by now as concentration camps. The German word was *Konzentrationslager*, or KZ. The opening of one such camp had occurred on March 22, 1933, its existence revealed at a press conference held by a thirty-two-year-old former chicken farmer turned commander of the Munich police, Heinrich Himmler. The camp occupied an old munitions factory a brief train ride from Munich, just outside the charming village of Dachau, and now housed hundreds of prisoners, possibly thousands—no one knew—most arrested not on specific charges but rather for "protective custody." These were not Jews, not yet, but communists and members of the liberal Social Democratic Party, all held in conditions of strict discipline.

Martha grew annoyed at Schultz's effort to tarnish her rosy view, but she liked Schultz and saw that she would make a valuable friend, given her vast range of contacts among journalists and diplomats. They parted amicably, but with Martha unshaken in her view that the revolution unfolding around her was a heroic episode that could yield a new and healthy Germany.

"I didn't believe all her stories," Martha wrote later. "I thought she was exaggerating and a bit hysterical."

When Martha left her hotel she witnessed no violence, saw no one cowering in fear, felt no oppression. The city was a delight. What Goebbels condemned she adored. A short walk from the hotel, to the right, away from the cool green of the Tiergarten, took her to Potsdamer Platz, one of the busiest intersections in the world, with its famous five-way streetlight, believed to have been the first-ever stoplight installed in Europe. Berlin had only 120,000 cars, but at any given moment all of them seemed to collect here, like bees to a hive. One could watch the whirl of cars and people from an outdoor table at the Josty Café. Here too stood Haus Vaterland, a five-story nightclub capable of serving six thousand diners in twelve restaurant milieus, including a Wild West bar, with waiters in immense cowboy hats, and the Rhineland Wine Terrace, where each hour guests experienced a brief indoor thunderstorm complete with lightning, thunder, and, to the chagrin of women wearing true silk, a sprinkling of rain. "What a youthful, carefree, won't-go-home-till-morning, romantic, wonderful place!" one visitor wrote: "It is the jolliest place in Berlin."

For a twenty-four-year-old woman unencumbered by job and financial concern and soon to be freed of a dead marriage, Berlin was endlessly compelling. Within days she found herself going on an afternoon "tea date" with a famous American correspondent, H. R. Knickerbocker—"Knick" to his friends—who filed stories for the *New York Evening Post*. He took her to the Eden Hotel, the notorious Eden, where communist firebrand Rosa Luxemburg had been beaten nearly to death in 1919 before being driven into the adjacent Tiergarten and killed.

Now, in the Eden's tea room, Martha and Knick danced. He was skinny and short, with red hair and brown eyes, and led her across the floor with skill and grace. Inevitably, the conversation shifted to Germany. Like Sigrid Schultz, Knickerbocker tried to teach Martha a bit about the politics of the country and the character of its new leadership. Martha wasn't interested, and the conversation drifted elsewhere. What enthralled her were the German men and women around her. She loved "their funny stiff dancing, listening to their incomprehensible and guttural tongue, and watching their simple gestures, natural behavior and childlike eagerness for life."

She liked the Germans she had met thus far—more, certainly, than the French she had encountered during her studies in Paris. Unlike the French, she wrote, the Germans "weren't thieves, they weren't selfish, they weren't impatient or cold and hard."

MARTHA'S CHEERY VIEW of things was widely shared by outsiders visiting Germany and especially Berlin. The fact was that on most days in most neighborhoods the city looked and functioned as it always had. The cigar peddler in front of the Hotel Adlon, at Unter den Linden 1, continued to sell cigars as always (and Hitler continued to shun the hotel, preferring instead the nearby Kaiserhof). Every morning Germans crowded the Tiergarten, many on horseback, as thousands of others commuted into the city center on trains and trams from such neighborhoods as Wedding and Onkel Toms Hütte. Nicely dressed men and women sat in the Romanisches Café, drinking coffee and wine, and smoking cigarettes and cigars, and exercising the sharp wit for which Berliners were famed—the *Berliner Schnauze*, or "Berlin snout." At the Katakombe cabaret, Werner Finck continued poking fun at the new regime, despite the risk of arrest. During one show a member of the audience called him a "lousy yid," to which he responded, "I'm not Jewish. I only look intelligent." The audience laughed with gusto.

Nice days were still nice. "The sun shines," wrote Christopher Isherwood in his *Berlin Stories*, "and Hitler is the master of this city. The sun shines, and dozens of my friends . . . are in prison, possibly dead." The prevailing normalcy was seductive. "I catch sight of my face in the mirror of a shop, and am shocked to see that I am smiling," Isherwood wrote. "You can't help smiling, in such beautiful weather." The trams moved as usual, as did the pedestrians passing on the street; everything around him had "an air of curious familiarity, of striking resemblance to something one remembers as normal and pleasant in the past—like a very good photograph."

Beneath the surface, however, Germany had undergone a rapid and sweeping revolution that reached deep into the fabric of daily life. It had occurred quietly and largely out of easy view. At its core was a government campaign called *Gleichschaltung*—meaning "Coordination"—to bring citizens, government ministries, universities, and cultural and social institutions in line with National Socialist beliefs and attitudes.

"Coordination" occurred with astonishing speed, even in sectors of life not directly targeted by specific laws, as Germans willingly placed themselves under the sway of Nazi rule, a phenomenon that became known as *Selbstgleichschaltung*, or "self-coordination." Change came to Germany so quickly and across such a wide front that German citizens who left the country for business or travel returned to find everything around them altered, as if they were characters in a horror movie who come back to find that people who once were their friends, clients, patients, and customers have become different in ways hard to discern. Gerda Laufer, a socialist, wrote that she felt "deeply shaken that people whom one regarded as friends, who were known for a long time, from one hour to the next transformed themselves."

Neighbors turned surly; petty jealousies flared into denunciations made to the SA—the Storm Troopers—or to the newly founded Geheime Staatspolizei, only just becoming known by its acronym, Gestapo (GEheime STAatsPOlizei), coined by a post office clerk seeking a less cumbersome way of identifying the agency. The Gestapo's reputation for omniscience and malevolence arose from a confluence of two phenomena: first, a political climate in which merely criticizing the government could get one arrested, and second, the existence of a populace eager not just to step in line and become coordinated but also to use Nazi sensitivities to satisfy individual needs and salve jealousies. One study of Nazi records found that of a sample of 213 denunciations, 37 percent arose not from heartfelt political belief but from private conflicts, with the trigger often breathtakingly trivial. In October 1933, for example, the clerk at a grocery store turned in a cranky customer who had stubbornly insisted on receiving three pfennigs in change. The clerk accused her of failure to pay taxes. Germans denounced one another with such gusto that senior Nazi officials urged the populace to be more discriminating as to what circumstances might justify a report to the police. Hitler himself acknowledged, in a remark to his minister of justice, "we are living at present in a sea of denunciations and human meanness."

A central element of Coordination was the insertion into Germany's civil service law of the "Aryan clause," which effectively banned Jews from government jobs. Additional regulations and local animosities severely restricted Jews from practicing medicine and becoming lawyers. As onerous and dramatic as these restrictions were for Jews, they made little impression on tourists and other casual observers, partly because so few Jews lived in Germany. As of January 1933 only about 1 percent of Germany's sixty-five million people were Jewish, and most lived in major cities, leaving a negligible presence throughout the rest of the country. Nearly a third—just over 160,000—lived in Berlin alone, but they constituted less than

4 percent of the city's overall population of 4.2 million, and many lived in close-knit neighborhoods not typically included on visitors' itineraries.

Yet even many Jewish residents failed to grasp the true meaning of what was occurring. Fifty thousand did see, and left Germany within weeks of Hitler's ascension to chancellor, but most stayed. "Hardly anyone thought that the threats against the Jews were meant seriously," wrote Carl Zuckmayer, a Jewish writer. "Even many Jews considered the savage anti-Semitic rantings of the Nazis merely a propaganda device, a line the Nazis would drop as soon as they won governmental power and were entrusted with public responsibilities." Although a song popular among Storm Troopers bore the title "When Jewish Blood Spurts from My Knife," by the time of the Dodds' arrival violence against Jews had begun to wane. Incidents were sporadic, isolated. "It was easy to be reassured," wrote historian John Dippel in a study of why many Jews decided to stay in Germany. "On the surface, much of daily life remained as it had been before Hitler came to power. Nazi attacks on the Jews were like summer thunderstorms that came and went quickly, leaving an eerie calm."

The most visible marker of the Coordination campaign was the sudden appearance of the Hitler salute, or *Hitlergruss*. It was sufficiently new to the outside world that Consul General Messersmith devoted an entire dispatch to the subject, dated August 8, 1933. The salute, he wrote, had no modern precedent, save for the more narrowly required salute of soldiers in the presence of superior officers. What made the practice unique was that everyone was expected to salute, even in the most mundane of encounters. Shopkeepers saluted customers. Children were required to salute their teachers several times a day. At the close of theatrical performances, a newly established custom demanded that audiences stand and salute as they sang first the German national anthem, "Deutschland über Alles," and second the Storm Trooper anthem, the "Horst Wessel Lied," or "Horst Wessel Song," named for its composer, an SA thug killed by communists but whom Nazi propaganda subsequently transformed into a hero. The German public had so avidly embraced the salute as to make the act of incessantly saluting almost comical, especially in the corridors of public buildings where everyone from the lowliest messenger to the loftiest official saluted and *Heiled* one another, turning a walk to the men's room into an exhausting affair.

Messersmith refused to salute and merely stood at attention, but he understood that for ordinary Germans that would not have sufficed. At times even he felt real pressure to conform. At the close of a luncheon he attended in the port city of Kiel, all the guests stood and with right arms extended sang the national anthem and the "Horst Wessel Song." Messersmith stood respectfully, as he would have in America for the "Star-Spangled Banner." Many of the other guests, including a number of Storm Troopers, glared at him and whispered among themselves as if trying to divine his identity. "I felt really quite fortunate that the incident took place within doors and among on the whole intelligent people," he wrote, "for if it had been in a street gathering or in an outdoor demonstration, no questions would have been asked as to who I was, and that I would have been mishandled is almost unquestionable." Messersmith recommended that American visitors try to anticipate when the songs and salute would be required and leave early.

He did not think it funny when now and then Ambassador Dodd threw him a mock salute.

DURING HER SECOND WEEK in Berlin, Martha discovered that she had not shed her past as completely as she had hoped.

Bassett, her husband, arrived in the city on what he privately called his "Mission to Berlin," hoping to win Martha back.

He checked in at the Hotel Adlon. They saw each other several times, but Bassett did not get the tear-filled rapprochement he had hoped for. Rather, he found a cordial indifference. "You remember our bicycle ride through the park," he wrote later. "You were friendly, but I sensed a difference between us."

To make matters worse, toward the end of his stay Bassett caught a severe cold. It laid him flat, just in time for Martha's last visit before his departure.

He knew that his Mission to Berlin had failed the moment Martha arrived in his room. She had brought her brother, Bill.

It was a moment of casual cruelty. She knew Bassett would interpret it correctly. She was tired. She had loved him once, but their relationship had been too fraught with misunderstandings and conflicting imperatives. Where there had been love, as Martha later put it, there were now only "embers," and these were not enough.

Bassett understood. "You had had it," he wrote. "And who could blame you!"

He sent her flowers, acknowledging defeat. The card that accompanied them began, "To my charming and lovely ex-wife."

He left for America, for Larchmont, New York, and a suburban life of lawn mowing and tending the copper beech in his backyard and evening drinks and potlucks and a train commute to his job at the bank. He wrote later, "I'm not at all sure you would have been happy as the wife of a bank economist, preoccupied with the Bank Letter, bringing up a family of children, PTA, and all that."

MARTHA'S CONNECTION WITH Sigrid Schultz soon began to pay off. Schultz threw a welcome party for Martha on July 23, 1933, and invited a number of her closest friends, among them still another correspondent, Quentin Reynolds, who wrote for the Hearst News Service. Martha and Reynolds hit it off instantly. He was big and cheerful, with curly hair and eyes that always seemed to convey a sense of impending laughter—though he had a reputation, as well, for being hard-nosed, skeptical, and smart.

They met again five days later in the bar at the Esplanade, along with her brother, Bill. Like Schultz, Reynolds knew everyone and had managed to befriend a number of Nazi officials, including a confidant of Hitler with the tongue-twisting name Ernst Franz Sedgwick Hanfstaengl. A Harvard graduate with an American-born mother, Hanfstaengl was known to play piano for Hitler late at night to soothe the dictator's nerves. No Mozart or Bach. Mostly Wagner and Verdi, Liszt and Grieg, some Strauss and Chopin.

Martha wanted to meet him; Reynolds knew of a party to be thrown by a fellow correspondent where Hanfstaengl was expected to be a guest and offered to bring her along.

CHAPTER 7

Hidden Conflict

Dodd walked from the Esplanade to his office each morning, a fifteen-minute stroll along Tiergartenstrasse, the street that formed the southern boundary of the park. On the south side stood mansions with lush grounds and wrought-iron fences, many belonging to embassies and consulates; on the north sprawled the park itself, dense with trees and statuary, its paths inked with morning shade. Dodd called it "the most beautiful park I have ever seen," and the walk quickly became his favorite part of the day. His office was in the embassy chancery on a street just off the park called Bendler-strasse, which also contained the "Bendler Block," a collection of squat, pale, rectangular buildings that served as the headquarters of the regular German army, the Reichswehr.

A photograph of Dodd at work in his office during his first week or so in Berlin shows him seated at a large, elaborately carved desk before a soaring tapestry hung on the wall behind him, with a large and complicated phone to his left at a reach of maybe five feet. There is something comical about the image: Dodd, slight of frame, his collar stiff and white, hair pomaded and severely parted, stares with a stern expression into the camera, utterly dwarfed by the opulence that surrounds him. The photograph caused a good deal of mirth back at the State Department among those who disapproved of Dodd's appointment. Undersecretary Phillips closed a letter to Dodd: "A photograph of you seated at your desk in front of a gorgeous tapestry has had quite a wide circulation and looks most impressive."

At every turn Dodd seemed to violate some aspect of embassy

custom, at least in the eyes of his counselor of embassy, George Gordon. Dodd insisted on walking to meetings with government officials. Once, in paying a call on the nearby Spanish embassy, he made Gordon walk with him, both men dressed in morning coats and silk hats. In a letter to Thornton Wilder evoking the scene, Martha wrote that Gordon had "rolled in the gutter in an apoplectic fit." When Dodd drove anywhere, he took the family's Chevrolet, no match for the Opels and Mercedeses favored by senior Reich officials. He wore plain suits. He cracked wry jokes. On Monday, July 24, he committed a particularly egregious sin. Consul General Messersmith had invited him and Gordon to a meeting with a visiting U.S. congressman, to be held in Messersmith's office at the American consulate, which occupied the first two floors of a building across the street from the Esplanade Hotel. Dodd arrived at Messersmith's office before Gordon; a few minutes later the telephone rang. What Dodd gleaned from Messersmith's end of the conversation was that Gordon was now refusing to come. The reason: pure pique. In Gordon's view Dodd had "degraded" himself and his post by stooping to attend a meeting in the office of a man of inferior rank. Dodd observed in his diary, "Gordon is an industrious career man with punctilio developed to the nth degree."

Dodd could not immediately present his credentials—his "Letters of Credence"—to President Hindenburg, as demanded by diplomatic protocol, for Hindenburg was unwell and had retreated to his estate at Neudeck in East Prussia to convalesce; he was not expected to return until the end of the summer. Dodd, therefore, was not yet officially recognized as ambassador and used this period of quiet to familiarize himself with such basic functions as the operation of the embassy phones, its telegraphic codes, and the typical departure times of diplomatic pouches. He met with a group of American correspondents and then with some twenty German reporters, who—as Dodd feared—had seen the report in the Jewish *Hamburger Israelitisches Familienblatt* claiming that he had "come to Germany to rectify the wrongs to the Jews." Dodd read them what he described as a "brief disavowal."

He quickly got a taste of life in the new Germany. On his first full day in Berlin, Hitler's cabinet enacted a new law, to take effect January 1, 1934, called the Law for the Prevention of Offspring with Hereditary Diseases, which authorized the sterilization of individuals suffering various physical and mental handicaps. He also learned that staff at the embassy and at Messersmith's consulate had become convinced that German authorities were intercepting incoming and outgoing mail and that this had prompted Messersmith to take extraordinary measures to ensure that the most sensitive correspondence reached America unopened. The consul general now dispatched messengers to hand such mail directly to the captains of ships bound for America, who would be met dockside by U.S. agents.

ONE OF THE EARLIEST TASKS that Dodd assigned himself was to gain a grasp of the talents and deficits of the embassy's officers, known as first and second secretaries, and the various clerks, stenographers, and other employees who worked out of the chancery. From the start Dodd found their work habits to be less than desirable. His more senior people came in each day at whatever hour seemed to please them and periodically disappeared to hunt or play golf. Almost all, he found, were members of a golf club in the Wannsee district southwest of central Berlin. Many were independently wealthy, in keeping with the traditions of the Foreign Service, and spent money with abandon, their own and the embassy's. Dodd was particularly appalled at how much they spent on international cables. The messages were long and rambling and thus needlessly expensive.

In notes for a personnel report, he wrote brief descriptions of key people. He observed that Counselor Gordon's wife had a "large income" and that Gordon tended to be temperamental. "Emotional. Too hostile to Germans . . . his irritations have been many and exasperating." In his sketch of one of the embassy's first secretaries, also wealthy, Dodd jotted the shorthand observation that he "loves to pass upon [the] color of men's socks." Dodd noted that the woman who ran the embassy reception room, Julia Swope Lewin, was ill suited to the task, as she was "very anti-German" and this was "not good for receiving German callers."

Dodd also learned the contours of the political landscape beyond the embassy's walls. The world of Messersmith's dispatches now came alive outside his windows under the bright sky of a summer's day. There were banners everywhere in a striking arrangement of colors: red background, white circle, and always a bold, black "broken cross," or *Hakenkreuz*, at the center. The word "swastika" was not yet the term of choice within the embassy. Dodd learned the significance of the various colors worn by the men he encountered during his walks. Brown uniforms, seemingly omnipresent, were worn by the Storm Troopers of the SA; black, by a smaller, more elite force called the Schutzstaffel, or SS; blue, by the regular police. Dodd learned as well about the mounting power of the Gestapo and its young chief, Rudolf Diels. He was slender, dark, and considered handsome despite an array of facial scars accumulated when, as a university student, he had engaged in the bare-blade dueling once practiced by young German men seeking to prove their manhood. Although his appearance was as sinister as that of a villain in a campy film, Diels had proved thus far—according to Messersmith—to be a man of integrity, helpful and rational where his superiors, Hitler, Göring, and Goebbels, most decidedly were not.

In many other ways, as well, this new world was proving to be far more nuanced and complex than Dodd had expected.

Deep fault lines ran through Hitler's government. Hitler had been chancellor since January 30, 1933, when he was appointed to the post by President Hindenburg as part of a deal crafted by senior conservative politicians who believed they could keep him under control, a notion that by the time of Dodd's arrival had been proved delusional. Hindenburg—known widely as the Old Gentleman—remained the last counterbalance to Hitler's power and several days before Dodd's departure had made a public declaration of displeasure at Hitler's attempts to suppress the Protestant Church. Declaring himself an "Evangelical Christian," Hindenburg in a published letter to Hitler warned of growing "anxiety for the inner freedom of the church" and that if things continued as they had, "the gravest damage must result to our people and fatherland, as well as injury to national unity." In addition to holding the constitutional author-

ity to appoint a new chancellor, Hindenburg commanded the loyalty of the regular army, the Reichswehr. Hitler understood that if
the nation began falling back into chaos, Hindenburg might feel
compelled to replace the government and declare martial law. He
also recognized that the most likely source of future instability was
the SA, commanded by his friend and longtime ally, Captain Ernst
Röhm. Increasingly Hitler saw the SA as an undisciplined and radical force that had outlasted its purpose. Röhm thought otherwise:
he and his Storm Troopers had been pivotal in bringing about the
National Socialist revolution and now, for their reward, wanted control of all the nation's military, including the Reichswehr. The army
found this prospect loathsome. Fat, surly, admittedly homosexual,
and thoroughly dissipated, Röhm had none of the soldierly bearing
the army revered. He did, however, command a fast-growing legion
of over one million men. The regular army was only one-tenth the
size but far better trained and armed. The conflict simmered.

Elsewhere in the government, Dodd thought he detected a new
and decidedly moderate bent, at least by comparison to Hitler,
Göring, and Goebbels, whom he described as "adolescents in the
great game of international leadership." It was in the next tier down,
the ministries, that he found cause for hope. "These men wish to
stop all Jewish persecution, to co-operate with remnants of German
Liberalism," he wrote, and added: "Since the day of our arrival here
there has been a struggle between these groups."

Dodd's assessment arose in large part from an early encounter with
Germany's minister of foreign affairs, Konstantin Freiherr von Neurath, whom Dodd—at least for now—perceived to be a member of
the moderate camp.

On Saturday, July 15, Dodd paid a visit to Neurath at his ministry
on Wilhelmstrasse, a boulevard that paralleled the eastern edge of
the Tiergarten. So many key Reich offices lined the street that Wilhelmstrasse became a shorthand means of referring to the German
government.

Neurath was a handsome man whose silver-gray hair, dark eyebrows, and close-trimmed gray mustache gave him the look of an
actor who played fatherly roles. Martha would soon meet him as well

and be struck by his ability to mask his interior emotions: "his face," she wrote, "was utterly expressionless—the proverbial poker-face." Like Dodd, Neurath enjoyed taking walks and began each day with a stroll through the Tiergarten.

Neurath saw himself as a sobering force in the government and believed he could help control Hitler and his party. As one peer put it, "He was trying to train the Nazis and turn them into really serviceable partners in a moderate nationalist regime." But Neurath also thought it likely that Hitler's government eventually would do itself in. "He always believed," one of his aides wrote, "that if he would only stay in office, do his duty, and preserve foreign contacts, one fine day he would wake up and find the Nazis gone."

Dodd thought him "most agreeable," a judgment that affirmed Dodd's resolve to be as objective as possible about all that was occurring in Germany. Dodd assumed that Hitler must have other officials of the same caliber. In a letter to a friend he wrote, "Hitler will fall into line with these wiser men and ease up on a tense situation."

THE VERY NEXT DAY, at about 1:30 p.m. in Leipzig, the city where Dodd had gotten his doctorate, a young American by the name of Philip Zuckerman was taking a Sunday stroll with his German wife and her father and sister. Given that they were Jews, this was perhaps an imprudent thing to do on that particular weekend, when some 140,000 Storm Troopers had flooded the town for one of the SA's frequent orgies of marching, drilling, and, inevitably, drinking. That Sunday afternoon a massive parade began surging through the heart of the city, under Nazi banners of red, white, and black that fluttered seemingly from every building. At one thirty a company of these SA men broke off from the main formation and veered into an intersecting avenue, Nikolaistrasse, where the Zuckermans happened to be walking.

As the SA detachment moved past, a group of men at the rear of the column decided the Zuckermans and kin had to be Jews and without warning surrounded them, knocked them to the ground, and launched upon them a cyclone of furious kicks and punches. Eventually the Storm Troopers moved on.

Zuckerman and his wife were severely injured, enough so that both had to be hospitalized, first in Leipzig and then again in Berlin, where the U.S. consulate got involved. "It is not unlikely that [Zuckerman] has suffered serious internal injuries from which he may never altogether recover," Consul General Messersmith wrote in a dispatch to Washington about the attack. He warned that the United States might be compelled to seek monetary damages for Zuckerman but pointed out that nothing could be done officially on his wife's behalf because she was not an American. Messersmith added, "It is interesting to note that she was obliged, as the result of the attack made on her at the same time, to go to a hospital where her baby of some months had to be removed." As a result of the operation, he wrote, Mrs. Zuckerman would never be able to bear another child.

Attacks of this nature were supposed to have come to an end; government decrees had urged restraint. The Storm Troopers appeared not to have paid attention.

In another dispatch on the case, Messersmith wrote, "It has been a favorite pastime of the SA men to attack the Jews and one cannot avoid the plain language of stating that they do not like to be deprived of their prey."

It was his insider's understanding of this and other phenomena of the new Germany that made him so frustrated with the failure of visitors to grasp the true character of Hitler's regime. Many American tourists returned home perplexed by the dissonance between the horrors they had read about in their hometown newspapers—the beatings and arrests of the preceding spring, the book pyres and concentration camps—and the pleasant times they actually experienced while touring Germany. One such visitor was a radio commentator named H. V. Kaltenborn—born Hans von Kaltenborn in Milwaukee—who soon after Dodd's arrival passed through Berlin with his wife, daughter, and son. Known as the "dean of commentators," Kaltenborn reported for the Columbia Broadcasting Service and had become famous throughout America, so famous that in later years he would have cameo roles as himself in Mr. Smith Goes to Washington and the science-fiction thriller The Day the Earth Stood Still. Before his departure for Germany, Kaltenborn had stopped in at the State Department and been allowed to read some of Consul

General Messersmith's dispatches. At the time he believed them to be exaggerated. Now, after four or five days in Berlin, he told Messersmith that he stood by his original conclusion and called the dispatches "inaccurate and overdrawn." He suggested that Messersmith must have relied on faulty sources.

Messersmith was shocked. He had no doubt that Kaltenborn was sincere but attributed the commentator's view to the fact that he "was a German by origin and he couldn't believe that Germans could carry on and do things that were happening every day and every hour in Berlin and all over the country."

It was a problem Messersmith had noticed time and again. Those who lived in Germany and who paid attention understood that something fundamental had changed and that a darkness had settled over the landscape. Visitors failed to see it. In part, Messersmith wrote in a dispatch, this was because the German government had begun a campaign "to influence Americans coming to Germany in forming a favorable opinion concerning happenings in the country." He saw evidence of this in the curious behavior of Samuel Bossard, an American attacked on August 31 by members of the Hitler Youth. Bossard had promptly filed an affidavit with the U.S. consulate and had spoken angrily about the incident to a number of correspondents in Berlin. Then, suddenly, he stopped speaking. Messersmith called him just before his return to America to ask how he was doing and found him unwilling to discuss the incident. Suspicious, Messersmith made inquiries and learned that the Ministry of Propaganda had toured Bossard through Berlin and Potsdam and otherwise showered him with courtesy and attention. The effort appeared to have paid off, Messersmith noted. Upon Bossard's arrival in New York, according to a news report, Bossard declared "that if Americans in Germany are subject to any kind of attacks, it can only be due to misunderstandings. . . . Many Americans do not seem to understand the changes which have taken place in Germany and through their awkwardness [have] acted in such a way as to invite attacks." He vowed to return to Germany the following year.

Messersmith sensed an especially deft hand behind the government's decision to cancel a ban on Rotary Clubs in Germany. Not only could the clubs continue; more remarkably, they were allowed to retain their Jewish members. Messersmith himself belonged to the Berlin Rotary. "The fact that Jews are permitted to continue membership in Rotary is being used as propaganda among the Rotary clubs throughout the world," he wrote. The underlying reality was that many of those Jewish members had lost their jobs or were finding their ability to practice within their professions severely limited. In his dispatches Messersmith reprised one theme again and again: how impossible it was for casual visitors to understand what was really happening in this new Germany. "The Americans coming to Germany will find themselves surrounded by influences of the Government and their time so taken up by pleasant entertainment, that they will have little opportunity to learn what the real situation is."

Messersmith urged Kaltenborn to get in touch with some of the American correspondents in Berlin, who would provide ample confirmation of his dispatches.

Kaltenborn dismissed the idea. He knew a lot of these correspondents. They were prejudiced, he claimed, and so was Messersmith.

He continued his journey, though in short order he would be forced in a most compelling way to reevaluate his views.

CHAPTER 8

Meeting Putzi

With the help of Sigrid Schultz and Quentin Reynolds, Martha inserted herself readily into the social fabric of Berlin. Smart, flirtatious, and good-looking, she became a favorite among the younger officers of the foreign diplomatic corps and a sought-after guest at the informal parties, the so-called bean parties and beer evenings, held after the obligatory functions of the day had concluded. She also became a regular at a nightly gathering of twenty or so correspondents who convened in an Italian restaurant, Die Taverne, owned by a German and his Belgian wife. The restaurant always set aside a big, round table in a corner for the group—a *Stammtisch*, meaning a table for regulars—whose members, including Schultz, typically began to arrive at about ten in the evening and might linger until as late as four the next morning. The group had achieved a kind of fame. "Everybody else in the restaurant is watching them and trying to overhear what they are saying," wrote Christopher Isherwood in *Goodbye to Berlin*. "If you have a piece of news to bring them—the details of an arrest, or the address of a victim whose relatives might be interviewed—then one of the journalists leaves the table and walks up and down with you outside, in the street." The table often drew cameo visits from the first and second secretaries of foreign embassies and various Nazi press officials, and on occasion even Gestapo chief Rudolf Diels. William Shirer, a later member of the group, saw Martha as a worthy participant: "pretty, vivacious, a mighty arguer."

In this new world, the calling card was the crucial currency. The character of an individual's card reflected the character of the individual, his perception of himself, or how he wanted the world to perceive him. The Nazi leadership invariably had the largest cards with the most imposing titles, usually printed in some bold Teutonic font. Prince Louis Ferdinand, son of Germany's crown prince, a sweet-tempered young man who had worked in a Ford assembly plant in America, had the tiniest of cards, with only his name and title. His father, on the other hand, had a large card with a photograph of himself on one side, in full princely regalia, the other side blank. Cards were versatile. Notes scrawled on cards served as invitations to dinner or cocktails or more compelling assignations. By simply crossing out the last name, a man or woman conveyed friendship, interest, even intimacy.

Martha accumulated dozens of cards, and saved them. Cards from Prince Louis, soon to become a suitor and friend; from Sigrid Schultz, of course; and from Mildred Fish Harnack, who had been present on the station platform when Martha and her parents arrived in Berlin. A correspondent for the United Press, Webb Miller, wrote on his card, "If you have nothing more important to do why not have dinner with me." He provided his hotel and room number.

AT LAST SHE MET her first senior Nazi. As promised, Reynolds took her to the party of his English friend, "a lavish and fairly drunken affair." Well after their arrival, an immense man with a brick of coal-black hair slammed into the room— "in a sensational manner," Martha later recalled—passing his card left and right, with a decided emphasis on recipients who were young and pretty. At six feet four inches in height, he was a head taller than most men in the room and weighed easily 250 pounds. A female observer once described him as "supremely awkward-looking—an enormous puppet on slack strings." Even amid the din of the party his voice stood out like thunder over rain.

This, Reynolds told Martha, was Ernst Hanfstaengl. Officially, as stated on his card, he was *Auslandspressechef*—foreign press chief—of the National Socialist Party, though in fact this was largely a made-up job with little real authority, a sop granted by Hitler to acknowledge

Hanfstaengl's friendship ever since the early days, when Hitler often came to Hanfstaengl's home.

Upon being introduced, Hanfstaengl told Martha, "Call me Putzi." It was his childhood nickname, used universally by his friends and acquaintances and by all the city's correspondents.

This was the giant that Martha by now had heard so much about— he of the unpronounceable, unspellable last name, adored by many correspondents and diplomats, loathed and distrusted by many others, this latter camp including George Messersmith, who claimed "an instinctive dislike" for the man. "He is totally insincere, and one cannot believe a word he says," Messersmith wrote. "He pretends the closest friendship with those whom he is at the same time trying to undermine or whom he may be directly attacking."

Martha's friend Reynolds at first liked Hanfstaengl. In contrast with other Nazis, the man "went out of his way to be cordial to Americans," Reynolds recalled. Hanfstaengl offered to arrange interviews that otherwise might be impossible to get and sought to present himself to the city's correspondents as one of the boys, "informal, hail-fellow-well-met, charming." Reynolds's affection for Hanfstaengl eventually cooled, however. "You had to know Putzi to really dislike him. That," he noted, "came later."

Hanfstaengl spoke English beautifully. At Harvard he had been a member of the Hasty Pudding Club, a theatrical group, and forever bent the minds of his audience when for one performance he dressed as a Dutch girl named Gretchen Spootsfeiffer. He had come to know classmate Theodore Roosevelt Jr., eldest son of Teddy Roosevelt, and had become a regular visitor to the White House. One story held that Hanfstaengl had played a piano in the White House basement with such verve that he broke seven strings. As an adult he had run his family's art gallery in New York, where he had met his wife-to-be. After moving to Germany, the couple had grown close to Hitler and made him godfather of their newborn son, Egon. The boy called him "Uncle Dolf." Sometimes when Hanfstaengl played for Hitler, the dictator wept.

Martha liked Hanfstaengl. He was not at all what she expected a senior Nazi official to be, "so blatantly proclaiming his charm and talent." He was big and full of energy, with giant, long-fingered hands—hands that Martha's friend Bella Fromm would describe as being "of almost frightening dimensions"—and a personality that bounded readily from one extreme to another. Martha wrote, "He had a soft, ingratiating manner, a beautiful voice which he used with conscious artistry, sometimes whispering low and soft, the next minute bellowing and shattering the room." He dominated any social milieu. "He could exhaust anyone and, from sheer perseverance, out-shout or out-whisper the strongest man in Berlin."

Hanfstaengl took a liking to Martha as well but did not think much of her father. "He was a modest little Southern history professor, who ran his embassy on a shoestring and was probably trying to save money out of his pay," Hanfstaengl wrote in a memoir. "At a time when it needed a robust millionaire to compete with the flamboyance of the Nazis, he teetered round self-effacingly as if he were still on his college campus." Hanfstaengl dismissively referred to him as "Papa" Dodd.

"The best thing about Dodd," Hanfstaengl wrote, "was his attractive blond daughter, Martha, whom I got to know very well." Hanfstaengl found her charming, vibrant, and clearly a woman of sexual appetite.

Which gave him an idea.

CHAPTER 9

Death Is Death

Dodd sought to maintain his objective stance despite early encounters with visitors who had experienced a Germany very different from the cheery, sun-dappled realm he walked through each morning. One such visitor was Edgar A. Mowrer, at the time the most famous correspondent in Berlin and the center of a maelstrom of controversy. In addition to reporting for the *Chicago Daily News*, Mowrer had written a best-selling book, *Germany Puts the Clock Back*, which had angered Nazi officials to the point where Mowrer's friends believed he faced mortal danger. Hitler's government wanted him out of the country. Mowrer wanted to stay and came to Dodd to ask him to intercede.

Mowrer had long been a target of Nazi ire. In his dispatches from Germany he had managed to cut below the patina of normalcy to capture events that challenged belief, and he used novel reporting techniques to do it. One of his foremost sources of information was his doctor, a Jew who was the son of the grand rabbi of Berlin. Every two weeks or so Mowrer would make an appointment to see him, ostensibly for a persistent throat complaint. Each time the doctor would give him a typed report of the latest Nazi excesses, a method that worked until the doctor came to suspect that Mowrer was being followed. The two arranged a new rendezvous point: every Wednesday at 11:45 a.m. they met in the public restroom underneath Potsdamer Platz. They stood at adjacent urinals. The doctor would drop the latest report, and Mowrer would pick it up.

Putzi Hanfstaengl tried to undermine Mowrer's credibility by spreading a false rumor that the reason his reports were so aggressively critical was that he was a "secret" Jew. In fact, the same thought had occurred to Martha. "I was inclined to think him Jewish," she wrote; she "considered his animus to be prompted only by his racial self-consciousness."

Mowrer was appalled at the failure of the outside world to grasp what was really happening in Germany. He found that even his own brother had come to doubt the truth of his reports.

Mowrer invited Dodd to dinner at his apartment overlooking the Tiergarten and tried to clue him in to certain hidden realities. "To no purpose," Mowrer wrote. "He knew better." Even the periodic assaults against Americans appeared not to have moved the ambassador, Mowrer recalled: "Dodd announced he had no wish to mix in Germany's affairs."

Dodd for his part assessed Mowrer as being "almost as vehement, in his way, as the Nazis."

Threats against Mowrer increased. Within the Nazi hierarchy there was talk of inflicting physical harm on the correspondent. Gestapo chief Rudolf Diels felt compelled to warn the U.S. embassy that Hitler became enraged whenever Mowrer's name was mentioned. Diels worried that some fanatic might kill Mowrer or otherwise "eliminate him from the picture," and claimed to have assigned certain Gestapo men "of responsibility" to stand discreet watch over the correspondent and his family.

When Mowrer's boss, Frank Knox, owner of the *Chicago Daily News*, learned of these threats, he resolved to transfer Mowrer out of Berlin. He offered him the paper's bureau in Tokyo. Mowrer accepted, grudgingly, aware that sooner or later he would be expelled from Germany, but he insisted on staying until October, partly just to demonstrate that he would not bow to intimidation, but mainly because he wanted to cover the annual Nazi Party spectacle in Nuremberg set to begin September 1. This next rally, the "Party Day of Victory," promised to be the biggest yet.

The Nazis wanted him gone immediately. Storm Troopers appeared outside his office. They followed his friends and made threats against his bureau staff. In Washington, Germany's ambassador to the United States notified the State Department that because of the "people's righteous indignation" the government could no longer hope to keep Mowrer free from harm.

At this point even his fellow correspondents became concerned. H. R. Knickerbocker and another reporter went to see Consul General Messersmith to ask him to persuade Mowrer to leave. Messersmith was reluctant. He knew Mowrer well and respected his courage in facing down Nazi threats. He feared that Mowrer might view his intercession as a betrayal. Nonetheless, he agreed to try.

It was "one of the most difficult conversations I ever had," Messersmith wrote later. "When he saw that I was joining his other friends in trying to persuade him to leave, tears came into his eyes and he looked at me reproachfully." Nonetheless, Messersmith felt it was his duty to convince Mowrer to leave.

Mowrer gave up "with a gesture of despair" and left Messersmith's office.

Now Mowrer took his case directly to Ambassador Dodd, but Dodd too believed he should leave, not just for his safety but because his reporting imparted an extra layer of strain to what was already a very challenging diplomatic environment.

Dodd told him, "If you were not being moved by your paper anyway, I would go to the mat on this issue. . . . Won't you do this to avoid complications?"

Mowrer gave in. He agreed to leave on September 1, the first full day of the Nuremberg rally he so wanted to cover.

Martha wrote later that Mowrer "never quite forgave my father for this advice."

ANOTHER OF DODD'S EARLY visitors was, as Dodd wrote, "perhaps the foremost chemist in Germany," but he did not look it. He was smallish in size and egg bald, with a narrow gray mustache above full lips. His complexion was sallow, his air that of a much older man.

He was Fritz Haber. To any German the name was well known and revered, or had been until the advent of Hitler. Until recently, Haber had been director of the famed Kaiser Wilhelm Institute for Physical Chemistry. He was a war hero and a Nobel laureate. Hoping to break the stalemate in the trenches during the Great War, Haber had invented poison chlorine gas. He had devised what became known as Haber's rule, a formula, $C \times t = k$, elegant in its lethality: a low exposure to gas over a long period will have the same result as a high exposure over a short period. He also invented a means to distribute his poison gas at the front and was himself present in 1915 for its first use against French forces at Ypres. On a personal level, that day at Ypres cost him dearly. His wife of thirty-two years, Clara, had long condemned his work as inhumane and immoral and demanded he stop, but to such concerns he gave a stock reply: death was death, no matter the cause. Nine days after the gas attack at Ypres, she committed suicide. Despite international outcry over his poison-gas research, Haber was awarded the 1918 Nobel Prize for chemistry for discovering a means of mining nitrogen from air and thus allowing the manufacture of plentiful, cheap fertilizer—and, of course, gunpowder.

Despite a prewar conversion to Protestantism, Haber was classified under the new Nazi laws as non-Aryan, but an exception granted to Jewish war veterans allowed him to remain director of the institute. Many Jewish scientists on his staff did not qualify for the exemption, however, and on April 21, 1933, Haber was ordered to dismiss them. He fought the decision but found few allies. Even his friend Max Planck offered tepid consolation. "In this profound dejection," Planck wrote, "my sole solace is that we live in a time of catastrophe such as attends every revolution, and that we must endure much of what happens as a phenomenon of nature, without agonizing over whether things could have turned out differently."

Haber didn't see it that way. Rather than preside over the dismissal of his friends and colleagues, he resigned.

Now—Friday, July 28, 1933—with few choices remaining, he came to Dodd's office for help, bearing a letter from Henry Morgenthau Jr., head of Roosevelt's Federal Farm Board (and future Treasury secretary). Morgenthau was Jewish and an advocate for Jewish refugees.

As Haber told his story he "trembled from head to foot," Dodd

wrote in his diary, calling Haber's account "the saddest story of
Jewish persecution I have yet heard." Haber was sixty-five years
old, with a failing heart, and was now being denied the pension
that had been guaranteed him under the laws of the Weimar Republic, which immediately preceded Hitler's Third Reich. "He
wished to know the possibilities in America for emigrants with
distinguished records here in science," Dodd wrote. "I could only
say that the law allowed none now, the quota being filled." Dodd
promised to write to the Labor Department, which administered
immigration quotas, to ask "if any favorable ruling might be made
for such people."

They shook hands. Haber warned Dodd to be careful about talking of his case to others, "as the consequences might be bad." And
then Haber left, a small gray chemist who once had been one of
Germany's most important scientific assets.

"Poor old man," Dodd recalled thinking—then caught himself,
for Haber was in fact only one year older than he was. "Such treatment," Dodd wrote in his diary, "can only bring evil to the government which practices such terrible cruelty."

Dodd discovered, too late, that what he had told Haber was simply
incorrect. The next week, on August 5, Dodd wrote to Isador Lubin,
chief of the U.S. Bureau of Labor Statistics: "You know the quota
is already full and you probably realize that a large number of very
excellent people would like to migrate to the United States, even
though they have to sacrifice their property in doing so." In light
of this, Dodd wanted to know whether the Labor Department had
discovered any means through which "the most deserving of these
people can be admitted."

Lubin forwarded Dodd's letter to Colonel D. W. MacCormack,
commissioner of immigration and naturalization, who on August 23
wrote back to Lubin and told him, "The Ambassador appears to have
been misinformed in this connection." In fact only a small fraction
of the visas allotted under the German quota had been issued, and
the fault, MacCormack made clear, lay with the State Department
and Foreign Service, and their enthusiastic enforcement of the
clause that barred entry to people "likely to become a public charge."

Nothing in Dodd's papers explains how he came to believe the quota was full.

All this came too late for Haber. He left for England to teach at Cambridge University, a seemingly happy resolution, but he found himself adrift in an alien culture, torn from his past, and suffering the effects of an inhospitable climate. Within six months of leaving Dodd's office, during a convalescence in Switzerland, he suffered a fatal heart attack, his passing unlamented in the new Germany. Within a decade, however, the Third Reich would find a new use for Haber's rule, and for an insecticide that Haber had invented at his institute, composed in part of cyanide gas and typically deployed to fumigate structures used for the storage of grain. At first called Zyklon A, it would be transformed by German chemists into a more lethal variant: Zyklon B.

DESPITE THIS ENCOUNTER, Dodd remained convinced that the government was growing more moderate and that Nazi mistreatment of Jews was on the wane. He said as much in a letter to Rabbi Wise of the American Jewish Congress, whom he had met at the Century Club in New York and who had been a fellow passenger on his ship to Germany.

Rabbi Wise was startled. In a July 28 reply from Geneva, he wrote, "How I wish I could share your optimism! I must, however, tell you that everything, every word from scores of refugees in London and Paris within the last two weeks leads me to feel that far from there having been, as you believe, an improvement, things are becoming graver and more oppressive for German Jews from day to day. I am certain that my impression would be borne out by the men whom you met at the little conference at the Century Club." He was reminding Dodd of the meeting in New York that had been attended by Wise, Felix Warburg, and other Jewish leaders.

Privately, in a letter to his daughter, Wise wrote that Dodd "is being lied to."

Dodd stood by his view. In a response to Wise's letter, Dodd countered that "the many sources of information open to the office here seem to me to indicate a desire to ease up on the Jewish problem. Of course, many incidents of very disagreeable character continue to be reported. These I think are the hangovers from the earlier agitation. While I am in no sense disposed to excuse or apologize for such conditions, I am quite convinced that the leading element in the Government inclines to a milder policy as soon as possible."

He added, "Of course you know our Government cannot intervene in such domestic matters. All one can do is to present the American point of view and stress the unhappy consequences of such a policy as has been pursued." He told Wise he opposed open protest. "It is my judgment . . . that the greatest influence we can exercise on behalf of a more kindly and humane policy is to be applied unofficially and through private conversations with men who already begin to see the risks involved."

Wise was so concerned about Dodd's apparent failure to grasp what was really occurring that he offered to come to Berlin and, as he told his own daughter, Justine, "tell him the truth which he would not otherwise hear." At the time, Wise was traveling in Switzerland. From Zurich he "again begged Dodd by telephone to make possible my air flight to Berlin."

Dodd refused. Wise was too well known in Germany and too widely hated. His photograph had appeared in the *Völkischer Beobachter* and *Der Stürmer* too often. As Wise recounted in a memoir, Dodd feared "I might be recognized, particularly because of my unmistakable passport, and give rise to an 'unpleasant incident' at a landing place such as Nuremberg." The ambassador was unswayed by Wise's suggestion that an embassy official meet him at the airport and keep him in sight for the duration of his trip.

While in Switzerland, Wise attended the World Jewish Conference in Geneva, where he introduced a resolution that called for a world boycott of German commerce. The resolution passed.

WISE WOULD HAVE BEEN heartened to learn that Consul General Messersmith held a much darker view of events than Dodd. While

Messersmith agreed that incidents of outright violence against Jews had fallen off sharply, he saw that these had been superseded by a form of persecution that was far more insidious and pervasive. In a dispatch to the State Department, he wrote, "Briefly it may be said that the situation of the Jews in every respect except that of personal safety, is constantly growing more difficult and that the restrictions in effect are becoming daily more effective in practice and that new restrictions are constantly appearing."

He cited several new developments. Jewish dentists were now barred from taking care of patients under Germany's social insurance system, an echo of what had happened to Jewish doctors earlier in the year. A new "German fashion office" had just excluded Jewish dressmakers from participating in an upcoming fashion show. Jews and anyone who had even the appearance of a non-Aryan were forbidden to become policemen. And Jews, Messersmith reported, were now officially banned from the bathing beach at Wannsee.

Even more systemic persecution was on the way, Messersmith wrote. He had learned that a draft existed of a new law that would effectively deprive Jews of their citizenship and all civil rights. Germany's Jews, he wrote, "look upon this proposed law as the most serious moral blow which could be delivered to them. They have and are being deprived of practically all means of making a livelihood and understand that the new citizenship law is to practically deprive them of all civil rights."

The only reason it hadn't become law already, Messersmith had learned, was that for the moment the men behind it feared "the unfavorable public sentiment it would arouse abroad." The draft had been circulating for nine weeks, and this prompted Messersmith to end his dispatch with a bit of wishful thinking. "The fact that the law has been under consideration for such a long time," he wrote, "may be an indication that in its final form it will be less radical than that still contemplated."

DODD REITERATED HIS COMMITMENT to objectivity and understanding in an August 12 letter to Roosevelt, in which he wrote that while he did not approve of Germany's treatment of Jews or Hitler's drive to restore the country's military power, "fundamentally, I believe a people has a right to govern itself and that other peoples must exercise patience even when cruelties and injustices are done. Give men a chance to try their schemes."

CHAPTER 10

Tiergartenstrasse 27a

Martha and her mother set out to find the family a house to lease, so that they could move out of the Esplanade—escape its opulence, in Dodd's view—and lead a more settled life. Bill Jr., meanwhile, enrolled in a doctoral program at the University of Berlin. To improve his German as speedily as possible, he arranged to live during the school week with the family of a professor.

The matter of housing the U.S. ambassador in Berlin had long been an embarrassment. Some years earlier the State Department had acquired and renovated a large and lavish building, the Blücher Palace, on Pariser Platz behind the Brandenburg Gate, to provide an ambassador's residence and consolidate in one location all the other diplomatic and consular offices spread throughout the city, and also to raise America's physical presence nearer to that of Britain and France, whose embassies had long been ensconced in majestic palaces on the plaza. However, just before Dodd's predecessor, Frederic Sackett, was to move in, fire had gutted the building. It had stood as a forlorn wreck ever since, forcing Sackett and now Dodd to find alternative lodging. On a personal level, Dodd was not unhappy about this. Though he reviled the waste of all the money thus far expended on the palace—the government, he wrote, had paid an "exorbitant" price for the building, but "you know it was in 1928 or 1929, when everybody was crazy"—he liked the idea of having a home outside the embassy itself. "Personally, I would rather have my residence a half-hour's walk away than to have it in the Palais," he wrote. He acknowledged that having a building large enough to house junior officials would be a good thing, "but any of us who have to see people would find that the residence alongside of our offices would deprive us practically of all privacy—which is sometimes very essential."

Martha and her mother toured greater Berlin's lovely residential neighborhoods and discovered the city to be full of parks and gardens, with planters and flowers seemingly on every balcony. In the farthest districts they saw what appeared to be tiny farms, possibly just the thing for Martha's father. They encountered squads of uniformed young people happily marching and singing, and more threatening formations of Storm Troopers with men of all sizes in ill-fitting uniforms, the centerpiece of which was a brown shirt of spectacularly unflattering cut. More rarely they spotted the leaner, better-tailored men of the SS, in night black accented with red, like some species of oversized blackbird.

The Dodds found many properties to choose from, though at first they failed to ask themselves why so many grand old mansions were available for lease so fully and luxuriously furnished, with ornate tables and chairs, gleaming pianos, and rare vases, maps, and books still in place. One area they particularly liked was the district immediately south of the Tiergarten along Dodd's route to work, where they found gardens, plentiful shade, a quiet atmosphere, and an array of handsome houses. A property in the district had become available, which they learned of through the embassy's military attaché, who had been told of its availability directly by the owner, Alfred Panofsky, the wealthy Jewish proprietor of a private bank and one of the many Jews—some sixteen thousand, or about 9 percent of Berlin's Jews—who lived within the district. Even though Jews were being evicted from their jobs throughout Germany, Panofsky's bank continued in operation and, surprisingly, with official indulgence.

Panofsky promised the rent would be very reasonable. Dodd, by now ruing but still adhering to his vow to live within his salary, was interested and toward the end of July went to take a look.

THE HOUSE, AT TIERGARTENSTRASSE 27A, was a four-story mansion of stone that had been built for Ferdinand Warburg of the famed Warburg dynasty. The park was across the street. Panofsky and his mother showed the Dodds the property, and now Dodd learned that in fact Panofsky was not offering the whole house, only the first three floors. The banker and his mother planned to occupy the top floor and reserved as well the use of the mansion's electric elevator.

Panofsky was sufficiently wealthy that he did not need the income from the lease, but he had seen enough since Hitler's appointment as chancellor to know that no Jew, no matter how prominent, was safe from Nazi persecution. He offered 27a to the new ambassador with the express intention of gaining for himself and his mother an enhanced level of physical protection, calculating that surely even the Storm Troopers would not risk the international outcry likely to arise from an attack on the house shared by the American ambassador. The Dodds, for their part, would gain all the amenities of a freestanding house, yet for a fraction of the cost, in a structure whose street presence was sufficiently impressive to communicate American power and prestige and whose interior spaces were grand enough to allow the entertainment of government and diplomatic guests without embarrassment. In a letter to President Roosevelt, Dodd exulted, "We have one of the best residences in Berlin at $150 a month—due to the fact the owner is a wealthy Jew, most willing to let us have it."

Panofsky and Dodd signed a one-page "gentleman's agreement," though Dodd still had a few qualms about the place. While he loved the quiet, the trees, the garden, and the prospect of continuing to walk to work each morning, he judged the house too opulent and called it, derisively, "our new mansion."

A plaque bearing the image of an American eagle was affixed to the iron gate at the entrance to the property, and on Saturday, August 5, 1933, Dodd and his family left the Esplanade behind and moved into their new home.

Dodd conceded later that if he had known Panofsky's actual intentions for the use of the fourth floor, beyond simply lodging himself and his mother, he never would have agreed to the lease.

TREES AND GARDENS FILLED the yard, which was surrounded with a high iron fence set in a knee-high wall of brick. Anyone arriving on foot reached the front entrance through doorlike gates built of vertical bars of iron; by car, through a tall master gate topped with an elaborate ironwork arch with a translucent orb at its center. The front doorway of the house was invariably in shadow and formed a black rectangle at the base of a rounded, towerlike facade that rose the full height of the building. The mansion's most peculiar architectural feature was an imposing protrusion about one and a half stories tall that jutted from the front of the house to form a porte cochere over the entry driveway and served as a gallery for the display of paintings.

The main entrance and foyer were on the ground floor, at the rear of which lay the operational soul of the house—servants' quarters, laundry, ice storage, various supply rooms and cupboards, a pantry, and a huge kitchen, which Martha described as being "twice the size of an average New York apartment." Upon entering the house, the Dodds walked first into a large vestibule flanked on both sides by cloakrooms and then up an elaborate staircase to the main floor.

It was here that the true drama of the house became evident. At the front, behind the curved facade, was a ballroom with an oval dance floor of gleaming wood and a piano covered in rich, fringed fabric, its bench upholstered and gilded. Here, on the piano, the Dodds placed an elaborate vase full of tall flowers and, beside this, a framed photographic portrait of Martha in which she looked exceptionally beautiful and overtly sexual, an odd choice, perhaps, for the ballroom of an ambassadorial residence. One reception room had walls covered in dark green damask, another, pink satin. A vast dining room had walls sheathed in red tapestry.

The Dodds' bedroom was on the third floor. (Panofsky and his mother were to live on the floor above this, the attic floor.) The master bathroom was immense, so elaborate and overdone as to be comical, at least in Martha's view. Its floors and walls were "entirely done in gold and colored mosaics." A large tub stood on a raised platform, like something on display in a museum. "For weeks," Martha wrote, "I roared with laughter whenever I saw the bathroom and occasionally as a lark would take my friends up to see it, when my father was away."

Though the house still struck Dodd as overly luxurious, even he had to concede that its ballroom and reception rooms would come in handy for diplomatic functions, some of which he knew—and dreaded—would require the invitation of scores of guests so as not to offend an overlooked ambassador. And he loved the *Wintergarten* at the south end of the main floor, a glassed-in chamber that opened onto a tiled terrace overlooking the garden. Inside he would lie reading in a recliner; on fine days he sat outside in a cane chair, a book in his lap, as he caught the southern sun.

The family's overall favorite room was the library, which offered the prospect of cozy winter nights beside a fire. It was walled with dark, gleaming wood and red damask, and had a great old fireplace whose black-enameled mantel was carved with forests and human figures. The shelves were full of books, many of which Dodd judged to be ancient and valuable. At certain times of day the room was bathed in colored light cast from stained glass set high in one wall. A glass-topped table displayed valuable manuscripts and letters left there by Panofsky. Martha especially liked the library's roomy brown leather sofa, soon to become an asset in her romantic life. The size of the house, the remoteness of its bedrooms, the quiet of its fabric-sheathed walls—these too would prove valuable, as would her parents' habit of retiring early despite the prevailing Berlin custom of staying up to all hours.

On that Saturday in August when the Dodds moved in, the Panofskys graciously placed fresh flowers throughout the house, prompting Dodd to write a thank-you note. "We are convinced that, thanks to your kind efforts and thoughtfulness, we shall be very happy in your lovely house."

Among the diplomatic community, the house at Tiergartenstrasse 27a quickly became known as a haven where people could speak their minds without fear. "I love going there because of Dodd's brilliant mind, his sharp gift of observation and trenchantly sarcastic tongue," wrote Bella Fromm, the society columnist. "I like it also because there is no rigid ceremony as observed in other diplomatic houses." One regular visitor was Prince Louis Ferdinand, who in a memoir described the house as his "second home." He often joined the Dodds for dinner. "When the servants were out of sight we opened our hearts," he wrote. Sometimes the prince's candor was too much even for Ambassador Dodd, who warned him, "If you don't try to be more careful with your talk, Prince Louis, they will hang you one of these days. I'll come to your funeral all right, but that won't do you much good, I am afraid."

As the family settled in, Martha and her father fell into an easy camaraderie. They traded jokes and wry observations. "We love each other," she wrote in a letter to Thornton Wilder, "and I am told state secrets. We laugh at the Nazis and ask our sweet butler if he has Jewish blood." The butler, named Fritz—"short, blond, obsequious, efficient"—had worked for Dodd's predecessor. "We talk mostly politics at table," she continued. "Father reads chapters of his *Old South* to the guests. They almost perish of chagrin and mystification."

She noted that her mother—whom she called "Her Excellency"—was in good health "but a bit nervous [and] rather enjoying it all." Her father, she wrote, was "flourishing incredibly," and seemed "slightly pro-German." She added, "We sort of don't like the Jews anyway."

Carl Sandburg sent her a maundering letter of greeting, typed on two very thin sheets of paper, with spaces instead of punctuation marks: "Now the hegira begins the wanderjahre the track over the sea and the zig-zag over the continent and the center and the home in berlin where are many ragged arithmetics and torn testaments   thru the doors will pass all the garbs and tongues and tales of europe   the jews the communists the atheists the non-aryans the proscribed will not always come as such but they will come in guises disguises disgeeses . . . some will arrive with strange songs and a few with lines we have known and loved   correspondents casual and permanent   international spies   spindrift   beach combers   aviators   heroes . . ."

The Dodds soon learned they had a prominent and much-feared neighbor farther along Tiergartenstrasse, on a side street called Standartenstrasse: Captain Röhm himself, commander of the Storm Troopers. Every morning he could be seen riding a large black horse in the Tiergarten. Another nearby building, a lovely two-story mansion that housed Hitler's personal chancellery, would soon become the home of a Nazi program to euthanize people with severe mental or physical disabilities, code-named Aktion (Action) T-4, for the address, Tiergartenstrasse 4.

To the horror of Counselor Gordon, Ambassador Dodd continued his practice of walking to work, alone, unguarded, in his plain business suits.

NOW, SUNDAY, AUGUST 13, 1933, with Hindenburg still convalescing on his estate, Dodd still an unofficial ambassador, and the matter of establishing a new household at last resolved, the family, accompanied by Martha's new friend, correspondent Quentin Reynolds, set off to see a little of Germany. They traveled first by car—the Dodds' Chevrolet—but planned to separate at Leipzig, about ninety miles south of Berlin, where Dodd and his wife planned to linger awhile and visit landmarks from his days at Leipzig University.

Martha, Bill Jr., and Reynolds continued south, with the aim of eventually reaching Austria. Theirs would prove to be a journey laden with incident that would provide the first challenge to Martha's rosy view of the new Germany.

PART III

Lucifer in the Garden

Rudolf Diels   Martha Dodd

CHAPTER 11

Strange Beings

They drove south through lovely countryside and small, neat villages, everything looking very much the same as it had thirty-five years earlier when Dodd previously had passed this way, with the salient exception that in town after town the facades of public buildings were hung with banners bearing the red, white, and black insignia of the Nazi Party, with the inevitable broken cross at the center. At eleven o'clock they arrived at their first stop, the Schlosskirche, or Castle Church, in Wittenberg, where Martin Luther nailed his "95 Theses" to the door and launched the Reformation. As a student Dodd had traveled to Wittenberg from Leipzig and had sat in on services within the church; now he found its doors locked. A Nazi parade moved through the city's streets.

The group paused in Wittenberg for only an hour, then continued to Leipzig, where they arrived at one o'clock, and made their way directly to one of the most famous restaurants in Germany, Auerbachs Keller, a favorite haunt of Goethe, who used the restaurant as a setting for an encounter between Mephistopheles and Faust, during which Mephisto's wine turned to fire. Dodd gauged the meal excellent, especially its price: three marks. He drank neither wine nor beer. Martha, Bill, and Reynolds, on the other hand, consumed stein after stein.

Now the party split into two groups. The young ones headed off by car toward Nuremberg; Dodd and his wife checked into a hotel, rested for several hours, then went out for supper, another good meal at an even better price: two marks. They continued touring the next day, then caught a train back to Berlin, where they arrived at five o'clock and took a taxi back to their new home at Tiergartenstrasse 27a.

DODD HAD BEEN HOME little more than twenty-four hours when another attack occurred against an American. The victim this time was a thirty-year-old surgeon named Daniel Mulvihill, who lived in Manhattan but practiced at a hospital on Long Island and was in Berlin to study the techniques of a famed German surgeon. Messersmith, in a dispatch on the incident, said Mulvihill was "an American citizen of a fine type and is not a Jew."

The attack followed a pattern that would become all too familiar: On the evening of Tuesday, August 15, Mulvihill was walking along Unter den Linden on his way to a drugstore when he stopped to watch the approach of a parade of uniformed SA members. The Storm Troopers were reenacting for a propaganda film the great march through the Brandenburg Gate that took place on the night of Hitler's appointment as chancellor. Mulvihill looked on, unaware that one SA man had left the parade and was headed his way. The trooper, without preamble, struck Mulvihill hard on the left side of his head, then calmly rejoined the parade. Bystanders told the stunned surgeon that the assault likely had occurred because of Mulvihill's failure to offer the Hitler salute as the parade passed. This was the twelfth violent attack on an American since March 4.

The U.S. consulate immediately protested, and by Friday evening the Gestapo claimed to have arrested the assailant. The next day, Saturday, August 19, a senior government official notified Vice Consul Raymond Geist that an order had been issued to the SA and SS stating that foreigners were not expected to give or return the Hitler salute. The official also said that the head of the Berlin division of the SA, a young officer named Karl Ernst, would personally call on Dodd early the next week to apologize for the incident. Consul General Messersmith, who had met Ernst before, wrote that he was "very young, very energetic, direct, enthusiastic" but exuded "an atmosphere of brutality and force which is characteristic of the SA."

Ernst arrived as promised. He clicked his heels and saluted and barked "Heil Hitler." Dodd acknowledged the salute but did not return it. He listened to Ernst's "confessions of regret" and heard him promise that no such attack would occur again. Ernst appeared to think he had done all he needed to do, but Dodd now sat him down and, lapsing into his familiar roles as both father and professor, gave Ernst a severe lecture on the bad behavior of his men and its potential consequences.

Ernst, discomfited, insisted that he really did intend to try to stop the attacks. He then rose, snapped to rigid attention, saluted again, "made a Prussian bow," and left.

"I was not a little amused," Dodd wrote.

That afternoon he told Messersmith that Ernst had delivered an appropriate apology.

Messersmith said: "The incidents will go on."

ALL ALONG THE ROUTE to Nuremberg, Martha and her companions encountered groups of men in the brown uniform of the SA, young and old, fat and skinny, parading and singing and holding Nazi banners aloft. Often, as the car slowed to pass through narrow village streets, onlookers turned toward them and made the Hitler salute, shouting "Heil Hitler," apparently interpreting the low number on the license plate—traditionally America's ambassador to Germany had number 13—as proof that those within must be the family of some senior Nazi official from Berlin. "The excitement of the people was contagious and I 'Heiled' as vigorously as any Nazi," Martha wrote in her memoir. Her behavior dismayed her brother and Reynolds, but she ignored their sarcastic jibes. "I felt like a child, ebullient and careless, the intoxication of the new regime working like wine in me."

At about midnight they pulled to a stop in front of their hotel in Nuremberg. Reynolds had been to Nuremberg before and knew it to be a sleepy place this late at night, but now, he wrote, they found the street "filled with an excited, happy crowd." His first thought was that these revelers were participants in a festival of the city's legendary toy industry.

Inside the hotel Reynolds asked the registration clerk, "Is there going to be a parade?"

The clerk, cheerful and pleasant, laughed with such delight that the tips of his mustache shook, Reynolds recalled. "It will be a kind of a parade," the clerk said. "They are teaching someone a lesson."

The three took their bags to their rooms, then set out for a walk to see the city and find something to eat.

The crowd outside had grown larger and was infused with good cheer. "Everyone was keyed up, laughing, talking," Reynolds saw. What struck him was how friendly everyone was—far more friendly, certainly, than an equivalent crowd of Berliners would have been. Here, he noted, if you bumped into someone by accident, you got a polite smile and cheerful forgiveness.

From a distance they heard the coarse, intensifying clamor of a still larger and more raucous crowd approaching on the street. They heard distant music, a street band, all brass and noise. The crowd pressed inward in happy anticipation, Reynolds wrote. "We could hear the roar of the crowd three blocks away, a laughing roar that swelled toward us with the music."

The noise grew, accompanied by a shimmery tangerine glow that fluttered on the facades of buildings. Moments later the marchers came into view, a column of SA men in brown uniforms carrying torches and banners. "Storm Troopers," Reynolds noted. "Not doll makers."

Immediately behind the first squad there followed two very large troopers, and between them a much smaller human captive, though Reynolds could not at first tell whether it was a man or a woman. The troopers were "half-supporting, half-dragging" the figure along the street. "Its head had been clipped bald," Reynolds wrote, "and face and head had been coated with white powder." Martha described the face as having "the color of diluted absinthe."

They edged closer, as did the crowd around them, and now Reynolds and Martha saw that the figure was a young woman—though Reynolds still was not completely certain. "Even though the figure wore a skirt, it might have been a man dressed as a clown," Reynolds wrote. "The crowd around me roared at the spectacle of this figure being dragged along."

The genial Nurembergers around them became transformed and taunted and insulted the woman. The troopers at her sides abruptly lifted her to her full height, revealing a placard hung around her neck. Coarse laughter rose from all around. Martha, Bill, and Reynolds deployed their halting German to ask other bystanders what was happening and learned in fragments that the girl had been associating with a Jewish man. As best Martha could garner, the placard said, "I HAVE OFFERED MYSELF TO A JEW."

As the Storm Troopers went past, the crowd surged from the sidewalks into the street behind and followed. A two-decker bus became stranded in the mass of people. Its driver held up his hands in mock surrender. Passengers on the top deck pointed at the girl and laughed. The troopers again lifted the girl—"their toy," as Reynolds put it—so that the riders could have a better view. "Then someone got the idea of marching the thing into the lobby of our hotel," Reynolds wrote. He learned that the "thing" had a name: Anna Rath.

The band stayed out on the street, where it continued to play in a loud, caustic manner. The Storm Troopers emerged from the lobby and dragged the woman away toward another hotel. The band struck up the "Horst Wessel Song," and suddenly in all directions along the street the crowd came to attention, right arms extended in the Hitler salute, all singing with vigor.

When the song ended, the procession moved on. "I wanted to follow," Martha wrote, "but my two companions were so repelled that they pulled me away." She too had been shaken by the episode, but she did not let it tarnish her overall view of the country and the revival of spirit caused by the Nazi revolution. "I tried in a self-conscious way to justify the action of the Nazis, to insist that we should not condemn without knowing the whole story."

The three retreated to the bar of their hotel, Reynolds vowing to get savagely drunk. He asked the bartender, quietly, about what had just occurred. The bartender told the story in a whisper: In defiance of Nazi warnings against marriage between Jews and Aryans, the young woman had planned to marry her Jewish fiancé. This would have been risky anywhere in Germany, he explained, but nowhere more so than in Nuremberg. "You have heard of Herr S., whose home is here?" the bartender said.

Reynolds understood. The bartender was referring to Julius Streicher, whom Reynolds described as "Hitler's circus master of anti-Semitism." Streicher, according to Hitler biographer Ian Kershaw, was "a short, squat, shaven-headed bully . . . utterly possessed by demonic images of Jews." He had founded the virulently anti-Semitic newspaper *Der Stürmer*.

Reynolds recognized that what he, Martha, and Bill had just witnessed was an event that had far more significance than its particular details. Foreign correspondents in Germany had reported on abuses of Jews, but so far their stories had been based on after-the-fact investigation that relied on the accounts of witnesses. Here was an act of anti-Jewish brutality that a correspondent had witnessed firsthand. "The Nazis had all along been denying the atrocities that were occasionally reported abroad, but here was concrete evidence," Reynolds wrote. "No other correspondent," he claimed, "had witnessed any atrocities."

His editor agreed it was an important story but feared that if Reynolds tried to send it by cable it would be intercepted by Nazi censors. He told Reynolds to send it by mail and recommended that he omit any reference to the Dodd children in order to avoid causing difficulties for the new ambassador.

Martha begged him not to write the story at all. "It was an isolated case," she argued. "It was not really important, would create a bad impression, did not reveal actually what was going on in Germany, overshadowed the constructive work they were doing."

Martha, Bill, and Reynolds continued south into Austria, where they spent another week before returning to Germany and making their way back along the Rhine. When Reynolds returned to his office, he found an urgent summons from foreign-press chief Ernst Hanfstaengl.

Hanfstaengl was furious, unaware as yet that Martha and Bill also had witnessed the incident.

"There isn't one damned word of truth in your story!" he raged. "I've talked with our people in Nuremberg and they say nothing of the sort happened there."

Reynolds quietly informed Hanfstaengl that he had watched the parade in the company of two important witnesses whom he had omitted from the story but whose testimony was unassailable. Reynolds named them.

Hanfstaengl sank into his chair and held his head. He complained that Reynolds should have told him sooner. Reynolds invited him to call the Dodds to confirm their presence, but Hanfstaengl waved away the suggestion.

At a press conference soon afterward, Goebbels, the propaganda minister, did not wait for a reporter to raise the issue of abuse against Jews but did so himself. He assured the forty or so reporters in the room that such incidents were rare, committed by "irresponsible" men.

One correspondent, Norman Ebbutt, chief of the London *Times*'s bureau in Berlin, interrupted. "But, Herr Minister, you must surely have heard of the Aryan girl, Anna Rath, who was paraded through Nuremberg just for wanting to marry a Jew?"

Goebbels smiled. It utterly transformed his face, though the result was neither pleasant nor engaging. Many in the room had encountered this effect before. There was something freakish about the extent to which the muscles of the bottom half of his face became engaged in the production of his smile and how abruptly his expressions could shift.

"Let me explain how such a thing might occasionally happen," Goebbels said. "All during the twelve years of the Weimar Republic our people were virtually in jail. Now our party is in charge and they are free again. When a man has been in jail for twelve years and he is suddenly freed, in his joy he may do something irrational, perhaps even brutal. Is that not a possibility in your country also?"

Ebbutt, his voice even, noted a fundamental difference in how England might approach such a scenario. "If it should happen," he said, "we would throw the man right back in jail."

Goebbels's smile disappeared, then just as quickly returned. He looked around the room. "Are there any more questions?"

The United States made no formal protest of the incident. Nonetheless, an official of the German foreign office apologized to Martha. He dismissed the incident as isolated and one that would be severely punished.

Martha was inclined to accept his view. She remained enthralled with life in the new Germany. In a letter to Thornton Wilder, she gushed, "The youth are bright faced and hopeful, they sing to the noble ghost of Horst Wessel with shining eyes and unerring tongues. Wholesome and beautiful lads these Germans, good, sincere, healthy, mystic brutal, fine, hopeful, capable of death and love, deep, rich wondrous and strange beings—these youths of modern *Hakenkreuz* Germany."

IN THE MEANTIME, Dodd received an invitation from the German foreign office to attend the upcoming party rally in Nuremberg, set to begin in earnest on September 1. The invitation troubled him.

He had read of the Nazi Party's penchant for staging these elaborate displays of party force and energy, and saw them not as official events sponsored by the state but as party affairs that had nothing to do with international relations. He could not imagine himself attending such a rally any more than he could envision the German ambassador to America attending a Republican or Democratic convention. Moreover, he feared that Goebbels and his propaganda ministry would seize on the fact of his attendance and portray it as an endorsement of Nazi policies and behavior.

On Tuesday, August 22, Dodd cabled the State Department to ask for advice. "I received a non-committal reply," he wrote in his diary. The department promised to support whatever decision he made. "I at once made up my mind not to go, even if all the other ambassadors went." The following Saturday he notified the German foreign office that he would not be attending. "I declined it on the grounds of pressure of work, though the main reason was my disapproval of a government invitation to a Party convention," he wrote. "I was also sure the behavior of the dominant group would be embarrassing."

An idea occurred to Dodd: if he could persuade his fellow ambassadors from Britain, Spain, and France also to rebuff the invitation, their mutual action would send a potent yet suitably indirect message of unity and disapproval.

Dodd first met with the Spanish ambassador, a session that Dodd described as "very pleasantly unconventional" because the Spaniard likewise had not yet been accredited. Even so, both approached the issue with caution. "I implied that I would not go," Dodd wrote. He provided the Spanish ambassador with a couple of historical precedents for snubbing such an invitation. The Spanish ambassador agreed that the rally was a party affair and not a state event but did not reveal what he planned to do.

Dodd learned, however, that he did at last send his regrets, as did the ambassadors from France and Britain, each citing an inescapable commitment of one kind or another.

Officially the State Department endorsed Dodd's demurral; unofficially, his decision rankled a number of senior officers, including Undersecretary Phillips and Western European affairs chief Jay Pierrepont Moffat. They viewed Dodd's decision as needlessly provocative, further proof that his appointment as ambassador had been a mistake. Forces opposed to Dodd began to coalesce.

CHAPTER 12

Brutus

In late August, President Hindenburg at last returned to Berlin from his convalescence at his country estate. And so, on Wednesday, August 30, 1933, Dodd put on a formal grasshopper cutaway and top hat and drove to the presidential palace to present his credentials.

The president was tall and broad, with a huge gray-white mustache that curled into two feathery wings. The collar of his uniform was high and stiff, his tunic riveted with medals, several of which were gleaming starbursts the size of Christmas-tree ornaments. Overall, he conveyed a sense of strength and virility that belied his eighty-five years. Hitler was absent, as were Goebbels and Göring, all presumably engaged in preparing for the party rally to begin two days later.

Dodd read a brief statement that emphasized his sympathy for the people of Germany and the nation's history and culture. He omitted any reference to the government and in so doing hoped to telegraph that he had no such sympathy for the Hitler regime. For the next fifteen minutes he and the Old Gentleman sat together on the "preferred couch" and conversed on an array of topics, ranging from Dodd's university experience in Leipzig to the dangers of economic nationalism. Hindenburg, Dodd noted later in his diary, "stressed the subject of international relations so pointedly that I thought he meant indirect criticism of the Nazi extremists." Dodd introduced his key embassy officers, and then all marched from the building to find soldiers of the regular army, the Reichswehr, lining both sides of the street.

This time Dodd did not walk home. As the embassy cars drove off, the soldiers stood at attention. "It was all over," Dodd wrote, "and I was at last a duly accepted representative of the United States in Berlin." Two days later, he found himself confronting his first official crisis.

ON THE MORNING of September 1, 1933, a Friday, H. V. Kaltenborn, the American radio commentator, telephoned Consul General Messersmith to express regret that he could not stop by for one more visit, as he and his family had finished their European tour and were preparing to head back home. The train to their ship was scheduled to depart at midnight.

He told Messersmith that he still had seen nothing to verify the consul's criticisms of Germany and accused him of "really doing wrong in not presenting the picture in Germany as it really was."

Soon after making the call, Kaltenborn and his family—wife, son, and daughter—left their hotel, the Adlon, to do a little last-minute shopping. The son, Rolf, was sixteen at the time. Mrs. Kaltenborn particularly wanted to visit the jewelry stores and silver shops on Unter den Linden, but their venture also took them seven blocks farther south to Leipziger Strasse, a busy east-west boulevard jammed with cars and trams and lined with handsome buildings and myriad small shops selling bronzes, Dresden china, silks, leather goods, and just about anything else one could desire. Here too was the famous Wertheim's Emporium, an enormous department store—a *Warenhaus*—in which throngs of customers traveled from floor to floor aboard eighty-three elevators.

As the family emerged from a shop, they saw that a formation of Storm Troopers was parading along the boulevard in their direction. The time was 9:20 a.m.

Pedestrians crowded to the edge of the sidewalk and offered the Hitler salute. Despite his sympathetic outlook, Kaltenborn did not wish to join in and knew that one of Hitler's top deputies, Rudolf Hess, had made a public announcement that foreigners were not obligated to do so. "This is no more to be expected," Hess had declared, "than that a Protestant cross himself when he enters a Catholic

Church." Nonetheless, Kaltenborn instructed his family to turn toward a shop window as if inspecting the goods on display.

Several troopers marched up to the Kaltenborns and demanded to know why they had their backs to the parade and why they did not salute. Kaltenborn in flawless German answered that he was an American and that he and his family were on their way back to their hotel.

The crowd began insulting Kaltenborn and became threatening, to the point where the commentator called out to two policemen standing ten feet away. The officers did not respond.

Kaltenborn and his family began walking back toward their hotel. A young man came from behind and without a word grabbed Kaltenborn's son and struck him in the face hard enough to knock him to the sidewalk. Still the police did nothing. One officer smiled.

Furious now, Kaltenborn grabbed the young assailant by the arm and marched him toward the policemen. The crowd grew more menacing. Kaltenborn realized that if he persisted in trying to get justice, he risked further attack.

At last an onlooker interceded and persuaded the crowd to leave the Kaltenborns alone, as they clearly were American. The parade moved on.

After reaching the safety of the Adlon, Kaltenborn called Messersmith. He was upset and nearly incoherent. He asked Messersmith to come to the Adlon right away.

For Messersmith, it was a troubling but darkly sublime moment. He told Kaltenborn he could not come to the hotel. "It just so happened that I had to be at my desk for the next hour or so," he recalled. He did, however, dispatch to the Adlon Vice Consul Raymond Geist, who arranged that the Kaltenborns would be escorted to the station that night.

"It was ironical that this was just one of the things which Kaltenborn said could not happen," Messersmith wrote later, with clear satisfaction. "One of the things that he specifically said I was incorrectly reporting on was that the police did not do anything to protect people against attacks." Messersmith acknowledged that the incident must have been a wrenching experience for the Kaltenborns, especially their son. "It was on the whole, however, a good thing that this happened because if it hadn't been for this incident, Kaltenborn would have gone back and told his radio audience how fine everything was in Germany and how badly the American officials were reporting to our government and how incorrectly the correspondents in Berlin were picturing developments in the country."

Messersmith met with Dodd and asked whether the time had come for the State Department to issue a definitive warning against travel in Germany. Such a warning, both men knew, would have a devastating effect on Nazi prestige.

Dodd favored restraint. From the perspective of his role as ambassador, he found these attacks more nuisance than dire emergency and in fact tried whenever possible to limit press attention. He claimed in his diary that he had managed to keep several attacks against Americans out of the newspapers altogether and had "otherwise tried to prevent unfriendly demonstrations."

On a personal level, however, Dodd found such episodes repugnant, utterly alien to what his experience as a student in Leipzig had led him to expect. During family meals he condemned the attacks, but if he hoped for a sympathetic expression of outrage from his daughter, he failed to get it.

Martha remained inclined to think the best of the new Germany, partly, as she conceded later, out of the simple perverseness of a daughter trying to define herself. "I was trying to find excuses for their excesses, and my father would look at me a bit stonily if tolerantly, and both in private and in public gently label me a young Nazi," she wrote. "That put me on the defensive for some time and I became temporarily an ardent defender of everything going on."

She countered that there was so much else that was good about Germany. In particular, she praised the enthusiasm of the country's young people and the measures Hitler was taking to reduce unemployment. "I felt there was something noble in the fresh, vigorous, strong young faces I saw everywhere, and would say so combatively every chance I got." In letters back to America she proclaimed that Germany was undergoing a thrilling rebirth, "and that the press reports and atrocity stories were isolated examples exaggerated by bitter, closed-minded people."

THE SAME FRIDAY that had begun so tumultuously with the attack on the Kaltenborns ended for Dodd in a far more satisfactory manner.

That evening correspondent Edgar Mowrer set out for Zoo Station to begin his long journey to Tokyo. His wife and daughter accompanied him to the station but only to see him off: they were to stay behind to oversee the packing of the family's household goods and would follow soon afterward.

Most of the foreign correspondents in the city converged on the station, as did a few stalwart Germans daring enough to let themselves be seen and identified by the agents who still kept Mowrer under surveillance.

A Nazi official assigned to make sure Mowrer actually got on the train came up to him and in a wheedling voice asked, "And when are you coming back to Germany, Herr Mowrer?"

With cinematic flare, Mowrer answered: "Why, when I can come back with about two million of my countrymen."

Messersmith embraced him in a display of support intended for the agents keeping watch. In a voice loud enough to be overheard, Messersmith promised that Mowrer's wife and daughter would follow unmolested. Mowrer was appreciative but had not forgiven Messersmith for failing to support his bid to stay in Germany. As Mowrer climbed aboard the train he turned to Messersmith with a slight smile and said: "And you too, Brutus."

For Messersmith it was a crushing remark. "I felt miserable and depressed," he wrote. "I knew it was the thing for him to do to leave and yet I hated the part that I had played in his leaving."

Dodd did not appear. He was glad Mowrer was gone. In a letter to a friend in Chicago, he wrote that Mowrer "was for a time, as you may know, somewhat of a problem here." Dodd conceded that Mowrer was a talented writer. "His experiences, however, after the publication of his book"—his notoriety and a Pulitzer Prize—"were such that he became rather more sharp and irritable than was best for all parties concerned."

Mowrer and his family made it safely to Tokyo. His wife, Lillian, recalled her great sorrow at having to leave Berlin. "Nowhere have I had such lovely friends as in Germany," she wrote. "Looking back on it all is like seeing someone you love go mad—and do horrible things."

THE DEMANDS OF PROTOCOL—in German, *Protokoll*—descended over Dodd's days like a black fog and kept him from the thing he loved most, his *Old South*. With his status as ambassador now official, his routine diplomatic responsibilities suddenly swelled, to a degree that caused him dismay. In a letter to Secretary of State Hull, he wrote, "The protokoll arbiters of one's social behavior follow precedent, and commit one to entertainments the early part of one's residence which are substantially useless, and which give every one of the various embassies and ministries the 'social' right to offer grand dinners."

It started almost immediately. Protocol required that he give a reception for the entire diplomatic corps. He expected forty to fifty guests but then learned that each diplomat planned to bring one or more members of his staff, causing the eventual attendance to rise to over two hundred. "So today the show began at five o'clock," Dodd wrote in his diary. "The Embassy rooms had been prepared; flowers abounded everywhere; a great punch bowl was filled with the accustomed liquors." Foreign Minister Neurath came, as did Reichsbank president Schacht, one of the few other men in Hitler's government whom Dodd saw as reasonable and rational. Schacht would become a frequent visitor to the Dodds' home, well liked by Mrs. Dodd, who often used him to avoid the awkward social moments that occurred when an expected guest suddenly canceled. She was fond of saying, "Well, if at the last minute another guest can't come, we can always invite Dr. Schacht." Overall, Dodd decided, "It was not a bad affair, and"—a point of special satisfaction—"cost 700 marks."

But now a flood of return invitations, both diplomatic and social, arrived on Dodd's desk and at his home. Depending on the importance of the event, these were often followed by an exchange of seating charts, given to protocol officers to ensure that no unfortunate

error of propinquity would mar the evening. The number of supposedly must-go banquets and receptions reached a point where even
veteran diplomats complained that attendance had become onerous
and exhausting. A senior official in the German foreign office said to
Dodd, "You people in the Diplomatic Corps will have to limit social
doings or we shall have to quit accepting invitations." And a British
official complained, "We simply cannot stand the pace."

It was not all drudgery, of course. These parties and banquets
yielded moments of fun and humor. Goebbels was known for his wit;
Martha, for a time, considered him charming. "Infectious and delightful, eyes sparkling, voice soft, his speech witty and light, it is
difficult to remember his cruelty, his cunning destructive talents."
Her mother, Mattie, always enjoyed being seated next to Goebbels
at banquets; Dodd considered him "one of the few men with a sense
of humor in Germany" and often engaged him in a brisk repartee of
quips and ironic comment. An extraordinary newspaper photograph
shows Dodd, Goebbels, and Sigrid Schultz at a formal banquet during a moment of what appears to be animated, carefree bonhomie.
Though doubtless useful for Nazi propaganda, the scene as played out
in the banquet hall was rather more complex than was captured on
film. In fact, as Schultz later explained in an oral-history interview,
she was trying *not* to speak to Goebbels but in the process "certainly
looked flirtatious." She explained (deploying the third person): "In
this picture Sigrid won't give him the time of day, you see. He's turning on a thousand watts of charm, but he knows and she knows that
she has no use for him." When Dodd saw the resulting photograph,
she said, he "laughed his head off."

Göring too seemed a relatively benign character, at least as compared with Hitler. Sigrid Schultz found him the most tolerable of the
senior Nazis because at least "you felt you could be in the same room
with the man," whereas Hitler, she said, "kind of turned my stomach." One of the American embassy's officers, John C. White, said
years later, "I was always rather favorably impressed by Göring. . . . If
any Nazi was likeable, I suppose he came nearest to it."

At this early stage, diplomats and others found Göring hard to
take seriously. He was like an immense, if exceedingly dangerous,

little boy who delighted in creating and wearing new uniforms. His great size made him the brunt of jokes, although such jokes were told only well out of his hearing.

One night Ambassador Dodd and his wife went to a concert at the Italian embassy, which Göring also attended. In a vast white uniform of his own design, he looked especially huge—"three times the size of an ordinary man," as daughter Martha told the story. The chairs set out for the concert were tiny gilded antiques that seemed far too fragile for Göring. With fascination and no small degree of anxiety, Mrs. Dodd watched Göring choose the chair directly in front of hers. She immediately found herself transfixed as Göring attempted to fit his gigantic "heart-shaped" rump onto the little chair. Throughout the concert she feared that at any moment the chair would collapse and Göring's great bulk would come crashing into her lap. Martha wrote, "She was so distracted at the sight of the huge loins rolling off the sides and edges of the chair, so perilously near to her, she couldn't remember a single piece that was played."

DODD'S BIGGEST COMPLAINT about the diplomatic parties thrown by other embassies was how much money was wasted in the process, even by those countries laid low by the Depression.

"To illustrate," he wrote to Secretary Hull, "last night we went at 8:30 to dine at the 53-room house of the Belgian minister (whose country is supposed to be unable to meet its lawful obligations)." Two servants in uniform met his car. "Four lackeys stood on the stairways, dressed in the style of Louis XIV servants. Three other servants in knee breeches took charge of our wraps. Twenty-nine people sat down in a more expensively furnished dining room than any room in the White House that I have seen. Eight courses were served by four uniformed waiters on silver dishes and platters. There were three wine glasses at every plate and when we rose, I noticed that many glass[es] were half full of wine which was to be wasted. The people at the party were agreeable enough, but there was no conversation of any value at all at my part of the table (this I have noted at all other large parties). . . . Nor was there any serious, informative or even witty talk after dinner." Martha attended as well and described how "all the women were covered with diamonds or other precious stones—I had never seen such a lavish display of wealth." She noted also that she and her parents left at ten thirty, and in so doing caused a minor scandal. "There was a good deal of genteel raising of eyebrows, but we braved the storm and went home." It was bad form, she discovered later, to leave a diplomatic function before eleven.

Dodd was shocked to learn that his independently wealthy predecessors in Berlin had spent up to one hundred thousand dollars a year on entertaining, more than five times Dodd's total salary. On some occasions they had tipped their servants more than what Dodd paid in rent each month. "But," he vowed to Hull, "we shall not return these hospitalities in larger than ten or twelve-guest parties, with four servants at most and they modestly clad"—meaning, presumably, that they would be fully clothed but forgo the knee breeches of the Belgians. The Dodds kept three servants, had a chauffeur, and hired an extra servant or two for parties attended by more than ten guests.

The embassy's cupboard, according to a formal inventory of government-owned property made for its annual "Post Report," contained:

Dinner plates 10½"	4 doz.
Soup plates 9½"	2 doz.
Entree plates 9½"	2 doz.
Dessert plates	2 doz.
Salad plates 5⁵⁄₁₆"	2 doz.
Bread/butter plates 6³⁄₁₆"	2 doz.
Teacups 3½"	2 doz.
Saucers 5¹¹⁄₁₆"	2 doz.
Bouillon cups 3½"	2 doz.
Saucers 5¹¹⁄₁₆"	2 doz.
After-dinner cups 2½"	2 doz.
Saucers 4¾"	2 doz.
Chop dishes	2 doz.
Platters, various sizes	4 doz.

Goblets	3 doz.
Tall sherbert	3 doz.
Low sherbert	3 doz.
Small tumblers	3 doz.
Tall tumblers	3 doz.
Finger bowls	3 doz.
Finger bowl plates	3 doz.

"We shall not use silver platters nor floods of wines nor will there be card tables all about the place," Dodd told Hull. "There will always be an effort to have some scholar or scientist or literary person present and some informatory talk; and it is understood that we retire at 10:30 to 11:00. We make no advertisement of these things but it is known that we shall not remain here when we find that we can not make both ends meet on the salary allowed."

In a letter to Carl Sandburg he wrote, "I can never adapt myself to the usual habit of eating too much, drinking five varieties of wine and saying nothing, yet talking, for three long hours." He feared he was a disappointment to his wealthier junior men, who threw lavish parties at their own expense. "They can not understand me," he wrote, "and I am sorry for them." He wished Sandburg all speed in completing his book on Lincoln, then lamented, "My half-completed Old South will probably be buried with me."

He closed the letter ruefully, "Once more: Greetings from Berlin!"

At least his health was good, though he had his usual bouts of hay fever, indigestion, and bowel upsets. But as if foreshadowing what was to come, his doctor in Chicago, Wilber E. Post—with an office, appropriately enough, in the People's Gas Building—sent Dodd a memorandum that he had written after his last thorough examination a decade earlier, for Dodd to use as a baseline against which to compare the results of future examinations. Dodd had a history of migraines, Post wrote, "with attacks of headaches, dizziness, fatigue, low spirits, and irritability of intestinal tract," the latter condition being best treated "by physical exercise in the open air and freedom from nervous strain and fatigue." His blood pressure was excellent, 100 systolic, 60 diastolic, more what one would expect from an athlete than from a man in late middle age. "The outstanding clinical feature has been that Mr. Dodd's health has been good when he has had the opportunity to get plenty of open air exercise and a comparatively bland non-irritating diet without too much meat."

In a letter appended to the report, Dr. Post wrote, "I trust that you will have no occasion to use it but it might be helpful in case you do."

THAT FRIDAY EVENING a special train, a *Sonderzug*, made its way from Berlin through the night landscape toward Nuremberg. The train carried the ambassadors of an array of minor nations, among them the ministers to Haiti, Siam, and Persia. It also carried protocol officers, stenographers, a doctor, and a cadre of armed Storm Troopers. This was the train that was to have carried Dodd and the ambassadors of France, Spain, and Britain. Originally the Germans had planned on fourteen railcars, but as the regrets came in, they scaled back to nine.

Hitler was already in Nuremberg. He had arrived the night before for a welcome ceremony, his every moment choreographed, right down to the gift presented to him by the city's mayor—a famous print by Albrecht Dürer entitled *Knight, Death and the Devil*.

CHAPTER 13

My Dark Secret

Martha delighted in the very entertainments that so wore on her father. As the daughter of the American ambassador she possessed instant cachet and in short order found herself sought after by men of all ranks, ages, and nationalities. Her divorce from her banker husband, Bassett, was still pending, but all that remained were the legal formalities. She considered herself free to behave as she wished and to disclose or not disclose the legal reality of her marriage. She found secrecy a useful and engaging tool: outwardly she looked the part of a young American virgin, but she knew sex and liked it, and especially liked the effect when a man learned the truth. "I suppose I practiced a great deception on the diplomatic corps by not indicating that I was a married woman at that time," she wrote. "But I must admit I rather enjoyed being treated like a maiden of eighteen knowing all the while my dark secret."

She had ample opportunity to meet new men. The house on Tiergartenstrasse was always full of students, German officials, embassy secretaries, correspondents, and men from the Reichswehr, the SA, and the SS. The Reichswehr officers carried themselves with aristocratic élan and confessed to her their secret hopes for a restoration of the German monarchy. She found them "extremely pleasant, handsome, courteous, and uninteresting."

She caught the attention of Ernst Udet, a flying ace from the Great War, who in the years since had become famous throughout Germany as an aerial adventurer, explorer, and stunt pilot. She went falcon hunting with Udet's fellow ace, Göring, at his vast estate,

Carinhall, named for his dead Swedish wife. Martha had a brief affair with Putzi Hanfstaengl, or so his son, Egon, later claimed. She was frankly sexual and put the house to good use, taking full advantage of her parents' habit of going to bed early. Eventually she would have an affair with Thomas Wolfe when the writer visited Berlin; Wolfe would tell a friend later that she was "like a butterfly hovering around my penis."

One of her lovers was Armand Berard, third secretary of the French embassy—six and a half feet tall and "incredibly handsome," Martha recalled. Before Berard asked her out on their first date, he asked Ambassador Dodd for permission, an act that Martha found both charming and amusing. She did not tell him of her marriage, and as a consequence, much to her secret delight, he treated her at first as a sexual ingenue. She knew that she possessed great power over him and that even some casual act or comment could drive him to despair. In their estranged periods she would see other men—and make sure he knew it.

"You are the only person on earth who can break me," he wrote at one point, "but how well you know it and how you seem to rejoice in doing so." He begged her not to be so hard. "I can't stand it," he wrote. "If you realized how unhappy I am, you would probably pity me."

For one suitor, Max Delbrück, a young biophysicist, the recollection of her skill at manipulation remained fresh even four decades later. He was slender and had a cleanly sculpted chin and masses of dark, neatly combed hair, for a look that evoked a young Gregory Peck. He was destined for great things, including a Nobel Prize that would be awarded in 1969.

In a late-life exchange of letters, Martha and Delbrück reminisced about their time together in Berlin. She recalled their innocence as they sat together in one of the reception rooms and wondered if he did as well.

"Of course I remember the green damask room off the dining room in the Tiergartenstrasse," he wrote. But his recollection diverged a bit from hers: "We did not only sit there modestly."

With a bit of dusty pique he reminded her of one rendezvous at the Romanisches Café. "You came terribly late and then yawned away, and explained that you did that because you felt relaxed in my company, and that it was a compliment to me."

With no small degree of irony, he added, "I became quite enthusiastic about this idea (after first getting upset), and have been yawning at my friends ever since."

Martha's parents gave her full independence, with no restrictions on her comings or goings. It was not uncommon for her to stay out until early in the morning with all manner of escorts, yet family correspondence is surprisingly free of censorious comment.

Others noticed, however, and disapproved, among them Consul General George Messersmith, who communicated his distaste to the State Department, thereby adding fuel to the quietly growing campaign against Dodd. Messersmith knew of Martha's affair with Udet, the flying ace, and believed she had been involved in romantic affairs with other ranking Nazis, including Hanfstaengl. In a "personal and confidential" letter to Jay Pierrepont Moffat, the Western European affairs chief, Messersmith wrote that these affairs had become grist for gossip. He assessed them as mostly harmless—except in the case of Hanfstaengl. He feared that Martha's relationship with Hanfstaengl and her seeming lack of discretion caused diplomats and other informants to be more reticent about what they told Dodd, fearing that their confidences would make their way back to Hanfstaengl. "I often felt like saying something to the Ambassador about it," Messersmith told Moffat, "but as it was rather a delicate matter, I confined myself to making it clear as to what kind of a person Hanfstaengl really is."

Messersmith's view of Martha's behavior hardened over time. In an unpublished memoir he wrote that "she had behaved so badly in so many ways, especially in view of the position held by her father."

The Dodds' butler, Fritz, framed his own criticism succinctly: "That was not a house, but a house of ill repute."

MARTHA'S LOVE LIFE took a dark turn when she was introduced to Rudolf Diels, the young chief of the Gestapo. He moved with ease and confidence, yet unlike Putzi Hanfstaengl, who invaded a room, he entered unobtrusively, seeping in like a malevolent fog. His arrival at a party, she wrote, "created a nervousness and tension that no other man possibly could, even when people did not know his identity."

What most drew her attention was the tortured landscape of his face, which she described as "the most sinister, scar-torn face I have ever seen." One long scar in the shape of a shallow "V" marked his right cheek; others arced below his mouth and across his chin; an especially deep scar formed a crescent at the bottom of his left cheek. His overall appearance was striking, that of a damaged Ray Milland—a "cruel, broken beauty," as Martha put it. His was the opposite of the bland handsomeness of the young Reichswehr officers, and she was drawn to him immediately, his "lovely" lips, his "jet-black luxuriant hair," and his penetrating eyes.

She was hardly alone in feeling this attraction. Diels was said to have great charm and to be sexually talented and experienced. As a student he had gained a reputation as a drinker and philanderer, according to Hans Bernd Gisevius, a Gestapo man who had been a student at the same university. "Involved affairs with women were a regular thing with him," Gisevius wrote in a memoir. Men also acknowledged Diels's charm and manner. When Kurt Ludecke, an early associate of Hitler's, found himself under arrest and summoned to Diels's office, he found the Gestapo chief unexpectedly cordial. "I felt at ease with this tall, slender, and polished young man, and found his consideration instantly comforting," Ludecke wrote. "It was an occasion when good manners were doubly welcome." He noted, "I went back to my cell feeling I'd rather be shot by a gentleman than drubbed by a churl." Nonetheless, Ludecke ultimately wound up imprisoned, under "protective custody," at a concentration camp in Brandenburg an der Havel.

What Martha also found compelling about Diels was the fact that everyone else was afraid of him. He was often referred to as the "Prince of Darkness," and, as Martha learned, he did not mind at all. "He took a vicious joy in his Mephistophelian manners and always wanted to create a hush by his melodramatic entrance."

Diels early on had allied himself closely with Göring, and when Hitler became chancellor, Göring, as the new Prussian minister of the interior, rewarded Diels's loyalty by making him head of the newly created Gestapo, despite the fact that Diels was not a member of the Nazi Party. Göring installed the agency in an old art school at Prinz-Albrecht-Strasse 8, roughly two blocks from the U.S. consulate on Bellevuestrasse. By the time of the Dodds' arrival in Berlin, the Gestapo had become a terrifying presence, though it was hardly the all-knowing, all-seeing entity that people imagined it to be. Its roster of employees was "remarkably small," according to historian Robert Gellately. He cites the example of the agency's Düsseldorf branch, one of the few for which detailed records survive. It had 291 employees responsible for a territory encompassing four million people. Its agents, or "specialists," were not the sociopaths of popular depiction, Gellately found. "Most of them were neither crazed, demented, nor superhuman, but terribly ordinary."

The Gestapo enhanced its dark image by keeping its operations and its sources of information secret. Out of the blue people received postcards requesting that they appear for questioning. These were uniquely terrifying. Despite their prosaic form, such summonses could not be discarded or ignored. They put citizens in the position of having to turn themselves in at that most terrifying of buildings to respond to charges of offenses about which they likely had no inkling, with the potential—often imagined but in many cases quite real—that by day's end they would find themselves in a concentration camp, under "protective custody." It was this accumulation of unknowns that made the Gestapo so fearsome. "One can evade a danger that one recognizes," wrote historian Friedrich Zipfel, "but a police working in the dark becomes uncanny. Nowhere does one feel safe from it. While not omnipresent, it *could* appear, search, arrest. The worried citizen no longer knows whom he ought to trust."

Yet under Diels the Gestapo played a complex role. In the weeks following Hitler's appointment as chancellor, Diels's Gestapo acted as a curb against a wave of violence by the SA, during which Storm Troopers dragged thousands of victims to their makeshift prisons. Diels led raids to close them and found prisoners in appalling conditions, beaten and garishly bruised, limbs broken, near starvation, "like a mass of inanimate clay," he wrote, "absurd puppets with lifeless eyes, burning with fever, their bodies sagging."

Martha's father liked Diels. To his surprise, he found the Gestapo chief to be a helpful intermediary for extracting foreign nationals and others from concentration camps and for exerting pressure on police authorities outside Berlin to find and punish the SA men responsible for attacks against Americans.

Diels was no saint, however. During his tenure as chief, thousands of men and women were arrested, many tortured, some murdered. On Diels's watch, for example, a German communist named Ernst Thälmann was imprisoned and interrogated at Gestapo headquarters. Thälmann left a vivid account. "They ordered me to take off my pants and then two men grabbed me by the back of the neck and placed me across a footstool. A uniformed Gestapo officer with a whip of hippopotamus hide in his hand then beat my buttocks with measured strokes. Driven wild with pain I repeatedly screamed at the top of my voice."

In Diels's view, violence and terror were valuable tools for the preservation of political power. During a gathering of foreign correspondents at Putzi Hanfstaengl's home, Diels told the reporters, "The value of the SA and the SS, seen from my viewpoint of inspector-general responsible for the suppression of subversive tendencies and activities, lies in the fact that they spread terror. That is a wholesome thing."

MARTHA AND DIELS TOOK walks together in the Tiergarten, which was fast becoming recognized as the one place in central Berlin where a person could feel at ease. Martha especially loved strolling through the park in autumn, amid what she termed "the golden death of the Tiergarten." They went to movies and nightclubs and drove for hours through the countryside. That they became lovers seems likely, despite the fact that both were married, Martha in technical terms only, Diels in name only, given his penchant for adultery. Martha loved being known as the woman who slept with the devil—and that she did sleep with him seems beyond doubt, though it is equally likely that Dodd, like naive fathers everywhere and in every time, had no idea. Messersmith suspected it, and so did Raymond Geist, his second in command. Geist complained to Wilbur Carr, head of consular services in Washington, that Martha was a "most indiscreet" young lady who had been "in the habit of constantly going about at night with the head of the Nazi Secret Police, a married man." Geist himself had heard her call Diels, in public, a variety of affectionate names, among them "dearie."

The more Martha came to know Diels, the more she saw that he too was afraid. He felt "he was constantly facing the muzzle of a gun," she wrote. He was most at ease during their drives, when no one could overhear their conversations or monitor their behavior. They would stop and walk through forests and have coffee in remote, little-known cafés. He told her stories of how everyone in the Nazi hierarchy distrusted everyone else, how Göring and Goebbels loathed each other and spied on each other, how both spied on Diels, and how Diels and his men spied on them in turn.

It was through Diels that she began for the first time to temper her idealistic view of the Nazi revolution. "There began to appear before my romantic eyes . . . a vast and complicated network of espionage, terror, sadism and hate, from which no one, official or private, could escape."

Not even Diels, as events soon would demonstrate.

CHAPTER 14

The Death of Boris

There was still another lover in Martha's life, the most important of all, a doomed Russian who would shape the rest of her life.

She first caught a glimpse of him in mid-September 1933 at one of the many parties Sigrid Schultz held at her apartment, where she lived with her mother and her two dogs. Schultz typically served sandwiches, baked beans, and sausages prepared by her mother and provided a lot of beer, wine, and liquor, which tended to cause even Nazi guests to shed doctrine in favor of fun and gossip. In the midst of a conversation, Martha happened to glance across the room and saw a tall, good-looking man at the center of a group of correspondents. He was not handsome in a conventional sense but very attractive— maybe thirty, short blond-brown hair, strikingly luminous eyes, and an easy, fluid manner. He moved his hands as he spoke, and Martha saw that he had long and supple fingers. "He had an unusual mouth, and upper lip," recalled one of Martha's friends, Agnes Knicker-bocker, wife of correspondent H. R. "Knick" Knickerbocker. "I can't describe it other than to say that it could go from sternness to laughter in an exploding split second."

As Martha watched him, he turned and looked at her. She held his gaze a few moments, then looked away and became involved in other conversations. (In a later unpublished account she recalled minute details of this moment and others to follow.) He turned away as well—but when the morning came and the night distilled to its essential elements, this meeting of glances was the thing that both remembered.

Several weeks later they encountered each other again. Knick and his wife invited Martha and a few other friends to join them for a night of drinks and dancing at Ciro's, a popular nightclub that employed black jazz musicians, a twofold act of defiance given the Nazi Party's obsession with racial purity and its condemnation of jazz— in party jargon, "nigger-Jew jazz"—as degenerate music.

Knick introduced Martha to the tall man she had seen at Sigrid Schultz's party. His name, she now learned, was Boris Winogradov (pronounced "Vinogradov"). A few moments later, Boris appeared before her table, smiling and self-conscious. "Gnädiges Fräulein," he began, offering the customary German greeting, meaning "dear young lady." He asked her to dance.

She was struck immediately by the beauty of his voice, which she described as falling somewhere between baritone and tenor. "Mellifluous," she wrote. It moved her, "struck my heart and for a moment left me without words or breath." He held out a hand to guide her from the crowded table.

She quickly learned that his natural grace had limits. He walked her around the dance floor, "stepping on my toes, bumping into people, his left arm stuck out stiffly, turning his head from side to side trying to avoid further collisions."

He told her, "I don't know how to dance."

It was such an obvious fact that Martha burst out laughing.

Boris laughed too. She liked his smile and his overall "aura of gentleness."

A few moments later he said to her, "I am with the Soviet embassy. Haben Sie Angst?"

She laughed again. "Of course not, why should I be afraid? Of what?"

"Correct," he said, "you're a private person, and with you I am too."

He held her closer. He was slender and broad shouldered and had eyes she deemed gorgeous, blue-green flecked with gold. He had irregular teeth that somehow enhanced his smile. He was quick to laugh.

"I have seen you several times before," he said. The last occasion, he reminded her, had been at Schultz's home. "Erinnern Sie sich?" Do you remember?

Contrarian by nature, Martha did not want to seem too easy a mark. She kept her voice "non-committal" but did concede the fact. "Yes," she said, "I remember."

They danced a while longer. When he returned her to the Knickerbockers' table, he leaned close and asked, "Ich möchte Sie sehr wiederzusehen. Darf ich Sie anrufen?"

The meaning was clear to Martha despite her limited German—Boris was asking if he could see her again.

She told Boris, "Yes, you may call."

Martha danced with others. At one point she looked back toward her table and spotted the Knickerbockers with Boris seated beside them. Boris watched her.

"Incredible as it sounds," she wrote, "I had the sensation after he left that the air around me was more luminous and vibrant."

SEVERAL DAYS LATER Boris did call. He drove to the Dodds' house; introduced himself to Fritz, the butler; then went charging up the stairs to the main floor carrying a bouquet of autumn flowers and a disc for a record player. He did not kiss her hand, a good thing, for that particular German ritual always annoyed her. After a brief preamble, he held out the record.

"You don't know Russian music, do you, *gnädiges Fräulein?* Have you ever heard 'The Death of Boris,' by Mussorgsky?"

He added, "I hope it's not my death I am going to play for you."

He laughed. She did not. It struck her even then as "a portent" of something dark to come.

They listened to the music—the death scene from Modest Mussorgsky's opera *Boris Godunov*, sung by the famous Russian bass Fyodor Chaliapin—and then Martha gave Boris a tour of the house, finishing in the library. At one end was her father's desk, immense and dark, its drawers always locked. The late autumn sun broke through the high stained-glass window in pleats of many-hued light. She led him to her favorite couch.

Boris was delighted. "This is our corner, *gnädiges Fräulein!*" he exclaimed. "Better than all the others."

Martha sat on the couch; Boris pulled over a chair. She rang for Fritz and asked him to bring beer and a casual fare of pretzels, sliced carrots and cucumbers, and hot cheese sticks, foods she usually ordered when she entertained unofficial visitors.

Fritz brought the food, his step very quiet, almost as if he were attempting to listen in. Boris guessed, correctly, that Fritz too had Slavic roots. The two men traded pleasantries.

Taking a cue from Boris's easy manner, Fritz quipped, "Did you communists really burn the Reichstag?"

Boris gave him an arch smile and winked. "Of course we did," he said, "you and I together. Don't you recall the night we were at Göring's and were shown the secret passageway to the Reichstag?" This was an allusion to a widely believed theory that a team of Nazi incendiaries had secretly made their way from Göring's palace to the Reichstag via an underground tunnel between the two buildings. Such a tunnel did, in fact, exist.

All three laughed. This mock complicity in the Reichstag fire would remain a joke between Boris and Fritz, repeated often in varying forms to the great delight of Martha's father—even though Fritz, Martha believed, was "almost surely an agent of the secret police."

Fritz returned with vodka. Boris poured himself a large drink and quickly downed it. Martha settled back in the couch. This time Boris sat beside her. He drank a second vodka but showed no obvious sign of its effect.

"From the first moment I saw you—" he began. He hesitated, then said, "Can it be, I wonder?"

She understood what he was trying to say and in fact she too felt a powerful, instant attraction, but she was not inclined to concede it this early in the game. She looked at him, blank.

He grew serious. He launched into a lengthy interrogation. What did she do in Chicago? What were her parents like? What did she want to do in the future?

The exchange had more in common with a newspaper interview than a first-date conversation. Martha found it vexing but answered with patience. For all she knew, this was how all Soviet men behaved. "I had never before met a *real* Communist, or a *Russian* for that matter," she wrote, "so I imagined this must be their way of knowing someone."

As the conversation wore on, both consulted pocket dictionaries. Boris knew some English, but not much, and conversed mainly in German. Martha knew no Russian, so deployed a mix of German and English.

Though it took a good deal of effort, she told Boris that her parents were both offspring of old southern landowning families, "each as well ancestored as the other, and almost pure British: Scotch-Irish, English, and Welsh."

Boris laughed. "That's not so pure, is it?"

With an unconscious note of pride in her voice, she added that both families had once owned slaves—"Mother's about twelve or so, Father's five or six."

Boris went quiet. His expression shifted abruptly to one of sorrow. "Martha," he said, "surely you are not proud that your ancestors owned the lives of other human beings."

He took her hands and looked at her. Until this moment the fact that her parents' ancestors had owned slaves had always seemed merely an interesting element of their personal history that testified to their deep roots in America. Now, suddenly, she saw it for what it was—a sad chapter to be regretted.

"I didn't mean to boast," she said. "I suppose it sounded like that to you." She apologized and immediately hated herself for it. She was, she conceded, "a combative girl."

"But we do have a long tradition in America," she told him. "We are not newcomers."

Boris found her defensiveness hilarious and laughed with unrestrained delight.

In the next instant, he adopted a look and tone that she recalled as being "solemn in the extreme."

"Congratulations, my noble, gracious, little Marta! I too am also of ancient lineage, even older than yours. I am a direct descendant of Neanderthal man. And pure? Yes, *pure human*."

They collapsed against each other with laughter.

✦ ✦ ✦

THEY BECAME REGULAR COMPANIONS, though they tried to keep
their emerging relationship as discreet as possible. The United States
had not yet recognized the Soviet Union (and would not do so until
November 16, 1933). To have the daughter of the American ambassador openly consorting with a first secretary of the Soviet embassy
at official functions would have constituted a breach of protocol that
would have put both her father and Boris at risk of criticism from
inside and outside their respective governments. She and Boris left
diplomatic receptions early, then met for secret meals at such fine
restaurants as Horcher's, Pelzer, Habel, and Kempinski. To cut costs
a bit, Boris also cultivated the chefs of small, inexpensive restaurants
and instructed them on how to prepare foods he liked. After dinner
he and Martha would go dancing at Ciro's or at the club on the roof
of the Eden Hotel, or to political cabarets such as the Kabarett der
Komiker.

Some nights Martha and Boris would join the correspondents
gathered at Die Taverne, where Boris was always welcomed. The reporters liked him. The now-exiled Edgar Mowrer had found Boris a
refreshing change from other officials in the Soviet embassy. Boris,
he recalled, spoke his mind without slavish adherence to party doctrine and "seemed totally unintimidated by the kind of censorship
which seemed to silence other members of the Embassy."

Like Martha's other suitors, Boris sought to escape Nazi intrusion
by taking her on long drives into the countryside. He drove a Ford
convertible, which he loved dearly. Agnes Knickerbocker recalled
that he "made some ceremony of putting on his fine leather gloves
before taking the wheel." He was "an unswerving communist," she
wrote, but "he liked the so-called good things in life."

He almost always kept the top down, closing it only on the cold-
est nights. As his relationship with Martha deepened, he insisted
on placing his arm around her as he drove. He seemed to need her
touch at all times. He would place her hand on his knee or insert
her fingers into his glove. On occasion they took these drives late at
night, sometimes staying out until dawn, Martha wrote, "to welcome
the rising sun in the black-green forests spangled with autumn gold."

Though his English was limited, he learned and adored the word "darling" and used it every chance he got. He also deployed Russian endearments, which he refused to translate, claiming that to do so would diminish their beauty. In German, he called her "my little girl," or "my sweet child," or "my little one." She mused that he did so partly because of her height, partly because of his overall perception of her character and maturity. "He once said I had a naïveté and idealism he could not easily understand," she wrote. She sensed that he found her too "flighty" to even attempt to indoctrinate her in the tenets of communism. This was a period, she acknowledged, when "I must have appeared a most naive and stubborn young American, a vexation to all sensible people I knew."

She found that Boris also took the world lightly, at least outwardly. "At thirty-one," she wrote, "Boris had a childlike gaiety and faith, a mad-cap humor and charm not often found in mature men." Now and then, however, reality intruded on what Martha called their "personal dream-world of dinners and concerts, theaters and joyous festivities." She sensed in him a seam of tension. He was especially dismayed to see how readily the world accepted Hitler's protestations of peace even as he so obviously girded the country for war. The Soviet Union seemed a likely target. Another source of stress was his own embassy's disapproval of his relationship with Martha. His superiors issued a reprimand. He ignored it.

Martha, meanwhile, experienced pressure of a less official variety. Her father liked Boris, she thought, but he was often reticent in Boris's presence, "even antagonistic at times." She attributed this mainly to his fear that she and Boris might get married.

"My friends and family are disturbed about us," she told Boris. "What can come of it? Only complications, some joy now, and then perhaps long despair."

FOR ONE OF THEIR September dates, Boris and Martha packed a picnic lunch and drove into the countryside. They found a private glade, where they spread their blanket. The air was suffused with the scent of freshly cut grass. As Boris lay on the blanket, smiling at the sky, Martha plucked a length of wild mint and used it to tickle his face.

He saved it, as she later discovered. He was a romantic, a collec-
tor of treasures. Even this early in their relationship he was deeply
smitten—and, as it happens, closely watched.

Martha appeared at this point to have no knowledge of what many
correspondents suspected: that Boris was no mere first secretary of
embassy, but rather an operative for Soviet intelligence, the NKVD,
precursor to the KGB.

CHAPTER 15

The "Jewish Problem"

As ambassador, Dodd's main point of contact in the German government was Foreign Minister Neurath. Spurred by the Kaltenborn incident, Dodd arranged to meet with Neurath on Thursday morning, September 14, 1933, to make a formal protest, against not just that episode but also the many other attacks on Americans and the regime's apparent unwillingness to bring the perpetrators to justice.

Their conversation took place in Neurath's office in the Foreign Ministry on Wilhelmstrasse.

It began amiably enough with a discussion of economic matters, but the atmosphere quickly grew tense as Dodd broached the subject of "SA brutalities" and reviewed for Neurath half a dozen incidents. The most recent had occurred on August 31 in Berlin—the Samuel Bossard incident, in which Bossard was assaulted by members of the Hitler Youth after failing to offer the Hitler salute. A week earlier another American, Harold Dahlquist, had been struck by a Storm Trooper for failing to stop to watch an SA parade. Overall the frequency of such attacks had decreased as compared with the preceding spring, but incidents continued to occur at a steady rate of one or two a month. Dodd warned Neurath that press accounts of these attacks had caused real damage to Germany's reputation in America and noted that this happened despite his own efforts to mute negative coverage by American correspondents. "I may say to you that the embassy has endeavored successfully on several occasions to prevent unimportant events from being reported and also warned reporters from exaggerating their stories," he told Neurath.

He revealed now that on one occasion his own car had been stopped and searched, apparently by an SA officer, but that he had kept the incident from being publicized "to prevent widespread discussions which as you know would have been inevitable."

Neurath thanked him and said he was aware of Dodd's efforts to temper press coverage of Storm Trooper violence, including the incident that Martha and Bill Jr. had witnessed in Nuremberg. He professed to be very grateful.

Dodd turned to the Kaltenborn episode. He told Neurath that the reaction in the United States could have been far worse if Kaltenborn himself had been inclined to publicize it. "He was generous enough, however, to ask us not to allow any report of the episode to get out, and both Mr. Messersmith and I urged the American press not to mention this story," Dodd said. "It did, however, get out and did Germany incalculable injury."

Neurath, though renowned for his lack of public affect, grew visibly perturbed, a novelty worth recording, as Dodd did in a "strictly confidential" memorandum he composed later that day. Neurath claimed to know Kaltenborn personally and condemned the attack as brutal and without justification.

Dodd watched him. Neurath seemed sincere, but lately the foreign minister had been displaying a penchant for agreeing and then doing nothing.

Dodd warned that if the attacks continued and if the assailants still evaded punishment, the United States might indeed be forced to "publish a statement which would greatly damage the rating of Germany all over the world."

Neurath's complexion turned a deeper red.

Dodd continued as if lecturing a wayward student: "I cannot see how your officials can allow such behavior or how they fail to see that it is one of the most serious things affecting our relations."

Neurath claimed that during the preceding week he had raised the issue directly with Göring and Hitler. Both, he said, had assured him that they would use their influence to prevent further attacks. Neurath vowed to do likewise.

Dodd pressed on, now venturing into even more charged territory: the Jewish "problem," as Dodd and Neurath both termed it.

Neurath asked Dodd whether the United States "did not have a Jewish problem" of its own.

"You know, of course," Dodd said, "that we have had difficulty now and then in the United States with Jews who had gotten too much of a hold on certain departments of intellectual and business life." He added that some of his peers in Washington had told him confidentially that "they appreciated the difficulties of the Germans in this respect but that they did not for a moment agree with the method of solving the problem which so often ran into utter ruthlessness."

Dodd described his encounter with Fritz Haber, the chemist.

"Yes," Neurath said, "I know Haber and recognize him as one of the greatest chemists in all Europe." Neurath agreed that Germany's treatment of Jews was wrongheaded and said his ministry was urging a more humane approach. He claimed to see signs of change. Just that week, he said, he had gone to the races at Baden-Baden and three prominent Jews had sat with him on the platform along with other government officials, "and there were no unfriendly expressions."

Dodd said, "You cannot expect world opinion of your conduct to moderate so long as eminent leaders like Hitler and Goebbels announce from platforms, as in Nuremberg, that all Jews must be wiped off the earth."

Dodd rose to leave. He turned to Neurath. "Shall we have a war?" he asked.

Again Neurath flushed: "Never!"

At the door, Dodd said, "You must realize that Germany would be ruined by another war."

Dodd left the building, "a little concerned that I had been so frank and critical."

THE VERY NEXT DAY, the American consul in Stuttgart, Germany, sent a "strictly confidential" communiqué to Berlin in which he reported that the Mauser Company, in his jurisdiction, had sharply increased its production of arms. The consul wrote, "No doubt can be entertained any longer that large scale preparation for a renewal of aggression against other countries is being planned in Germany."

Soon afterward the same consul reported that German police had begun close surveillance of highways, routinely stopping travelers and subjecting them, their cars, and their baggage to detailed search.

On one notorious occasion the government ordered a nation-wide halt of all traffic between noon and 12:40 so that squads of police could search all trains, trucks, and cars then in transit. The official explanation, quoted by German newspapers, was that the police were hunting for weapons, foreign propaganda, and evidence of communist resistance. Cynical Berliners embraced a different theory then making the rounds: that what the police really hoped to find, and confiscate, were copies of Swiss and Austrian newspapers carrying allegations that Hitler himself might have Jewish ancestry.

CHAPTER 16

A Secret Request

The attacks against Americans, his protests, the unpredictability of Hitler and his deputies, and the need to tread with so much delicacy in the face of official behavior that anywhere else might draw time in prison—all of it wore Dodd down. He was plagued by headaches and stomach troubles. In a letter to a friend he described his ambassadorship as "this disagreeable and difficult business."

On top of it all came the quotidian troubles that even ambassadors had to cope with.

In mid-September the Dodds became aware of a good deal of noise coming from the fourth floor of their house on Tiergartenstrasse, which supposedly was occupied only by Panofsky and his mother. With no advance notice to Dodd, a team of carpenters arrived and, starting at seven o'clock each day, began hammering and sawing and otherwise raising a clamor, and continued doing so for two weeks. On September 18, Panofsky wrote a brief note to Dodd: "Herewith I am informing you that at the beginning of the coming month my wife and my children will return from their stay in the countryside back to Berlin. I am convinced that the comfort of your excellency and of Mrs. Dodd will not be impaired, as it is my aspiration to make your stay in my house as comfortable as possible."

Panofsky moved his wife and children into the fourth floor, along with several servants.

Dodd was shocked. He composed a letter to Panofsky, which he then edited heavily, crossing out and modifying every other line, clearly aware that this was more than a routine landlord-tenant matter. Panofsky was bringing his family back to Berlin because Dodd's presence ensured their safety. Dodd's first draft hinted that he might now have to move his own family and chided Panofsky for not having disclosed his plans in July. Had he done so, Dodd wrote, "we should not [have] been in such an embarrassing position."

Dodd's final draft was softer. "We are very happy indeed to hear that you are reunited with your family," he wrote, in German. "Our only concern would be that your children won't be able to use their own home as freely as they would like. We bought our house in Chicago so that our children could experience the advantages of the outdoors. It would sadden me to have the feeling that we might hinder this entitled freedom and bodily movement of your children. If we had known about your plans in July, we would not have been in this tight spot right now."

The Dodds, like abused tenants everywhere, resolved at first to be patient and to hope that the new din of children and servants would subside.

It did not. The clatter of comings and goings and the chance appearances of small children caused awkward moments, especially when the Dodds entertained diplomats and senior Reich officials, the latter already disposed to belittle Dodd's frugal habits—his plain suits, the walks to work, the old Chevrolet. And now the unexpected arrival of an entire household of Jews.

"There was too much noise and disturbance, especially since the duties of my office required frequent entertainments," Dodd wrote in a memorandum. "I think anyone would have said it was an act of bad faith."

Dodd consulted a lawyer.

His landlord troubles and the mounting demands of his post made it increasingly difficult for Dodd to find time to work on his *Old South*. He was able to write only for brief intervals in the evening and on weekends. He struggled to acquire books and documents that would have been simple to locate in America.

The thing that weighed on him most, however, was the irrationality of the world in which he now found himself. To some extent he was a prisoner of his own training. As a historian, he had come to view the world as the product of historical forces and the decisions of more or less rational people, and he expected the men around him to behave in a civil and coherent manner. But Hitler's government was neither civil nor coherent, and the nation lurched from one inexplicable moment to another.

Even the language used by Hitler and party officials was weirdly inverted. The term "fanatical" became a positive trait. Suddenly it connoted what philologist Victor Klemperer, a Jewish resident of Berlin, described as a "happy mix of courage and fervent devotion." Nazi-controlled newspapers reported an endless succession of "fanatical vows" and "fanatical declarations" and "fanatical beliefs," all good things. Göring was described as a "fanatical animal lover." *Fanatischer Tierfreund.*

Certain very old words were coming into darkly robust modern use, Klemperer found. *Übermensch:* superman. *Untermensch:* sub-human, meaning "Jew." Wholly new words were emerging as well, among them *Strafexpedition*—"punitive expedition"—the term Storm Troopers applied to their forays into Jewish and communist neighborhoods.

Klemperer detected a certain "hysteria of language" in the new flood of decrees, alarms, and intimidation—"This perpetual threatening with the death penalty!"—and in strange, inexplicable episodes of paranoid excess, like the recent nationwide search. In all this Klemperer saw a deliberate effort to generate a kind of daily suspense, "copied from American cinema and thrillers," that helped keep people in line. He also gauged it to be a manifestation of insecurity among those in power. In late July 1933 Klemperer saw a newsreel in which Hitler, with fists clenched and face contorted, shrieked, "On 30 January they"—and here Klemperer presumed he meant the Jews—"laughed at me—that smile will be wiped off their faces!" Klemperer was struck by the fact that although Hitler was trying to convey omnipotence, he appeared to be in a wild, uncontrolled rage, which paradoxically had the effect of undermining his boasts that the new Reich would last a thousand years and that all his enemies would be annihilated. Klemperer wondered, Do you talk with such blind rage "if you are so sure of this endurance and this annihilation"?

He left the theater that day "with what almost amounted to a glimmer of hope."

IN THE WORLD OUTSIDE Dodd's windows, however, the shadows steadily deepened. Another attack occurred against an American, a representative of the Woolworth dime-store chain named Roland Velz, who was assaulted in Düsseldorf on Sunday, October 8, 1933, as he and his wife strolled along one of the city's main streets. Like so many victims before them, they had committed the sin of failing to acknowledge an SA parade. An incensed Storm Trooper struck Velz twice, hard, in the face, and moved on. When Velz tried to get a policeman to arrest the man, the officer declined. Velz then complained to a police lieutenant standing nearby, but he also refused to act. Instead, the officer provided a brief lesson on how and when to salute.

Dodd sent two notes of protest to the foreign office in which he demanded immediate action to arrest the attacker. He received no reply. Once again Dodd weighed the idea of asking the State Department to "announce to the world that Americans are not safe in Germany and that travelers had best not go there," but he ultimately demurred.

Persecution of Jews continued in ever more subtle and wide-ranging form as the process of Gleichschaltung advanced. In September the government established the Reich Chamber of Culture, under the control of Goebbels, to bring musicians, actors, painters, writers, reporters, and filmmakers into ideological and, especially, racial alignment. In early October the government enacted the Editorial Law, which banned Jews from employment by newspapers and publishers and was to take effect on January 1, 1934. No realm was too petty: The Ministry of Posts ruled that henceforth when trying to spell a word over the telephone a caller could no longer say "D as in David," because "David" was a Jewish name. The caller had to use "Dora." "Samuel" became "Siegfried." And so forth. "There has been nothing in social history more implacable, more heartless and more devastating than the present policy in Germany against the Jews," Consul General Messersmith told Undersecretary Phillips in a long letter dated September 29, 1933. He wrote, "It is definitely the aim of the Government, no matter what it may say to the outside or in Germany, to eliminate the Jews from German life."

For a time Messersmith had been convinced that Germany's economic crisis would unseat Hitler. No longer. He saw now that Hitler, Göring, and Goebbels were firmly in power. They "know practically nothing concerning the outside world," he wrote. "They know only that in Germany they can do as they will. They feel their power within the country and are to that extent drunk with it."

Messersmith proposed that one solution might be "forcible intervention from the outside." But he warned that such an action would have to come soon. "If there were intervention by other powers now, probably about half of the population would still look upon it as deliverance," he wrote. "If it is delayed too long, such intervention might meet a practically united Germany."

One fact was certain, Messersmith believed: Germany now posed a real and grave threat to the world. He called it "the sore spot which may disturb our peace for years to come."

DODD BEGAN TO EXHIBIT the first signs of discouragement and a deep weariness.

"There is nothing here that seems to offer much promise," he wrote to his friend Colonel Edward M. House, "and I am, between us again, not a little doubtful of the wisdom of my having intimated last spring that I might be of service in Germany. I have one volume of *The Old South* ready or nearly ready for publication. There are to be three more. I have worked twenty years on the subject and dislike to run too great a risk of never finishing it." He closed: "Now I am here, sixty-four years old, and engaged ten to fifteen hours a day! Getting nowhere. Yet, if I resigned, that fact would complicate matters." To his friend Jane Addams, the reformer who founded Hull House in Chicago, he wrote, "It defeats my history work and I am far from sure I was right in my choice last June."

On October 4, 1933, barely three months into his stay, Dodd sent Secretary Hull a letter marked "confidential and for you alone."

Citing the dampness of Berlin's autumn and winter climate and his lack of a vacation since March, Dodd requested permission to take a lengthy leave early in the coming year so that he could spend time on his farm and do some teaching in Chicago. He hoped to depart Berlin at the end of February and return three months later.

He asked Hull to keep his request secret. "Please do not refer to others if you have doubts yourself."

Hull granted Dodd's leave request, suggesting that at this time Washington did not share Messersmith's assessment of Germany as a serious and growing threat. The diaries of Undersecretary Phillips and Western European affairs chief Moffat make clear that the State Department's main concern about Germany remained its huge debt to American creditors.

CHAPTER 17

Lucifer's Run

With the approach of autumn, the challenge for Martha of juggling the suitors in her life became a bit less daunting, albeit for a disturbing reason. Diels disappeared.

One night in early October, Diels was working late at his office at Prinz-Albrecht-Strasse 8 when, around midnight, he received a telephone call from his wife, Hilde, who sounded deeply distressed. As he recounted in a later memoir, *Lucifer Ante Portas—Lucifer at the Gate*—his wife told him that "a horde" of armed men in black uniforms had broken into their apartment, locked her in a bedroom, and then conducted an aggressive search, collecting diaries, letters, and various other files that Diels kept at home. Diels raced to his apartment and managed to piece together enough information to identify the intruders as a squad of SS under the command of one Captain Herbert Packebusch. Packebusch was only thirty-one years old, Diels wrote, but already had a "harshness and callousness written deep into his face." Diels called him "the very prototype and image of the later concentration-camp commandants."

Although the brazen nature of Packebusch's raid surprised Diels, he understood the forces at work behind it. The regime seethed with conflict and conspiracy. Diels stood primarily in Göring's camp, with Göring holding all police power in Berlin and the surrounding territory of Prussia, the largest of the German states. But Heinrich Himmler, in charge of the SS, was rapidly gaining control over secret police agencies throughout the rest of Germany. Göring and Himmler loathed each other and competed for influence.

Diels acted quickly. He called a friend in charge of the Tiergarten station of the Berlin police and marshaled a force of uniformed officers armed with machine guns and hand grenades. He led them to an SS stronghold on Potsdamer Strasse and directed the men to surround the building. The SS guarding the door were unaware of what had taken place and helpfully led Diels and a contingent of police to Packebusch's office.

The surprise was total. As Diels entered he saw Packebusch at his desk in shirtsleeves, the black jacket of his uniform hanging on an adjacent wall, along with his belt and holstered pistol. "He sat there, brooding over the papers on his desk like a scholar working into the night," Diels wrote. Diels was outraged. "They were my papers he was working on, and defacing, as I soon discovered, with inept annotations." Diels found that Packebusch even saw evil in the way Diels and his wife had decorated their apartment. In one note Packebusch had scrawled the phrase "furnishing style a la Stresemann," a reference to the late Gustav Stresemann, a Weimar-era opponent of Hitler.

"You're under arrest," Diels said.

Packebusch looked up abruptly. One instant he had been reading Diels's personal papers, and the next, Diels was standing before him. "Packebusch had no time to recover from his surprise," Diels wrote. "He stared at me as if I were an apparition."

Diels's men seized Packebusch. One officer took the SS captain's pistol from his gun belt on the wall, but apparently no one bothered to conduct a more thorough search of Packebusch himself. Police officers moved through the building to arrest other men whom Diels believed had taken part in the raid on his apartment. All the suspects were transported to Gestapo headquarters; Packebusch was brought to Diels's office.

There, in the early hours of morning, Diels and Packebusch sat facing each other, both livid. Diels's Alsatian wolf dog—in that time the official name for German shepherds—stood nearby, watchful.

Diels vowed to put Packebusch in prison.

Packebusch accused Diels of treason.

Infuriated by Packebusch's insolence, Diels rocketed from his chair in a flare of anger. Packebusch loosed his own freshet of obscenities and pulled a hidden pistol from a back pocket of his pants. He aimed it at Diels, finger on the trigger.

Diels's dog hurtled into the scene, leaping toward Packebusch, according to Diels's account. Two uniformed officers grabbed Packebusch and wrenched the gun from his hand. Diels ordered him placed in the Gestapo's house prison, in the basement.

In short order, Göring and Himmler got involved and struck a compromise. Göring removed Diels as head of the Gestapo and made him assistant police commissioner in Berlin. Diels recognized that the new job was a demotion to a post with no real power—at least not the kind of power he would need to hold his own against Himmler if the SS chief chose to seek further revenge. Nonetheless he accepted the arrangement, and so things stood until one morning later that month, when two loyal employees flagged him down as he drove to work. They told him that agents of the SS were waiting for him in his office with an arrest order.

Diels fled. In his memoir he claims that his wife recommended he bring along a friend, an American woman, "who could be helpful when crossing borders." She lived in "a flat on Tiergartenstrasse," he wrote, and she liked risk: "I knew her enthusiasm for danger and adventure."

His clues bring Martha immediately to mind, but she made no mention of such a journey in her memoir or in any of her other writings.

Diels and his companion drove to Potsdam, then south to the border, where he left his car in a garage. He carried a false passport. They crossed the border into Czechoslovakia and proceeded to the spa city of Carlsbad, where they checked into a hotel. Diels also took along some of his more sensitive files, as insurance.

"From his retreat in Bohemia," wrote Hans Gisevius, the Gestapo memoirist, "he threatened embarrassing revelations, and asked a high price for keeping his mouth shut."

WITH DIELS GONE, many in Martha's growing circle of friends doubtless breathed a little more easily, especially those who harbored sympathy for communists or mourned the lost freedoms of the Weimar past. Her social life continued to blossom.

Of all her new friends, the one she found most compelling was Mildred Fish Harnack, whom she had first encountered on the train platform upon arriving in Berlin. Mildred spoke flawless German and by most accounts was a beauty, tall and slender, with long blond hair that she wore in a thick coil and large, serious blue eyes. She shunned all makeup. Later, after a certain secret of hers was revealed, a description of her would surface in Soviet intelligence files that sketched her as "very much the German Frau, an intensely Nordic type and very useful."

She stood out not just because of her looks, Martha saw, but also because of her manner. "She was slow to speak and express opinions," Martha wrote; "she listened quietly, weighing and evaluating the words, thoughts and motivations in conversation. . . . Her words were thoughtful, sometimes ambiguous when it was necessary to feel people out."

This art of parsing the motives and attitudes of others had become especially important given how she and her husband, Arvid Harnack, had spent the preceding few years. The two had met in 1926 at the University of Wisconsin, where Mildred was an instructor. They married that August, moved to Germany, and eventually settled in Berlin. Along the way they demonstrated a talent for bringing people together. At each stop they formed a salon that convened at regular intervals for meals, conversation, lectures, even group readings of Shakespeare's plays, all echoes of a famous group they had joined in Wisconsin, the Friday Niters, founded by John R. Commons, a professor and leading Progressive who one day would become known as the "spiritual father" of Social Security.

In Berlin, in the winter of 1930–31, Arvid founded yet another group, this devoted to the study of Soviet Russia's planned economy. As the Nazi Party gained sway, his field of interest became decidedly problematic, but he nonetheless arranged and led a tour of the Soviet Union for some two dozen German economists and engineers. While abroad he was recruited by Soviet intelligence to work secretly against the Nazis. He agreed.

When Hitler came to power, Arvid felt compelled to disband his planned-economy group. The political climate had grown lethal. He and Mildred retreated to the countryside, where Mildred spent her time writing and Arvid took a job as a lawyer for the German airline Lufthansa. After the initial spasm of anticommunist terror subsided, the Harnacks returned to their apartment in Berlin. Surprisingly, given his background, Arvid got a job within the Ministry of Economics and began a rapid rise that prompted some of Mildred's friends in America to decide that she and Arvid had "gone Nazi."

Early on, Martha knew nothing of Arvid's covert life. She loved visiting the couple's apartment, which was bright and cozy and pasteled with comforting hues: "dove tans, soft blues, and greens." Mildred filled large vases with lavender cosmos and placed them in front of a pale yellow wall. Martha and Mildred came to see each other as kindred spirits, both deeply interested in writing. By late September 1933 the two had arranged to write a column on books for an English-language newspaper called *Berlin Topics*. In a September 25, 1933, letter to Thornton Wilder, Martha described the newspaper as "lousy" but said she hoped it might serve as a catalyst "to build up a little colony in the English-speaking group here. . . . Get people together who like books and authors."

When the Harnacks traveled, Mildred sent Martha postcards upon which she wrote poetic observations of the scenery before her and warm expressions of affection. On one card Mildred wrote, "Martha, you know that I love you and think of you through it all." She thanked Martha for reading and critiquing some of her writing. "It shows a gift in you," she wrote.

She closed with an inked sigh: "Oh my Dear, my Dear . . . life—" The ellipsis was hers.

To Martha these cards were like petals falling from an unseen place. "I prized these post-cards and short letters with their delicate, almost tremblingly sensitive prose. There was nothing studied or affected about them. Their feeling sprang simply from her full and joyous heart and had to be expressed."

Mildred became a regular guest at embassy functions, and by November she was earning extra pay typing the manuscript of the first volume of Dodd's *Old South*. Martha, in turn, became a regular attendee at a new salon that Mildred and Arvid established, the Berlin equivalent of the Friday Niters. Ever the organizers, they accumulated a society of loyal friends—writers, editors, artists, intellectuals—who convened at their apartment several times a month for weekday suppers and Saturday-afternoon teas. Here, Martha noted in a letter to Wilder, she met the writer Ernst von Salomon, notorious for having played a role in the 1922 assassination of Weimar foreign minister Walter Rathenau. She loved the cozy atmosphere Mildred conjured, despite having little money to spare. There were lamps, candles and flowers, and a tray of thin bread, cheese, liverwurst, and sliced tomatoes. Not a banquet, but enough. Her host, Martha told Wilder, was "the kind of person who has the sense or nonsense to put a candle behind a bunch of pussy willows or alpen rosen."

The talk was bright, smart, and daring. Too daring at times, at least in the view of Salomon's wife, whose perspective was shaped partly by the fact she was Jewish. She was appalled at how casually the guests would call Himmler and Hitler "utter fools" in her presence, without knowing who she was or where her sympathies lay. She watched one guest pass a yellow envelope to another and then wink like an uncle slipping a piece of forbidden candy to a nephew. "And there I sit on the sofa," she said, "and can hardly breathe."

Martha found it thrilling and gratifying, despite the group's anti-Nazi bent. She staunchly defended the Nazi revolution as offering the best way out of the chaos that had engulfed Germany ever since the past war. Her participation in the salon reinforced her sense of herself as a writer and intellectual. In addition to attending the correspondents' *Stammtisch* at Die Taverne, she began spending a lot of time in the great old Berlin cafés, those still not fully "coordinated," such as the Josty on Potsdamer Platz and the Romanisches on the Kurfürstendamm. The latter, which could seat up to a thousand people, had a storied past as a haven for the likes of Erich Maria Remarque, Joseph Roth, and Billy Wilder, though all by now had been driven from Berlin. She went out to dinner often and to nightclubs like Ciro's and the Eden roof. Ambassador Dodd's papers are silent on the matter, but given his frugality he must have found Martha to be an unexpectedly, and alarmingly, costly presence on the family ledger.

Martha hoped to stake a place in Berlin's cultural landscape all her own, not just by dint of her friendship with the Harnacks, and she wanted that place to be a prominent one. She brought Salomon to one staid U.S. embassy function, clearly hoping to cause a stir. She succeeded. In a letter to Wilder she exulted in the crowd's reaction as Salomon appeared: "the astonishment (there was a little hushed gasping and whispering behind hands from the oh so proper gathering) . . . Ernst von Salomon! accomplice in the Rathenau murder . . ."

She coveted attention and got it. Salomon described the guests gathered at one U.S. embassy party—possibly the same one—as "the capital's jeunesse dorée, smart young men with perfect manners . . . smiling attractively or laughing gaily at Martha Dodd's witty sallies."

She grew bolder. The time had come, she knew, to start throwing some parties of her own.

MEANWHILE DIELS, STILL ABROAD and living well at a swank hotel in Carlsbad, began putting out feelers to gauge the mood back in Berlin, whether it was safe yet for him to return; for that matter, whether it would ever be safe.

CHAPTER 18

Warning from a Friend

Martha grew increasingly confident about her social appeal, enough so that she organized her own afternoon salon, modeled on the teas and evening discussion groups of her friend Mildred Fish Harnack. She also threw herself a birthday party. Both events unfolded in ways markedly different from what she had hoped for.

In selecting guests for her salon she used her own contacts as well as Mildred's. She invited several dozen poets, writers, and editors, for the ostensible purpose of meeting a visiting American publisher. Martha hoped "to hear amusing conversation, some exchange of stimulating views, at least conversation on a higher plane than one is accustomed to in diplomatic society." But the guests brought an unexpected companion.

Instead of forming a lively and vibrant company with her at its center, the crowd became atomized, small groups here and there. A poet sat in the library with several guests clustered near. Others gathered tightly around the guest of honor, exhibiting what Martha termed "a pathetic eagerness to know what was happening in America." Her Jewish guests looked especially ill at ease. The talk lagged; the consumption of food and alcohol surged. "The rest of the guests were standing around drinking heavily and devouring plates of food," Martha wrote. "Probably many of them were poor and actually ill-fed, and the others were nervous and anxious to conceal it."

In all, Martha wrote, "it was a dull and, at the same time, tense afternoon." The uninvited guest was fear, and it haunted the gathering. The crowd, she wrote, was "so full of frustration and misery . . .

of tension, broken spirits, doomed courage or tragic and hated cowardice, that I vowed never to have such a group again in my house."

Instead she resigned herself to helping the Harnacks with their regular soirees and teas. They did have a gift for gathering loyal and compelling friends and holding them close. The idea that one day it would kill them would have seemed at the time, to Martha, utterly laughable.

THE GUEST LIST for her birthday party, set for October 8, her actual birth date, included a princess, a prince, several of her correspondent friends, and various officers of the SA and SS, "young, heel-clicking, courteous almost to the point of absurdity." Whether Boris Winogradov attended is unclear, though by now Martha was seeing him "regularly." It's possible, even likely, that she didn't invite him, for the United States still had not recognized the Soviet Union.

Two prominent Nazi officials made appearances at the party. One was Putzi Hanfstaengl, the other Hans Thomsen, a young man who served as liaison between the Foreign Ministry and Hitler's chancellery. He had never exhibited the overheated swoon so evident in other Nazi zealots, and as a consequence he was well liked by members of the diplomatic corps and a frequent visitor to the Dodds' home. Martha's father often spoke with him in terms more blunt than diplomatic protocol allowed, confident that Thomsen would relay his views to senior Nazi officials, possibly even to Hitler himself. At times Martha had the impression that Thomsen might harbor personal reservations about Hitler. She and Dodd called him "Tommy."

Hanfstaengl arrived late, as was his custom. He craved attention, and by dint of his immense height and energy always got it, no matter how crowded the room. He had become immersed in conversation with a musically knowledgeable guest about the merits of Schubert's *Unfinished Symphony* when Martha walked to the family's Victrola and put on a recording of the Nazi hymn to Horst Wessel, the anthem she had heard sung in Nuremberg by the parading Storm Troopers.

Hanfstaengl seemed to enjoy the music. Hans Thomsen clearly did not. He stood abruptly, then marched to the record player and switched it off.

In her most innocent manner, Martha asked him why he didn't like the music.

Thomsen glared, his face hard. "That is not the sort of music to be played for mixed gatherings and in a flippant manner," he scolded. "I won't have you play our anthem, with its significance, at a social party."

Martha was stunned. This was her house, her party, and, moreover, American ground. She could do as she pleased.

Hanfstaengl looked at Thomsen with what Martha described as "a vivid look of amusement tinged with contempt." He shrugged his shoulders, then sat down at the piano and began hammering away with his usual boisterous élan.

Later, Hanfstaengl took Martha aside. "Yes," he said, "there are some people like that among us. People who have blind spots and are humorless—one must be careful not to offend their sensitive souls."

For Martha, however, Thomsen's display had a lingering effect of surprising power, for it eroded—albeit slightly—her enthusiasm for the new Germany, in the way a single ugly phrase can tilt a marriage toward decline.

"Accustomed all my life to the free exchange of views," she wrote, "the atmosphere of this evening shocked me and struck me as a sort of violation of the decencies of human relationship."

DODD TOO WAS FAST GAINING an appreciation of the prickly sensitivities of the day. No event provided a better measure of these than a speech he gave before the Berlin branch of the American Chamber of Commerce on Columbus Day, October 12, 1933. His talk managed to stir a furor not only in Germany but also, as Dodd was dismayed to learn, within the State Department and among the many Americans who favored keeping the nation from entangling itself in European affairs.

Dodd believed that an important part of his mission was to exert quiet pressure toward moderation or, as he wrote in a letter to the Chicago lawyer Leo Wormser, "to continue to persuade and entreat men here not to be their own worst enemies." The invitation to speak seemed to present an ideal opportunity.

His plan was to use history to telegraph criticism of the Nazi regime, but obliquely, so that only those in the audience with a good grasp of ancient and modern history would understand the underlying message. In America a speech of this nature would have seemed anything but heroic; amid the mounting oppression of Nazi rule, it was positively daring. Dodd explained his motivation in a letter to Jane Addams. "It was because I had seen so much of injustice and domineering little groups, as well as heard the complaints of so many of the best people of the country, that I ventured as far as my position would allow and by historical analogy warned men as solemnly as possible against half-educated leaders being permitted to lead nations into war."

He gave the talk the innocuous title "Economic Nationalism." By citing the rise and fall of Caesar and episodes from French, English, and U.S. history, Dodd sought to warn of the dangers "of arbitrary and minority" government without ever actually mentioning contemporary Germany. It was not the kind of thing a traditional diplomat might have undertaken, but Dodd saw it as simply fulfilling Roosevelt's original mandate. In defending himself later, Dodd wrote, "The President told me pointedly that he wanted me to be a standing representative and spokesman (on occasion) of American ideals and Philosophy."

He spoke in a banquet room at the Adlon Hotel before a large audience that included a number of senior government officials, including Reichsbank president Hjalmar Schacht and two men from Goebbels's ministry of propaganda. Dodd knew he was about to step upon very sensitive terrain. He understood as well, given the many foreign correspondents in the room, that the talk would get wide press coverage in Germany, America, and Britain.

As he began to read, he sensed a quiet excitement permeate the hall. "In times of great stress," he began, "men are too apt to abandon too much of their past social devices and venture too far upon uncharted courses. And the consequence has always been reaction, sometimes disaster." He stepped into the deep past to begin his allusive journey with the examples of Tiberius Gracchus, a populist leader, and Julius Caesar. "Half-educated statesmen today swing violently away from the ideal purpose of the first Gracchus and think they find salvation for their troubled fellows in the arbitrary modes of the man who fell an easy victim to the cheap devices of the lewd Cleopatra." They forget, he said, that "the Caesars succeeded only for a short moment as measured by the test of history."

He described similar moments in English and French history and here offered the example of Jean-Baptiste Colbert, the powerful minister of finance under Louis XIV. In an apparent allusion to the relationship between Hitler and Hindenburg, he told his audience how Colbert "was granted despotic powers. He dispossessed hundreds of great families of newly rich folk, handed their properties over to the Crown, condemned thousands to death because they resisted him. . . . The recalcitrant landed aristocracy was everywhere subdued, parliaments were not allowed to assemble." Autocratic rule persisted in France until 1789, the start of the French Revolution, when "with a crash and a thunder" it collapsed. "Governments from the top fail as often as those from the bottom; and every great failure brings a sad social reaction, thousands and millions of helpless men laying down their lives in the unhappy process. Why may not statesmen study the past and avoid such catastrophes?"

After a few more allusions, he came to his ending. "In conclusion," he said, "one may safely say that it would be no sin if statesmen learned enough of history to realize that no system which implies control of society by privilege seekers has ever ended in any other way than collapse." To fail to learn from such "blunders of the past," he said, was to end up on a course toward "another war and chaos."

The applause, Dodd said in his diary, "was extraordinary." In describing the moment to Roosevelt, Dodd noted that even Schacht "applauded extravagantly," as did "all other Germans present. I have never noted more unanimous approval." He wrote to Secretary Hull, "When the thing was over about every German present showed and expressed a kind of approval which revealed the thought: 'You have said what all of us have been denied the right to say.'" An official of the Deutsche Bank called to express his own agreement. He told Dodd, "Silent, but anxious Germany, above all the business and University Germany, is entirely with you and most thankful that you are here and can say what we can not say."

That these listeners understood the true intent of Dodd's speech was obvious. Afterward, Bella Fromm, the society columnist for the *Vossische Zeitung*, who was fast becoming a friend of the Dodd family, told him, "I enjoyed all these nicely disguised hints against Hitler and Hitlerism."

Dodd gave her an arch grin. "I had no delusions about Hitler when I was appointed to my post in Berlin," he answered. "But I had at least hoped to find some decent people around Hitler. I am horrified to discover that the whole gang is nothing but a horde of criminals and cowards."

Fromm later chided the French ambassador to Germany, André François-Poncet, for missing the speech. His response encapsulated a fundamental quandary of traditional diplomacy. "The situation is very difficult," he said, with a smile. "One is at once a diplomat and must hide one's feelings. One must please one's superiors at home and yet not be expelled from here but I too am glad that his Excellency Mr. Dodd cannot be subverted by flattery and high honor."

Dodd was heartened by the response from his audience. He told Roosevelt, "My interpretation of this is that all liberal Germany is with us—and more than half of Germany is at heart liberal."

The response elsewhere was decidedly less positive, as Dodd quickly found. Goebbels blocked publication of the speech, although three large newspapers published excerpts anyway. The next day, Friday, Dodd arrived at Foreign Minister Neurath's office for a previously scheduled meeting, only to be told Neurath could not see him—a clear breach of diplomatic custom. In a cable to Washington that afternoon, Dodd told Secretary Hull that Neurath's action seemed "to constitute a serious affront to our Government." Dodd finally got to see Neurath at eight o'clock that night. Neurath claimed to have been too busy to see him during the day, but Dodd knew that the minister had been free enough from pressing obligations to have

lunch with a minor diplomat. Dodd wrote in his diary that he suspected Hitler himself might have forced the postponement "as a sort
of rebuke for my speech of yesterday."

To his greater surprise, he also sensed a groundswell of criticism
from America and took steps to defend himself. He promptly sent
Roosevelt a verbatim copy and told the president he was doing so
because he feared "that some embarrassing interpretations may have
been put out at home." That same day he also sent a copy to Undersecretary Phillips, "in the hope that you, acquainted with all the
precedents, may explain to Secretary Hull—i.e., if he or anybody
else in the Department seems to think I have done our cause here
any harm."

If he expected Phillips to rise to his defense, he was mistaken.

Phillips and other senior men in the State Department, including Moffat, the Western European affairs chief, were becoming increasingly unhappy with the ambassador. These ranking members
of Hugh Wilson's "pretty good club" seized upon Dodd's speech as
further evidence that he was the wrong man for the post. Moffat in
his diary likened Dodd's performance to "the schoolmaster lecturing
his pupils." Phillips, master of the art of palace whisper, took delight
in Dodd's discomfort. He ignored several of Dodd's letters, in which
the ambassador sought official advice on whether to accept future
public-speaking offers. At last Phillips did reply, with apologies, explaining "that I was in doubt whether any words from me could be of
help or guidance to you who are living in a world so wholly different
from that in which most ambassadors find themselves."

Though he congratulated Dodd on the "high art" he exhibited
in crafting a speech that let him speak his mind yet avoid giving
direct offense, Phillips also offered a quiet rebuke. "In brief, my feeling is that an Ambassador, who is a privileged guest of the country to
which he is accredited, should be careful not to give public expression to anything in the nature of criticism of his adopted country,
because in so doing, he loses ipso facto the confidence of those very
public officials whose good-will is so important to him in the success
of his mission."

Dodd still seemed unaware of it, but several members of the Pretty

Good Club had begun stepping up their campaign against him, with the ultimate aim of ousting him from their ranks. In October his longtime friend Colonel House sent him a quiet, sidesaddle warning. First came the good news. House had just met with Roosevelt. "It was delightful to hear the President say that he was pleased beyond measure with the work you are doing in Berlin."

But then House had visited the State Department. "In the strictest confidence, they did not speak of you with the same enthusiasm as the President," he wrote. "I insisted on something concrete and all that I could get was that you did not keep them well informed. I am telling you this so you may be guided in the future."

ON SATURDAY, OCTOBER 14, two days after his Columbus Day address, Dodd was in the middle of a dinner party he was hosting for military and naval attachés when he received startling news. Hitler had just announced his decision to withdraw Germany from the League of Nations and from a major disarmament conference that had been under way in Geneva, off and on, since February 1932.

Dodd found a radio and immediately heard the coarse voice of the chancellor, though he was struck by the absence of Hitler's usual histrionics. Dodd listened intently as Hitler portrayed Germany as a well-meaning, peace-seeking nation whose modest desire for equality of armaments was being opposed by other nations. "It was not the address of a thinker," Dodd wrote in his diary, "but of an emotionalist claiming that Germany had in no way been responsible for the World War and that she was the victim of wicked enemies."

It was a stunning development. In one stroke, Dodd realized, Hitler had emasculated the League and virtually nullified the Treaty of Versailles, clearly declaring his intention to rearm Germany. He announced as well that he was dissolving the Reichstag and would hold new elections on November 12. The ballot also would invite the public to pass judgment upon his foreign policy through a yes-or-no plebiscite. Secretly Hitler also gave orders to General Werner von Blomberg, his minister of defense, to prepare for possible military action by League members seeking to enforce the Treaty of

Versailles—although Blomberg knew full well that Germany's small army could not hope to prevail against a combined action by France, Poland, and Czechoslovakia. "That the allies at this time could easily have overwhelmed Germany is as certain as it is that such an action would have brought the end of the Third Reich in the very year of its birth," wrote William Shirer in his classic work, *The Rise and Fall of the Third Reich*, but Hitler "knew the mettle of his foreign adversaries as expertly and as uncannily as he had sized up that of his opponents at home."

Though Dodd continued to nurture the hope that the German government would grow more civil, he recognized that Hitler's two decisions signaled an ominous shift away from moderation. The time had come, he knew, to meet with Hitler face-to-face.

Dodd went to bed that night deeply troubled.

SHORTLY BEFORE NOON ON TUESDAY, October 17, 1933, Roosevelt's "standing liberal" set out in top hat and tails for his first meeting with Adolf Hitler.

CHAPTER 19

Matchmaker

Putzi Hanfstaengl knew of Martha's various romantic relationships, but by the fall of 1933 he had begun to imagine for her a new partner.

Having come to feel that Hitler would be a much more reasonable leader if only he fell in love, Hanfstaengl appointed himself match-maker. He knew this would not be easy. As one of Hitler's closest as-sociates, he recognized that the history of Hitler's relationships with women was an odd one, marred by tragedy and persistent rumors of unsavory behavior. Hitler liked women, but more as stage decoration than as sources of intimacy and love. There had been talk of numer-ous liaisons, typically with women much younger than he—in one case a sixteen-year-old named Maria Reiter. One woman, Eva Braun, was twenty-three years his junior and had been an intermittent com-panion since 1929. So far, however, Hitler's only all-consuming affair had been with his young niece, Geli Raubal. She was found shot to death in Hitler's apartment, his revolver nearby. The most likely explanation was suicide, her means of escaping Hitler's jealous and oppressive affection—his "clammy possessiveness," as historian Ian Kershaw put it. Hanfstaengl suspected that Hitler once had been attracted to his own wife, Helena, but she assured him there was no cause for jealousy. "Believe me," she said, "he's an absolute neuter, not a man."

Hanfstaengl telephoned Martha at home.

"Hitler needs a woman," he said. "Hitler should have an American woman—a lovely woman could change the whole destiny of Europe."

He got to the point: "Martha," he said, "you are the woman!"

PART IV

How the Skeleton Aches

The Tiergarten, January 1934

CHAPTER 20

The Führer's Kiss

Dodd walked up a broad stairway toward Hitler's office, at each bend encountering SS men with their arms raised "Caesar style," as Dodd put it. He bowed in response and at last entered Hitler's waiting room. After a few moments the black, tall door to Hitler's office opened. Foreign Minister Neurath stepped out to welcome Dodd and to bring him to Hitler. The office was an immense room, by Dodd's estimate fifty feet by fifty feet, with ornately decorated walls and ceiling. Hitler, "neat and erect," wore an ordinary business suit. Dodd noted that he looked better than newspaper photographs indicated.

Even so, Hitler did not cut a particularly striking figure. He rarely did. Early in his rise it was easy for those who met him for the first time to dismiss him as a nonentity. He came from plebeian roots and had failed to distinguish himself in any way, not in war, not in work, not in art, though in this last domain he believed himself to have great talent. He was said to be indolent. He rose late, worked little, and surrounded himself with the lesser lights of the party with whom he felt most comfortable, an entourage of middle-brow souls that Putzi Hanfstaengl derisively nicknamed the "Chauffeureska," consisting of bodyguards, adjutants, and a chauffeur. He loved movies—*King Kong* was a favorite—and he adored the music of Richard Wagner. He dressed badly. Apart from his mustache and his eyes, the features of his face were indistinct and unimpressive, as if begun in clay but never fired. Recalling his first impression of Hitler, Hanfstaengl wrote, "Hitler looked like a suburban hairdresser on his day off."

Nonetheless the man had a remarkable ability to transform him-self into something far more compelling, especially when speaking in public or during private meetings when some topic enraged him. He had a knack as well for projecting an aura of sincerity that blinded onlookers to his true motives and beliefs, though Dodd had not yet come to a full appreciation of this aspect of his character.

First Dodd raised the subject of the many attacks against Ameri-cans. Hitler was cordial and apologetic and assured Dodd that the perpetrators of all such attacks would be "punished to the limit." He promised as well to publicize widely his prior decrees exempting for-eigners from giving the Hitler salute. After some bland conversation about Germany's debts to American creditors, Dodd moved to the topic most on his mind, the "all-pervasive question of the German thunderbolt of last Saturday"—Hitler's decision to withdraw from the League of Nations.

When Dodd asked him why he had pulled Germany from the League, Hitler grew visibly angry. He attacked the Treaty of Versailles and France's drive to maintain superiority in arms over Germany. He railed against the "indignity" of keeping Germany in an unequal state, unable to defend herself against her neighbors.

Hitler's sudden rage startled Dodd. He tried to appear unfazed, less a diplomat now than a professor dealing with an overwrought student. He told Hitler, "There is evident injustice in the French attitude; but defeat in war is always followed by injustice." He raised the example of the aftermath of the American Civil War and the North's "terrible" treatment of the South.

Hitler stared at him. After a brief period of silence, the conver-sation resumed, and for a few moments the two men engaged in what Dodd described as "an exchange of niceties." But now Dodd asked whether "an incident on the Polish, Austrian or French border which drew an enemy into the Reich" would be enough for Hitler to launch a war.

"No, no," Hitler insisted.

Dodd probed further. Suppose, he asked, such an incident were to involve the Ruhr Valley, an industrial region about which Germans were particularly sensitive. France had occupied the Ruhr from

1923 to 1925, causing great economic and political turmoil within Germany. In the event of another such incursion, Dodd asked, would Germany respond militarily on its own or call for an international meeting to resolve the matter?

"That would be my purpose," Hitler said, "but we might not be able to restrain the German people."

Dodd said, "If you would wait and call a conference, Germany would regain her popularity outside."

Soon the meeting came to an end. It had lasted forty-five minutes. Though the session had been difficult and strange, Dodd nonetheless left the chancellery feeling convinced that Hitler was sincere about wanting peace. He was concerned, however, that he might again have violated the laws of diplomacy. "Perhaps I was too frank," he wrote later to Roosevelt, "but I had to be honest."

At 6:00 p.m. that day he sent a two-page cable to Secretary Hull summarizing the meeting and closed by telling Hull, "The total effect of the interview was more favorable from the point of view of the maintenance of world peace than I had expected."

Dodd also conveyed these impressions to Consul General Messersmith, who then sent Undersecretary Phillips a letter—at eighteen pages, a characteristically long one—in which he seemed intent on undermining Dodd's credibility. He challenged the ambassador's appraisal of Hitler. "The Chancellor's assurances were so satisfying and so unexpected that I think they are on the whole too good to be true," Messersmith wrote. "We must keep in mind, I believe, that when Hitler says anything he for the moment convinces himself that it is true. He is basically sincere; but he is at the same time a fanatic."

Messersmith urged skepticism regarding Hitler's protestations. "I think for the moment he genuinely desires peace but it is a peace of his own kind and with an armed force constantly becoming more effective in reserve, in order to impose their will when it may become essential." He reiterated his belief that Hitler's government could not be viewed as a rational entity. "There are so many pathological cases involved that it would be impossible to tell from day to day what will happen any more than the keeper of a madhouse is able to tell what his inmates will do in the next hour or during the next day."

He urged caution, in effect warning Phillips to be skeptical of Dodd's conviction that Hitler wanted peace. "I think for the present moment . . . we must guard against any undue optimism which may be aroused by the apparently satisfying declarations of the Chancellor."

ON THE MORNING of the rendezvous that Putzi Hanfstaengl had arranged for Martha with Hitler, she dressed carefully, seeing as she had been "appointed to change the history of Europe." To her it seemed a lark of the first order. She was curious to meet this man she once had dismissed as a clown but whom she now was convinced was "a glamorous and brilliant personality who must have great power and charm." She decided to wear her "most demure and intriguing best," nothing too striking or revealing, for the Nazi ideal was a woman who wore little makeup, tended her man, and bore as many children as possible. German men, she wrote, "want their women to be seen and not heard, and then seen only as appendages of the splendid male they accompany." She considered wearing a veil.

Hanfstaengl picked her up in his huge car and drove to the Kaiserhof, seven blocks away on Wilhelmplatz, just off the southeast corner of the Tiergarten. A grand hotel with a cavernous lobby and arched entrance portico, the Kaiserhof had been Hitler's home until his ascension to chancellor. Now Hitler often had lunch or tea in the hotel surrounded by his Chauffeureska.

Hanfstaengl had arranged that he and Martha would be joined for lunch by another party, a Polish tenor, Jan Kiepura, thirty-one years old. Hanfstaengl, well known and unmistakable, was treated with deference by the restaurant's staff. Once seated, Martha and the two men chatted over tea and waited. In time a commotion arose at the entrance to the dining room, and soon came the inevitable rumble of chairs shoved back and shouts of "Heil Hitler."

Hitler and his party—including, indeed, his chauffeur—took seats at an adjacent table. First, Kiepura was ushered to Hitler's side. The two spoke about music. Hitler seemed unaware that Kiepura under Nazi law was classified as Jewish, by maternal heritage. A few moments later Hanfstaengl came over and bent low to Hitler's ear. He barreled back to Martha with the news that Hitler would now see her.

She walked to Hitler's table and stood there a moment as Hitler rose to greet her. He took her hand and kissed it and spoke a few quiet words in German. She got a close look at him now: "a weak, soft face, with pouches under the eyes, full lips and very little bony facial structure." At this vantage, she wrote, the mustache "didn't seem as ridiculous as it appeared in pictures—in fact, I scarcely noticed it." What she did notice were his eyes. She had heard elsewhere that there was something piercing and intense about his gaze, and now, immediately, she understood. "Hitler's eyes," she wrote, "were startling and unforgettable—they seemed pale blue in color, were intense, unwavering, hypnotic."

Yet his manner was gentle—"excessively gentle," she wrote—more that of a shy teenager than an iron dictator. "Unobtrusive, communicative, informal, he had a certain quiet charm, almost a tenderness of speech and glance," she wrote.

Hitler now turned back to the tenor and with what seemed to be real interest rekindled their conversation about music.

He "seemed modest, middle class, rather dull and self-conscious—yet with this strange tenderness and appealing helplessness," Martha wrote. "It was hard to believe that this man was one of the most powerful men in Europe."

Martha and Hitler shook hands once again, and for the second time he kissed hers. She returned to her table and to Hanfstaengl.

They remained a while longer, over tea, eavesdropping on the continuing conversation between Kiepura and Hitler. Now and then Hitler would look her way, with what she judged to be "curious, embarrassed stares."

That night, over dinner, she told her parents all about the day's encounter and how charming and peaceful the *Führer* had been. Dodd was amused and conceded "that Hitler was not an unattractive man personally."

He teased Martha and told her to be sure to take note of exactly where Hitler's lips had touched her hand, and he recommended that if she "must" wash that hand, that she do so with care and only around the margins of the kiss.

She wrote, "I was a little angry and peeved."

Martha and Hitler never repeated their encounter, nor had she seriously expected they would, though as would become clear some years later, Martha did enter Hitler's mind on at least one more occasion. For her part, all she had wanted was to meet the man and satisfy her own curiosity. There were other men in her circle whom she found infinitely more compelling.

One of these had come back into her life, with an invitation for a most unusual date. By the end of October, Rudolf Diels had returned to Berlin and to his old post as chief of the Gestapo, paradoxically with even more power than before his exile to Czechoslovakia. Himmler had not only apologized for the raid on Diels's home; he had promised to make Diels a *Standartenführer*, or colonel, in the SS.

Diels sent him a fawning thank-you: "By promoting me to the *Obersturmbannführer der SS*, you have brought so much joy to me that it cannot be expressed in these short words of thanks."

Safe at least for the time being, Diels invited Martha to attend an upcoming session of the Reichstag arson trial, which had been under way in the Supreme Court in Leipzig for nearly a month but was about to reconvene in Berlin, at the scene of the crime. The trial was supposed to have been a short one and to conclude with convictions and, ideally, death sentences for all five defendants, but it was not proceeding as Hitler had hoped.

Now a special "witness" was scheduled to appear.

CHAPTER 21

The Trouble with George

Within Germany, a great flywheel had been set in motion that drove the country inexorably toward some dark place alien to Dodd's recollection of the old Germany he had known as a student. As the autumn advanced and color filled the Tiergarten, he came more and more to realize just how correct he had been back in Chicago, in the spring, when he had observed that his temperament was ill suited to "high diplomacy" and playing the liar on bended knee. He wanted to have an effect: to awaken Germany to the dangers of its current path and to nudge Hitler's government onto a more humane and rational course. He was fast realizing, however, that he possessed little power to do so. Especially strange to him was the Nazi fixation on racial purity. A draft of a new penal code had begun to circulate that proposed to make it a key buttress of German law. The American vice consul in Leipzig, Henry Leverich, found the draft an extraordinary document and wrote an analysis: "For the first time, therefore, in German legal history the draft code contains definite suggestions for protection of the German Race from what is considered the disintegration caused by an intermixture of Jewish and colored blood." If the code became law—and he had no doubt it would—then henceforth "it shall be considered as a crime for a gentile man or woman to marry a Jewish or colored man or woman." He noted also that the code made paramount the protection of the family and thus outlawed abortion, with the exception that a court could authorize the procedure when the expected offspring was a mix of German and Jewish or colored blood. Vice Consul Leverich wrote, "Judging from newspaper comment, this portion of the draft will almost certainly be transacted into law."

Another newly proposed law caught Dodd's particular attention—a law "to permit killing incurables," as he described it in a memorandum to the State Department dated October 26, 1933. Seriously ill patients could ask to be euthanized, but if unable to make the request, their families could do so for them. This proposal, "together with legislation already enacted governing the sterilization of persons affected by hereditary imbecility and other similar defects, is in line with Hitler's aim to raise the physical standard of the German people," Dodd wrote. "According to Nazi philosophy only Germans who are physically fit belong in the Third Reich, and they are the ones who are expected to raise large families."

Attacks against Americans continued, despite Dodd's protests, and the prosecution of past cases seemed languid at best. On November 8 Dodd received notice from the German foreign office that no arrest would be made in the assault on H. V. Kaltenborn's son, because the senior Kaltenborn "could remember neither the name nor the number of the Party identification card of the culprit, and as no other clues which might be useful in the investigation could be found."

Perhaps because of his mounting sense of futility, Dodd shifted his focus from the realm of international affairs to the state of affairs within his own embassy. Dodd found himself—his frugal, Jeffersonian self—drawn more and more to concentrate on the failings of his staff and the extravagance of embassy business.

He intensified his campaign against the cost of telegrams and the length and redundancy of dispatches, all of which he believed to be consequences of having so many rich men in the department. "Wealthy staff people want to have cocktail parties in the afternoon, card parties in the evening and get up next day at 10 o'clock," he wrote to Secretary Hull. "That tends to reduce effective study and work . . . and also to cause men to be indifferent to the cost of their reports and telegrams." Telegrams should be cut in half, he wrote. "Long habit here resists my efforts to shorten telegrams to the point where men have 'fits' when I erase large parts. I shall have to write them myself. . . ."

What Dodd had failed as yet to fully appreciate was that in complaining about the wealth, dress, and work habits of embassy officers, he was in fact attacking Undersecretary Phillips, Western European Affairs Chief Moffat, and their colleagues, the very men who sustained and endorsed the foreign-service culture—the Pretty Good Club—that Dodd found so distressing. They saw his complaints about costs as offensive, tedious, and confounding, especially given the nature of his posting. Were there not matters of greater importance that demanded his attention?

Phillips in particular took umbrage and commissioned a study by the State Department's communications division to compare the volume of cables from Berlin with that of other embassies. The chief of the division, one D. A. Salmon, found that Berlin had sent three fewer telegrams than Mexico City and only four more messages than the tiny legation at Panama. Salmon wrote, "It would seem that in view of the acute situation existing in Germany the telegraphing from the American Embassy at Berlin had been very light since Ambassador Dodd assumed charge."

Phillips sent the report to Dodd with a three-sentence cover letter in which, with an aristocratic sniff, he cited Dodd's recent mention of "the extravagance in the telegraphic business in the Embassy at Berlin." Phillips wrote: "Thinking it would be of interest to you, I enclose a copy of it herewith."

Dodd replied, "Do not think that Mr. Salmon's comparison of my work with that of my friend Mr. Daniels in Mexico in any sense affects me. Mr. Daniels and I have been friends since I was 18 years old; but I know that he does not know how to condense reports!"

DODD BELIEVED THAT one artifact of past excess—"another curious hangover," he told Phillips—was that his embassy had too many personnel, in particular, too many who were Jewish. "We have six or eight members of the 'chosen race' here who serve in most useful but conspicuous positions," he wrote. Several were his best workers, he acknowledged, but he feared that their presence on his staff impaired the embassy's relationship with Hitler's government and thus impeded the day-to-day operation of the embassy. "I would not for a moment consider transfer. However, the number is too great and one of them"—he meant Julia Swope Lewin, the embassy receptionist—"is so ardent and in evidence every day that I hear echoes from semi-official circles." He also cited the example of the embassy's bookkeeper, who, while "very competent," was also "one of the 'Chosen People' and that puts him at some disadvantage with the Banks here."

In this respect, oddly enough, Dodd also had concerns about George Messersmith. "His office is important and he is very able," Dodd wrote to Hull, "but German officials have said to one of the staff here: 'he is also a Hebrew.' I am no race antagonist, but we have a large number here and it affects the service and adds to my load."

For the moment, at least, Dodd seemed unaware that Messersmith was not in fact Jewish. He had fallen, apparently, for a rumor launched by Putzi Hanfstaengl after Messersmith had publicly chastised him during an embassy function for making an unwelcome advance on a female guest.

Dodd's assumption would have outraged Messersmith, who found it hard enough to listen to the speculation of Nazi officials as to who was or was not Jewish. On Friday, October 27, Messersmith held a lunch at his house at which he introduced Dodd to a number of especially rabid Nazis, to help Dodd gain a sense of the true character of the party. One seemingly sober and intelligent Nazi stated as fact a belief common among party members that President Roosevelt and his wife had nothing but Jewish advisers. Messersmith wrote the next day to Undersecretary Phillips: "They seem to believe that because we have Jews in official positions or that important people at home have Jewish friends, our policy is being dictated by the Jews alone and that particularly the President and Mrs. Roosevelt are conducting anti-German propaganda under the influence of Jewish friends and advisers." Messersmith reported how this had caused him to bristle. "I told them that they must not think that because there is an anti-Semitic movement in Germany, well-thinking and well-meaning people in the United States were going to give up associating with Jews. I said that the arrogance of some of the party leaders here was their greatest defect, and the feeling that they had that they could impose their views on the rest of the world, was one of their greatest weaknesses."

He cited such thinking as an example of the "extraordinary mentality" that prevailed in Germany. "It will be hard for you to believe that such notions actually exist among worthwhile people in the German Government," he told Phillips, "but that they do was made clear to me and I took the opportunity in no uncertain language to make clear how wrong they were and how much such arrogance injured them."

Given Phillips's own dislike of Jews, it is tantalizing to imagine what he really thought of Messersmith's observations, but on this the historical record is silent.

What is known, however, is that among the population of Americans who expressed anti-Semitic leanings, a common jibe described the presidency of Franklin Roosevelt as the "Rosenberg administration."

DODD'S WILLINGNESS TO BELIEVE that Messersmith was Jewish had little do with his own rudimental anti-Semitism but seemed rather to be a symptom of deeper misgivings that he had begun to harbor with regard to the consul general. Increasingly he wondered whether Messersmith was wholly on his side.

He never questioned Messersmith's competence or his courage in speaking out when American citizens and interests were harmed, and he acknowledged that Messersmith "has many sources of information which I do not have." But in two letters to Undersecretary Phillips, composed two days apart, Dodd suggested that Messersmith had outstayed his assignment in Berlin. "I must add that he has been here three or four years in the midst of very exciting and troublous times," Dodd wrote in one of the letters, "and I think he has developed a sensitiveness, and perhaps even an ambition, which tend to make him restless and discontented. This may be too strong, but I think not."

Dodd gave little evidence for his appraisal. He isolated only one flaw with any clarity, and that was Messersmith's penchant for writing dispatches of great length on all things, grave or mundane. Dodd told Phillips that the size of Messersmith's dispatches could be halved "without the slightest injury" and that the man needed to be more judicious in his choice of subject. "Hitler could not have left his hat in a flying machine without an account of it."

The reports, however, were for Dodd merely a target of convenience, a proxy for sources of displeasure that were harder for him to isolate. By mid-November, his dissatisfaction with Messersmith had begun to veer toward distrust. He sensed that Messersmith coveted his own job, and he saw his unceasing production of reports as a manifestation of his ambitions. "It occurs to me," Dodd told Phillips, "that he feels that a promotion is due and I think that his services demand it; but I am not sure but that the most useful period of his work here has passed. You know as well as I do that circumstances and conditions and sometimes disappointments make it wise to transfer even the ablest of Government officials." He urged Phillips to discuss the matter with consular-service chief Wilbur Carr "and see whether some such thing can not be done."

He closed, "I need hardly say that I hope all this will be kept entirely confidential."

That Dodd imagined Phillips would retain this confidence suggests he was unaware that Phillips and Messersmith maintained a regular and frequent exchange of correspondence outside the stream of official reportage. When Phillips replied to Dodd in late November, he added his usual dash of irony, the tone light and agreeable to an extent that suggested he was merely humoring Dodd, responsive yet at the same time dismissive. "The letters and dispatches of your Consul General are full of interest, but should be cut in half—as you say. More strength to your elbow! I look to you to spread this much needed reform."

ON SUNDAY, OCTOBER 29, at about noon, Dodd was walking along Tiergartenstrasse, on his way to the Hotel Esplanade. He spotted a large procession of Storm Troopers in their telltale brown shirts marching toward him. Pedestrians stopped and shouted the Hitler salute.

Dodd turned and walked into the park.

CHAPTER 22

The Witness Wore Jackboots

The weather chilled and with each day the northern dusk seemed to make a noticeable advance. There was wind, rain, and fog. That November the weather station at Tempelhof Airport would record periods of fog on fourteen of thirty days. The library at Tiergartenstrasse 27a became irresistibly cozy, the books and damask walls turned amber by the flames in the great hearth. On November 4, a Saturday at the end of an especially dreary weak of rain and wind, Martha set out for the Reichstag building, where a makeshift courtroom had been constructed for the Berlin session of the great arson trial. She carried a ticket provided by Rudolf Diels.

Police with carbines and swords ringed the building—"swarms" of them, according to one observer. Everyone who tried to enter was stopped and checked. Eighty-two foreign correspondents crammed the press gallery at the back of the chamber. The five judges, led by presiding judge Wilhelm Bünger, wore scarlet robes. Throughout the audience were men in SS black and SA brown, as well as civilians, government officials, and diplomats. Martha was startled to find that her ticket placed her not just on the main floor but at the front of the courtroom among various dignitaries. "I walked in, my heart in my throat, as I was seated much too close to the front," she recalled.

The day's installment was scheduled to begin at nine fifteen, but the star witness, Hermann Göring, was late. For possibly the first time since testimony had begun in September there was real suspense in the room. The trial was supposed to have been short and to have provided the Nazis with a world stage upon which they could condemn the evils of communism and at the same time challenge the widely held belief that they themselves had set the fire. Instead, despite clear evidence that the presiding judge favored the prosecution, the trial had proceeded like a real trial, with both sides presenting great masses of evidence. The state hoped to prove that all five defendants had played a role in the arson, despite Marinus van der Lubbe's insistence that he alone was responsible. Prosecutors brought forth innumerable experts in an attempt to demonstrate that the damage to the building was far too extensive, with too many small fires in too many places, to have been the work of a single arsonist. In the process, according to Fritz Tobias, author of the seminal account of the fire and its aftermath, what was to have been an exciting, revealing trial instead became "a yawning abyss of boredom."

Until now.

Göring was due at any moment. Famously volatile and outspoken, given to flamboyant dress and always seeking attention, Göring was expected to add spark to the trial. The chamber filled with the wheeze of shifting flannel and mohair as people turned to look back toward the entrance.

A half hour passed, and still Göring did not appear. Diels too was nowhere in sight.

To pass the time, Martha watched the defendants. There was Ernst Torgler, a Communist Party deputy to the Reichstag before Hitler's ascension, looking pale and tired. Three were Bulgarian communists—Georgi Dimitrov, Simon Popov, and Vassili Tanev—who "looked wiry, tough, indifferent." The key defendant, van der Lubbe, presented "one of the most awful sights I have yet seen in human form. Big, bulky, sub-human face and body, he was so repulsive and degenerate that I could scarcely bear to look at him."

An hour elapsed. The tension in the room grew still greater as impatience and expectation merged.

A clamor arose at the back of the room—boots and commands, as Göring and Diels entered amid a spearhead of uniformed men. Göring, forty years old, 250 pounds or more, strode confidently to the front of the room in a brown hunting jacket, jodhpurs, and gleaming brown boots that came to his knees. None of it could mask his great girth or the resemblance he bore to "the hind end of an elephant," as one U.S. diplomat described him. Diels, in a handsome dark suit, was like a slender shadow.

"Everyone jumped up as if electrified," a Swiss reporter observed, "and all Germans, including the judges, raised their arms to give the Hitler salute."

Diels and Göring stood together at the front of the chamber, very near Martha. The two men spoke quietly.

The presiding judge invited Göring to speak. Göring stepped forward. He appeared pompous and arrogant, Martha recalled, but she sensed also a subcurrent of unease.

Göring launched into a prepared harangue that lasted nearly three hours. In a voice hard and coarse, rising now and then to a shout, he raged against communism, the defendants, and the act of arson they had perpetrated against Germany. Cries of "Bravo!" and loud applause filled the chamber.

"With one hand he gestured wildly," wrote Hans Gisevius in his Gestapo memoir; "with the perfumed handkerchief in his other hand he wiped the perspiration from his brow." Attempting to capture a sense of the moment, Gisevius described the faces of the three most important actors in the room—"Dimitrov's full of scorn, Göring's contorted with rage, Presiding Judge Bünger's pale with fright."

And there was Diels, sleek, dark, his expression unreadable. Diels had helped interrogate van der Lubbe on the night of the fire and concluded that the suspect was a "madman" who had indeed set the fire all by himself. Hitler and Göring, however, had immediately decided that the Communist Party was behind it and that the fire was the opening blow of a larger uprising. On that first night Diels had watched Hitler's face grow purple with rage as he cried that every communist official and deputy was to be shot. The order was rescinded, replaced by mass arrests and impromptu acts of Storm Trooper violence.

Now Diels stood with one elbow against the judge's bench. From time to time he changed position as if to get a better view of Göring. Martha became convinced that Diels had planned Göring's performance, perhaps even written his speech. She recalled that Diels had been "especially anxious to have me present on this day, almost as if he were showing off his own craftsmanship."

Diels had warned against holding a trial of anyone other than van der Lubbe and had predicted the acquittal of the other defendants. Göring had failed to listen, although he did recognize what lay at stake. "A botch," Göring had acknowledged, "could have intolerable consequences."

NOW DIMITROV ROSE TO SPEAK. Wielding sarcasm and quiet logic, he clearly hoped to ignite Göring's famed temper. He charged that the police investigation of the fire and the initial court review of the evidence had been influenced by political directives from Göring, "thus preventing the apprehension of the real incendiaries."

"If the police were allowed to be influenced in a particular direction," Göring said, "then, in any case, they were only influenced in the proper direction."

"That is your opinion," Dimitrov countered. "My opinion is quite different."

Göring snapped, "But mine is the one that counts."

Dimitrov pointed out that communism, which Göring had called a "criminal mentality," controlled the Soviet Union, which "has diplomatic, political and economic contacts with Germany. Her orders provide work for hundreds of thousands of German workers. Does the Minister know that?"

"Yes I do," Göring said. But such debate, he said, was beside the point. "Here, I am only concerned with the Communist Party of Germany and with the foreign communist crooks who come here to set the Reichstag on fire."

The two continued sparring, with the presiding judge now and then interceding to warn Dimitrov against "making communist propaganda."

Göring, unaccustomed to challenge from anyone he deemed an inferior, grew angrier by the moment.

Dimitrov calmly observed, "You are greatly afraid of my questions, are you not, Herr Minister?"

At this Göring lost control. He shouted, "You will be afraid when I catch you. You wait till I get you out of the power of the court, you crook!"

The judge ordered Dimitrov expelled; the audience erupted in applause; but it was Göring's closing threat that made headlines. The moment was revealing in two ways—first, because it betrayed Göring's fear that Dimitrov might indeed be acquitted, and second, because it provided a knife-slash glimpse into the irrational, lethal heart of Göring and the Hitler regime.

The day also caused a further erosion of Martha's sympathy for the Nazi revolution. Göring had been arrogant and threatening, Dimitrov cool and charismatic. Martha was impressed. Dimitrov, she wrote, was "a brilliant, attractive, dark man emanating the most amazing vitality and courage I have yet seen in a person under stress. He was alive, he was burning."

THE TRIAL SETTLED back into its previous bloodless state, but the damage had been done. The Swiss reporter, like dozens of other foreign correspondents in the room, recognized that Göring's outburst had transformed the proceeding: "For the world had been told that, no matter whether the accused was sentenced or acquitted by the Court, his fate had already been sealed."

CHAPTER 23

Boris Dies Again

As winter neared, Martha focused her romantic energies primarily on Boris. They logged hundreds of miles in his Ford convertible, with forays into the countryside all around Berlin.

On one such drive Martha spotted an artifact of the old Germany, a roadside shrine to Jesus, and insisted they stop for a closer look. She found within a particularly graphic rendition of the Crucifixion. The face of Jesus was contorted in an expression of agony, his wounds garish with blood. After a few moments, she glanced back at Boris. Though she never would have described herself as terribly religious, she was shocked by what she saw.

Boris stood with his arms stretched out, his ankles crossed, and his head drooping to his chest.

"Boris, stop it," she snapped. "What are you doing?"

"I'm dying for you, darling. I am willing to, you know."

She declared his parody not funny and stepped away.

Boris apologized. "I didn't mean to offend you," he said. "But I can't understand why Christians adore the sight of a tortured man."

That wasn't the point, she said. "They adore his sacrifice for his beliefs."

"Oh, do they really?" he said. "Do you believe that? Are there so many ready to die for their beliefs, following his example?"

She cited Dimitrov and his bravery in standing up to Göring at the Reichstag trial.

Boris gave her an angelic smile. "Yes, *liebes Fräulein*, but *he* was a communist."

CHAPTER 24

Getting Out the Vote

On Sunday morning, November 12—cold, with drizzle and fog—the Dodds encountered a city that seemed uncannily quiet, given that this was the day Hitler had designated for the public referendum on his decision to leave the League of Nations and to seek equality of armaments. Everywhere the Dodds went they saw people wearing little badges that indicated not only that they had voted but that they had voted yes. By midday nearly everyone on the streets seemed to be wearing such insignia, suggesting that voters had arisen early in order to get the deed done and thereby avoid the danger almost certain to arise if they were perceived to have failed in their civic duty.

Even the date of the election had been chosen with care. November 12 was the day after the fifteenth anniversary of the signing of the armistice that ended the Great War. Hitler, who flew around Germany campaigning for a positive vote, told one audience, "On an eleventh of November the German people formally lost its honor; fifteen years later came a twelfth of November and then the German people restored its honor to itself." President Hindenburg too lobbied for a positive vote. "Show tomorrow your firm national unity and your solidarity with the government," he said in a speech on November 11. "Support with me and the Reich Chancellor the principle of equal rights and of peace with honor."

The ballot had two main components. One asked Germans to elect delegates to a newly reconstituted Reichstag but offered only Nazi candidates and thus guaranteed that the resulting body would be a cheering section for Hitler's decisions. The other, the foreign-policy question, had been composed to ensure maximum support. Every German could find a reason to justify voting yes—if he wanted peace, if he felt the Treaty of Versailles had wronged Germany, if he believed Germany ought to be treated as an equal by other nations, or if he simply wished to express his support for Hitler and his government.

Hitler wanted a resounding endorsement. Throughout Germany, the Nazi Party apparatus took extraordinary measures to get people to vote. One report held that patients confined to hospital beds were transported to polling places on stretchers. Victor Klemperer, the Jewish philologist in Berlin, took note in his diary of the "extravagant propaganda" to win a yes vote. "On every commercial vehicle, post office van, mailman's bicycle, on every house and shopwindow, on broad banners, which are stretched across the street—quotations from Hitler are everywhere and always 'Yes' for peace! It is the most monstrous of hypocrisies."

Party men and the SA monitored who voted and who did not; laggards got a visit from a squad of Storm Troopers who emphasized the desirability of an immediate trip to the polls. For anyone dense enough to miss the point, there was this item in the Sunday-morning edition of the official Nazi newspaper, *Völkischer Beobachter*: "In order to bring about clarity it must be repeated again. He who does not attach himself to us today, he who does not vote and vote 'yes' today, shows that he is, if not our bloody enemy, at least a product of destruction and that he is no more to be helped."

Here was the kicker: "It would be better for him and it would be better for us if he no longer existed."

Some 45.1 million Germans were qualified to vote, and 96.5 percent did so. Of these, 95.1 percent voted in favor of Hitler's foreign policy. More interesting, however, was the fact that 2.1 million Germans—just shy of 5 percent of the registered electorate—made the dangerous decision to vote no.

Hitler issued a proclamation afterward thanking the German people for the "historically unique acknowledgment they have made in favor of real love of peace, at the same time also their claim to our honor and to our eternal equal rights."

The outcome was clear to Dodd well before the votes were counted. He wrote to Roosevelt, "The election here is a farce."

Nothing indicated this more clearly than the vote within the camp at Dachau: 2,154 of 2,242 prisoners—96 percent—voted in favor of Hitler's government. On the fate of the 88 souls who either failed to vote or voted no, history is silent.

ON MONDAY, NOVEMBER 13, President Roosevelt took a few moments to compose a letter to Dodd. He complimented him on his letters thus far and, in an apparent allusion to Dodd's concerns after his interview with Hitler, told Dodd, "I am glad you have been frank with certain people. I think that is a good thing."

He mused on an observation by columnist Walter Lippmann that a mere 8 percent of the world's population, meaning Germany and Japan, was able "because of imperialistic attitude" to prevent peace and disarmament for the rest of the world.

"I sometimes feel," the president wrote, "that the world problems are getting worse instead of better. In our own country, however, in spite of sniping, 'chiseling' and growling by the extreme right and by the extreme left, we are actually putting people back to work and raising values."

He closed with a jovial "Keep up the good work!"

IN WASHINGTON, SECRETARY HULL and other senior officials, including Undersecretary Phillips, spent the first half of the month consumed by planning for the impending visit of Maxim Litvinov, the Soviet commissar for foreign affairs, who was to begin discussions with Roosevelt aimed at U.S. recognition of the Soviet Union. The idea was deeply unpopular with America's isolationists, but Roosevelt saw important strategic benefits, such as opening Russia to American investment and helping check Japanese ambitions in Asia. The "Roosevelt-Litvinov conversations," often difficult and frustrating for both parties, ultimately resulted in Roosevelt's asserting formal recognition on November 16, 1933.

Seven days later, Dodd once again put on his cutaway and stove-pipe and paid his first official visit to the Soviet embassy. An Associated Press photographer asked for a picture of Dodd standing beside his Soviet counterpart. The Russian was willing, but Dodd begged off, fearing "that certain reactionary papers in America would exaggerate the fact of my call and repeat their attacks upon Roosevelt for his recognition."

CHAPTER 25

The Secret Boris

Now Martha and Boris felt freer about revealing their relationship to the world, though both recognized that discretion was still necessary given the continuing disapproval of Boris's superiors and Martha's parents. Their affair grew steadily more serious, despite Martha's efforts to keep things light and noncommittal. She continued to see Armand Berard of the French embassy, and possibly Diels, and to accept dates from potential new suitors, and this drove Boris wild with jealousy. He sent a blizzard of notes, flowers, and music and telephoned her repeatedly. "I wanted to love him only lightly," Martha wrote, in an unpublished account; "I tried to treat him as casually as I did other friends. I forced myself to be indifferent to him one week; then the next, I became stupidly jealous. I was forgetful of him, then absorbed in him. It was an unbearable contradiction, grievous and frustrating to us both."

Martha was still committed to seeing the best in the Nazi revolution, but Boris had no illusions about what was occurring around them. To Martha's irritation, he was always looking for the underlying motives that governed the actions of Nazi leaders and the various figures who visited the U.S. embassy.

"You always see the bad things," she said angrily. "You should try to see the positive things in Germany, and in our visitors, not always suspect them of ulterior motives."

She suggested that at times he too was guilty of hiding his motives—"I think you're jealous of Armand," she said, "or anyone else who takes me out."

The next day, she received a package from Boris. Inside she found three ceramic monkeys and a card that read, "See no Evil, Hear no Evil, Speak no Evil." Boris closed the note: "I love you."

Martha laughed. In return, she sent him a small carved-wood figure of a nun, along with a note that assured him she was following the monkeys' orders.

Behind it all was that looming question: where could their relationship possibly go? "I could not bear to think of the future, either with or without him," she wrote. "I loved my family, my country, and did not want to face the possibility of separation from either."

This tension led to misunderstandings and grief. Boris suffered.

"Martha!" he wrote in one pain-flushed letter. "I am so sad that I cannot find the right words for everything that happened. Forgive me if I have done something mean or bad to you. I did not mean or wish to do so. I understand you, but not completely, and I do not know what I ought to do. What shall I do?

"Farewell, Martha, be happy without me, and do not think bad about me."

Always they came back together. Each separation seemed to intensify their attraction all the more but also amplified the moments of misunderstanding and anger—until one Sunday afternoon in late November their relationship underwent a material change. She recalled it all in fine-grained detail.

A bleak day, the sky like smudged charcoal, the air cold, but not so cold as to prompt Boris to raise the top on his Ford. They set out for a cozy restaurant they both loved that was housed in a boathouse on pilings over a lake in the Wannsee district. A fragrant pine forest walled the shoreline.

They found the restaurant to be almost empty but still charming. Wood tables surrounded a small dance floor. When the jukebox wasn't playing, the sound of water gently smacking the pilings outside was clearly audible.

Martha ordered onion soup, salad, and beer; Boris chose vodka, shashlik, and herring immersed in sour cream and onions. And more vodka. Boris loved food, Martha noted, but never seemed to gain *ein Pfund.*

After lunch they danced. Boris was improving but still tended to treat dancing and walking as interchangeable phenomena. At one point as their bodies came together, both became very still, Martha recalled; she felt suddenly radiant with heat.

Boris pulled away abruptly. He took her arm and led her outside onto a wooden deck that jutted over the water. She looked at him and saw pain—eyebrows drawn together, lips compressed. He seemed agitated. They stood together at the rail watching a squadron of white swans.

He turned to her, his expression almost somber. "Martha," he said, "I love you." He confessed now that he had felt that way ever since the first time he had seen her at Sigrid Schultz's apartment. He held her before him, his hands firmly vised around her elbows. The madcap gaiety was gone.

He stepped back and looked at her. "Don't play with me, darling," he said. *"Du hast viele Bewerber."* You have a lot of suitors. "You should not decide yet. But don't treat me lightly. I could not bear it."

She looked away. "I love you, Boris. You know it. And you know how hard I try not to."

Boris turned to watch the water. "Yes, I know it," he said with sorrow. "It is not easy for me either."

Boris could never be subdued for long, however. His smile reappeared—that explosive smile. "But," he said, "your country and mine are now friends, officially, and that makes it better, makes anything possible, doesn't it?"

Yes, but . . .

There was another obstacle. Boris had been keeping a secret. Martha knew it but had not yet told him so. Now, facing him, she made her voice very quiet.

"Also," she said, "you are married."

Once again Boris stepped away. His complexion, already flushed from the cold, grew perceptibly redder. He moved to the railing and leaned on his elbows. His long frame formed a slender and graceful arc. Neither spoke.

"I'm sorry," he said. "I should have told you. I thought you knew. Forgive me."

She told him that she had not known at first, not until Armand and her parents showed her Boris's entry in the diplomatic directory published by the German foreign office. Next to Boris's name was a reference to his wife, who was "*abwesend*." Meaning absent.

"She is not 'absent,'" Boris said. "We are separated. We have not been happy together for a long time. The next diplomatic listing will have nothing in that space." He revealed as well that he had a daughter, whom he adored. It was only through her, he said, that he continued to have contact with his wife.

Martha noticed tears in his eyes. He had cried in her presence before, and she always found it moving but also discomfiting. A crying man—this was new to her. In America, men did not cry. Not yet. Up until now she had seen her father with tears in his eyes only once, upon the death of Woodrow Wilson, whom he counted as a good friend. There would be one other occasion, but that was to come in a few years' time.

They went back into the restaurant, to their table. Boris ordered another vodka. He seemed relieved. They held hands across the table.

But now Martha offered a revelation of her own.

"I too am married," she said.

The intensity of his response startled her. His voice fell and darkened. "Martha, no!" He continued to hold her hands, but his expression changed to one of puzzlement and pain. "Why didn't *you* tell *me?*"

She explained that her marriage had been a secret from the start, to all but her family—that her husband was a banker in New York, she had loved him once, and deeply, but now they were legally separated, with only the technicalities of divorce remaining.

Boris dropped his head to his arms. Under his breath he said something in Russian. She stroked his hair.

He stood abruptly and walked back outside. Martha stayed seated. A few moments later, Boris returned.

"Ach, dear God," he said. He laughed. He kissed her head. "Oh, what a mess we're in. A married woman, a banker, a foreign diplomat's daughter—I don't think it could be worse. But we'll figure it out somehow. Communists are used to doing the impossible. But you must help me."

It was nearly sundown when they left the restaurant and began their drive back toward the city, the top still down. The day had been an important one. Martha recalled small details—the onrushing wind that tore her hair loose from its coil at the back of her head, and how Boris drove with his right arm over her shoulder, his hand cupping her breast, as was often his custom. The dense forests along the roads grew darker in the fading light and exuded a rich autumnal fragrance. Her hair flew behind her in tendrils of gold.

Though neither said so directly, both understood that something fundamental had occurred. She had fallen deeply for this man and could no longer treat him in the same way she treated her other conquests. She had not wanted this to happen, but it had, and with a man whom the rest of the world saw as unsuitable in the extreme.

CHAPTER 26

The Little Press Ball

Every November the Foreign Press Association in Berlin threw a dinner and ball at the Hotel Adlon, a glamorous affair to which many of the city's most prominent officials, diplomats, and personalities were invited. The event was nicknamed the Little Press Ball because it was smaller and far less constrained than the annual banquet hosted by Germany's domestic press, which had become even stuffier than usual due to the fact that the country's newspapers were by now almost wholly under the control of Joseph Goebbels and his Ministry of Public Enlightenment. For the foreign correspondents the Little Press Ball had immense practical value. Wrote Sigrid Schultz, "It is always easier to pump a man for a story after he and his wife—if he has one—have been your guests and danced at your ball than if you see him only in business hours." In 1933 the Little Press Ball was held on the evening of Friday, November 24, six days before the city's American population would celebrate Thanksgiving.

Shortly before eight o'clock, the Adlon began receiving the first of a long procession of big cars, many with headlights the size of halved melons. Out stepped an array of senior Nazis, ambassadors, artists, filmmakers, actresses, writers, and of course the foreign correspondents themselves, from countries large and small, all bundled in big coats and furs against the damp, near-freezing air. Among the arrivals were the German state secretary Bernhard von Bülow; Foreign Minister Neurath; French ambassador François-Poncet; Sir Eric Phipps, the British ambassador; and of course the ubiquitous and gigantic Putzi Hanfstaengl. Here too came Bella Fromm, the "Auntie Voss"

society columnist, for whom the banquet would prove to be edged
with darkest tragedy, albeit of a kind grown increasingly common
in the Berlin beyond public view. The Dodds—all four—arrived in
their old Chevrolet; Hitler's vice-chancellor, Franz von Papen, came
in a significantly larger and fancier car and, like Dodd, also brought
his wife, daughter, and son. Louis Adlon, beaming in tux and tails,
greeted each splendid arrival, while bellmen took away furs, coats,
and top hats.

As Dodd was about to find out, in a milieu as supercharged as
Berlin, where every public action of a diplomat accrued exaggerated
symbolic weight, even a mere bit of conversational sparring across a
banquet table could become the stuff of minor legend.

THE GUESTS MOVED into the hotel, first to the elegant drawing
rooms for cocktails and hors d'oeuvres, then to the winter-garden
hall, beclouded with thousands of hothouse chrysanthemums. The
room was always "painfully crowded," in Schultz's appraisal, but tradition required that the ball always be held at the Adlon. Custom
also called for guests to arrive in formal wear but "without any display
of orders or official rank," as Fromm wrote in her diary, though a few
guests anxious to display their enthusiasm for the National Socialist
Party wore the drab brown of the Storm Troopers. One guest, a
duke named Eduard von Koburg, commander of the SA's Motorized
Forces, walked around wearing a dagger given him by Mussolini.

The guests were shown to their seats at tables of a kind favored by
banquet organizers in Berlin, so agonizingly narrow they put guests
in arm's reach of their peers at the opposite side. Such close quarters
had the potential to create awkward social and political situations—
putting, say, the mistress of an industrialist across from the man's
wife—so the hosts of each table made sure their seating plans were
reviewed by various protocol officials. Some juxtapositions simply
could not be avoided. The most important German officials had to
be seated not only at the head table, which this year was hosted
by the American correspondents, but also close to the captains of
the table, Schultz and Louis Lochner, chief of the Berlin bureau of

the Associated Press, and to the table's most prominent U.S. figure, Ambassador Dodd. Thus Vice-Chancellor Papen wound up sitting directly opposite Schultz, despite the fact that Papen and Schultz were known to dislike each other.

Mrs. Dodd also took a prominent seat, as did State Secretary Bülow and Putzi Hanfstaengl; Martha and Bill Jr. and numerous other guests filled out the table. Photographers circled and took picture after picture, the flare from their "flashlights" illuminating whorls of cigar smoke.

Papen was a handsome man—he resembled the character Topper as played on television years later by the actor Leo G. Carroll. But he had an unsavory reputation as an opportunist and betrayer of trust and was deemed by many to be arrogant in the extreme. Bella Fromm called him the "Gravedigger of the Weimar Republic," alluding to Papen's role in engineering the appointment of Hitler as chancellor. Papen was a protégé of President Hindenburg, who affectionately called him Fränzchen, or Little Franz. With Hindenburg in his camp, Papen and fellow intriguers had imagined they could control Hitler. "I have Hindenburg's confidence," Papen once crowed. "Within two months we will have pushed Hitler so far into a corner that he'll squeak." It was possibly the greatest miscalculation of the twentieth century. As historian John Wheeler-Bennett put it, "Not until they had riveted the fetters upon their own wrists did they realize who indeed was captive and who captor."

Dodd too viewed Papen with distaste, but for reasons stemming from treachery of a more concrete variety. Shortly before the United States had entered the past world war, Papen had been a military attaché assigned to the German embassy in Washington, where he had planned and abetted various acts of sabotage, including the dynamiting of rail lines. He had been arrested and thrown out of the country.

Once all were seated, conversation ignited at various points along the table. Dodd and Mrs. Papen talked about the American university system, which Mrs. Papen praised for its excellence: during the Papens' tenure in Washington, their son had attended Georgetown University. Putzi was his usual boisterous self. Even seated he towered above the guests around him. A strained silence occupied the cleft of linen, crystal, and china that separated Schultz and Papen. That a chill existed between them was obvious to all. "When he arrived he was as suave and polite as his reputation required," Schultz wrote, "but all through the first four courses of the dinner the gentleman ignored [me] with remarkable consistency." She noted: "This was not easy to do because it was a narrow table and I sat just about three feet opposite him."

She did all she could to draw Papen into conversation, only to be rebuffed. She had promised herself that she would "try to be the perfect hostess and steer clear of controversial subjects," but the more Papen ignored her, the less inclined she was to do so. Her resolve, she wrote, "wore thin in the face of Papen's obvious bad manners."

After the fourth course, when she could resist no longer, she looked at Papen and, deploying what she described as "the most naive sounding tones" she could muster, said, "Mr. Chancellor, there is something in the Memoirs of President von Hindenburg which I am sure you can elucidate for me."

Papen gave her his attention. His eyebrows were flared upward at the ends like feathers and imparted to his gaze the cold focus of a raptor.

Schultz kept her expression cherubic and continued: "He complains that in the last war, in 1917, the German High Command never heard anything about the peace suggestions of President Wilson and that if he had known about them the dangerous submarine campaign would not have been launched. How was that possible?"

Despite the quiet of her voice, suddenly everyone at the table within eavesdropping distance became silent and intent. Dodd watched Papen; State Secretary Bülow leaned in toward the conversation with what Schultz described as "a gleam of wicked amusement in his eyes."

Papen said brusquely, "There never was such a thing as a peace suggestion by President Wilson."

A very foolish thing to say, Schultz knew, given the presence of Ambassador Dodd, an expert on Wilson and the period in question.

Quietly but firmly, his voice bearing the lingual mists of North Carolina—"every bit the Southern gentleman," Schultz recalled—Dodd looked at Papen and said, "Oh yes there was." And gave the precise date.

Schultz was delighted. "Papen's long horsey teeth grew longer," she wrote. "He did not even try to emulate the quiet tone of Ambassador Dodd."

Instead, Papen "just snarled" his reply: "I never understood anyhow why America and Germany got to grips in that war." He looked at the faces around him "triumphantly proud of the arrogance of his tone," Schultz wrote.

In the next instant Dodd won Shultz's "undying admiration and gratitude."

MEANWHILE, AT ANOTHER TABLE, Bella Fromm experienced an anxiety unrelated to the conversations around her. She had come to the ball because it was always great fun and very useful for her column on Berlin's diplomatic community, but this year she arrived suppressing a deep uneasiness. Though she was enjoying herself, at odd moments her mind returned to her best friend, Wera von Huhn, also a prominent columnist, whom most everyone knew by her nickname, "Poulette," French for "young hen," derived from her last name, Huhn, which in German means "chicken."

Ten days earlier, Fromm and Poulette had gone for a drive through the Grunewald, an eleven-thousand-acre forest preserve west of Berlin. Like the Tiergarten, it had become a haven for diplomats and others seeking respite from Nazi surveillance. The act of driving in the forest provided Fromm one of the few moments when she felt truly safe. "The louder the motor," she wrote in her diary, "the more I feel at ease."

There was nothing carefree about this latest drive, however. Their conversation centered on the law passed the preceding month that barred Jews from editing and writing for German newspapers and required members of the domestic press to present documentation from civil and church records to prove they were "Aryan." Certain Jews could retain their jobs, namely those who had fought in the past war or lost a son in battle or who wrote for Jewish newspapers, but only a small number qualified for these exemptions. Any unregistered journalist caught writing or editing faced up to one year in prison. The deadline was January 1, 1934.

Poulette sounded deeply troubled. Fromm found this perplexing. She herself knew about the requirement, of course. Being Jewish, she had resigned herself to the fact that she would be out of a job by the new year. But Poulette? "Why should *you* worry?" Fromm asked.

"I have reason, Bella darling. I wrote for my papers, chased all over the place getting them. Finally I found out that my grandmother was Jewish."

With that news her life had been abruptly, irrevocably altered. Come January she would join a wholly new social stratum consisting of thousands of people stunned to learn they had Jewish relatives somewhere in their past. Automatically, no matter how thoroughly they had identified themselves as Germans, they became reclassified as non-Aryan and found themselves consigned to new and meager lives on the margins of the Aryans-only world being constructed by Hitler's government.

"Nobody knew anything about it," Poulette told Fromm. "Now I lose my living."

By itself the discovery was bad enough, but it also coincided with the anniversary of the death of Poulette's husband. To Fromm's surprise, Poulette decided not to attend the Little Press Ball; she was feeling too sad to go.

Fromm hated to leave her alone that night but went to the ball all the same after resolving that the next day she would visit Poulette and bring her back to her house, where Poulette loved to play with Fromm's dogs.

Throughout the evening, in the moments when her mind wasn't engaged by the antics of those around her, Fromm found herself haunted by thoughts of her friend's uncharacteristic depression.

TO DODD, PAPEN'S REMARK ranked as one of the most idiotic he had heard since his arrival in Berlin. And he had heard many. An odd kind of fanciful thinking seemed to have bedazzled Germany, to the highest levels of government. Earlier in the year, for example, Göring had claimed with utter sobriety that three hundred German Americans had been murdered in front of Independence Hall in Philadelphia at the start of the past world war. Messersmith, in a dispatch, observed that even smart, well-traveled Germans will "sit and calmly tell you the most extraordinary fairy tales."

Now here was the nation's vice-chancellor claiming not to understand why the United States had entered the world war against Germany.

Dodd looked at Papen. "I can tell you that," he said, his voice just as level and even as before. "It was through the sheer, consummate stupidity of German diplomats."

Papen looked stunned. His wife, according to Sigrid Schultz, looked strangely pleased. A new silence filled the table—not one of anticipation, as before, but a charged emptiness—until suddenly everyone sought to fill the chasm with flecks of diverting conversation.

In another world, another context, it would have been a minor incident, a burst of caustic banter readily forgotten. Amid the oppression and *Gleichschaltung* of Nazi Germany, however, it was something far more important and symbolic. After the ball, as had become custom, a core group of guests retired to Schultz's flat, where her mother had prepared piles of sandwiches and where the story of Dodd's verbal swordplay was recounted with great and no doubt drunken flourish. Dodd himself was not present, inclined as he was to leave banquets as early as protocol allowed and head for home to close out the night with a glass of milk, a bowl of stewed peaches, and the comfort of a good book.

DESPITE HER MOMENTS of upwelling anxiety, Bella Fromm found the ball delightful. Such a pleasure to see how Nazis behaved after a few drinks and to listen in as they julienned one another with lacerating commentary delivered in a whisper. At one point the dagger-carrying duke, Koburg, happened to strut past Fromm as she was conversing with Kurt Daluege, a police official whom she described as "brutal and ruthless." The duke seemed to want to project arrogance, but the effect, Fromm noted, was comically undermined by "his stooped, dwarf-like figure." Daluege told Fromm, "That Koburg walks as though he were on stilts," then added with menace: "It might leak out that his grandmother deceived the Grand Duke with that Jewish court banker."

At ten the next morning, Fromm telephoned Poulette but only reached her elderly maid, who said, "The Baroness has left a note in the kitchen that she is not to be disturbed."

Poulette never slept this late. "Suddenly I understood," Fromm wrote.

Poulette wouldn't be the first Jew or newly classified non-Aryan to try suicide in the wake of Hitler's rise. Rumors of suicides were common, and indeed a study by the Berlin Jewish Community found that in 1932–34 there were 70.2 suicides per 100,000 Jews in Berlin, up sharply from 50.4 in 1924–26.

Fromm raced to her garage and drove as quickly as possible to Poulette's home.

At the door the servant told her Poulette was still asleep. Fromm brushed past and continued on until she reached Poulette's bedroom. The room was dark. Fromm opened the curtains. She found Poulette lying in bed, breathing, but with difficulty. Beside the bed, on a night table, were two empty tubes of a barbiturate, Veronal.

Fromm also found a note addressed to her. "I can't live anymore because I know I will be forced to give up my work. You have been my best friend, Bella. Please take all my files and use them. I thank you for all the love you gave me. I know you are brave, braver than I am, and you must live because you have a child to think of, and I am sure that you will bear the struggle far better than I could."

The household came alive. Doctors arrived but could do nothing.

The next day an official of the foreign office called Fromm to convey his sorrow and an oblique message. "Frau Bella," he said, "I am deeply shocked. I know how terrible your loss is. Frau von Huhn died of pneumonia."

"Nonsense!" Fromm snapped. "Who told you that? She committed—"

"Frau Bella, please understand, our friend had pneumonia. Further explanations are undesirable. In your interest, as well."

MOST GUESTS HAD FOUND the ball to be a lovely diversion. "We all had a really good time," wrote Louis Lochner in a letter to his daughter at school in America, "and the party was a jolly one." Ambassador Dodd, predictably, had a different assessment: "The dinner was a bore, though the company present might under other circumstances have been most informing."

One result was unexpected. Instead of embittered estrangement between Dodd and Papen, there grew instead a warm and lasting association. "From that day on," Sigrid Schultz observed, "Papen himself cultivated the friendship of Ambassador Dodd with the greatest assiduity." Papen's behavior toward Schultz also improved. He seemed to have decided, she wrote, that "it was better to display his Sunday manners toward me." This, she found, was typical of a certain kind of German. "Whenever they come up against someone who will not stand for their arrogance, they climb down from their perch and behave," she wrote. "They respect character when they meet it, and if more people had shown firmness to Hitler's handyman Papen and his acolytes in small every day contacts, as well as in big affairs of state, the Nazi growth could have been slowed up."

RUMOR SPREAD ABOUT THE true cause of Poulette's death. After the funeral, Fromm was accompanied home by a good friend to whom she felt a daughterly bond—"Mammi" von Carnap, wife of a former chamberlain to the kaiser and long an excellent source of information for Fromm's column. Although loyal to the old Germany, the Carnaps were sympathetic to Hitler and his campaign to restore the nation's strength.

Mammi seemed to have something on her mind. After a few moments, she said, "Bellachen, we are all so shocked that the new regulations should have this effect!"

Fromm was startled. "But Mammi," Fromm said, "don't you realize? This is only the beginning. This thing will turn against all of you who helped to create it."

Mammi ignored the remark. "Frau von Neurath advises you to hurry up and get baptized," she said. "They are very anxious at the foreign office to avoid a second *casus* Poulette."

Fromm found this astonishing—that someone could be so ignorant of the new realities of Germany as to think that mere baptism could restore one's status as an Aryan.

"Poor old fool!" Fromm wrote in her diary.

CHAPTER 27

O Tannenbaum

It was almost Christmas. The winter sun, when it shone at all, climbed only partway into the southern sky and cast evening shadows at midday. Frigid winds came in off the plains. "Berlin is a skeleton which aches in the cold," wrote Christopher Isherwood, describing the winters he experienced during his tenure in 1930s Berlin: "It is my own skeleton aching. I feel in my bones the sharp ache of the frost in the girders of the overhead railway, in the ironwork of balconies, in bridges, tramlines, lamp-standards, latrines. The iron throbs and shrinks, the stone and the bricks ache dully, the plaster is numb."

The gloom was leavened somewhat by the play of lights on wet streets—sidewalk lamps, storefronts, headlights, the warmly lit interiors of countless streetcars—and by the city's habitual embrace of Christmas. Candles appeared in every window and large trees lit with electric lights graced squares and parks and the busiest street corners, reflecting a passion for the season that even the Storm Troopers could not suppress and in fact used to their financial advantage. The SA monopolized the sale of Christmas trees, selling them from rail yards, ostensibly for the benefit of the Winterhilfe—literally, Winter Help—the SA's charity for the poor and jobless, widely believed by cynical Berliners to fund the Storm Troopers' parties and banquets, which had become legendary for their opulence, their debauchery, and the volume of champagne consumed. Troopers went door-to-door carrying red donation boxes. Donors received little badges to pin on their clothing to show they had given money, and they made sure to wear them, thereby putting oblique pressure on those brave or foolhardy souls who failed to contribute.

Another American ran afoul of the government, due to a false denunciation by "persons who had a grudge against him," according to a consulate report. It was the kind of moment that decades hence would become a repeated motif in films about the Nazi era.

At about four thirty in the morning on Tuesday, December 12, 1933, an American citizen named Erwin Wollstein stood on a train platform in Breslau waiting for a train to Oppeln in Upper Silesia, where he planned to conduct some business. He was leaving so early because he hoped to return later that same day. In Breslau he shared an apartment with his father, who was a German citizen.

Two men in suits approached and called him by name. They identified themselves as officers of the Gestapo and asked him to accompany them to a police post located in the train station.

"I was ordered to remove my overcoat, coat, shoes, spats, collar and necktie," Wollstein wrote in an affidavit. The agents then searched him and his belongings. This took nearly half an hour. They found his passport and quizzed him on his citizenship. He confirmed that he was an American citizen and asked that they notify the American consulate in Breslau of his arrest.

The agents then took him by car to the Breslau Central Police Station, where he was placed in a cell. He was given "a frugal breakfast." He remained in his cell for the next nine hours. In the meantime, his father was arrested and their apartment searched. The Gestapo confiscated personal and business correspondence and other documents, including two expired and canceled American passports.

At five fifteen that afternoon the two Gestapo agents took Wollstein upstairs and at last read him the charges filed against him, citing denunciations by three people whom Wollstein knew: his landlady, a second woman, and a male servant who cleaned the apartment. His landlady, Miss Bleicher, had charged that two months earlier he had said, "All Germans are dogs." His servant, Richard Kuhne, charged that Wollstein had declared that if another world war occurred, he would join the fight against Germany. The third, a Miss Strausz, charged that Wollstein had loaned her husband "a communistic book." The book, as it happened, was *Oil!* by Upton Sinclair.

Wollstein spent the night in jail. The next morning he was permitted to confront his denouncers face-to-face. He accused them of having lied. Now, unprotected by the veil of anonymity, the witnesses wavered. "The witnesses themselves appeared to be confused and not sure of their ground," Wollstein recalled in his affidavit.

Meanwhile, the U.S. consul in Breslau reported the arrest to the consulate in Berlin. Vice Consul Raymond Geist in turn complained to Gestapo chief Rudolf Diels and requested a full report on Wollstein's arrest. That evening, Diels telephoned and told Geist that on his orders Wollstein would be released.

Back in Breslau, the two Gestapo men ordered Wollstein to sign a statement declaring that he would never "be an enemy to the German State." The document included a magnanimous offer: that if he ever felt his safety endangered, he could report for arrest under protective custody.

He was released.

MARTHA ASSIGNED HERSELF the task of trimming the family tree, an enormous fir placed in the ballroom on the second floor of the house. She enlisted the help of Boris, Bill, butler Fritz, the family chauffeur, and various friends who stopped by to help. She resolved to have a tree that was entirely white and silver and so bought silver balls, silver tinsel, a large silver star, and white candles, eschewing electric lights for the more traditional and infinitely more lethal approach. "In those days," she wrote, "it was heresy to think of electric lights for a tree." She and her helpers kept pails of water nearby.

Her father, she wrote, was "bored with all this foolishness" and avoided the project, as did her mother, who was busy with myriad other holiday preparations. Bill was helpful to a point but had a tendency to drift away in search of more engaging pursuits. The project took two days and two evenings.

Martha found it funny that Boris was willing to help, given that he claimed not to believe in the existence of God. She smiled as she watched him at work atop a stepladder dutifully helping her trim a symbol of the foremost holy day of the Christian faith.

"My darling atheist," she recalled telling him, "why do you help me decorate a Christmas tree to celebrate the birth of Christ?"

He laughed. "This isn't for Christians or for Christ, *liebes Kind*," he said, "only for pagans like you and me. Anyway, it is very beautiful. What would you like?" He sat at the apex of the ladder. "Do you want me to put my white orchids on top? Or would you prefer a handsome red star?"

She insisted on white.

He protested. "But red *is* a more beautiful color than white, darling."

Despite the tree and Boris and the overall cheer of the season, Martha felt that a fundamental element was absent from her life in Berlin. She missed her friends—Sandburg and Wilder and her colleagues at the *Tribune*—and her comfortable house in Hyde Park. By now her friends and neighbors would be gathering for cozy parties, caroling sessions, and mulled wine.

On Thursday, December 14, she wrote a long letter to Wilder. She felt keenly the withering of her connection to him. Just knowing him gave her a sense of credibility, as if by refraction she too possessed literary cachet. But she had sent him a short story of hers, and he had said nothing. "Have you lost even your literary interest in me or shall I say your interest in the literary me (what there is left of it, if there was anything to begin with). And your trip to Germany. Has it been definitely passed up. Gosh, you have certainly given me the slip, to lapse back into Berlin slang for a moment!"

She had done little other writing, she told him, though she had found a certain satisfaction in talking and writing about books, thanks to her new friendship with Arvid and Mildred Harnack. Together, she told Wilder, "we have concluded we are the only people in Berlin genuinely interested in writers." Mildred and she had begun their book column. "She is tall and beautiful with a heavy burden of honey colored hair—dark honey in some lights. . . . Very poor and real and fine and not much in favor though the family is old and respected. An oasis really to me mad with thirst."

She alluded to her father's sense that a conspiracy was mounting against him from within the State Department. "Mazes of hate and intrigue in our Embassy have as yet failed to trap us," she wrote.

Hatreds of a more personal kind had touched her as well. In America her secret marriage to Bassett and her equally secret effort to divorce him had become public knowledge. "Nasty what my enemies cooked up about me in Chicago," she told Wilder. One woman in particular, whom Martha identified as Fanny, had begun spreading especially unpleasant rumors out of what Martha believed to be jealousy over Martha's publication of a short story. "She insists that you and I have had an affair and it has come back to me from two people. I wrote to her the other day pointing out the dangers of slander unfounded and indicated the mess she might get into." She added, "I feel sorry for her, but it does not alter the fact that she is a rather slimy mouthed bitch."

She sought to capture for Wilder a sense of the wintry city outside her windows, this new world in which she found herself. "The snow is soft and deep lying here—a copper smoke mist over Berlin by day and the brilliance of the falling moon by night. The gravel squeaks under my window at night—the sinister faced, lovely lipped and gaunt Diels of the Prussian Secret Police must be watching and the gravel spits from under his soft shoes to warn me. He wears his deep scars as proudly as I would fling about in a wreath of edelweiss."

She expressed a deep and pervading sorrow. "The smell of peace is abroad, the air is cold, the skies are brittle, and the leaves have finally fallen. I wear a pony coat with skin like watered silk and muff of lamb. My fingers lie in depths of warmth. I have a jacket of silver sequins and heavy bracelets of rich corals. I wear about my neck a triple thread-like chain of lapis lazulis and pearls. On my face is softness and content like a veil of golden moonlight. And I have never in all my lives been so lonely."

THOUGH MARTHA'S REFERENCE to "mazes of hate" was a bit strong, Dodd had indeed begun to sense that a campaign was gathering against him within the State Department and that its participants were the men of wealth and tradition. He suspected also that they were assisted by one or more people on his own staff providing intelligence in sotto voce fashion about him and the operation of the embassy. Dodd grew increasingly suspicious and guarded, so much so that he began writing his most sensitive letters in longhand because he did not trust the embassy stenographers to keep their contents confidential.

He had reason to be concerned. Messersmith continued his back-channel correspondence with Undersecretary Phillips. Raymond Geist, Messersmith's number-two officer (another Harvard man) also kept watch on the affairs of Dodd and the embassy. During a stop in Washington, Geist had a long and secret conversation with Wilbur Carr, chief of consular services, during which Geist provided a wide range of intelligence, including details about unruly parties thrown by Martha and Bill that sometimes lasted until five in the morning. "On one occasion the hilarity was so great," Geist told Carr, that it drew a written complaint to the consulate. This prompted Geist to call Bill into his office, where he warned him, "If there was a repetition of that conduct it would have to be reported officially." Geist also offered a critique of Ambassador Dodd's performance: "The Ambassador is mild mannered and unimpressive whereas the only kind of person who can deal successfully with the Nazi Government is a man of intelligence and force who is willing to assume a dictatorial attitude with the Government and insist upon his demands being met. Mr. Dodd is unable to do this."

The arrival in Berlin of a new man, John C. White, to replace George Gordon as counselor of embassy could only have increased Dodd's wariness. In addition to being wealthy and prone to hosting elaborate parties, White also happened to be married to the sister of Western European affairs chief Jay Pierrepont Moffat. The two brothers-in-law carried on a chummy correspondence, calling each other "Jack" and "Pierrepont." Dodd would not have found the opening line of one of White's first letters from Berlin to be terribly reassuring: "There appears to be a spare typewriter round here, so I can write you without other witnesses." In one reply, Moffat called Dodd "a curious individual whom I find it almost impossible to diagnose."

To make matters even more claustrophobic for Dodd, another new officer, Orme Wilson, who arrived at about the same time to become a secretary of embassy, was Undersecretary Phillips's nephew.

When the *Chicago Tribune* printed an article about Dodd's request for leave in the coming year, along with conjecture that he might quit his post, Dodd complained to Phillips that someone within the department must have revealed his leave request, intending harm. What especially galled Dodd was a comment in the article attributed to an unnamed State Department spokesman. The article stated: "Permanent retirement from the post of Ambassador to Germany is not contemplated by Professor Dodd, it was insisted here." With the perverse logic of publicity, the denial actually raised the question of Dodd's fate—would he retire or was he being forced from his post? The situation in Berlin was difficult enough without such specula-tion, Dodd told Phillips. "I believe von Neurath and his colleagues would be considerably displeased if this report were forwarded to them."

Phillips replied, with his now-familiar textual smirk, "I cannot imagine who gave the *Tribune* information regarding your possible leave next Spring," he wrote. "Certainly no one has asked the ques-tion of me. . . . One of the principal joys of the newspaper world is to start gossip about resignations. At times we all suffer from that phobia and do not take it seriously."

In closing, Phillips noted that Messersmith, who was then in Washington on leave, had visited the department. "Messersmith has been with us for a few days and we have had some good talks on the various phases of the German situation."

Dodd would have been right to read those last lines with a degree of anxiety. During one of these visits to Phillips's office, Messersmith provided what Phillips described in his diary as "an inside glimpse of conditions in the Embassy in Berlin." Here too the subject of Martha and Bill came up. "Apparently," Phillips wrote, "the Ambassador's son and daughter are not assisting the Embassy in any way and are too much inclined to running around to night clubs with certain Germans of not particularly good standing and with the press."

Messersmith also met with Moffat and Moffat's wife. The three spent an afternoon talking about Germany. "We went over it from all angles," Moffat wrote in his diary. The next day he and Messer-smith had lunch, and several weeks later they met again. During one conversation, according to Moffat's diary, Messersmith claimed to be "much concerned at letters received from Dodd indicating that he was turning against his staff."

Dodd's recently departed counselor, George Gordon, happened to be on a lengthy leave in the United States at the same time as Messersmith. Though Gordon's relationship with Dodd had begun badly, by now Dodd grudgingly had come to see Gordon as an asset. Gordon wrote to Dodd, "Our mutual friend G.S.M."—meaning Messersmith—"has been staging a most active campaign in support of his candidacy for the Legation at Prague." (Messersmith had long hoped to leave the Foreign Service behind and become a full-fledged diplomat; now, with the embassy in Prague available, he saw an opportunity.) Gordon noted that a torrent of letters and newspaper editorials testifying to Messersmith's "sterling work" had begun flowing into the department. "A familiar touch was imparted to all this," Gordon wrote, "when I heard that he had told one of the high officials that he really was a little embarrassed by all the press eulogies of himself because he did not like that kind of thing!!!!"

Gordon added, in longhand: "O sancta virginitas simplicitasque," Latin for "Such pious maidenly innocence!"

ON DECEMBER 22, a Friday, Dodd got a visit from Louis Lochner, who brought troubling news. The visit itself was not unusual, for by now Dodd and the Associated Press bureau chief had become friends and met often to discuss events and exchange information. Lochner told Dodd that an official high in the Nazi hierarchy had informed him that the next morning the court in the Reichstag trial would declare its verdict, and that all but van der Lubbe would be acquitted. This was stunning news by itself and, if true, would constitute a serious blow to the prestige of Hitler's government and in particular to Göring's standing. It was precisely the "botch" Göring had feared. But Lochner's informant also had learned that Göring, still incensed at Dimitrov's impudence during their courtroom confrontation, now wanted Dimitrov dead. His death was to occur soon after the end of the trial. Lochner refused to identify his source but told Dodd that in conveying the information the source hoped to prevent further damage to Germany's already poor international reputation. Dodd believed the informant to be Rudolf Diels.

Lochner had come up with a plan to scuttle the assassination by publicizing it but wanted first to run the idea past Dodd, in case Dodd felt the diplomatic repercussions would be too great. Dodd approved but in turn consulted Sir Eric Phipps, the British ambassador, who also agreed that Lochner should go ahead.

Lochner weighed precisely how to execute his plan. Oddly enough, the initial idea of publicizing the impending assassination had been brought to him by Göring's own press adjutant, Martin Sommerfeldt, who also had learned of the imminent murder. His source, according to one account, was Putzi Hanfstaengl, though it is entirely possible that Hanfstaengl learned of it from Diels. Sommerfeldt told Lochner that he knew from experience that "there is one way of dissuading the general. When the foreign press claims one thing about him, he stubbornly does the opposite." Sommerfeldt proposed that Lochner attribute the story to an "unimpeachable source" and stress that the murder would have "far reaching international consequences." Lochner faced a quandary, however. If he published so inflammatory a report through the Associated Press, he risked enraging Göring to the point where Göring might shut down the AP's Berlin bureau. It was far better, Lochner reasoned, to have the story break in a British newspaper. He, Sommerfeldt, and Hanfstaengl revised their plan.

Lochner knew that a very green reporter had just joined the Berlin bureau of Reuters. He invited him out for drinks at the Adlon Hotel, where Hanfstaengl and Sommerfeldt soon joined them. The new reporter savored his luck at this apparently chance convergence of senior officials.

After a few moments, Lochner mentioned to Sommerfeldt the rumor of a threat against Dimitrov. Sommerfeldt, as per plan, feigned surprise—surely Lochner had gotten it wrong, for Göring was a man of honor and Germany was a civilized land.

The Reuters reporter knew this was a big story and asked Sommerfeldt for permission to quote his denial. With a great show of reluctance, Sommerfeldt agreed.

The Reuters man raced off to file his story.

Late that afternoon, the report made the papers in Britain, Lochner told Dodd. Lochner also showed Dodd a telegram to the foreign press from Goebbels, in which Goebbels, acting as spokesman for the government, denied the existence of any plot to murder Dimitrov. Göring issued his own denial, dismissing the allegation as a "horrid rumor."

On December 23, as Lochner had forecast, the presiding judge in the Reichstag trial announced the court's verdict, acquitting Dimitrov, Torgler, Popov, and Tanev but finding van der Lubbe guilty of "high treason, insurrectionary arson and attempted common arson." The court condemned him to death, while also stating—despite masses of testimony to the contrary—"that van der Lubbe's accomplices must be sought in the ranks of the Communist Party, that communism is therefore guilty of the Reichstag fire, that the German people stood in the early part of the year 1933 on the brink of chaos into which the Communists sought to lead them, and that the German people were saved at the last moment."

Dimitrov's ultimate fate, however, remained unclear.

AT LAST CAME CHRISTMAS DAY. Hitler was in Munich; Göring, Neurath, and other senior officials likewise had left Berlin. The city was quiet, truly at peace. Streetcars evoked toys under a tree.

At midday all the Dodds set out in the family Chevrolet and paid a surprise visit to the Lochners. Louis Lochner wrote in a round-robin letter to his daughter in America, "We were sitting together drinking our coffee, when suddenly the whole Dodd family—the Ambassador, Mrs. Dodd, Martha, and young Mr. Dodd—snowed in on us just to wish us Merry Christmas. That was awfully nice of them, wasn't it? I like Mr. Dodd the more I work with him; he's a man of profound culture and endowed with one of the keenest minds I have come in contact with." Lochner described Mrs. Dodd as "a sweet, womanly woman who . . . like her husband far rather visits with a family of friends than go through all the diplomatic shallow stuff. The Dodds don't pretend to be social lions, and I admire them for it."

Dodd spent a few moments admiring the Lochners' tree and other decorations, then took Lochner aside and asked for the latest news of the Dimitrov affair.

Dimitrov thus far appeared to have escaped harm, Lochner said.

He also reported that his highly placed source—whose identity he still would not reveal to Dodd—had thanked him for handling the matter so deftly.

Dodd feared further repercussions, however. He remained convinced that Diels had played a key role in revealing the plot. Dodd continued to be surprised by Diels. He knew his reputation as a cynic and opportunist of the first order, but he found him time and again to be a man of integrity and worthy of respect. It was Diels, indeed, who earlier in the month had persuaded Göring and Hitler to decree a Christmas amnesty for inmates of concentration camps who were not hardened criminals or clearly dangerous to state security. Diels's precise motives cannot be known, but he considered that time, as he went from camp to camp selecting prisoners to be freed, one of the best moments of his career.

Dodd feared that Diels might have gone too far. In his diary entry for Christmas Day, Dodd wrote, "The Secret Police Chief did a most dangerous thing and I shall not be surprised later to hear that he has been sent to prison."

In traveling about the city that day, Dodd was struck anew by the "extraordinary" German penchant for Christmas display. He saw Christmas trees everywhere, in every public square and every window.

"One might think," he wrote, "the Germans believed in Jesus or practiced his teachings!"

1934

PART V
Disquiet

Hitler and Röhm

CHAPTER 28

January 1934

On January 9 the primary defendant in the Reichstag trial, Marinus van der Lubbe, received word from the public prosecutor that he was to be beheaded the next day.

"Thank you for telling me," van der Lubbe said. "I shall see you tomorrow."

The executioner wore top hat and tails and, in a particularly fastidious touch, white gloves. He used a guillotine.

Van der Lubbe's execution provided a clear if gory punctuation point to the Reichstag fire saga and thereby quelled a source of turbulence that had roiled Germany since the preceding February. Now anyone who felt the need for an ending could point to an official act of state: van der Lubbe had set the fire, and now van der Lubbe was dead. Dimitrov, still alive, was to be flown to Moscow. The way was clear for the restoration of Germany.

As the year opened, Germany did seem on a superficial level to have grown more stable, much to the disappointment of foreign observers and diplomats who still nurtured the belief that economic pressures would cause the collapse of the Hitler regime. At the end of his first year as chancellor, Hitler seemed more rational, almost conciliatory, and went so far as to hint that he might support some form of nonaggression pact with France and Britain. Anthony Eden, Britain's Lord Privy Seal, traveled to Germany to meet with him and, like Dodd, came away impressed with Hitler's sincerity in wanting peace. Sir Eric Phipps, Britain's ambassador to Germany, wrote in his diary, "Herr Hitler seemed to feel a genuine sympathy for Mr. Eden, who certainly succeeded in bringing to the surface of that strange being certain human qualities which for me had hitherto remained obstinately dormant." In a letter to Thornton Wilder, Martha wrote: "Hitler is improving definitely."

This sense of looming normalcy was apparent in other spheres as well. The official tally of unemployed workers showed a rapid decline, from 4.8 million in 1933 to 2.7 million in 1934, although a good deal of this was due to such measures as assigning one-man jobs to two men and an aggressive propaganda campaign that sought to discourage women from working. The "wild" concentration camps had been closed, thanks in part to Gestapo chief Rudolf Diels. Within the Reich Ministry of the Interior there was talk of doing away with protective custody and concentration camps altogether.

Even Dachau seemed to have become civilized. On February 12, 1934, a representative of the Quakers, Gilbert L. MacMaster, set out to visit the camp, after having been granted permission to see an inmate, a sixty-two-year-old former deputy of the Reichstag named George Simon, who had been arrested because he was a socialist. MacMaster caught a train in Munich and half an hour later got off in the village of Dachau, which he described as an "artists village." From there he walked another half hour to reach the camp.

He was surprised by what he found. "More atrocity reports have come from this camp than any other one in Germany," he wrote. "The outward appearance though is better than any camp I have seen." The former gunpowder plant in which the camp was located had been built during the past world war. "There were good houses for the chemists and the officers; the barracks for the workers were more stable, and the whole plant was steam heated," MacMaster saw. "This makes Dachau seem better equipped for the comfort of the prisoners, especially in cold weather, than the provisional camp in an old factory or farm house. In fact the appearance of the whole is more that of a permanent institution than that of a camp."

The inmate, Simon, was soon brought to the guardhouse to meet with MacMaster. He wore a gray prison suit and seemed well. "He had no complaint," MacMaster wrote, "except that he was suffering a great deal from acute rheumatism."

Later that day MacMaster spoke to a police official who told him the camp housed two thousand prisoners. Only twenty-five were Jews, and these, the official insisted, were held for political offenses, not because of their religion. MacMaster, however, had heard reports that at least five thousand prisoners were housed within and that forty to fifty were Jews, of whom only "one or two" had been arrested for political offenses; others had been arrested following denunciations by people "who wanted to injure them in business and others because they were accused of associating with non-Jewish girls." He was surprised to hear the official say that he saw the camps "as temporary and would welcome the day when they could be done away with."

MacMaster found Dachau even had a certain beauty. "It was a very cold morning," he wrote. "There had been such a dense fog the night before that I had had a hard time finding my hotel. This morning there was a perfect blue sky, Bavarian colors were white, for the clouds, and blue for the Bavarian sky, and the fog of the night before covered the trees with a thick hoar-frost." Everything was coated with a glistening lace of ice crystals that gave the camp an ethereal look, like something from a fable. In the sun the birches of the surrounding moor became spires of diamond.

But as in so many situations in the new Germany, the outward appearance of Dachau was misleading. The cleanliness and efficiency of the camp had little to do with a desire to treat the inmates in a humane fashion. The preceding June an SS officer named Theodor Eicke had taken command of Dachau and composed a set of regulations that later became the model for all camps. Issued on October 1, 1933, the new rules codified the relationship between guards and prisoners and in so doing removed the act of punishment from the realm of impulse and caprice to a plane where discipline became systematic, dispassionate, and predictable. Now everyone at least knew the rules, but the rules were harsh and explicitly left no room for pity.

"Tolerance means weakness," Eicke wrote in the introduction to his rules. "In the light of this conception, punishment will be mercilessly handed out whenever the interests of the fatherland warrant it." Minor offenses drew beatings with a cane and stints in solitary confinement. Even irony was costly. Eight days' solitary and "twenty-five strokes" were meted out to "anyone making depreciatory or ironical remarks to a member of the SS, deliberately omitting the prescribed marks of respect, or in any other way demonstrating unwillingness to submit himself to disciplinary measures." A catch-all clause, Article 19, dealt with "incidental punishments," which were to include reprimands, beatings, and "tying to stakes." Another section laid out the rules for hangings. Death was the penalty for anyone who, "for the purpose of agitating," discussed politics or was caught meeting with others. Even collecting "true or false information about the concentration camp" or receiving such information or talking about it with others could get an inmate hanged. "If a prisoner attempts to escape," Eicke wrote, "he is to be shot without warning." Gunfire also was the required response to prisoner uprisings. "Warning shots," Eicke wrote, "are forbidden on principle."

Eicke made sure all new guards were fully indoctrinated, as one of his trainees, Rudolf Höss, would later attest. Höss became a guard at Dachau in 1934 and recalled how Eicke repeatedly drummed home the same message. "Any pity whatsoever for 'enemies of the State' was unworthy of an SS-man. There was no place in the ranks of the SS for men with soft hearts and any such would do well to retire quickly to a monastery. He could only use hard, determined men who ruthlessly obeyed every order." An adept pupil, Höss went on to become commandant at Auschwitz.

AT FIRST GLANCE, persecution of Jews seemed also to have eased. "Outwardly Berlin presented during my recent stay there a normal appearance," wrote David J. Schweitzer, a senior official with the American Joint Distribution Committee, nicknamed the Joint, a Jewish relief organization. "The air is not charged, general courtesy prevails." Jews who had fled during the previous year now actually had begun returning, he wrote. Some ten thousand Jews who had left in early 1933 had returned by the start of 1934, though outbound emigration—four thousand Jews in 1934—continued as well. "So much is this the actual situation or so well masked is it that I heard an American, one who has just spent a week passing on to a neighboring country, remark that he could not see that anything has actually happened that so stirred the outside world."

But Schweitzer understood this was in large part an illusion. Overt violence against Jews did appear to have receded, but a more subtle oppression had settled in its place. "What our friend had failed to see from outward appearances is the tragedy that is befalling daily the job holders who are gradually losing their positions," Schweitzer wrote. He gave the example of Berlin's department stores, typically owned and staffed by Jews. "While on the one hand one can observe a Jewish department store crowded as usual with non-Jews and Jews alike, one can observe in the very next department store the total absence of a single Jewish employee." Likewise the situation varied from community to community. One town might banish Jews, while in the next town over Jews and non-Jews continued "to live side by side with their neighbors and pursue their occupations as best they can unmolested."

Likewise Schweitzer detected divergent outlooks among Berlin's Jewish leaders. "The one tendency is that there is nothing to hope for, that things are bound to get worse," he wrote. "The other tendency, however, is quite the opposite but just as definite, namely a tendency resulting from thinking in terms of March 1934 instead of March 1933, reconciling themselves to the present situation, accepting the status of the inevitable, adjusting themselves to move in their own restricted circles and hoping that just as things have changed from March 1933 to March 1934 they will continue to improve in a favorable manner."

HITLER'S CONTINUED PROTESTATIONS of peace constituted the most blatant official deception. Anyone who made an effort to travel the countryside outside Berlin knew it at once. Raymond Geist, acting consul general, routinely made such journeys, often on a bicycle. "Before the end of 1933, during my frequent excursions, I discovered outside of Berlin on nearly every road leaving from the city new large military establishments, including training fields, airports, barracks, proving grounds, anti-aircraft stations and the like."

Even the newly arrived Jack White recognized the true reality of what was occurring. "Any one motoring out in the country of a Sunday can see brown shirts drilling in the woods," he told his brother-in-law, Moffat.

White was astonished to learn that the young daughter of a friend was required to spend every Wednesday afternoon practicing the art of throwing hand grenades.

THE SUPERFICIAL NORMALCY of Germany also masked the intensifying conflict between Hitler and Röhm. Dodd and others who had spent time in Germany knew full well that Hitler was intent on increasing the size of the regular army, the Reichswehr, despite the explicit prohibitions of the Treaty of Versailles, and that Captain Röhm of the SA wanted any increase to include the incorporation of entire SA units, part of his campaign to gain control of the nation's military. Defense Minister Blomberg and the army's top generals loathed Röhm and disdained his uncouth legions of brown-shirted Storm Troopers. Göring hated Röhm as well and saw his drive for power as a threat to Göring's own control of Germany's new air force, his pride and joy, which he was now quietly but energetically working to construct.

What remained unclear was where exactly Hitler stood on the matter. In December 1933, Hitler made Röhm a member of his cabinet. On New Year's Eve he sent Röhm a warm greeting, published in the press, in which he praised his longtime ally for building so effective a legion. "You must know that I am grateful to destiny, which has allowed me to call such a man as you my friend and brother-in-arms."

Soon afterward, however, Hitler ordered Rudolf Diels to compile a report on the outrages committed by the SA and on the homosexual practices of Röhm and his circle. Diels later claimed that Hitler also asked him to kill Röhm and certain other "traitors" but that he refused.

President Hindenburg, the supposed last restraint against Hitler, seemed oblivious to the pressures building below. On January 30, 1934, Hindenburg issued a public statement congratulating Hitler on the "great progress" Germany had made in the year since his ascension to chancellor. "I am confident," he wrote, "that in the coming year you and your fellow workers will successfully continue, and with God's help complete, the great work of German reconstruction which you have so energetically begun, on the basis of the new happily attained national unity of the German people."

And so the year began, with an outward sense of better times ahead and, for the Dodds, a fresh round of parties and banquets. Formal invitations arrived on printed cards in envelopes, followed as always by seating diagrams. The Nazi leadership favored an awkward arrangement in which tables formed a large rectangular horseshoe with guests arrayed along the inside and outside of the configuration. Those seated along the inside flank spent the evening in an abyss of social discomfort, watched from behind by their fellow guests. One such invitation arrived for Dodd and his family from their neighbor Captain Röhm.

Martha later would have cause to save a copy of the seating chart. Röhm, the *Hausherr*, or host, sat at the top of the horseshoe and had full view of everyone seated before him. Dodd sat on Röhm's right, in a position of honor. Directly across the table from Röhm, in the most awkward seat of the horseshoe, was Heinrich Himmler, who loathed him.

CHAPTER 29

Sniping

In Washington, Undersecretary Phillips called Jay Pierrepont Moffat into his office "to read a whole series of letters from Ambassador Dodd," as Moffat noted in his diary. Among these were recent letters in which Dodd repeated his complaints about the wealth of Foreign Service officers and the number of Jews on his staff, and one that dared to suggest a foreign policy that America should pursue. The nation, Dodd had written, must discard its "righteous aloofness" because "another life and death struggle in Europe would bother us all—especially if it was paralleled by a similar conflict in the Far East (as I believe is the understanding in secret conclaves)." Dodd acknowledged Congress's reluctance to become entangled abroad but added, "I do, however, think facts count; even if we hate them."

Although Phillips and Moffat were disenchanted with Dodd, they recognized that they had limited power over him because of his relationship with Roosevelt, which allowed Dodd to skirt the State Department and communicate directly with the president whenever he wished. Now, in Phillips's office, they read Dodd's letters and shook their heads. "As usual," Moffat wrote in his diary, "he is dissatisfied with everything." In one letter Dodd had described two of his embassy officers as "competent but unqualified"—prompting Moffat to snipe, "Whatever that may mean."

On Wednesday, January 3, Phillips, his tone remote and supercilious, wrote to Dodd to address some of Dodd's complaints, one of which centered on the transfer of Phillips's nephew, Orme Wilson, to Berlin. Wilson's arrival the previous November had caused an upwelling of competitive angst within the embassy. Phillips now chided Dodd for not managing the situation better. "I hope it will not be difficult for you to discourage any further talk of an undesirable nature amongst the members of your staff."

As to Dodd's repeated complaint about the work habits and qualifications of Foreign Service men, Phillips wrote, "I confess I am at a loss to understand your feeling that 'somebody in the Department is encouraging people in mistaken attitudes and conduct.'"

He cited Dodd's past observation that there were too many Jews on the embassy's clerical staff but professed to be "somewhat confused" as to how to resolve the issue. Dodd previously had told him he did not want to transfer anyone out, but now it appeared he did. "Do you desire any transfers?" Phillips asked. He added, "If . . . the racial question is one that needs correction in view of the special conditions in Germany, it will be perfectly possible for the Department to do this upon definite recommendation from you."

THAT SAME WEDNESDAY, in Berlin, Dodd wrote a letter to Roosevelt that he deemed so sensitive he not only wrote it in longhand but also sent it first to his friend Colonel House, so that House could give it to the president in person. Dodd urged that Phillips be removed from his position as undersecretary and given a different sort of posting, perhaps as an ambassador somewhere. He suggested Paris and added that Phillips's departure from Washington "would limit a little the favoritisms that prevail there."

He wrote, "Do not think I have any personal axe to grind or any personal grievances about anything. I hope"—*hope*—"it is the public service alone that motivates [this] letter."

CHAPTER 30

Premonition

Martha became consumed with Boris. Her French lover, Armand Berard, upon finding himself consigned to the background, grieved. Diels too receded, though he remained a frequent companion.

Early in January, Boris arranged a tryst with Martha that yielded one of the most unusual romantic encounters she had ever experienced, though she had no advance warning of what was to occur other than Boris's plea that she wear his favorite dress—gold silk, off the shoulders, deep and revealing neckline, close fitted at the waist. She added a necklace of amber and a corsage that Boris had provided, of gardenias.

Fritz, the butler, greeted Boris at the front door, but before he could announce the Russian's presence, Boris went bounding up the stairway to the main floor. Fritz followed. Martha was just then walking along the hall toward the stairs, as she wrote in a detailed recollection of the evening. Upon seeing her, Boris dropped to one knee.

"Oh my darling!" he said, in English. Then, in German: "You look wonderful."

She was delighted and mildly embarrassed. Fritz grinned. Boris led her out to his Ford—the top raised, mercifully, against the cold—and drove them to Horcher's restaurant on Lutherstrasse, a few blocks south of the Tiergarten. It was one of Berlin's finest restaurants, specializing in game, and was said to be Göring's favorite place to dine. It was identified also, in a 1929 short story by then-popular writer Gina Kaus, as the place to go if your goal was seduction. You could be seated on one of its leather banquettes and a few tables over, there would be Göring, resplendent in his uniform of the moment. In another time there might have been famous writers, artists, and musicians and prominent Jewish financiers and scientists, but by this point most had fled or else had found themselves suddenly isolated in circumstances that did not permit costly nights on the town. The restaurant endured, however, as if unmindful that anything had changed in the world outside.

Boris had reserved a private room, where he and Martha dined lavishly on smoked salmon, caviar, turtle soup, and chicken in the style coming to be known as "Kievsky." For dessert they had brandied Bavarian cream. They drank champagne and vodka. Martha loved the food, the drink, the lofty setting, but was perplexed. "Why all this, Boris?" she asked him. "What are we celebrating?"

In answer he gave only a smile. After dinner, they drove north and turned onto Tiergartenstrasse as if heading for the Dodds' house, but instead of stopping there, Boris kept driving. They tooled along the darkly forested boundary of the park until they reached the Brandenburg Gate and Unter den Linden, its two-hundred-foot width clogged with automobiles whose headlights transformed it into a sluiceway of platinum. One block east of the gate, Boris pulled to a stop at the Soviet embassy, at Unter den Linden 7. He led Martha into the building and along several corridors, then up a flight of stairs, until they stood before an unmarked door.

He smiled and opened the door, then stepped aside to let her pass. He switched on a table lamp and lit two red candles. The room reminded her at first of a student's residence in a dormitory, though Boris had done what he could to make it something more. She saw a straight-backed chair, two armchairs, and a bed. Over the pillow he had spread an embroidered cloth that he identified as coming from the Caucasus. A samovar for making tea occupied a table by the window.

In one corner of the room, in a bookcase, Martha found a collection of photographs of Vladimir Lenin centered around a single large portrait that showed him in a manner Martha had not seen before, like a friend captured in a snapshot, not the stern-visaged Lenin of Soviet propaganda. Here too lay a number of pamphlets in Russian, one with the scintillating title, as translated by Boris, "Workers and Peasant Inspection Teams." Boris identified all this as his "Lenin corner," his Soviet equivalent of the religious images that Orthodox Russians traditionally hung high in one corner of a room. "My people, as you may have read in the Russian novels you love, used to have, and still have, icon corners," he told her. "But I am a modern Russian, a communist!"

In another corner she found a second shrine, but the centerpiece of this one, she saw, was herself. Boris called it his "Martha corner." A photograph of her stood on a small table, shimmying in the red flicker of one of Boris's candles. He also had set out several of her letters and more photographs. An enthusiastic amateur photographer, he had taken many pictures during their travels around Berlin. There were keepsakes as well—a linen handkerchief she had given him and that stalk of wild mint from their picnic in September 1933, now dried but still exuding a faint tang. And here too was the carved wooden statue of a nun that she had sent to him as a reply to his three "see no evil" monkeys—except Boris had accessorized the nun by adding a tiny halo fashioned out of fine gold wire.

More recently he had added pinecones and freshly cut evergreen boughs to his Martha shrine, and these filled the room with the scent of forest. He included these, he told her, to symbolize that his love for her was "ever green."

"My God, Boris," she laughed, "you are a romantic! Is this a proper thing for a tough communist like you to do?"

Next to Lenin, he told her, "I love you most." He kissed her bare shoulder and suddenly became very serious. "But in case you don't understand yet," he said, "my party and country must always come first."

The sudden shift, the look on his face—again Martha laughed. She told Boris she understood. "My father thinks of Thomas Jefferson almost the way you do about Lenin," she said.

They were getting cozy, when suddenly, quietly, the door opened and in stepped a blond girl whom Martha guessed to be about nine years old. She knew at once this had to be Boris's daughter. Her eyes were just like her father's—"extraordinary, luminous eyes," Martha wrote—though in most other ways she seemed very unlike him. Her face was plain and she lacked her father's irrepressible mirth. She looked somber. Boris rose and went to her.

"Why is it so dark in here?" his daughter said. "I don't like it."

She spoke in Russian, with Boris translating. Martha suspected the girl knew German, given her schooling in Berlin, but that she spoke Russian now out of petulance.

Boris turned on an overhead light, a bare bulb. Its harsh glow instantly dispersed the romantic air he had managed to create with his candles and shrines. He told his daughter to shake Martha's hand, and the girl did so, though with obvious reluctance. Martha found the girl's hostility unpleasant but understandable.

The girl asked her, in Russian, "Why are you so dressed up?"

Boris explained that this was the Martha he had told her about. She was dressed so nicely, he said, because this was her very first visit to the Soviet embassy and thus a special occasion.

The girl appraised Martha. A hint of a smile appeared. "She is very pretty," the girl said. "But she's too thin."

Boris explained that nonetheless Martha was healthy.

He checked his watch. The time was almost ten o'clock. He sat his daughter in his lap, held her close, and gently ran his hand through her hair. He and Martha spoke of trivial matters as the girl stared at Martha. After a few moments Boris stopped stroking her hair and gave her a hug, his signal that it was time for her to go to bed. She curtsied and in grudging, quiet German said, "Auf Wiedersehen, Fräulein Marta."

Boris took the girl's hand and walked her from the room.

In his absence, Martha gave his quarters a closer examination, and she continued doing so after his return. Now and then she glanced in his direction.

"Lenin was very human," he said, smiling. "He would have understood *your* corner."

They lay on the bed and held each other. He told her of his life—how his father had abandoned his family, and how at sixteen he had joined the Red Guard. "I want my daughter to have an easier life," he said. He wanted the same for his country. "We've had nothing but tyranny, war, revolution, terror, civil war, starvation. If we aren't attacked again, we may have a chance to build something new and unique in human history. You understand?"

At times as he told his story tears slipped down his cheeks. She was used to it now. He told her his dreams for the future.

"Then he held me close to his body," she wrote. "From below his collarbone to his navel, his honey-colored hair covered him, as soft as down. . . . Truly, it was beautiful to me, and gave me a deep feeling of warmth, comfort and closeness."

As the evening came to an end, he made tea and poured it into the traditional cup—clear glass in a metal frame.

"Now, my darling," he said, "in the last few hours you have had a small taste of a *Russian* evening."

"HOW COULD I TELL HIM," she wrote later, "that it was one of the strangest evenings I had ever spent in my life?" A sense of foreboding tempered her enjoyment. She wondered whether Boris, by becoming so involved with her—establishing his Martha corner in the embassy and daring to bring her to his private quarters—had somehow transgressed an unwritten prohibition. She sensed that some "malevolent eye" had taken note. "It was," she recalled, "as if a dark wind had entered the room."

Late that night Boris drove her home.

CHAPTER 31

Night Terrors

The lives of the Dodds underwent a subtle change. Where once they had felt free to say anything they wished within their own home, now they experienced a new and unfamiliar constraint. In this their lives reflected the broader miasma suffusing the city beyond their garden wall. A common story had begun to circulate: One man telephones another and in the course of their conversation happens to ask, "How is Uncle Adolf?" Soon afterward the secret police appear at his door and insist that he prove that he really does have an Uncle Adolf and that the question was not in fact a coded reference to Hitler. Germans grew reluctant to stay in communal ski lodges, fearing they might talk in their sleep. They postponed surgeries because of the lip-loosening effects of anesthetic. Dreams reflected the ambient anxiety. One German dreamed that an SA man came to his home and opened the door to his oven, which then repeated every negative remark the household had made against the government. After experiencing life in Nazi Germany, Thomas Wolfe wrote, "Here was an entire nation . . . infested with the contagion of an ever-present fear. It was a kind of creeping paralysis which twisted and blighted all human relations."

Jews, of course, experienced it most acutely. A survey of those who fled Germany, conducted from 1993 through 2001 by social historians Eric A. Johnson and Karl-Heinz Reuband, found that 33 percent had felt "constant fear of arrest." Among those who had lived in small towns, more than half recalled feeling such fear. Most non-Jewish citizens, however, claimed to have experienced little fear—in Berlin, for example, only 3 percent described their fear of arrest as constant—but they did not feel wholly at ease. Rather, most Germans experienced a kind of echo of normality. There arose among them a recognition that their ability to lead normal lives "depended on their acceptance of the Nazi regime and their keeping their heads down and not acting conspicuously." If they fell into line, allowed themselves to be "coordinated," they would be safe—though the survey also found a surprising tendency among non-Jewish Berliners to occasionally step out of line. Some 32 percent recalled telling anti-Nazi jokes, and 49 percent claimed to have listened to illegal radio broadcasts from Britain and elsewhere. However, they only dared to commit such infractions in private or among trusted friends, for they understood that the consequences could be lethal.

For the Dodds, at first, it was all so novel and unlikely as to be almost funny. Martha laughed the first time her friend Mildred Fish Harnack insisted they go into a bathroom for a private conversation. Mildred believed that bathrooms, being sparsely furnished, were more difficult to fit with listening devices than a cluttered living room. Even then Mildred would "whisper almost inaudibly," Martha wrote.

It was Rudolf Diels who first conveyed to Martha the unfunny reality of Germany's emerging culture of surveillance. One day he invited her to his office and with evident pride showed her an array of equipment used for recording telephone conversations. He led her to believe that eavesdropping apparatus had indeed been installed in the chancery of the U.S. embassy and in her home. Prevailing wisdom held that Nazi agents hid their microphones in telephones to pick up conversations in the surrounding rooms. Late one night, Diels seemed to confirm this. Martha and he had gone dancing. Afterward, upon arrival at her house, Diels accompanied her upstairs to the library for a drink. He was uneasy and wanted to talk. Martha grabbed a large pillow, then walked across the room toward her father's desk. Diels, perplexed, asked what she was doing. She told him she planned to put the pillow over the telephone. Diels nodded slowly, she recalled, and "a sinister smile crossed his lips."

She told her father about it the next day. The news surprised him.

Though he accepted the fact of intercepted mail, tapped telephones and telegraph lines, and the likelihood of eavesdropping at the chancery, he never would have imagined a government so brazen as to place microphones in a diplomat's private residence. He took it seriously, however. By now he had seen enough unexpected behavior from Hitler and his underlings to show him that anything was possible. He filled a cardboard box with cotton, Martha recalled, and used it to cover his own telephone whenever a conversation in the library shifted to confidential territory.

As time passed the Dodds found themselves confronting an amorphous anxiety that infiltrated their days and gradually altered the way they led their lives. The change came about slowly, arriving like a pale mist that slipped into every crevice. It was something everyone who lived in Berlin seemed to experience. You began to think differently about whom you met for lunch and for that matter what café or restaurant you chose, because rumors circulated about which establishments were favorite targets of Gestapo agents—the bar at the Adlon, for example. You lingered at street corners a beat or two longer to see if the faces you saw at the last corner had now turned up at this one. In the most casual of circumstances you spoke carefully and paid attention to those around you in a way you never had before. Berliners came to practice what became known as "the German glance"—*der deutsche Blick*—a quick look in all directions when encountering a friend or acquaintance on the street.

The Dodds' home life became less and less spontaneous. They grew especially to distrust their butler, Fritz, who had a knack for moving soundlessly. Martha suspected that he listened in when she had friends and lovers in the house. Whenever he appeared in the midst of a family conversation, the talk would wither and become desultory, an almost unconscious reaction.

After vacations and weekends away, the family's return was always darkened by the likelihood that in their absence new devices had been installed, old ones refreshed. "There is no way on earth one can describe in the coldness of words on paper what this espionage can do to the human being," Martha wrote. It suppressed routine discourse—"the family's conferences and freedom of speech and action were so circumscribed we lost even the faintest resemblance to a normal American family. Whenever we wanted to talk we had to look around corners and behind doors, watch for the telephone and speak in whispers." The strain of all this took a toll on Martha's mother. "As time went on, and the horror increased," Martha wrote, "her courtesy and graciousness towards the Nazi officials she was forced to meet, entertain, and sit beside, became so intense a burden she could scarcely bear it."

Martha eventually found herself deploying rudimentary codes in communications with friends, an increasingly common practice throughout Germany. Her friend Mildred used a code for letters home in which she crafted sentences that meant the opposite of what the words themselves indicated. That such practices had become usual and necessary was difficult for outsiders to understand. An American professor who was a friend of the Dodds, Peter Olden, wrote to Dodd on January 30, 1934, to tell him he had received a message from his brother-in-law in Germany in which the man described a code he planned to use in all further correspondence. The word "rain," in any context, would mean he had been placed in a concentration camp. The word "snow" would mean he was being tortured. "It seems absolutely unbelievable," Olden told Dodd. "If you think that this is really something in the nature of a bad joke, I wonder if you could mention so in a letter to me."

Dodd's careful reply was a study in deliberate omission, though his meaning was clear. He had come to believe that even diplomatic correspondence was intercepted and read by German agents. A subject of growing concern was the number of German employees who worked for the consulate and the embassy. One clerk in particular had drawn the attention of consular officials: Heinrich Rocholl, a longtime employee who helped prepare reports for the American commercial attaché, whose offices were on the first floor of the Bellevuestrasse consulate. In his spare time Rocholl had founded a pro-Nazi organization, the Association of Former German Students in America, which issued a publication called *Rundbriefe*. Lately Rocholl had been discovered trying "to find out the contents of confidential reports of the Commercial Attaché," according to a memorandum that

Acting Consul General Geist sent to Washington. "He has also had conversations with other German members of the staff who assist in the reporting work, and intimated to these that their work should be in every respect favorable to the present regime." In one issue of the *Rundbriefe* Geist found an article in which "disparaging allusions were made to the Ambassador as well as to Mr. Messersmith." For Geist this was the last straw. Citing the clerk's "overt act of disloyalty to his chiefs," Geist fired him.

Dodd realized that the best way to have a truly private conversation with anyone was to meet in the Tiergarten for a walk, as Dodd often did with his British counterpart, Sir Eric Phipps. "I shall be walking at 11:30 on the Hermann-Göring-Strasse alongside the Tiergarten," Dodd told Phipps in a telephone call at ten o'clock one morning. "Would you be able to meet me there and talk for a while?" And Phipps, on another occasion, sent Dodd a handwritten note asking, "Could we meet tomorrow morning at 12 o'clock in the Siegesallee between the Tiergartenstrasse & the Charlottenburger Chaussee, on the right side (going from here)?"

WHETHER LISTENING DEVICES TRULY laced the embassy and the Dodds' home cannot be known, but the salient fact was that the Dodds came to see Nazi surveillance as omnipresent. Despite the toll this perception increasingly took on their lives, they believed they had one significant advantage over their German peers—that no physical harm would come to them. Martha's own privileged status offered no protection to her friends, however, and here Martha had particular cause for concern because of the nature of the men and women she befriended.

She had to be especially watchful in her relationship with Boris— as a representative of a government reviled by the Nazis, he was beyond doubt a target of surveillance—and with Mildred and Arvid Harnack, both of whom had grown increasingly opposed to the Nazi regime and were taking their first steps toward building a loose association of men and women committed to resisting Nazi power. "If I had been with people who had been brave or reckless enough to talk in opposition to Hitler," Martha wrote in her memoir, "I spent sleepless nights wondering if a Dictaphone or a telephone had registered the conversation, or if men had followed and overheard."

In that winter of 1933–34, her anxiety blossomed into a kind of terror that "bordered on the hysterical," as she described it. Never had she been more afraid. She lay in her own bed, in her own room, with her parents upstairs, objectively as safe as could be, and yet as shadows cast by the dim streetlamps outside played across her ceiling, she could not keep the terror from staining the night.

She heard, or imagined she heard, the grating of hard-soled shoes on the gravel in the drive below, the sound tentative and intermittent, as if someone was watching her bedroom. By day the many windows in her room brought light and color; at night, they conjured vulnerability. Moonlight cast moving shadows on the lawns and walks and beside the tall pillars of the entrance gate. Some nights she imagined hearing whispered conversations, even distant gunshots, though by day she was able to dismiss these as the products of wind blowing across gravel and engine backfires.

But anything was possible. "I often felt such terror," she wrote, "that occasionally I would wake up my mother and ask her to come and sleep in my room."

CHAPTER 32

Storm Warning

In February 1934 rumors reached Dodd that suggested the conflict between Hitler and Captain Röhm had attained a new level of intensity. The rumors were well founded.

Toward the end of the month, Hitler appeared before a gathering of the top officers of Röhm's SA, Heinrich Himmler's SS, and the regular army, the Reichswehr. Present with him on the dais were Röhm and Minister of Defense Blomberg. The atmosphere in the room was charged. All present knew of the simmering conflict between the SA and the army and expected Hitler to address the issue.

First Hitler spoke of broader matters. Germany, he declared, needed more room in which to expand, "more living space for our surplus population." And Germany, he said, must be ready to take it. "The Western powers will never yield this vital space to us," Hitler said. "That is why a series of decisive blows may become necessary— first in the West, and then in the East."

After further elaboration, he turned to Röhm. All in the room knew of Röhm's ambitions. A few weeks earlier Röhm had made a formal proposal that the Reichswehr, SA, and SS be consolidated under a single ministry, leaving unsaid but implied that he himself should be the minister in charge. Now, looking directly at Röhm, Hitler said, "The SA must limit itself to its political task."

Röhm maintained an expression of indifference. Hitler continued, "The Minister of War may call upon the SA for border control and for premilitary instruction."

This too was a humiliation. Not only was Hitler consigning the

SA to the decidedly inglorious tasks of border control and training, but he was explicitly placing Röhm in an inferior position to Blomberg as the recipient of orders, not the originator. Röhm still did not react.

Hitler said, "I expect from the SA loyal execution of the work entrusted to it."

After concluding his speech, Hitler turned to Röhm, took his arm, and grasped his hand. Each looked into the other's eyes. It was an orchestrated moment, meant to convey reconciliation. Hitler left. Acting his part, Röhm now invited the gathered officers to lunch at his quarters. The banquet, in typical SA style, was lavish, accompanied by a torrent of champagne, but the atmosphere was anything but convivial. At an appropriate moment, Röhm and his SA men stood to signal that the luncheon had come to an end. Heels clicked, a forest of arms shot outward in the Hitler salute, *Heils* were barked, and the army leaders made their exit.

Röhm and his men remained behind. They drank more champagne, but their mood was glum.

For Röhm, Hitler's remarks constituted a betrayal of their long association. Hitler seemed to have forgotten the crucial role the Storm Troopers had played in bringing him to power.

Now, to no one in particular, Röhm said, "That was a new Versailles Treaty." A few moments later, he added, "Hitler? If only we could get rid of that limp rag."

The SA men lingered a while longer, trading angry reactions to Hitler's speech—all this witnessed by a senior SA officer named Viktor Lutze, who found it deeply troubling. A few days later, Lutze reported the episode to Rudolf Hess, at this point one of Hitler's closest aides, who urged Lutze to see Hitler in person and tell him everything.

Upon hearing Lutze's account, Hitler replied, "We'll have to let the thing ripen."

CHAPTER 33

"Memorandum of a Conversation with Hitler"

Dodd's happy anticipation of his upcoming leave was marred by two unexpected demands. The first came on Monday, March 5, 1934, when he was summoned to the office of Foreign Minister Neurath, who angrily demanded that he do something to halt a mock trial of Hitler set to take place two days later in New York's Madison Square Garden. The trial was organized by the American Jewish Congress, with support from the American Federation of Labor and a couple of dozen other Jewish and anti-Nazi organizations. The plan so outraged Hitler that he ordered Neurath and his diplomats in Berlin and Washington to stop it.

One result was a sequence of official protests, replies, and memoranda that revealed both Germany's sensitivity to outside opinion and the lengths U.S. officials felt compelled to go to avoid direct criticism of Hitler and his party. The degree of restraint would have been comical if the stakes had not been so high and raised a question: why were the State Department and President Roosevelt so hesitant to express in frank terms how they really felt about Hitler at a time when such expressions clearly could have had a powerful effect on his prestige in the world?

GERMANY'S EMBASSY IN WASHINGTON had first gotten wind of the planned trial several weeks earlier, in February, through advertisements in the *New York Times*. Germany's ambassador to the United States, Hans Luther, promptly complained to Secretary of State Hull, whose response was careful: "I stated that I was sorry to see these differences arise between persons in his country and in mine; that I would give the matter all due attention such as might be possible and justifiable in all of the circumstances."

On March 1, 1934, the German embassy's number-two man, Rudolf Leitner, met with a State Department official named John Hickerson and urged him to "do something to prevent this trial because of its lamentable effect on German public opinion if it should take place." Hickerson replied that owing to "our constitutional guarantees of freedom of expression" the federal government could do nothing to stop it.

Leitner found this difficult to fathom. He told Hickerson "that if the circumstances were reversed the German Government would certainly find a way of 'stopping such a proceeding.'"

On this point Hickerson had no doubt. "I replied," Hickerson wrote, "that it is my understanding that the German Government is not so limited in the action which it can take in such matters as the American government."

The next day, Friday, March 2, Ambassador Luther had a second meeting with Secretary Hull to protest the trial.

Hull himself would have preferred that the mock trial not occur. It complicated things and had the potential of further reducing Germany's willingness to pay its debts. At the same time, he disliked the Nazi regime. Although he avoided any direct statement of criticism, he took a certain pleasure in telling the German ambassador that the men slated to speak at the trial "were not in the slightest under the control of the Federal Government," and therefore the State Department was powerless to intervene.

It was then that Foreign Minister Neurath summoned Dodd to his office. Neurath kept him waiting ten minutes, which Dodd "noticed and resented." The delay reminded him of Neurath's snub the previous October after his Columbus Day speech about Gracchus and Caesar.

Neurath handed him an aide-mémoire—a written statement given by one diplomat to another, typically on a serious matter where verbal delivery might distort the intended message. This one was unexpectedly intemperate and threatening. It called the planned mock trial a "malicious demonstration" and cited a pattern of similarly "insulting expressions" that had taken place in the United States throughout the preceding year, describing these as "a combat tantamount to direct interference in the internal affairs of another country." The document also attacked an ongoing Jewish American boycott of German goods promoted by the American Jewish Congress. Playing to America's fears of a German bond default, it claimed the boycott had reduced Germany's balance of payments with the United States to such an extent that "the fulfillment of the obligations of German companies to their American creditors has only been partially possible."

Neurath ended the aide-mémoire by declaring that because of the mock trial "maintenance of friendly relations, sincerely desired by both Governments, is rendered extremely difficult thereby."

After reading it, Dodd explained quietly that in America "nobody could suppress a private or public meeting," a point the Germans seemed utterly unable to grasp. Dodd also hinted that Germany had brought these public relations troubles upon itself. "I reminded the Minister that many things still occur here shocking to foreign public opinion."

After the meeting, Dodd cabled Secretary Hull and told him the mock trial had made "an extraordinary impression" on the German government. Dodd ordered his staff to translate Neurath's aide-mémoire and only then sent it to Hull, by mail.

On the morning before the mock trial, German ambassador Luther tried again to stop it. This time he called on Undersecretary William Phillips, who also told him nothing could be done. Luther demanded that the department announce immediately "that nothing which was to be said at the meeting would represent the views of the Government."

Here too Phillips demurred. Not enough time remained to prepare such a statement, he explained; he added that it would be inappropriate for the secretary of state to attempt to anticipate what the speakers would or would not say at the trial.

Luther made one last try and asked that the State Department at least issue such a disavowal on the morning after the trial.

Phillips said he could not commit the department but would "take the matter under consideration."

The trial took place as planned, guarded by 320 uniformed New York City policemen. Inside Madison Square Garden, forty plain-clothes detectives circulated among the twenty thousand people in attendance. The twenty "witnesses" who testified during the trial included Rabbi Stephen Wise, Mayor Fiorello La Guardia, and a former secretary of state, Bainbridge Colby, who delivered the opening remarks. The trial found Hitler guilty: "We declare that the Hitler government is compelling the German people to turn back from civilization to an antiquated and barbarous despotism which menaces the progress of mankind toward peace and freedom, and is a present threat against civilized life throughout the world."

At a press conference the next day Phillips stated that he had "no comment other than to re-emphasize the private nature of the gathering and that no member of the Administration was present."

Phillips and fellow officials turned their attention to other matters. As would soon become apparent, however, Germany was not yet willing to let the matter drop.

THE SECOND DISTASTEFUL TASK that Dodd had to complete before his departure was to meet with Hitler. He had received an order from Secretary Hull directing him to convey to the chancellor America's dismay at a burst of Nazi propaganda recently unleashed within the United States. Putzi Hanfstaengl arranged the meeting, which was to be private and secret—just Hitler and Dodd—and so, on Wednesday, March 7, shortly before one o'clock in the afternoon, Dodd once again found himself in the Reich chancellery making his way to Hitler's office past the usual cadre of guards clicking and saluting.

First Dodd asked Hitler whether he had a personal message for Roosevelt that Dodd might deliver in person when he met with the president in Washington.

Hitler paused. He looked at Dodd a moment.

"I am very much obliged to you," he said, "but this takes me by

surprise and I wish you would give me time to think the subject over
and let me talk with you again."

Dodd and Hitler conversed a few moments about innocuous
things before Dodd turned to the matter at hand—"the unfortunate
propaganda which has been made in the United States," as Dodd
recounted in a memorandum he composed after the meeting.

Hitler "pretended astonishment," Dodd wrote, and then asked for
details.

Within the last ten days, Dodd told him, a Nazi pamphlet had
begun circulating in the United States that contained what Dodd
described as "an appeal to Germans in other countries to think
themselves always as Germans and owing moral, if not political, allegiance to the fatherland." Dodd likened it to similar propaganda
distributed in the United States in 1913, well before America entered the past war.

Hitler flared. "*Ach*," he snapped, "that is all Jewish lies; if I find
out who does that, I will put him out of the country at once."

With this the conversation veered into a broader, more venomous
discussion of the "Jewish problem." Hitler condemned all Jews and
blamed them for whatever bad feeling had arisen in America toward
Germany. He became enraged and exclaimed, "Damn the Jews!"

Given Hitler's fury, Dodd thought it prudent to refrain from raising the subject of the mock trial, which would take place later that
day, New York time. Hitler didn't mention it either.

Instead, Dodd turned to how the Jewish situation might be resolved peacefully and humanely. "You know there is a Jewish problem
in other countries," Dodd told Hitler. Dodd proceeded to describe
how the State Department was providing unofficial encouragement
to a new organization established by the League of Nations under
the direction of James G. McDonald, newly appointed high commissioner for refugees from Germany, to relocate Jews, as Dodd put it,
"without too much suffering."

Hitler dismissed it out of hand. The effort would fail, he said, no
matter how much money the commission raised. The Jews, he said,
would turn it into a weapon to "attack Germany and make endless
trouble."

Dodd countered that Germany's current approach was doing great damage to the country's reputation in America. Oddly, Dodd now sought to find a kind of middle ground with the dictator. He told Hitler, "You know a number of high positions in our country are at present occupied by Jews, both in New York and Illinois." He named several "eminent fair-minded Hebrews," including Henry Morgenthau Jr., Roosevelt's secretary of the Treasury since January. Dodd explained to Hitler "that where the question of over-activity of Jews in university or official life made trouble, we had managed to redistribute the offices in such a way as not to give great offense, and that wealthy Jews continued to support institutions which had limited the number of Jews who held high positions." Dodd cited one such example in Chicago and added, "The Jews in Illinois constituted no serious problem."

Dodd in his memorandum explained: "My idea was to suggest a different procedure from that which has been followed here—of course never giving pointed advice."

Hitler shot back that "59 percent of all offices in Russia were held by Jews; that they had ruined that country and that they intended to ruin Germany." More furious now than ever, Hitler proclaimed, "If they continue their activity, we shall make a complete end to all of them in this country."

It was a strange moment. Here was Dodd, the humble Jeffersonian schooled to view statesmen as rational creatures, seated before the leader of one of Europe's great nations as that leader grew nearly hysterical with fury and threatened to destroy a portion of his own population. It was extraordinary, utterly alien to his experience.

Dodd calmly turned the conversation back to American perceptions and told Hitler "that public opinion in the United States is firmly convinced that the German people, if not their Government, are militaristic, if not actually warlike" and that "most people of the United States have the feeling that Germany is aiming one day to go to war." Dodd asked, "Is there any real basis for that?"

"There is absolutely no basis," Hitler said. His rage seemed to subside. "Germany wants peace and will do everything in her power to keep the peace; but Germany demands and will have equality of rights in the matter of armaments."

Dodd cautioned that Roosevelt placed high importance on respect for existing national boundaries.

On that score, Hitler said, Roosevelt's attitude matched his own, and for that he professed to be "very grateful."

Well then, Dodd asked, would Germany consider taking part in a new international disarmament conference?

Hitler waved off the question and again attacked the Jews. It was they, he charged, who had promoted the perception that Germany wanted war.

Dodd steered him back. Would Hitler agree to two points: that "no nation should cross another nation's boundaries and that all European nations should agree to a supervisory commission and respect the rulings of such a body?"

Yes, Hitler said, and did so, Dodd observed, "heartily."

Later, Dodd wrote a description of Hitler in his diary. "He is romantic-minded and half-informed about great historical events and men in Germany." He had a "semi-criminal" record. "He has definitely said on a number of occasions that a people survives by fighting and dies as a consequence of peaceful policies. His influence is and has been wholly belligerent."

How, then, could one reconcile this with Hitler's many declarations of peaceful intent? As before, Dodd believed Hitler was "perfectly sincere" about wanting peace. Now, however, the ambassador had realized, as had Messersmith before him, that Hitler's real purpose was to buy time to allow Germany to rearm. Hitler wanted peace only to prepare for war. "In the back of his mind," Dodd wrote, "is the old German idea of dominating Europe through warfare."

DODD PREPARED FOR HIS VOYAGE. Though he would be gone two months, he planned to leave his wife, Martha, and Bill behind in Berlin. He would miss them, but he could hardly wait to get on that ship bound for America and his farm. Less cheery was the prospect of the meetings he would have to attend at the State Department immediately after his arrival. He planned to take the opportunity to continue his campaign to make the Foreign Service more egalitarian by confronting, directly, the members of the Pretty Good Club:

Undersecretary Phillips, Moffat, Carr, and an increasingly influential assistant secretary of state, Sumner Welles, another Harvard grad and a confidant of Roosevelt (a page, in fact, at Roosevelt's 1905 wedding) who had been instrumental in crafting the president's Good Neighbor policy. Dodd would have liked to return to America with some concrete proof that his approach to diplomacy—his interpretation of Roosevelt's mandate to serve as an exemplar of American values—had exerted a moderating influence on the Hitler regime, but all he had accrued thus far was repugnance for Hitler and his deputies and grief for the lost Germany of his recollection.

Shortly before his departure, however, there came a glint of light that heartened him and suggested that his efforts had not been wasted. On March 12 an official of Germany's foreign office, Hans-Heinrich Dieckhoff, announced at a meeting of the German Press Club that henceforth Germany would require that a warrant be issued before any arrest and that the notorious Columbia House prison would be closed. Dodd believed that he personally had much to do with the order.

He would have been less heartened to learn of Hitler's private reaction to their last meeting, as recorded by Putzi Hanfstaengl. "Dodd made no impression," Hanfstaengl wrote. "Hitler was almost pitying." After the meeting, Hitler had said: "*Der gute* Dodd. He can hardly speak German and made no sense at all."

Which accorded rather closely with the reaction, back in Washington, of Jay Pierrepont Moffat. In his diary Moffat wrote, "Ambassador Dodd, quite without instruction, took up with Hitler the President's non-aggression idea and asked him point-blank if he would attend an international conference to discuss this. Where the Ambassador got the idea that we wanted another international conference is a mystery."

With clear exasperation Moffat wrote, "I am glad he is soon returning on leave."

THE NIGHT BEFORE his departure Dodd went up to his bedroom and found Fritz, the butler, packing his suitcases. Dodd grew annoyed. He did not trust Fritz, but that wasn't the issue here. Rather, Fritz's efforts abraded his own Jeffersonian instincts. Dodd wrote in his diary, "I do not think it a disgrace for a man to pack his own bags."

On Tuesday, March 13, he and all his family drove to Hamburg, 180 miles northwest of Berlin, where he bade everyone good-bye and settled into his cabin aboard the SS *Manhattan* of the United States Lines.

DODD WAS HAPPILY AFLOAT when the German government's anger about the mock trial flared again. The Third Reich, it seemed, simply could not let the issue go.

On the day of Dodd's sailing, fully six days after the trial, Ambassador Luther in Washington again called on Secretary Hull. According to Hull's account, Luther protested "such offensive and insulting acts by the people of one country against the Government and its officials of another country."

By this point Hull was losing patience. After offering a pro forma expression of regret and reiterating that the mock trial had no connection to the U.S. government, he launched a sly attack. "I stated further that I trusted that the people of every country would, in the future, exercise such self-restraint as would enable them to refrain from excessive or improper manifestations or demonstrations on account of the action of peoples of another country. I sought to make this latter veiled reference to Germany plain. I then added generally that the world seems to be in a ferment to a considerable extent, with the result that the people in more countries than one are neither thinking nor acting normally."

Ten days later, amid a snowstorm, the German ambassador returned yet again, angrier than ever. As Luther entered Hull's office, the secretary quipped that he hoped the ambassador "was not feeling as cool as the snow falling outside."

Using language that Hull described as "almost violent," Luther spent the next forty-five minutes angrily citing a list of "abusive and insulting expressions of American citizens towards the Hitler Government."

Hull expressed his sorrow that America had become a target of German criticism but then noted that at least "my government was not alone in this situation; that virtually all the governments surrounding Germany and also those in and about his country seemed to be likewise in rather distinct disfavor on one account or another; and that his government as at present constituted seemed for some reason to be almost entirely isolated from all countries, although I did not intimate that it had been in the least at fault in a single instance. I said that it might be well, however, for his government to check its conditions of isolation and see where the trouble or fault lay."

Hull also pointed out that America's relationship with previous German governments had been "uniformly agreeable" and stated that "it was only during the control of the present government that the troubles complained of had arisen, much to our personal and official regret." He was careful to note that certainly this was mere "coincidence."

The whole problem would go away, Hull intimated, if Germany "could only bring about a cessation of these reports of personal injuries which had been coming steadily to the United States from Germany and arousing bitter resentment among many people here."

Hull wrote, "We were clearly referring to the persecution of the Jews throughout the conversation."

A week later, Secretary Hull launched what proved to be the final salvo on the matter. He had at last received the translation of the aide-mémoire Neurath had given to Dodd. It was Hull's turn now to be angry. He sent an aide-mémoire of his own, to be delivered in person to Neurath by the chargé d'affaires in Berlin, John C. White, who was running the embassy in Dodd's absence.

After chiding Neurath on the "tone of asperity unusual in diplomatic communication" that had pervaded the German's aide-mémoire, Hull gave him a brief lecture on American principles.

He wrote, "It is well known that the free exercise of religion, the freedom of speech and of the press, and the right of peaceable assembly, are not only guaranteed to our citizens by the Constitution of the United States, but are beliefs deep-seated in the political consciousness of the American people." And yet, Hull wrote, Neurath in his aide-mémoire had described incidents where Germany felt the U.S. government should have disregarded these principles. "It appears, therefore, that the points of view of the two Governments, with respect to the issues of free speech and assembly, are irreconcilable, and that any discussion of this difference could not improve relations which the United States Government desires to preserve on as friendly a basis as the common interest of the two peoples demands."

And thus at last the battle over the mock trial came to an end, with diplomatic relations chilly but intact. Once again no one in the U.S. government had made any public statement either supporting the trial or criticizing the Hitler regime. The question remained: what was everyone afraid of?

A U.S. senator, Millard E. Tydings of Maryland, tried to force Roosevelt to speak against Jewish persecution by introducing in the Senate a resolution that would have instructed the president "to communicate to the Government of the German Reich an unequivocal statement of the profound feelings of surprise and pain experienced by the people of the United States upon learning of discriminations and oppressions imposed by the Reich upon its Jewish citizens."

A State Department memorandum on the resolution written by Dodd's friend R. Walton Moore, assistant secretary of state, sheds light on the government's reluctance. After studying the resolution, Judge Moore concluded that it could only put Roosevelt "in an embarrassing position." Moore explained: "If he declined to comply with the request, he would be subjected to considerable criticism. On the other hand, if he complied with it he would not only incur the resentment of the German Government, but might be involved in a very acrimonious discussion with that Government which conceivably might, for example, ask him to explain why the negroes of this country do not fully enjoy the right of suffrage; why the lynching of negroes in Senator Tydings' State and other States is not prevented or severely punished; and how the anti-Semitic feeling in the United States, which unfortunately seems to be growing, is not checked."

The resolution failed. Secretary Hull, according to one historian, "exerted his influence with the Foreign Relations Committee to have it buried."

CHAPTER 34

Diels, Afraid

With the approach of spring, as temperatures at last broke the fifty-degree threshold, Martha began to notice a change in Diels. Usually so cool and suave, he seemed now to be on edge. He had good reason.

The stress of his post increased markedly as Captain Röhm pressed his demand for control of the military and as Heinrich Himmler sought to strengthen his grasp over secret-police operations throughout Germany. Diels had once said that his job required that he sit "on all sides of the fence at once," but now even he recognized his position was no longer tenable. His insider's view showed him the intensity of the passions at play and the unyielding character of the ambitions that underlay them. He knew as well that all parties involved viewed imprisonment and murder as useful political tools. He told Martha that even though he was now officially a colonel in Himmler's SS, he was hated by Himmler and his associates. He began to fear for his life and at one point told Martha and Bill that he could be shot at any moment. "We didn't take too seriously what he said," she recalled. He had a tendency to be overly melodramatic, she knew, though she acknowledged that "his job was one in which anyone might become hysterical or paranoiac." The strain did seem to be taking a toll on his health, however. He complained, she wrote, of "acute stomach and heart disorders."

Sensing that a political eruption of some sort was inevitable, Diels met with Hermann Göring, still nominally his boss, to ask for a leave from the Gestapo. He cited illness as the reason. In his later memoir he described Göring's reaction.

"You are sick?" Göring hissed. "You had better make up your mind to be *very* sick."

"Yes, I am truly ill," Diels said. He told Göring he had done all he could "to return the carriage of state to its proper path." But now, he said, "I cannot go on."

"All right, you are ill," Göring said. "Therefore, you cannot remain in service, not for a single day longer. You are confined to your home since you are ill. You will not make any long-distance calls or write any letters. Above all else, watch your step."

Prudence dictated an alternative course. Once again Diels left the country, but this time he checked himself into a sanatorium in Switzerland. Rumor held, not implausibly, that he had brought with him a cargo of damning secret files for delivery to a friend in Zurich who was to publish everything if Diels was shot.

A few weeks later Diels returned to Berlin, and soon afterward he invited Martha and Bill to his apartment. Diels's wife led the pair into the living room, where they found Diels lying on a couch looking anything but cured. A couple of pistols lay on a table beside him next to a large map. Diels dismissed his wife, whom Martha described as "a pathetic passive-looking creature."

The map, Martha saw, was covered with symbols and notations applied with inks of different colors that described a network of secret-police posts and agents. Martha found it terrifying, "a vast spider-web of intrigue."

Diels was proud of it. "You know most of this is my work," he said. "I have really organized the most effective system of espionage Germany has ever known."

If he possessed such power, Martha asked him, why was he so clearly afraid?

He answered, "Because I know too much."

Diels needed to shore up his defenses. He told Martha that the more he and she could be seen together in public, the safer he would feel. This was no mere line aimed at rekindling their romance. Even Göring was coming to see Diels as an asset of fading value. Amid the storm of clashing passions whirling through Berlin that spring, the gravest danger to Diels arose from the fact that he continued to resist choosing a side and as a result was distrusted in varying degrees by all camps. He grew sufficiently paranoid that he believed someone was trying to poison him.

Martha had no objection to spending more time with Diels. She liked being associated with him and having the insider's view he afforded her. "I was young and reckless enough to want to be as closely in on every situation as I possibly could," she wrote. But again, she possessed what Diels did not, the assurance that as the daughter of the American ambassador she was safe from harm.

A friend warned her, however, that in this case she was "playing with fire."

Over the weeks that followed, Diels stayed close to Martha and behaved, she wrote, "like a frightened rabbit," though she also sensed that a part of Diels—the old confident Lucifer—reveled in the game of extricating himself from his predicament.

"In some ways the danger he thought he was in was a challenge to his slyness and shrewdness," she recalled. "Could he outwit them or not, could he escape them or not?"

CHAPTER 35

Confronting the Club

Dodd's ship arrived at quarantine in New York harbor on Friday, March 23. He had hoped that his arrival would escape notice by the press, but once again his plans were frustrated. Reporters routinely met the great ocean liners of the day on the presumption, generally valid, that someone of importance would be aboard. Just in case, Dodd had prepared a brief, five-sentence statement, and he soon found himself reading it to two reporters who had spotted him. He explained that he had come back to America "on a short leave . . . in order to get some much-needed rest from the tense European atmosphere." He added, "Contrary to the predictions of many students of international problems, I feel fairly certain that we shall not have war in the near future."

He was heartened to find that the German vice consul in New York had come to meet the ship bearing a letter from Hitler for delivery to Roosevelt. Dodd was especially pleased that his friend Colonel House had sent his "handsome limousine" to pick him up and bring him to the colonel's Manhattan home at East Sixty-eighth Street and Park Avenue to wait for his train to Washington, D.C.—a lucky thing, Dodd wrote in his diary, because taxi drivers were on strike "and if I had gone to a hotel the newspaper folk would have pestered me until my train for Washington departed." Dodd and the colonel had a candid talk. "House gave me valuable information about unfriendly officials in the State Department with whom I would have to deal."

Best of all, soon after his arrival Dodd received the latest chapter of his *Old South*, freshly typed by Martha's friend Mildred Fish Harnack and sent via diplomatic pouch.

IN WASHINGTON, DODD CHECKED into the Cosmos Club, which at the time stood on Lafayette Square, just north of the White House. On his first morning in Washington, he walked to the State Department for the first of many meetings and lunches.

At eleven o'clock he met with Secretary Hull and Undersecretary Phillips. All three spent a good deal of time puzzling out how to respond to Hitler's letter. Hitler praised Roosevelt's efforts to restore America's economy and stated that "duty, readiness for sacrifice, and discipline" were virtues that should be dominant in any culture. "These moral demands which the President places before every individual citizen of the United States, are also the quintessence of the German State philosophy which finds its expression in the slogan, 'The Public Weal Transcends the Interests of the Individual.'"

Phillips called it a "strange message." To Dodd, as well as to Hull and Phillips, it was obvious that Hitler hoped to draw a parallel between himself and Roosevelt and that the obligatory U.S. reply would have to be drafted very carefully. That task fell to Phillips and Western European affairs chief Moffat, the goal being, Moffat wrote, "to prevent our falling into the Hitler trap." The resulting letter thanked Hitler for his kind words but noted that his message applied not to Roosevelt personally but rather to the American people as a whole, "who have freely and gladly made heroic efforts in the interest of recovery."

In his diary Phillips wrote, "We sought to sidestep the impression that the President was becoming a Fascist."

The next day, Monday, March 26, Dodd strolled to the White House for lunch with Roosevelt. They discussed a surge of hostility toward Germany that had arisen in New York in the wake of the mock trial earlier in the month. Dodd had heard one New Yorker express the fear that "there might easily be a little civil war" in New York City. "The president also spoke of this," Dodd wrote, "and asked me, if I would do so, to get Chicago Jews to call off their Mock Trial set for mid-April."

Dodd agreed to try. He wrote to Jewish leaders, including Leo Wormser, to ask them "to quiet things if possible" and wrote as well to Colonel House to ask him to exert his influence in the same direction.

As anxious as Dodd was to get to his farm, he did relish the prospect of a conference set for early that week at which he at last would have the opportunity to bring his criticism of the policies and practices of the Foreign Service directly to the boys of the Pretty Good Club.

HE SPOKE BEFORE an audience that included Hull, Moffat, Phillips, Wilbur Carr, and Sumner Welles. Unlike in his Columbus Day speech in Berlin, Dodd was blunt and direct.

The days of "Louis XIV and Victoria style" had passed, he told them. Nations were bankrupt, "including our own." The time had come "to cease grand style performances." He cited an American consular official who had shipped enough furniture to fill a twenty-room house—and yet had only two people in his family. He added that a mere assistant of his "had a chauffeur, a porter, a butler, a valet, two cooks and two maids."

Every official, he said, should be required to live within his salary, be it the $3,000 a year of a junior officer or the $17,500 that he himself received as a full-fledged ambassador, and everyone should be required to know the history and customs of his host country. The only men sent abroad should be those "who think of their country's interests, not so much about a different suit of clothes each day or sitting up at gay but silly dinners and shows every night until 1 o'clock."

Dodd sensed that this last point struck home. He noted in his diary, "Sumner Welles winced a little: the owner of a mansion in Washington which outshines the White House in some respects and is about as large." Welles's mansion, called by some the "house with a hundred rooms," stood on Massachusetts Avenue off Dupont Circle and was renowned for its opulence. Welles and his wife also owned a 255-acre country estate just outside the city, Oxon Hill Manor.

After Dodd concluded his remarks, his audience praised him and applauded. "I was not fooled, however, after two hours of pretended agreement."

Indeed, his lecture only deepened the ill feelings of the Pretty Good Club. By the time of his talk, some of its members, most notably Phillips and Moffat, privately had begun to express real hostility.

Dodd paid a visit to Moffat's office. Later that day Moffat wrote a brief assessment of the ambassador in his diary: "He is . . . by no means a clear thinker. He will express great dissatisfaction with a situation and then reject every proposal to remedy it. He dislikes all his staff but yet does not wish any transferred. He is suspicious by turns of nearly everyone with whom he comes in contact and a little jealous." Moffat called him "an unfortunate misfit."

Dodd seemed unaware that he might be conjuring forces that could endanger his career. Rather he delighted in pricking the clubby sensibilities of his opponents. With clear satisfaction he told his wife, "Their chief protector"—presumably he meant Phillips or Welles— "is not a little disturbed. If he attacks it certainly is not in the open."

CHAPTER 36

Saving Diels

The fear Diels felt grew more pronounced, to the point where in March he again went to Martha for help, this time in hopes of using her to acquire assistance from the U.S. embassy itself. It was a moment freighted with irony: the chief of the Gestapo seeking aid from American officials. Somehow Diels had gotten wind of a plan by Himmler to arrest him, possibly that very day. He had no illusions. Himmler wanted him dead.

Diels knew he had allies at the American embassy, namely Dodd and Consul General Messersmith, and believed they might be able to provide a measure of safety by expressing to Hitler's regime their interest in his continued well-being. But Dodd, he knew, was on leave. Diels asked Martha to speak with Messersmith, who by now had returned from his own leave, to see what he could do.

Despite Martha's inclination to view Diels as overly dramatic, this time she did believe he faced mortal peril. She went to see Messersmith at the consulate.

She was "obviously in a greatly perturbed situation," Messersmith recalled. She broke down in tears and told him that Diels was to be arrested that day "and that it was almost certain that he would be executed."

She composed herself, then pleaded with Messersmith to meet with Göring at once. She tried flattery, calling Messersmith the only man who could intercede "without being in danger of his own life."

Messersmith was unmoved. By now he had grown to dislike Martha. He found her behavior—her various love affairs—repugnant. Given her presumed relationship with Diels, Messersmith was not surprised that she had come to his office in "this hysterical state." He told her he could do nothing "and after a great deal of difficulty was able to get her out of my office."

After she left, however, Messersmith began to reconsider. "I began thinking about the matter and realized that she was correct in saying one thing, and that is that Diels after all was one of the best in the regime, as was Göring and that in case anything happened to Diels and Himmler came in, it would weaken the position of Göring and of the more reasonable element in the party." If Himmler ran the Gestapo, Messersmith believed, he and Dodd would have far more difficulty resolving future attacks against Americans, "for Himmler was known to be even more cold-blooded and ruthless than Dr. Diels."

Messersmith was scheduled to attend a luncheon that afternoon at the Herrenklub, a men's club for conservatives, hosted by two prominent Reichswehr generals, but now, recognizing that a talk with Göring was far more important, Messersmith saw that he might have to cancel. He called Göring's office to arrange the meeting and learned that Göring had just left for a luncheon of his own—at the Herrenklub. Messersmith hadn't known until then that Göring was to be the guest of honor at the generals' lunch.

He realized two things: first, that the task of speaking with Göring had suddenly become much simpler, and second, that the luncheon was a landmark: "It was the first time since the Nazis came to power that the highest ranking officers of the German Army . . . were going to sit down to a table with Göring or any high ranking member of the Nazi regime." It struck him that the lunch might signal that the army and government were closing ranks against Captain Röhm and his Storm Troopers. If so, it was an ominous sign, for Röhm was not likely to jettison his ambitions without a fight.

MESSERSMITH ARRIVED AT THE CLUB shortly after noon and found Göring conversing with the generals. Göring put his arm around Messersmith's shoulders and told the others, "Gentlemen, this is a man who doesn't like me at all, a man who doesn't think very much of me, but he is a good friend of our country."

Messersmith waited for an appropriate moment to take Göring aside. "I told him in very few words that a person in whom I had absolute confidence had called on me that morning and told me that Himmler was bent on getting rid of Diels during the course of the day and that Diels was actually to be bumped off."

Göring thanked him for the information. The two rejoined the other guests, but a few moments later Göring offered his regrets and left.

What happened next—what threats were made, what compromises struck, whether Hitler himself intervened—isn't clear, but by five o'clock that afternoon, April 1, 1934, Messersmith learned that Diels had been named *Regierungspräsident,* or regional commissioner, of Cologne and that the Gestapo would now be headed by Himmler.

Diels was saved, but Göring had suffered a significant defeat. He had acted not for the sake of past friendship but out of anger at the prospect of Himmler trying to arrest Diels in his own realm. Himmler, however, had won the greatest prize, the last and most important component of his secret-police empire. "It was," Messersmith wrote, "the first setback that Göring had had since the beginning of the Nazi regime."

A photograph of the moment when Himmler officially took control of the Gestapo, at a ceremony on April 20, 1934, shows Himmler speaking at the podium, his aspect bland as ever, as Diels stands nearby, facing the camera. His face seems swollen as if from excess drink or lack of sleep, and his scars are exceptionally pronounced. He is the portrait of a man under duress.

In a conversation with a British embassy official that occurred at about this time, quoted in a memorandum later filed with the foreign office in London, Diels delivered a monologue on his own moral unease: "The infliction of physical punishment is not every man's job, and naturally we were only too glad to recruit men who were prepared to show no squeamishness at their task. Unfortunately, we knew nothing about the Freudian side of the business, and it was only after a number of instances of unnecessary flogging and meaningless cruelty that I tumbled to the fact that my organization had been attracting all the sadists in Germany and Austria without my

knowledge for some time past. It had also been attracting unconscious sadists, i.e. men who did not know themselves that they had
sadist leanings until they took part in a flogging. And finally it had
been actually creating sadists. For it seems that corporal chastise-
ment ultimately arouses sadistic leanings in apparently normal men
and women. Freud might explain it."

APRIL BROUGHT STRANGELY LITTLE RAIN but a bumper crop of
fresh secrets. Early in the month, Hitler and Defense Minister Blomberg learned that President Hindenburg had become ill, gravely
so, and was unlikely to survive the summer. They kept the news to
themselves. Hitler coveted the presidential authority still possessed
by Hindenburg and planned upon his death to combine in himself
the roles of chancellor and president and thereby at last acquire absolute power. But two potential barriers remained: the Reichswehr
and Röhm's Storm Troopers.

In mid-April, Hitler flew to the naval port of Kiel and there
boarded a pocket battleship, the *Deutschland*, for a four-day voyage,
accompanied by Blomberg; Admiral Erich Raeder, head of the navy;
and General Werner von Fritsch, chief of the army command. Details are scarce, but apparently in the intimate quarters of the ship
Hitler and Blomberg crafted a secret deal, truly a devil's bargain,
in which Hitler would neutralize Röhm and the SA in return for
the army's support for his acquisition of presidential authority upon
Hindenburg's death.

The deal was of incalculable value to Hitler, for now he could go
forward without having to worry about where the army stood.

Röhm, meanwhile, became increasingly insistent on winning control over the nation's armed forces. In April, during one of his morning rides in the Tiergarten, he watched a group of senior Nazis pass
by, then turned to a companion. "Look at those people over there,"
he said. "The Party isn't a political force anymore; it's turning into
an old-age home. People like that . . . We've got to get rid of them
quickly."

He grew bolder about airing his displeasure. At a press conference on April 18, he said, "Reactionaries, bourgeois conformists, we feel like vomiting when we think of them."

He declared, "The SA is the National Socialist Revolution."

Two days later, however, a government announcement seemed to undercut Röhm's declarations of self-importance: the entire SA had been ordered to go on leave for the month of July.

ON APRIL 22, Heinrich Himmler appointed his young protégé Reinhard Heydrich, newly thirty, to fill Diels's job as chief of the Gestapo. Heydrich was blond, tall, slim, and considered handsome, save for a head described as disproportionately narrow and eyes spaced too closely. He spoke in a near falsetto that was perversely out of step with his reputation for being coolly and utterly ruthless. Hitler dubbed him "the Man with the Iron Heart," and yet Heydrich was said to play the violin with such passion that he would weep as he executed certain passages. Throughout his career he would battle rumors that he was in fact Jewish, despite an investigation by the Nazi Party that purported to find no truth to the allegation.

With Diels gone, the last trace of civility left the Gestapo. Hans Gisevius, the Gestapo memoirist, recognized at once that under Himmler and Heydrich the organization would undergo a change of character. "I could very well venture combat with Diels, the unsteady playboy who, conscious of being a bourgeois renegade, had a good many inhibitions holding him back from foul play," Gisevius wrote. "But as soon as Himmler and Heydrich entered the arena I should have prudently withdrawn."

TOWARD THE END OF APRIL the government at last revealed to the public the grave state of Hindenburg's health. Suddenly the question of who would succeed him became a matter of pressing conversation everywhere. All who were aware of the deepening split between Röhm and Hitler understood that a new element of suspense now propelled the narrative.

CHAPTER 37

Watchers

While all this was occurring, another nation's spies became interested in the Dodds. By April, Martha's relationship with Boris had caught the interest of his superiors in the NKVD. They sensed a rare opportunity. "Tell Boris Winogradov that we want to use him to carry out a project that interests us," one wrote in a message to the agency's Berlin chief.

Somehow—possibly through Boris—Moscow had come to understand that Martha's infatuation with the Nazi revolution was beginning to wane.

The message continued: "It has to do with the fact that, according to our information, the sentiments of his acquaintance (Martha Dodd) have fully ripened for her to be recruited once and for all to work for us."

CHAPTER 38

Humbugged

What most troubled Dodd during his leave was his sense that his opponents in the State Department were growing more aggressive. He became concerned about what he saw as a pattern of disclosures of confidential information that seemed aimed at undermining his standing. A troubling incident occurred on the night of Saturday, April 14, as he was leaving the annual Gridiron Club dinner in Washington. A young State Department officer, whom he did not know, approached him and began a conversation in which he openly challenged Dodd's appraisal of conditions in Germany, citing a confidential dispatch the ambassador had cabled from Berlin. The young man was much taller than Dodd and stood very close in a manner Dodd found physically intimidating. In an angry letter that Dodd planned to hand in person to Secretary Hull, he described the encounter as "an intentional affront."

Most distressing to Dodd, however, was the question of how the young man had gotten access to his dispatch. "It is my opinion," Dodd wrote, ". . . that there is a group somewhere in the Department who think of themselves and not the country and who, upon the slightest effort of any ambassador or minister to economize and improve, begin consorting together to discredit and defeat him. This is the third or fourth time entirely confidential information I have given has been treated as gossip—or made gossip. I am not in the service for any personal or social gain and/or status; I am ready to do anything possible for better work and co-operation; but I do not wish to work alone or become the object of constant intrigue and maneuver. I shall not resign, however, in silence, if this sort of thing continues."

Dodd decided not to give the letter to Hull after all. It ended up filed among papers he identified as "undelivered."

What Dodd apparently did not yet know was that he and fifteen other ambassadors had been the subject of a major article in the April 1934 issue of *Fortune* magazine. Despite the article's prominence and the fact that it must surely have been a topic of rabid conversation within the State Department, Dodd only learned of its existence much later, after his return to Berlin, when Martha brought home a copy she had received during an appointment with her Berlin dentist.

Entitled "Their Excellencies, Our Ambassadors," the article identified the appointees and indicated their personal wealth by placing dollar signs next to their names. Jesse Isidor Straus—ambassador to France and former president of R. H. Macy & Company—was identified as "$$$$ Straus." Dodd had a single "¢" next to his name. The article poked fun at his cheapskate approach to diplomacy and suggested that in renting his Berlin house at a discount from a Jewish banker he was seeking to profit from the plight of Germany's Jews. "So," the article stated, "the Dodds got a nice little house very cheap and managed to run it with only a few servants." The article noted that Dodd had brought his weary old Chevrolet to Berlin. "His son was supposed to run it for him evenings," the writer said. "But the son wanted to go the places and do the things sons have a habit of doing, and that left Mr. Dodd chauffeurless (though top-hatted) in his Chevrolet." Dodd, the article claimed, was left having to cadge rides from junior embassy officers, "the luckier of them in their chauffeured limousines."

The writer called Dodd "a square academic peg in a round diplomatic hole" who was hampered by his relative poverty and lack of diplomatic aplomb. "Morally a very courageous person, he is so intellectual, so divorced from run-of-mine human beings, that he talks in parables, as one gentleman and scholar to another; and the brown-shirted brethren of blood and steel can't understand him even when they care to. So Dodd boils inwardly, and when he tries to get tough, nobody pays much attention."

It was immediately clear to Dodd that one or more officials within the State Department and perhaps even his office in Berlin had revealed fine-grained details of his life in Germany. Dodd complained to Undersecretary Phillips. The article, he wrote, "reveals a strange and even unpatriotic attitude, so far as my record and efforts here are concerned. In my letter of acceptance I said to the president that it must be understood I was to live on my salary income. How and why so much discussion of this simple and obvious fact for me?" He cited diplomats from history who had lived modestly. "Why all this condemnation of my following such examples?" He told Phillips that he suspected people within his own embassy were leaking information and cited other news accounts that had carried distorted reports. "How all these false stories and no reference to real services I have attempted to render?"

Phillips waited nearly a month to respond. "With regard to that article in *Fortune*," he wrote, "I would not give it another thought. I cannot imagine where the information to which you refer came from any more than I can imagine how the Press gets hold of gossip (usually erroneous) in regard to myself and other colleagues of yours." He urged Dodd, "Don't let this particular item disturb you in the least."

DODD DID GET to spend a little time in the Library of Congress doing research for his *Old South* and managed to carve out two weeks on his farm, where he wrote and tended farm matters, and he was able to travel to Chicago as planned, but this did not yield the pleasant reencounter he had anticipated. "Once there," he wrote to Martha, "everybody wanted to see me: telephones, letters, visits, luncheons, dinners all the time." He fielded many inquiries about her and her brother, he wrote, "but only one about your problem in New York," meaning her divorce. A friend wanted to show him examples of "how decently Chicago papers treated it," but, he wrote, "I did not care to read clippings." He gave speeches and resolved faculty squabbles. In his diary he noted that he also met with two Jewish leaders whom he had contacted previously in fulfilling Roosevelt's directive to damp Jewish protest. The two men described "how they and their friends had calmed their fellows and prevented any violent demonstrations in Chicago as planned."

A personal crisis intruded. While in Chicago Dodd received a telegram relaying a message from his wife. After enduring the inevitable spasm of anxiety that telegrams from loved ones sparked, Dodd read that his old Chevy, icon of his ambassadorship, had been totaled by his chauffeur. The kicker: "THEREFORE HOPE YOU CAN BRING NEW CAR."

So now Dodd, while on his supposedly restorative leave, was being asked in the matter-of-fact language of telegraphy to buy a new car and arrange for its shipping to Berlin.

He wrote to Martha later, "I fear Mueller was driving carelessly, as I noted several times before I came away." Dodd could not understand it. He himself had driven between his farm and Washington, D.C., many times and had driven all over the city without ever having an accident. "While this may prove nothing, it suggests something. People who do not own the car are far less careful than those who do." In light of what was to happen a few years hence, Dodd's crowing about his own driving prowess can only raise a chill. He wanted a Buick but deemed the price—$1,350—too much to spend given the limited time his family expected to stay in Berlin. He also worried about the $100 he would have to pay to ship the car to Germany.

Ultimately he got his Buick. He instructed his wife to buy it from a dealer in Berlin. The car, he wrote, was a basic model that his embassy protocol experts disparaged as "ridiculously simple for an Ambassador."

DODD WAS ABLE to make one more visit to his farm, which cheered him but also made his final departure all the more painful. "This was a beautiful day," he wrote in his diary on Sunday, May 6, 1934. "The budding trees and the apple blooms were most appealing, especially since I must leave."

Three days later, Dodd's ship sailed from New York. He felt he had achieved a victory in getting Jewish leaders to agree to ease the intensity of their protests against Germany and hoped his efforts would bring further moderation on the part of Hitler's government. These hopes were chilled, however, when on Saturday, May 12, while in midocean, he got word via wireless of a speech just delivered by Goebbels in which the propaganda minister called Jews "the syphilis of all European peoples."

Dodd felt betrayed. Despite Nazi promises about arrest warrants and closure of the Columbia House prison, clearly nothing had changed. He feared that now he appeared naive. He wrote to Roosevelt of his dismay, after all the work he had done with American Jewish leaders. Goebbels's speech had rekindled "all the animosities of the preceding winter," he wrote, "and I was put in the position of having been humbugged, as indeed I was."

He reached Berlin on Thursday, May 17, at 10:30 p.m. and found a changed city. During his two months away, drought had browned the landscape to a degree he had never seen before, but there was something else. "I was delighted to be home," he wrote, "but the tense atmosphere was revealed at once."

PART VI
Berlin at Dusk

Göring's bedroom at Carinhall

CHAPTER 39

Dangerous Dining

The city seemed to vibrate with a background thrum of danger, as if an immense power line had been laid through its center. Everyone in Dodd's circle felt it. Partly this tension arose from the unusual May weather and the concomitant fears of a failed harvest, but the main engine of anxiety was the intensifying discord between Captain Röhm's Storm Troopers and the regular army. A popular metaphor used at the time to describe the atmosphere in Berlin was that of an approaching thunderstorm—that sense of charged and suspended air.

Dodd had little chance to settle back into the rhythms of work.

The day after his return from America, he faced the prospect of hosting a giant good-bye banquet for Messersmith, who had at last managed to secure for himself a loftier post, though not in Prague, his original target. Competition for that job had been robust, and although Messersmith had lobbied hard and persuaded allies of all stripes to write letters to bolster his bid, in the end the job went to someone else. Instead, Undersecretary Phillips had offered Messersmith another vacant post: Uruguay. If Messersmith had been disappointed, he had not shown it. He had counted himself lucky simply to be leaving the consular service behind. But then his luck had gotten better still. The post of ambassador to Austria suddenly had become vacant, and Messersmith was the obvious choice for the job. Roosevelt agreed. Now Messersmith truly was delighted. So too was Dodd, just to have him gone, though he'd have preferred to have him at the other side of the world.

There were many parties for Messersmith—for a time every dinner and luncheon in Berlin seemed to be in his honor—but the U.S. embassy's banquet on May 18 was the biggest and most official. While Dodd was in America, Mrs. Dodd, with the assistance of embassy protocol experts, had overseen the creation of a four-page, single-spaced list of guests that seemed to include everyone of import, except Hitler. To anyone knowledgeable about Berlin society, the real fascination was not who attended, but who did not. Göring and Goebbels sent their regrets, as did Vice-Chancellor Papen and Rudolf Diels. Defense Minister Blomberg came, but not SA chief Röhm.

Bella Fromm attended, and so did Sigrid Schultz and various of Martha's friends, including Putzi Hanfstaengl, Armand Berard, and Prince Louis Ferdinand. This mixture by itself added to the aura of tension in the room, for Berard still loved Martha and Prince Louis mooned for her, though her adoration remained utterly fixed on Boris (absent, interestingly, from the invitation list). Martha's handsome young Hitler liaison, Hans "Tommy" Thomsen, came, as did his ofttimes companion, the dark and lushly beautiful Elmina Rangabe, but there was a hitch this night—Tommy brought his wife. There was heat, champagne, passion, jealousy, and that background sense of something unpleasant building just over the horizon.

Bella Fromm chatted briefly with Hanfstaengl and recorded the encounter in her diary.

"I wonder why we were asked today," Hanfstaengl said. "All this excitement about Jews. Messersmith is one. So is Roosevelt. The party detests them."

"Dr. Hanfstaengl," Fromm said, "we've discussed this before. You don't have to put on that kind of an act with me."

"All right. Even if they are Aryan, you'd never know it from their actions."

At the moment Fromm was not feeling particularly solicitous of Nazi goodwill. Two weeks earlier her daughter, Gonny, had left for America, with Messersmith's help, leaving Fromm saddened but relieved. A week before that, the newspaper *Vossische Zeitung*—"Auntie Voss," where she had worked for years—had closed. She felt more and more that an epoch in which she once had thrived was coming to an end.

She said to Hanfstaengl, "Of course if you're going to do away with right and wrong, and make it Aryan and non-Aryan, it leaves people who happen to have rather old-fashioned notions about what is right and wrong, what is decent and what is obscene, without much ground to stand on."

She turned the conversation back to the subject of Messersmith, whom she described as being so revered by his colleagues "that he is practically regarded as having ambassadorial rank," a remark that would have irritated Dodd no end.

Hanfstaengl softened his voice. "All right, all right," he said. "I have lots of friends in the United States, and all of them side with the Jews, too. But since it is insisted on in the party program—" He stopped there in a kind of verbal shrug. He reached into his pocket, and pulled out a small bag of candy fruit drops. *Lutschbonbons*. Bella had loved them as a child.

"Have one," Hanfstaengl said. "They are made especially for the *Führer*."

She chose one. Just before she popped it into her mouth she saw that it was embossed with a swastika. Even fruit drops had been "coordinated."

The conversation turned to the political warfare that was causing so much unease. Hanfstaengl told her that Röhm coveted control not only of the German army but also of Göring's air force. "Hermann is in a rage!" Hanfstaengl said. "You can do anything to him except fool around with his Luftwaffe, and he could murder Röhm in cold blood." He asked: "Do you know Himmler?"

Fromm nodded.

Hanfstaengl said, "He was a chicken farmer, when he wasn't on duty spying for the Reichswehr. He kicked Diels out of the Gestapo. Himmler can't stand anybody, but Röhm least of all. Now they're all ganged up against Röhm: Rosenberg, Goebbels, and the chicken farmer." The Rosenberg he mentioned was Alfred Rosenberg, an ardent anti-Semite and head of the Nazi Party's foreign bureau.

After recounting the conversation in her diary, Fromm added,

"There is nobody among the officials of the National Socialist party who would not cheerfully cut the throat of every other official in order to further his own advancement."

IT WAS A MEASURE of the strange new climate of Berlin that another dinner party, wholly innocuous, should prove to have profoundly lethal consequences. The host was a wealthy banker named Wilhelm Regendanz, a friend of the Dodds, though happily the Dodds were not invited on this particular occasion. Regendanz held the dinner one evening in May at his luxurious villa in Dahlem, in the southwestern portion of greater Berlin known for its lovely homes and its proximity to the Grunewald.

Regendanz, father of seven, was a member of the Stahlhelm, or Steel Helmets, an organization of former army officers with a conservative bent. He liked bringing together men of diverse position for meals, discussions, and lectures. To this particular dinner Regendanz invited two prominent guests, French ambassador François-Poncet and Captain Röhm, both of whom had been to the house on past occasions.

Röhm arrived accompanied by three young SA officers, among them a curly-headed blond male adjutant nicknamed "Count Pretty," who was Röhm's secretary and, rumor held, his occasional lover. Hitler would later describe this meeting as a "secret dinner," though in fact the guests made no attempt to disguise their presence. They parked their cars in front of the house in full view of the street, with their tell-all license plates fully exposed.

The guests were an odd match. François-Poncet disliked the SA chief, as he made clear in his memoir, *The Fateful Years*. "Having always entertained the liveliest repugnance toward Röhm," he wrote, "I avoided him as much as possible despite the eminent role he played in the Third Reich." But Regendanz had "begged" François-Poncet to come.

Later, in a letter to the Gestapo, Regendanz tried to explain his insistence on getting the two men together. He laid the impetus for the dinner on François-Poncet, who, he claimed, had expressed frustration at not being able to meet with Hitler himself and had asked

Regendanz to speak with someone close to Hitler to communicate his desire for a meeting. Regendanz suggested that Röhm might prove a worthy intermediary. At the time of the dinner, Regendanz claimed, he was unaware of the rift between Röhm and Hitler—"on the contrary," he told the Gestapo, "it was assumed that Röhm was the man who absolutely had the confidence of the *Führer* and was his follower. In other words one believed that one was informing the *Führer* when one informed Röhm."

For dinner, the men were joined by Mrs. Regendanz and a son, Alex, who was preparing to become an international lawyer. After the meal, Röhm and the French ambassador retired to Regendanz's library for an informal conversation. Röhm talked of military matters and disclaimed any interest in politics, declaring that he saw himself only as a soldier, an officer. "The result of this conversation," Regendanz told the Gestapo, "was literally nothing."

The evening came to an end—mercifully, in François-Poncet's opinion. "The meal was dismal, the conversation insignificant," he recalled. "I found Röhm sleepy and heavy; he woke up only to complain of his health and the rheumatism he expected to nurse at Wiessee," a reference to Bad Wiessee, where Röhm planned a lakeside sojourn to take a cure. "Returning home," François-Poncet wrote, "I cursed our host for the evening's boredom."

How the Gestapo learned of the dinner and its guests isn't known, but by this point Röhm most certainly was under close surveillance. The license plates of the cars parked at Regendanz's house would have tipped any watcher off to the identities of the men within.

The dinner became infamous. Later, in midsummer, Britain's Ambassador Phipps would observe in his diary that of the seven people who sat down to dine at the Regendanz mansion that night, four had been murdered, one had fled the country under threat of death, and another had been imprisoned in a concentration camp.

Phipps wrote, "The list of casualties for one dinner party might make even a Borgia envious."

AND THERE WAS THIS:

On Thursday, May 24, Dodd walked to a luncheon with a senior official of the foreign ministry, Hans-Heinrich Dieckhoff, whom Dodd described as being "what amounts to Assistant Secretary of State." They met at a small, discreet restaurant on Unter den Linden, the wide boulevard that ran due east from the Brandenburg Gate, and there they engaged in a conversation that Dodd found extraordinary.

Dodd's main reason for wanting to see Dieckhoff was to express his dismay at having been made to seem naive by Goebbels's Jews-as-syphilis speech after all he had done to quiet Jewish protests in America. He reminded Dieckhoff of the Reich's announced intent to close the Columbia House prison and to require warrants for all arrests and of other assurances that Germany "was easing up on the Jewish atrocities."

Dieckhoff was sympathetic. He confessed to his own dim view of Goebbels and told Dodd he expected that soon Hitler would be overthrown. Dodd wrote in his diary that Dieckhoff "gave what he considered good evidence that the Germans would not much longer endure the system under which they were drilled everlastingly and semi-starved."

Such candor amazed Dodd. Dieckhoff spoke as freely as if he were in England or the United States, Dodd noted, even to the point of expressing the hope that Jewish protests in America would continue. Without them, Dieckhoff said, the chances of overthrowing Hitler would diminish.

Dodd knew that even for a man of Dieckhoff's rank such talk was dangerous. He wrote, "I felt the deep concern of a high official who could thus risk his life in criticism of the existing regime."

After exiting the restaurant, the two men walked west along Unter den Linden toward Wilhelmstrasse, the main government thoroughfare. They parted, Dodd wrote, "rather sadly."

Dodd returned to his office, worked a couple of hours, then took a long walk around the Tiergarten.

CHAPTER 40

A Writer's Retreat

The increasing evidence of social and political oppression came more and more to trouble Martha, in spite of her enthusiasm for the bright, blond young men whom Hitler attracted by the thousands. One of the most important moments in her education came in May when a friend, Heinrich Maria Ledig-Rowohlt, a regular in the salon of Mildred and Arvid Harnack, invited her and Mildred to accompany him for a visit to one of the few prominent authors who had not joined the great flight of artistic talent from Nazi Germany—an exodus that included Fritz Lang, Marlene Dietrich, Walter Gropius, Thomas and Heinrich Mann, Bertolt Brecht, Albert Einstein, and composer Otto Klemperer, whose son, actor Werner Klemperer, would go on to portray a kindly, befuddled Nazi prison-camp commandant in the TV series *Hogan's Heroes*. Ledig-Rowohlt was the illegitimate son of publisher Ernst Rowohlt and worked as an editor in his father's company. The author in question was Rudolf Ditzen, known universally by his pseudonym, Hans Fallada.

The visit was supposed to take place earlier in the year, but Fallada had postponed it until May because of his anxiety over the publication of his latest book, *Once a Jailbird*. By this point Fallada had achieved considerable fame worldwide for his novel *Little Man—What Now?*, about one couple's struggle during the economic and social upheaval of the Weimar Republic. What made *Once a Jailbird* a subject of such anxiety for Fallada was the fact that it was his first major work to be published since Hitler had become chancellor. He was uncertain of his standing in the eyes of Goebbels's Reich Literary

Chamber, which claimed the right to decide what constituted acceptable literature. To try to smooth the way for his new book, Fallada included in its introduction a statement that praised the Nazis for ensuring that the awful situation at the center of the book could no longer occur. Even his publisher, Rowohlt, thought Fallada had gone too far and told him the introduction "does seem rather TOO ingratiating." Fallada kept it.

In the months following Hitler's ascension to chancellor, the German writers who were not outright Nazis had quickly divided into two camps—those who believed it was immoral to remain in Germany and those who felt the best strategy was to stay put, recede as much as possible from the world, and wait for the collapse of the Hitler regime. The latter approach became known as "inner emigration," and was the path Fallada had chosen.

Martha asked Boris to come along as well. He agreed, despite his previously stated view that Mildred was someone Martha should avoid.

THEY SET OUT on the morning of Sunday, May 27, for the three-hour drive to Fallada's farmhouse in Carwitz, in the lake country of Mecklenburg north of Berlin. Boris drove his Ford and of course left the top down. The morning was cool and soft, the roads mostly free of traffic. Once outside the city, Boris accelerated. The Ford sped along country roads lined with chestnut and acacia, the air fragrant with spring.

Halfway through the drive, the landscape darkened. "Little sharp lines of lightning lit up the sky," Martha recalled, "and the scene was wild and violent with color, intense electric green and violet, lavender and gray." A sudden rain sent pellets of water exploding against the windscreen, but even here, to the delight of all, Boris kept the top down. The car raced along on a cloud of spray.

Abruptly the sky cleared, leaving sun-shafted steam and sudden color, as if they were driving through a painting. The scent of newly moist ground filled the air.

As they neared Carwitz, they entered a terrain of hills, meadows, and bright blue lakes, laced together with sandy paths. The houses and barns were simple boxes with steeply pitched roofs. They were only three hours from Berlin, yet the place seemed remote and hidden.

Boris brought the Ford to a stop at an old farmhouse beside a lake. The house stood at the base of a tongue of land called the Bohnenwerder that jutted into the lake and was mounded with hills.

Fallada emerged from the house trailed by a young boy of about four and Fallada's blond and buxom wife, who held their second child, a baby. A dog bounded out as well. Fallada was a boxy man with a square head, wide mouth, and cheekbones so round and hard they might have been golf balls implanted under his skin. His glasses had dark frames and circular lenses. He and his wife gave the new arrivals a brief tour of the farm, which they had bought using the proceeds from *Little Man*. Martha was struck by the apparent contentment of both.

It was Mildred who brought to the fore the questions that had been in the air since the group's arrival, though she was careful to shade them with nuance. As she and Fallada strolled to the lake, according to a detailed account by one of Fallada's biographers, she talked about her life in America and how she used to enjoy walking along the shore of Lake Michigan.

Fallada said, "It must be difficult for you to live in a foreign country, especially when your interest is literature and language."

True, she told him, "but it can also be difficult to live in one's own country when one's concern is literature."

Fallada lit a cigarette.

Speaking now very slowly, Fallada said, "I could never write in another language, nor live in any other place than Germany."

Mildred countered: "Perhaps, Herr Ditzen, it is less important where one lives than how one lives."

Fallada said nothing.

After a moment, Mildred asked, "Can one write what one wishes here these days?"

"That depends on one's point of view," he said. There were difficulties and demands, words to be avoided, but in the end language endured, he said. "Yes, I believe one can still write here in these times if one observes the necessary regulations and gives in a little. Not in the important things, of course."

Mildred asked: "What is important and what unimportant?"

THERE WAS LUNCH AND COFFEE. Martha and Mildred walked to the top of the Bohnenwerder to admire the view. A soft haze muted edges and colors and created an overall sense of peace. Down below, however, Fallada's mood had turned stormy. He and Ledig-Rowohlt played chess. The subject of Fallada's introduction to *Jailbird* came up, and Ledig-Rowohlt questioned its necessity. He told Fallada it had been a topic of conversation during the drive to Carwitz. Upon hearing this, Fallada grew angry. He resented being the subject of gossip and disputed whether anyone had a right to judge him, least of all a couple of American women.

When Martha and Mildred returned, the conversation continued, and Mildred joined in. Martha listened as best she could, but her German was not yet expert enough to allow her to pick up enough detail to make sense of it. She could tell, however, that Mildred was "gently probing" Fallada's retreat from the world. His unhappiness at being thus challenged was obvious.

Later, Fallada walked them through his house—it had seven rooms, electric light, a spacious attic, and various warming stoves. He showed them his library, with its many foreign editions of his own books, and then led them to the room in which his infant son now was napping. Martha wrote: "He revealed uneasiness and self-consciousness, though he tried to be proud and happy in the infant, in his self-tilled garden, in his simple buxom wife, in the many translations and editions of his books lining the shelves. But he was an unhappy man."

Fallada took photographs of the group; Boris did likewise. During the journey back to Berlin, the four companions again talked about Fallada. Mildred described him as cowardly and weak but then added, "He has a conscience and that is good. He is not happy, he is not a Nazi, he is not hopeless."

Martha recorded another impression: "I saw the stamp of naked fear on a writer's face for the first time."

FALLADA BECAME, ULTIMATELY, a controversial figure in German lit-erature, reviled in some quarters for his failure to stand up to the Nazis but defended in others for not choosing the safer path of exile. In the years that followed Martha's visit, Fallada found himself increasingly compelled to bend his writing to the demands of the Nazi state. He turned to preparing translations for Rowohlt, among them Clarence Day's *Life with Father*, then very popular in the United States, and to writing innocuous works that he hoped would not offend Nazi sensi-bilities, among them a collection of children's stories about a child's pull toy, *Hoppelpoppel, Wo bist du?* (Hoppelpoppel, Where Are You?).

He found his career briefly invigorated with publication in 1937 of a novel entitled *Wolf Among Wolves*, which party officials interpreted as a worthy attack on the old Weimar world and which Goebbels himself described as "a super book." Even so, Fallada made more and more concessions, eventually allowing Goebbels to script the ending of his next novel, *Iron Gustav*, which depicted the hardships of life during the past world war. Fallada saw this as a prudent concession. "I do not like grand gestures," he wrote; "being slaughtered before the tyrant's throne, senselessly, to the benefit of no one and to the detriment of my children, that is not my way."

He recognized, however, that his various capitulations took a toll on his writing. He wrote to his mother that he was not satisfied with his work. "I cannot act as I want to—if I want to stay alive. And so a fool gives less than he has."

Other writers, in exile, watched with disdain as Fallada and his fel-low inner emigrants surrendered to government tastes and demands. Thomas Mann, who lived abroad throughout the Hitler years, later wrote their epitaph: "It may be superstitious belief, but in my eyes, any books which could be printed at all in Germany between 1933 and 1945 are worse than worthless and not objects one wishes to touch. A stench of blood and shame attaches to them. They should all be pulped."

✢ ✢ ✢

THE FEAR AND OPPRESSION that Martha saw in Fallada crowned a rising mountain of evidence that throughout the spring had begun to erode her infatuation with the new Germany. Her blind endorsement of Hitler's regime first faded to a kind of sympathetic skepticism, but as summer approached, she felt a deepening revulsion.

Where once she had been able to wave away the beating incident in Nuremberg as an isolated episode, now she recognized that German persecution of Jews was a national pastime. She found herself repulsed by the constant thunder of Nazi propaganda that portrayed Jews as enemies of the state. Now when she listened to the anti-Nazi talk of Mildred and Arvid Harnack and their friends, she no longer felt quite so inclined to defend the "strange beings" of the fledgling revolution whom she once had found so entrancing. "By the spring of 1934," she wrote, "what I had heard, seen, and felt, revealed to me that conditions of living were worse than in pre-Hitler days, that the most complicated and heartbreaking system of terror ruled the country and repressed the freedom and happiness of the people, and that German leaders were inevitably leading these docile and kindly masses into another war against their will and their knowledge."

She was not yet willing, however, to openly declare her new attitude to the world. "I still attempted to keep my hostility guarded and unexpressed."

Instead, she revealed it obliquely by proclaiming in deliberately contrarian fashion a new and energetic interest in the Hitler regime's greatest enemy, the Soviet Union. She wrote, "A curiosity began to grow in me as to the nature of this government, so loathed in Germany, and its people, described as so utterly ruthless."

Against her parents' wishes, but with Boris's encouragement, she began planning a journey to the Soviet Union.

BY JUNE, DODD HAD COME to see that the "Jewish problem," as he continued to call it, was anything but improved. Now, he told Secretary Hull in a letter, "the prospect of a cessation appears far less hopeful." Like Messersmith, he saw that persecution was pervasive, even if it had changed character to become "more subtle and less advertised."

In May, he reported, the Nazi Party had launched a campaign against "grumblers and faultfinders" that was meant to reenergize *Gleichschaltung*. Inevitably it also increased pressure on Jews. Goebbels's newspaper *Der Angriff* began urging readers "to keep a sharp eye on the Jews and report any of their shortcomings," Dodd wrote. The Jewish owners of the *Frankfurter Zeitung* had been forced to abandon their controlling interest, as had the last Jewish owners of the famed Ullstein publishing empire. A large rubber company was told it must provide proof that it had no Jewish employees before it could submit bids to municipalities. The German Red Cross was suddenly required to certify that new contributors were of Aryan origin. And two judges in two different cities granted permission to two men to divorce their wives for the sole reason that the women were Jewish, reasoning that such marriages would yield mixed offspring that would only weaken the German race.

Dodd wrote: "These instances and others of lesser importance reveal a different method in the treatment of the Jews—a method perhaps less calculated to bring repercussions from abroad, but reflecting nonetheless the Nazis' determination to force the Jews out of the country."

Germany's Aryan population also experienced a new tightening of control. In another dispatch written the same day, Dodd described how the Ministry of Education had announced that the school week would be divided in such a way that Saturdays and Wednesday evenings would be devoted to the demands of the Hitler Youth.

Henceforth Saturday was to be called the Staatsjugendtag, the State's Day for Youth.

THE WEATHER REMAINED WARM, with scant rain. On Saturday, June 2, 1934, with temperatures in the eighties, Ambassador Dodd wrote in his diary: "Germany looks dry for the first time; trees and fields are yellow. The papers are full of accounts of the drought in Bavaria and in the United States as well."

In Washington, Moffat also took note of the weather. In his diary he called it "the great heat" and cited Sunday, May 20, as the day it had begun, with a high of ninety-three degrees. In his office.

No one knew it yet, of course, but America had entered the second of a series of cataclysmic droughts that soon would transform the Great Plains into the Dust Bowl.

CHAPTER 41

Trouble at the Neighbor's

As summer neared, the sense of unease in Berlin became acute. The mood was "tense and electric," Martha wrote. "Everyone felt there was something in the air but did not know what it was."

The strange atmosphere and the fragile condition of Germany were topics of conversation at a late-afternoon *Tee-Empfang*—a tea party—hosted by Putzi Hanfstaengl on Friday, June 8, 1934, which the Dodd family attended.

On their way home from the tea, the Dodds could not help but notice that something unusual was happening in Bendlerstrasse, the last side street they passed before reaching their house. There, in easy view, stood the buildings of the Bendler Block, army headquarters. Indeed, the Dodds and the army were almost back-fence neighbors—a man with a strong arm could throw a stone from the family's yard and expect to break one of the army's windows.

The change was obvious. Soldiers stood on the roofs of headquarters buildings. Heavily armed patrols moved along the sidewalks. Army trucks and Gestapo cars clogged the street.

These forces remained throughout Friday night and Saturday. Then, Sunday morning, June 10, the troops and trucks were gone.

At the Dodds' house a coolness spread outward from the forested ground of the Tiergarten. There were riders in the park, as always, and the thud of hooves was audible in the Sunday-morning quiet.

CHAPTER 42

Hermann's Toys

Amid the many rumors of coming upheaval, it remained difficult for Dodd and his peers in the diplomatic corps to imagine that Hitler, Göring, and Goebbels could endure much longer. Dodd still saw them as inept and dangerous adolescents—"16 year olds," as he now put it—who found themselves confronting an accumulation of daunting troubles. The drought grew steadily more severe. The economy showed little sign of improvement, other than the illusory decline in unemployment. The rift between Röhm and Hitler seemed to have deepened. And there continued to be moments—strange, ludicrous moments—that suggested that Germany was merely the stage set for some grotesque comedy, not a serious country in a serious time.

Sunday, June 10, 1934, provided one such episode, when Dodd, French ambassador François-Poncet, and Britain's Sir Eric Phipps, along with three dozen other guests, attended a kind of open house at Göring's vast estate an hour's drive north of Berlin. He had named it Carinhall for his dead Swedish wife, Carin, whom he revered; later in the month he planned to exhume her body from its resting place in Sweden, transport it to Germany, and entomb it in a mausoleum on the estate grounds. Today, however, Göring wanted merely to show off his forests and his new bison enclosure, where he hoped to breed the creatures and then turn them loose on his grounds.

The Dodds arrived late in their new Buick, which had betrayed them along the way with a minor mechanical failure, but they still managed to arrive before Göring himself. Their instructions called for them to drive to a particular point on the estate. To keep guests from getting lost, Göring had stationed men at each crossroads to provide directions. Dodd and his wife found the other guests gathered around a speaker who held forth on some aspect of the grounds. The Dodds learned they were at the edge of the bison enclosure.

At last Göring arrived, driving fast, alone, in what Phipps described as a racing car. He climbed out wearing a uniform that was partly the costume of an aviator, partly that of a medieval hunter. He wore boots of India rubber and in his belt had tucked a very large hunting knife.

Göring took the place of the first speaker. He used a microphone but spoke loudly into it, producing a jarring effect in the otherwise sylvan locale. He described his plan to create a forest preserve that would reproduce the conditions of primeval Germany, complete with primeval animals like the bison that now stood indolently in the near distance. Three photographers and a "cinematograph" operator captured the affair on film.

Elisabetta Cerruti, the beautiful Hungarian and Jewish wife of the Italian ambassador, recalled what happened next.

"Ladies and gentlemen," Göring said, "in a few minutes you will witness a unique display of nature at work." He gestured toward an iron cage. "In this cage is a powerful male bison, an animal almost unheard of on the Continent. . . . He will meet here, before your very eyes, the female of his species. Please be quiet and don't be afraid."

Göring's keepers opened the cage.

"Ivan the Terrible," Göring commanded, "I order you to leave the cage."

The bull did not move.

Göring repeated his command. Once again the bull ignored him.

The keepers now attempted to prod Ivan into action. The photographers readied themselves for the lustful charge certain to ensue.

Britain's Ambassador Phipps wrote in his diary that the bull emerged from the cage "with the utmost reluctance, and, after eyeing the cows somewhat sadly, tried to return to it." Phipps also described the affair in a later memorandum to London that became famous within the British foreign office as "the bison dispatch."

Next, Dodd and Mattie and the other guests climbed aboard thirty small, two-passenger carriages driven by peasants and set off on a long, meandering ride through forests and across meadows. Göring was in the lead in a carriage pulled by two great horses, with Mrs. Cerruti seated to his right. An hour later, the procession halted near a swamp. Göring climbed from his carriage and gave another speech, this on the glories of birds.

Once again the guests climbed into their carriages and, after another lengthy ride, came to a glade where their cars stood waiting. Göring levered his massive self into his car and raced off at high speed. The other guests followed at a slower pace and after twenty minutes came to a lake beside which stood an immense, newly constructed lodge that seemed meant to evoke the home of a medieval lord. Göring was waiting for them, dressed in a wholly new outfit, "a wonderful new white summer garb," Dodd wrote—white tennis shoes, white duck trousers, white shirt, and a hunting jacket of green leather, in whose belt the same hunting knife appeared. In one hand he held a long implement that seemed a cross between a shepherd's staff and a harpoon.

It was now about six o'clock, and the afternoon sun had turned the landscape a pleasing amber. Staff in hand, Göring led his guests into the house. A collection of swords hung just inside the main door. He showed off his "gold" and "silver" rooms, his card room, library, gym, and movie theater. One hallway was barbed with dozens of sets of antlers. In the main sitting room they found a live tree, a bronze image of Hitler, and an as-yet-unoccupied space in which Göring planned to install a statue of Wotan, the Teutonic god of war. Göring "displayed his vanity at every turn," Dodd observed. He noted that a number of guests traded amused but discreet glances.

Then Göring drew the party outside, where all were directed to sit at tables set in the open air for a meal orchestrated by the actress Emmy Sonnemann, whom Göring identified as his "private secretary," though it was common knowledge that she and Göring were romantically involved. (Mrs. Dodd liked Sonnemann and in coming months would become, as Martha noted, "rather attached to her.") Ambassador Dodd found himself seated at a table with

Vice-Chancellor Papen, Phipps, and François-Poncet, among others. He was disappointed in the result. "The conversation had no value," he wrote—though he found himself briefly engaged when the discussion turned to a new book about the German navy in World War I, during which far-too-enthusiastic talk of war led Dodd to say, "If people knew the truth of history there would never be another great war."

Phipps and François-Poncet laughed uncomfortably.

Then came silence.

A few moments later, talk resumed: "we turned," Dodd wrote, "to other and less risky subjects."

Dodd and Phipps assumed—*hoped*—that once the meal was over they would be able to excuse themselves and begin their journey back to Berlin, where both had an evening function to attend, but Göring now informed all that the climax of the outing—"this strange comedy," Phipps called it—was yet to come.

Göring led his guests to another portion of the lake shore some five hundred yards away, where he stopped before a tomb erected at the water's edge. Here Dodd found what he termed "the most elaborate structure of its kind I ever saw." The mausoleum was centered between two great oak trees and six large sarsen stones reminiscent of those at Stonehenge. Göring walked to one of the oaks and planted himself before it, legs apart, like some gargantuan wood sprite. The hunting knife was still in his belt, and again he wielded his medieval staff. He held forth on the virtues of his dead wife, the idyllic setting of her tomb, and his plans for her exhumation and reinterment, which was to occur ten days hence, on the summer solstice, a day that the pagan ideology of the National Socialists had freighted with symbolic importance. Hitler was to attend, as were legions of men from the army, SS, and SA.

At last, "weary of the curious display," Dodd and Phipps in tandem moved to say their good-byes to Göring. Mrs. Cerruti, clearly awaiting her own chance to bolt, acted with more speed. "Lady Cerruti saw our move," Dodd wrote, "and she arose quickly so as not to allow anybody to trespass upon her fight to lead on every possible occasion."

The next day Phipps wrote about Göring's open house in his diary. "The whole proceedings were so strange as at times to convey a feeling of unreality," he wrote, but the episode had provided him a valuable if unsettling insight into the nature of Nazi rule. "The chief impression was that of the most pathetic naïveté of General Göring, who showed us his toys like a big, fat, spoilt child: his primeval woods, his bison and birds, his shooting-box and lake and bathing beach, his blond 'private secretary,' his wife's mausoleum and swans and sarsen stones. . . . And then I remembered there were other toys, less innocent though winged, and these might some day be launched on their murderous mission in the same childlike spirit and with the same childlike glee."

CHAPTER 43

A Pygmy Speaks

Wherever Martha and her father now went they heard rumors and speculation that the collapse of Hitler's regime might be imminent. With each hot June day the rumors gained detail. In bars and cafés, patrons engaged in the decidedly dangerous pastime of composing and comparing lists of who would comprise the new government. The names of two former chancellors came up often: General Kurt von Schleicher and Heinrich Brüning. One rumor held that Hitler would remain chancellor but be kept under control by a new, stronger cabinet, with Schleicher as vice-chancellor, Brüning as foreign minister, and Captain Röhm as defense minister. On June 16, 1934, a month shy of the one-year anniversary of his arrival in Berlin, Dodd wrote to Secretary of State Hull, "Everywhere I go men talk of resistance, of possible putsches in big cities."

And then something occurred that until that spring would have seemed impossible given the potent barriers to dissent established under Hitler's rule.

On Sunday, June 17, Vice-Chancellor Papen was scheduled to deliver a speech in Marburg at the city's namesake university, a brief rail journey southwest of Berlin. He did not see the text until he was aboard his train, this owing to a quiet conspiracy between his speechwriter, Edgar Jung, and his secretary, Fritz Gunther von Tschirschky und Boegendorff. Jung was a leading conservative who had become so deeply opposed to the Nazi Party that he briefly considered assassinating Hitler. Until now he had kept his anti-Nazi views out of Papen's speeches, but he sensed that the growing conflict within the government offered a unique opportunity. If Papen himself spoke out against the regime, Jung reasoned, his remarks might at last prompt President Hindenburg and the army to eject the Nazis from power and quash the Storm Troopers, in the interest of restoring order to the nation. Jung had gone over the speech carefully with Tschirschky, but both men had deliberately kept it from Papen until the last moment so that he would have no choice but to deliver it. "The speech took months of preparation," Tschirschky later said. "It was necessary to find the proper occasion for its delivery, and then everything had to be prepared with the greatest possible care."

Now, in the train, as Papen read the text for the first time, Tschirschky saw a look of fear cross his face. It is a measure of the altered mood in Germany—the widespread perception that dramatic change might be imminent—that Papen, an unheroic personality, felt he could go ahead and deliver it and still survive. Not that he had much choice. "We more or less forced him to make that speech," Tschirschky said. Copies already had been distributed to foreign correspondents. Even if Papen balked at the last minute, the speech would continue to circulate. Clearly hints of its content already had leaked out, for when Papen arrived at the hall the place hummed with anticipation. His anxiety surely spiked when he saw that a number of seats were occupied by men wearing brown shirts and swastika armbands.

Papen walked to the podium.

"I am told," he began, "that my share in events in Prussia, and in the formation of the present Government"—an allusion to his role in engineering Hitler's appointment as chancellor—"has had such an important effect on developments in Germany that I am under an obligation to view them more critically than most people."

The remarks that followed would have earned any man of lesser stature a trip to the gallows. "The Government," Papen said, "is well aware of the selfishness, the lack of principle, the insincerity, the unchivalrous behavior, the arrogance which is on the increase under the guise of the German revolution." If the government hoped to establish "an intimate and friendly relationship with the people," he warned, "then their intelligence must not be underestimated, their trust must be reciprocated and there must be no continual attempt to browbeat them."

The German people, he said, would follow Hitler with absolute loyalty "provided they are allowed to have a share in the making and carrying out of decisions, provided every word of criticism is not immediately interpreted as malicious, and provided that despairing patriots are not branded as traitors."

The time had come, he proclaimed, "to silence doctrinaire fanatics."

The audience reacted as if its members had been waiting a very long time to hear such remarks. As Papen concluded his speech, the crowd leapt to its feet. "The thunder of applause," Papen noted, drowned out "the furious protests" of the uniformed Nazis in the crowd. Historian John Wheeler-Bennett, at the time a Berlin resident, wrote, "It is difficult to describe the joy with which it was received in Germany. It was as if a load had suddenly been lifted from the German soul. The sense of relief could almost be felt in the air. Papen had put into words what thousands upon thousands of his countrymen had locked up in their hearts for fear of the awful penalties of speech."

THAT SAME DAY, Hitler was scheduled to speak elsewhere in Germany on the subject of a visit he had just made to Italy to meet with Mussolini. Hitler turned the opportunity into an attack on Papen and his conservative allies, without mentioning Papen directly. "All these little dwarfs who think they have something to say against our idea will be swept away by its collective strength," Hitler shouted. He railed against "this ridiculous little worm," this "pygmy who imagines he can stop, with a few phrases, the gigantic renewal of a people's life."

He issued a warning to the Papen camp: "If they should at any time attempt, even in a small way, to move from their criticism to a new act of perjury, they can be sure that what confronts them today is not the cowardly and corrupt bourgeoisie of 1918 but the fist of the entire people. It is the fist of the nation that is clenched and will smash down anyone who dares to undertake even the slightest attempt at sabotage."

Goebbels acted immediately to suppress Papen's speech. He banned its broadcast and ordered the destruction of the gramophone records onto which it had been cast. He banned newspapers from publishing its text or reporting on its contents, though at least one newspaper, the *Frankfurter Zeitung*, did manage to publish extracts. So intent was Goebbels on stopping dissemination of the speech that copies of the paper "were snatched from the hands of the guests of restaurants and coffee houses," Dodd reported.

Papen's allies used the presses of Papen's own newspaper, *Germania*, to produce copies of the speech for quiet distribution to diplomats, foreign correspondents, and others. The speech caused a stir throughout the world. The *New York Times* requested that Dodd's embassy provide the full text by telegraph. Newspapers in London and Paris made the speech a sensation.

The event intensified the sense of disquiet suffusing Berlin. "There was something in the sultry air," wrote Hans Gisevius, the Gestapo memoirist, "and a flood of probable and wildly fantastic rumors spilled out over the intimidated populace. Insane tales were fondly believed. Everyone whispered and peddled fresh rumors." Men on both sides of the political chasm "became extremely concerned with the question of whether assassins had been hired to murder them and who these killers might be."

Someone threw a hand-grenade fuse from the roof of a building onto Unter den Linden. It exploded, but the only harm was to the psyches of various government and SA leaders who happened to be in the vicinity. Karl Ernst, the young and ruthless leader of the Berlin division of the SA, had passed by five minutes before the explosion and claimed he was its target and that Himmler was behind it.

In this cauldron of tension and fear, the idea of Himmler wishing to kill Ernst was utterly plausible. Even after a police investigation identified the would-be assassin as a disgruntled part-time worker, an aura of fear and doubt remained, like smoke drifting from a gun barrel. Wrote Gisevius, "There was so much whispering, so much winking and nodding of heads, that traces of suspicion remained."

The nation seemed poised at the climax of some cinematic thriller. "Tension was at the highest pitch," Gisevius wrote. "The tormenting uncertainty was harder to bear than the excessive heat and humidity. No one knew what was going to happen next and everyone felt that something fearful was in the air." Victor Klemperer, the Jewish philologist, sensed it as well. "Everywhere uncertainty, ferment, secrets," he wrote in his diary in mid-June. "We live from day to day."

FOR DODD, PAPEN'S MARBURG SPEECH seemed a marker of what he had long believed—that Hitler's regime was too brutal and irrational to last. Hitler's own vice-chancellor had spoken out against the regime and survived. Was this indeed the spark that would bring Hitler's government to an end? And if so, how strange that it should be struck by so uncourageous a soul as Papen.

"There is now great excitement all over Germany," Dodd wrote in his diary on Wednesday, June 20. "All old and intellectual Germans are highly pleased." Suddenly fragments of other news began to make more sense, including a heightened fury in the speeches of Hitler and his deputies. "All guards of the leaders are said to be showing signs of revolt," Dodd wrote. "At the same time, aircraft practice and military drills and maneuvers are reported to be increasingly common sights by those who drive about the country."

That same Wednesday, Papen went to Hitler to complain about the suppression of his speech. "I spoke at Marburg as an emissary of the president," he told Hitler. "Goebbels's intervention will force me to resign. I shall inform Hindenburg immediately."

To Hitler this was a serious threat. He recognized that President Hindenburg possessed the constitutional authority to unseat him and commanded the loyalty of the regular army, and that both these factors made Hindenburg the one truly potent force in Germany over which he had no control. Hitler understood as well that Hindenburg and Papen—the president's "Fränzchen"—maintained a close personal relationship and knew that Hindenburg had telegraphed Papen to congratulate him on his speech.

Papen now told Hitler he would go to Hindenburg's estate, Neudeck, and ask Hindenburg to authorize full publication of the speech.

Hitler tried to mollify him. He promised to remove the propaganda minister's ban on publication and told Papen he would go with him to Neudeck, so that they could meet with Hindenburg together. In a moment of surprising naïveté, Papen agreed.

THAT NIGHT, SOLSTICE REVELERS ignited bonfires throughout Germany. North of Berlin the funeral train carrying the body of Göring's wife, Carin, came to a stop at a station near Carinhall. Formations of Nazi soldiers and officials crowded the plaza in front of the station as a band played Beethoven's "Funeral March." First, eight policemen carried the coffin, then with great ceremony it was passed to another group of eight men, and so on, until at last it was placed aboard a carriage pulled by six horses for the final journey to Göring's lakeside mausoleum. Hitler joined the procession. Soldiers carried torches. At the tomb there were great bowls filled with flame. In an eerie, carefully orchestrated touch, the mournful cry of hunters' horns rose from the forest beyond the fire glow.

Himmler arrived. He was clearly agitated. He took Hitler and Göring aside and gave them unsettling news—untrue, as Himmler surely was aware, but useful as one more prod to get Hitler to act against Röhm. Himmler raged that someone had just tried to kill him. A bullet had pierced his windshield. He blamed Röhm and the SA. There was no time to waste, he said: the Storm Troopers clearly were on the verge of rebellion.

The hole in his windshield, however, had not been made by a bullet. Hans Gisevius got a look at the final police report. The damage was more consistent with what would have been caused by a stone kicked up from a passing car. "It was with cold calculation that [Himmler], therefore, blamed the attempted assassination on the SA," Gisevius wrote.

The next day, June 21, 1934, Hitler flew to Hindenburg's estate—without Papen, as certainly had been his intent all along. At Neudeck, however, he first encountered Defense Minister Blomberg. The general, in uniform, met him on the steps to Hindenburg's castle. Blomberg was stern and direct. He told Hitler that Hindenburg was concerned about the rising tension within Germany. If Hitler could not get things under control, Blomberg said, Hindenburg would declare martial law and place the government in the army's hands.

When Hitler met with Hindenburg himself, he received the same message. His visit to Neudeck lasted all of thirty minutes. He flew back to Berlin.

THROUGHOUT THE WEEK DODD heard talk of Vice-Chancellor Papen and his speech and of the simple miracle of his survival. Correspondents and diplomats made note of Papen's activities—what luncheons he attended, who spoke with him, who shunned him, where his car was parked, whether he still took his morning walk through the Tiergarten—looking for signs of what might lie ahead for him and for Germany. On Thursday, June 21, Dodd and Papen both attended a speech by Reichsbank president Hjalmar Schacht. Afterward, Dodd noticed, Papen seemed to get even more attention than the speaker. Goebbels was present as well. Dodd noted that Papen went to his table, shook hands with him, and joined him for a cup of tea. Dodd was amazed, for this was the same Goebbels "who after the Marburg speech would have ordered his prompt execution if Hitler and von Hindenburg had not intervened."

The atmosphere in Berlin remained charged, Dodd noted in his diary on Saturday, June 23. "The week closes quietly but with great uneasiness."

CHAPTER 44

The Message in the Bathroom

Papen moved about Berlin seemingly unperturbed and on June 24, 1934, traveled to Hamburg as Hindenburg's emissary to the German Derby, a horse race, where the crowd gave him a spirited ovation. Goebbels arrived and pushed through the crowd behind a phalanx of SS, drawing hisses and boos. Both men shook hands as photographers snapped away.

Edgar Jung, Papen's speechwriter, kept a lower profile. By now he had become convinced that the Marburg speech would cost him his life. Historian Wheeler-Bennett arranged a clandestine meeting with him in a wooded area outside Berlin. "He was entirely calm and fatalistic," Wheeler-Bennett recalled, "but he spoke with the freedom of a man who has nothing before him and therefore nothing to lose, and he told me many things."

The rhetoric of the regime grew more menacing. In a radio address on Monday, June 25, Rudolf Hess warned, "Woe to him who breaks faith, in the belief that through a revolt he can serve the revolution." The party, he said, would meet rebellion with absolute force, guided by the principle "If you strike, strike hard!"

The next morning, Tuesday, June 26, Edgar Jung's housekeeper arrived at his home to find it ransacked, with furniture upended and clothing and papers scattered throughout. On the medicine chest in his bathroom Jung had scrawled a single word: GESTAPO.

DIELS READIED HIMSELF to be sworn in as regional commissioner of Cologne. Göring flew to the city for the occasion. His white plane emerged from a clear cerulean sky on what Diels described as a "beautiful Rhineland summer day." At the ceremony Diels wore his black SS uniform; Göring wore a white uniform of his own design. Afterward, Göring took Diels aside and told him, "Watch yourself in the next few days."

Diels took it to heart. Adept now at timely exits, he left the city for a sojourn in the nearby Eifel Mountains.

CHAPTER 45

Mrs. Cerruti's Distress

In his diary entry for Thursday, June 28, 1934, Ambassador Dodd wrote, "During the last five days, stories of many kinds have tended to make the Berlin atmosphere more tense than at any time since I have been in Germany." Papen's speech continued to be a topic of daily conversation. With rising ferocity, Hitler, Göring, and Goebbels warned of dire consequences for anyone who dared to oppose the government. In a cable to the State Department, Dodd likened the atmosphere of threat to that of the French Revolution—"the situation was much as it was in Paris in 1792 when the Girondins and Jacobins were struggling for supremacy."

In his own household, there was an extra layer of strain that had nothing to do with weather or political upheaval. Against her parents' wishes, Martha continued planning her trip to Russia. She insisted that her interest had nothing to do with communism per se but rather arose out of her love for Boris and her mounting distaste for the Nazi revolution. She recognized that Boris was indeed a loyal communist, but she claimed he exerted influence over her political perspective only "by the example of his magnetism and simplicity, and his love of country." She confessed to feeling a gnawing ambivalence "regarding him, his beliefs, the political system in his country, our future together." She insisted on taking the trip without him.

She wanted to see as much of Russia as she could and ignored his advice to concentrate on only a few cities. He wanted her to gain a deep understanding of his homeland, not some glancing tourist's appreciation. He recognized also that travel in his country was not as quick or comfortable as in Western Europe, nor did its cities and towns have the obvious charm of the picturesque villages of Germany and France. Indeed, the Soviet Union was anything but the workers' paradise many left-leaning outsiders imagined it to be. Under Stalin, peasants had been forced into vast collectives. Many resisted, and an estimated five million people—men, women, and children—simply disappeared, many shipped off to far-flung work camps. Housing was primitive, consumer goods virtually nonexistent. Famine scoured the Ukraine. Livestock suffered a drastic decline. From 1929 to 1933 the total number of cattle fell from 68.1 million to 38.6 million; of horses, from 34 million to 16.6 million. Boris knew full well that to a casual visitor, the physical and social scenery and especially the drab workers' fashion of Russia could seem less than captivating, especially if that visitor happened to be exhausted by difficult travel and the mandatory presence of an Intourist guide.

Nonetheless, Martha chose Tour No. 9, the Volga-Caucasus-Crimea tour, set to begin on July 6 with a flight—her first ever—from Berlin to Leningrad. After two days in Leningrad, she would set out by train for Moscow, spend four days there, then proceed by overnight train to Gorki and, two hours after her 10:04 arrival, catch a Volga steamer for a four-day cruise with stops at Kazan, Samara, Saratov, and Stalingrad, where she was to make the obligatory visit to a tractor works; from Stalingrad, she would take a train to Rostov-on-Don, where she would have the option of visiting a state farm, though here her itinerary exuded just a whiff of capitalism, for the farm tour would require an "extra fee." Next, Ordzhonikidze, Tiflis, Batumi, Yalta, Sebastopol, Odessa, Kiev, and, at last, back to Berlin by train, where she was to arrive on August 7, the thirty-third day of her journey, at precisely—if optimistically—7:22 p.m.

Her relationship with Boris continued to deepen, though with its usual wild swings between passion and anger and the usual cascade of pleading notes and fresh flowers from him. At some point she returned his three "see no evil" ceramic monkeys. He sent them back.

"Martha!" he wrote, indulging his passion for exclamation:

"I thank you for your letters and for 'not forgetfulness.' Your three monkeys have grown (they have become big) and want to be with

you. I am sending them. I have to tell you very frankly: three monkeys have longed for you. And not only the three monkeys, I know
another handsome, blond (aryan!!) young man, who has longed to
be with you. This handsome boy (not older than 30)—is *me*.

"Martha! I want to see you, I need to tell you that I also have not
forgotten my little adorable lovely Martha!

"I love you, Martha! What do I have to do to establish more confidence in you?

"Yours, Boris."

In any era their relationship would have been likely to draw the attention of outsiders, but that June in Berlin everything took on added
gravitas. Everyone watched everyone else. At the time, Martha gave
little thought to the perceptions of others, but years later, in a letter
to Agnes Knickerbocker, the wife of her correspondent friend Knick,
she acknowledged how readily perception could distort reality. "I
never plotted the overthrow nor even the subversion of the U.S.
government, neither in Germany nor in the USA!" she wrote. "I
think however that just knowing and loving Boris would be enough
for some people to suspect the worst."

At the time there was nothing to suspect, she insisted. "Instead
it was one of those absorbing things that had no political base at
all, except that through him I came to know something about the
USSR."

FRIDAY, JUNE 29, 1934, brought the same atmosphere of impending storm that had marked the preceding weeks. "It was the hottest
day we had had that summer," recalled Elisabetta Cerruti, wife of
the Italian ambassador. "The air was so heavy with moisture that
we could hardly breathe. Black clouds loomed on the horizon, but a
merciless sun burned overhead."

That day the Dodds held a lunch at their home, to which they
had invited Vice-Chancellor Papen and other diplomatic and government figures, including the Cerrutis and Hans Luther, Germany's
ambassador to the United States, who at the time happened to be
in Berlin.

Martha also attended and watched as her father and Papen stepped away from the other guests for a private conversation in the library, in front of the now-dormant fireplace. Papen, she wrote, "seemed self-confident and as suave as usual."

At one point Dodd spotted Papen and Luther edging toward each other with a "rather tense attitude" between them. Dodd moved to intervene and steered them out to the lovely winter garden, where another guest joined them in conversation. Dodd, referring to the press photographs taken during the German Derby, said to Papen, "You and Dr. Goebbels seemed to be quite friendly at Hamburg the other day."

Papen laughed.

At lunch, Mrs. Cerruti sat on Dodd's right and Papen sat directly opposite, next to Mrs. Dodd. Mrs. Cerruti's anxiety was palpable, even to Martha, watching from a distance. Martha wrote, "She sat by my father in a state of near-collapse, hardly speaking, pale, pre-occupied, and jumpy."

Mrs. Cerruti told Dodd, "Mr. Ambassador, something terrible is going to happen in Germany. I feel it in the air."

A later rumor held that Mrs. Cerruti somehow knew in advance what was about to happen. She found this astonishing. Her remark to Dodd, she claimed years later, referred only to the weather.

IN AMERICA THAT FRIDAY the "great heat" worsened. In humid locales like Washington it became nearly impossible to work. Moffat noted in his diary: "Temperature 101 and ½ in the shade today."

The heat and humidity were so unbearable that as evening approached Moffat and Phillips and a third official went to the home of a friend of Moffat's to use his pool. The friend was away at the time. The three men undressed and climbed in. The water was warm and provided scant relief. No one swam. Instead the three simply sat there, talking quietly, only their heads showing above the water.

That Dodd was a subject of this conversation seems likely. Just a few days earlier Phillips had written in his diary about Dodd's un-relenting assault on the wealth of diplomats and consular officials.

"Presumably the Ambassador has been complaining to the President," Phillips groused in his diary. Dodd "always complains because of the fact that they are spending in Berlin more than their salaries. This he objects to strenuously, probably for the simple reason that he himself has not the money to spend beyond that of his salary. It is, of course, a small town attitude."

ODDLY ENOUGH, MOFFAT'S MOTHER, Ellen Low Moffat, was in Berlin that Friday, to visit her daughter (Moffat's sister), who was married to the embassy secretary, John C. White. That evening the mother attended a dinner party where she sat beside Papen. The vice-chancellor was, as she later told her son, "well and in extremely high spirits."

CHAPTER 46

Friday Night

That Friday evening, June 29, 1934, Hitler settled in at the Hotel Dreesen, a favorite of his, in the resort of Bad Godesberg, situated along the Rhine just outside central Bonn. He had traveled here from Essen, where he had received yet another dose of troubling news—that Vice-Chancellor Papen planned to make good on his threat and meet with President Hindenburg the next day, Saturday, June 30, to persuade the Old Gentleman to take steps to rein in Hitler's government and the SA.

This news, atop the accumulation of reports from Himmler and Göring that Röhm was planning a coup, convinced Hitler that the time had come for action. Göring left for Berlin to make ready. Hitler ordered the Reichswehr on alert, though the forces he intended to deploy were mostly SS units. Hitler telephoned one of Röhm's key deputies and ordered all SA leaders to attend a meeting Saturday morning in Bad Wiessee, near Munich, where Röhm was already comfortably ensconced in the Hotel Hanselbauer, taking his cure, which on that Friday night involved a good deal of drinking. His aide, Edmund Heines, bedded down with a handsome eighteen-year-old Storm Trooper.

Goebbels joined Hitler at Bad Godesberg. They spoke on the hotel terrace as a parade roared below. Blue flashes of lightning lit the sky over Bonn and thunder rumbled everywhere, amplified by the strange sonic physics of the Rhine Valley.

Goebbels later gave a melodramatic account of those heady moments before Hitler made his final decision. The air had grown still as the distant storm advanced. Suddenly, heavy rain began to fall. He and Hitler remained seated a few moments longer, enjoying the cleansing downpour. Hitler laughed. They went inside. Once the storm had passed, they returned to the terrace. "The *Führer* seemed in a thoughtful, serious mood," Goebbels said. "He stared out at the clear darkness of the night, which after the purification of the storm stretched peacefully across a vast, harmonious landscape."

The crowd on the street lingered despite the storm. "Not one of the many people standing below knows what is threatening to come," Goebbels wrote. "Even among those around the Leader on the terrace only a few have been informed. In this hour he is more than ever to be admired by us. Not a quiver on his face reveals the slightest sign of what is going on within him. Yet we few, who stand by him in all difficult hours, know how deeply he is grieved, but also how determined he is to stamp out mercilessly the reactionary rebels who are breaking their oath of loyalty to him, under the slogan of carrying out a second revolution."

It was after midnight when Himmler telephoned with more bad news. He told Hitler that Karl Ernst, commander of the Berlin division of the SA, had ordered his forces to go on alert. Hitler cried, "It's a putsch!"—though in fact, as Himmler surely knew, Ernst had just recently gotten married and was headed to the port of Bremen for the start of a honeymoon cruise.

AT 2:00 A.M. SATURDAY, June 30, 1934, Hitler left the Hotel Dreesen and was driven at high speed to the airport, where he boarded a Ju 52 airplane, one of two aircraft ready for his use. He was joined by two adjutants and a senior SA officer whom he trusted, Viktor Lutze. (It was Lutze who had told Hitler about Röhm's scathing remarks after Hitler's February 1934 speech to the leaders of the army and SA.) Hitler's chauffeurs also climbed aboard. The second aircraft contained a squad of armed SS men. Both planes flew to Munich, where they arrived at four thirty in the morning, just as the sun was beginning to rise. One of Hitler's drivers, Erich Kempka, was struck by the beauty of the morning and the freshness of the rain-scrubbed air, the grass "sparkling in the morning light."

Soon after landing, Hitler received a final bit of incendiary news—the day before, some three thousand Storm Troopers had raged through Munich's streets. He was not told, however, that this demonstration had been spontaneous, conducted by men loyal to him who were themselves feeling threatened and betrayed and who feared an attack against them by the regular army.

Hitler's fury peaked. He declared this "the blackest day of my life." He decided that he could not afford to wait even until the meeting of SA leaders set for later that morning at Bad Wiessee. He turned to Kempka: "To Wiessee, as fast as possible!"

Goebbels called Göring and gave him the code word to launch the Berlin phase of the operation—the innocent-sounding "*Kolibri.*" Hummingbird.

IN BERLIN, THE LAST of the late northern dusk lingered on the horizon as the Dodds settled in for a peaceful Friday night. Dodd read a book and consumed his usual digestif of stewed peaches and milk. His wife allowed her thoughts to dwell for a time on the grand lawn party she and Dodd planned for July 4, less than a week away, to which they had invited all the embassy staff and several hundred other guests. Bill Jr. stayed at the house that night and planned to take the family Buick for a drive the next morning. Martha looked forward to the morning as well, when she and Boris planned to set off on another countryside excursion, this time to picnic and sunbathe on a beach in the Wannsee district. In six days she would set out for Russia.

Outside, cigarettes twinkled in the park, and now and then a large, open car whooshed past on Tiergartenstrasse. In the park, insects speckled the halos cast by lamps, and the brilliant white statues in the Siegesallee—Avenue of Victory—gleamed like ghosts. Though hotter and more still, the night was very much like Martha's first in Berlin, peaceful, with that small-town serenity she had found so captivating.

PART VII

When Everything Changed

CHAPTER 47

"Shoot, Shoot!"

The next morning, Saturday, June 30, 1934, Boris drove to Martha's house in his open Ford and soon, armed with picnic larder and blanket, the two set out for the Wannsee district southwest of Berlin. As a setting for trysts it had a turbulent history. Here, on a lake named Kleiner Wannsee—Little Wannsee—the German poet Heinrich von Kleist shot himself in 1811, after first shooting his terminally ill lover. Martha and Boris were headed for a small, uncrowded lake well to the north called Gross Glienicke, Martha's favorite.

The city around them was sleepy with nascent heat. Though the day would be another difficult one for farmers and laborers, for anyone intent on lakeside sunbathing it promised to be ideal. As Boris drove toward the city's outskirts, everything seemed utterly normal. Other residents, looking back, made the same observation. Berliners "strolled serenely through the streets, went about their business," observed Hedda Adlon, wife of the proprietor of the Hotel Adlon. The hotel followed its usual rhythms, although the day's heat promised to compound the logistical challenges of catering a banquet for the king of Siam to be held later that day at the Schloss Bellevue— Bellevue Palace—at the northern edge of the Tiergarten, on the Spree. The hotel would have to shuttle its canapés and entrees in its catering van through traffic and heat, amid temperatures expected to rise into the nineties.

At the lake, Boris and Martha spread their blanket. They swam and lay in the sun, entangled in each other's arms until the heat drove them apart. They drank beer and vodka and dined on sandwiches.

"It was a beautiful serene blue day, the lake shimmering and glittering in front of us, and the sun spreading its fire over us," she wrote. "It was a silent and soft day—we didn't even have the energy or desire to talk politics or discuss the new tension in the atmosphere."

ELSEWHERE THAT MORNING, three far larger cars raced across the countryside between Munich and Bad Wiessee—Hitler's car and two others filled with armed men. They arrived at the Hotel Hanselbauer, where Captain Röhm lay asleep in his room. Hitler led a squad of armed men into the hotel. By one account he carried a whip, by another, a pistol. The men climbed the stairs in a thunder of bootheels.

Hitler himself knocked on Röhm's door, then burst inside, followed by two detectives. "Röhm," Hitler barked, "you are under arrest."

Röhm was groggy, clearly hungover. He looked at Hitler. "Heil, mein Führer," he said.

Hitler shouted again, "You are under arrest," and then stepped back into the hall. He advanced next to the room of Röhm's adjutant, Heines, and found him in bed with his young SA lover. Hitler's driver, Kempka, was present in the hall. He heard Hitler shout, "Heines, if you are not dressed in five minutes I'll have you shot on the spot!"

Heines emerged, preceded by, as Kempka put it, "an 18-year-old fair-haired boy mincing in front of him."

The halls of the hotel resounded with the shouts of SS men herding sleepy, stunned, and hungover Storm Troopers down to the laundry room in the hotel basement. There were moments that in another context might have been comical, as when one of Hitler's raiding party emerged from a hotel bedroom and reported, crisply, "Mein Führer! . . . The Police President of Breslau is refusing to get dressed!"

Or this: Röhm's doctor, an SA Gruppenführer named Ketterer, emerged from one room accompanied by a woman. To the astonishment of Hitler and his detectives, the woman was Ketterer's wife. Viktor Lutze, the trusted SA officer who had been in Hitler's plane that morning, persuaded Hitler that the doctor was a loyal ally. Hitler walked over to the man and greeted him politely. He shook hands with Mrs. Ketterer, then quietly recommended that the couple leave the hotel. They did so without argument.

IN BERLIN THAT MORNING, Frederick Birchall of the *New York Times* was awakened by the persistent ring of the telephone beside his bed. He had been out late the night before and at first was inclined to ignore the call. He speculated, wishfully, that it must be unimportant, probably only an invitation to lunch. The phone kept ringing. At length, acting on the maxim "It is never safe to despise a telephone call, especially in Germany," he picked up the receiver and heard a voice from his office: "Better wake up and get busy. Something doing here." What the caller said next captured Birchall's full attention: "Apparently a lot of people are being shot."

Louis Lochner, the Associated Press correspondent, learned from a clerical worker arriving late to the AP office that Prinz-Albrecht-Strasse, where the Gestapo was headquartered, had been closed to traffic and now was filled with trucks and armed SS, in their telltale black uniforms. Lochner made a few calls. The more he learned, the more disturbing it all seemed. As a precaution—believing that the government might shut down all outbound international telephone lines—Lochner called the AP's office in London and told its staff to call him every fifteen minutes until further notice, on the theory that inbound calls might still be allowed through.

Sigrid Schultz set off for the central government district, watching carefully for certain license plate numbers, Papen's in particular. She would work nonstop until four the next morning and then note in her daily appointments diary, "dead tired—[could] weep."

One of the most alarming rumors was of massed volleys of gunfire from the courtyard of the old cadet school in the otherwise peaceful enclave of Gross-Lichterfelde.

AT THE HOTEL HANSELBAUER, Röhm got dressed in a blue suit and emerged from his room, still confounded and apparently not yet terribly worried by Hitler's anger or the commotion in the hotel. A cigar projected from the corner of his mouth. Two detectives took him to the hotel lobby, where he sat in a chair and ordered coffee from a passing waiter.

There were more arrests, more men shoved into the laundry room. Röhm remained seated in the lobby. Kempka heard him request another cup of coffee, by now his third.

Röhm was taken away by car; the rest of the prisoners were loaded onto a chartered bus and driven to Munich, to Stadelheim Prison, where Hitler himself had spent a month in 1922. Their captors took back roads to avoid contact with any Storm Troopers seeking to effect rescue. Hitler and his ever-larger raiding party climbed back into their cars, now numbering about twenty, and raced off on a more direct route toward Munich, stopping any cars bearing SA leaders who, unaware of all that had just occurred, were still expecting to attend Hitler's meeting set for later that morning.

In Munich, Hitler read through a list of the prisoners and marked an "X" next to six names. He ordered all six shot immediately. An SS squad did so, telling the men just before firing, "You have been condemned to death by the *Führer! Heil Hitler.*"

The ever-obliging Rudolf Hess offered to shoot Röhm himself, but Hitler did not yet order his death. For the moment, even he found the idea of killing a longtime friend to be abhorrent.

SOON AFTER ARRIVING at his Berlin office that morning, Hans Gisevius, the Gestapo memoirist, tuned his radio to police frequencies and heard reports that sketched an action of vast scope. Senior SA men were being arrested, as were men who had no connection with the Storm Troopers. Gisevius and his boss, Kurt Daluege, set off in search of more detailed information and went directly to Göring's palace on Leipziger Platz, from which Göring was issuing commands. Gisevius stuck close to Daluege in the belief that he was safer in his company than alone. He also figured no one would think to look for him at Göring's residence.

Although the palace was an easy walk away, they drove. They were struck by the aura of utter calm on the streets, as though nothing unusual were taking place. They did note, however, the complete absence of Storm Troopers.

The sense of normalcy disappeared immediately when they turned a corner and arrived at Göring's palace. Machine guns jutted from every promontory. The courtyard was filled with police.

Gisevius wrote: "As I followed Daluege through the succession of guards and climbed the few steps to the huge lobby, I felt as if I could scarcely breathe. An evil atmosphere of haste, nervousness, tension, and above all of bloodshed, seemed to strike me in the face."

Gisevius made his way to a room next to Göring's study. Adjutants and messengers hurried past. An SA man sat quaking with fear, having been told by Göring that he was to be shot. Servants brought sandwiches. Although crowded, the room was quiet. "Everyone whispered as if he were in a morgue," Gisevius recalled.

Through an open doorway, he saw Göring conferring with Himmler and Himmler's new Gestapo chief, Reinhard Heydrich. Gestapo couriers arrived and left carrying white slips of paper on which, Gisevius presumed, were the names of the dead or soon-to-be dead. Despite the serious nature of the endeavor at hand, the atmosphere in Göring's office was closer to what could be expected at a racetrack. Gisevius heard crude and raucous laughter and periodic shouts of "Away!"

"Aha!"

"Shoot him."

"The whole crew of them seemed to be in the best humor," Gisevius recalled.

Now and then he caught a glimpse of Göring striding around the room dressed in a billowy white shirt and blue-gray trousers tucked into black jackboots that rose above his knees. "Puss-in-Boots," Gisevius thought suddenly.

At one point a red-faced police major burst from the study, followed by an equally enflamed Göring. Apparently a prominent target had escaped.

Göring shouted instructions.

"Shoot them! . . . Take a whole company. . . . Shoot them. . . . Shoot them at once!"

Gisevius found it appalling beyond description. "The written word

cannot reproduce the undisguised blood lust, fury, vicious vengeful-
ness, and, at the same time, the fear, the pure funk, that the scene
revealed."

DODD HEARD NOTHING about the cataclysm unfolding elsewhere
in the city until that Saturday afternoon when he and his wife sat
down for lunch in their garden. At almost the same moment, their
son, Bill, appeared, having just returned from his drive. He looked
troubled. He reported that a number of streets had been closed, including Unter den Linden at the heart of the government district,
and these were being patrolled by heavily armed squads of SS. He
had heard as well that arrests had been made at the headquarters of
the SA, located just blocks from the house.

Immediately Dodd and his wife experienced a spike of anxiety for
Martha, out for the day with Boris Winogradov. Despite his diplomatic status, Boris was a man whom the Nazis even in ordinary times
could be expected to view as an enemy of the state.

CHAPTER 48

Guns in the Park

Boris and Martha stayed at the beach all day, retreating to shade when the sun became too much but returning again for more. It was after five when they packed their things and with reluctance began the drive back to the city, "our heads giddy," Martha recalled, "and our bodies burning from the sun." They traveled as slowly as possible, neither wanting the day to end, both still relishing the oblivion of sunshine on water. The day had grown hotter as the ground cast its accumulated warmth back into the atmosphere.

They drove through a bucolic landscape softened by heat haze that rose from the fields and forests around them. Riders on bicycles overtook and passed them, some carrying small children in baskets over the front fenders or in wagons pulled alongside. Women carried flowers and men with knapsacks engaged in the German passion for a good, fast walk. "It was a homely, hot, and friendly day," Martha wrote.

To catch the late afternoon sun and the breezes that flowed through the open car, Martha hiked the hem of her skirt to the tops of her thighs. "I was happy," she wrote, "pleased with my day and my companion, full of sympathy for the earnest, simple, kindly German people, so obviously taking a hard-earned walk or rest, enjoying themselves and their countryside so intensely."

At six o'clock they entered the city. Martha sat up straight and dropped the hem of her skirt "as befits a diplomat's daughter."

The city had changed. They realized it in phases as they got closer and closer to the Tiergarten. There were fewer people on the street than might be considered normal, and these tended to gather in "curious static groups," as Martha put it. Traffic moved slowly. At the point where Boris was about to enter Tiergartenstrasse, the flow of cars all but stopped. They saw army trucks and machine guns and suddenly realized that the only people around them were men in uniform, mostly SS black and the green of Göring's police force. Noticeably absent were the brown uniforms of the SA. What made this especially odd was that the SA's headquarters and Captain Röhm's home were so near.

They came to a checkpoint. The license plate on Boris's car indicated diplomatic status. The police waved them through.

Boris drove slowly through a newly sinister landscape. Across the street from Martha's house, beside the park, stood a line of soldiers, weapons, and military trucks. Farther down Tiergartenstrasse, at the point where it intersected Standartenstrasse—Röhm's street— they saw more soldiers and a rope barrier marking the street's closure.

There was a sense of suffocation. Drab trucks blocked the vistas of the park. And there was heat. It was evening, well after six, but the sun was still high and hot. Once so alluring, the sun now to Martha was "broiling." She and Boris parted. She ran to her front door and quickly entered. The sudden darkness and stone-cool air of the entry foyer were so jarring she felt dizzy, "my eyes blinded for the moment by the lack of light."

She ascended the stairwell to the main floor and there found her brother. "We were worried about you," he said. He told her General Schleicher had been shot. Their father had gone to the embassy to prepare a message for the State Department. "We don't know what is happening," Bill said. "There is martial law in Berlin."

In that first instant, the name "Schleicher" brought no recognition. Then she remembered: Schleicher, the general, a man of military bearing and integrity, a former chancellor and minister of defense.

"I sat down, still confused and terribly distressed," Martha recalled. She could not understand why General Schleicher would be shot. She recalled him as being "courtly, attractive, clever."

Schleicher's wife had been shot as well, Bill told her. Both shot in the back, in their garden; both shot numerous times. The story would change over the next few days, but the irrevocable fact was that both Schleichers were dead.

Mrs. Dodd came downstairs. She, Bill, and Martha went into one of the reception rooms. They took seats close together and talked quietly. They noticed that Fritz appeared with unusual frequency. They closed all the doors. Fritz continued to bring word of new telephone calls from friends and correspondents. He seemed afraid, "white and scared," Martha wrote.

The story Bill told was a chilling one. Although a fog of rumor clouded every new revelation, certain facts were clear. The deaths of the Schleichers were just two of dozens, perhaps hundreds, of official murders committed so far that day, and the killing continued. Röhm was said to be under arrest, his fate uncertain.

Each new telephone call brought more news, much of it sounding too wild to be credible. Assassination squads were said to be roaming the country, hunting targets. Karl Ernst, chief of Berlin's SA, had been dragged from his honeymoon ship. A prominent leader in the Catholic Church had been murdered in his office. A second army general had been shot, as had a music critic for a newspaper. The killings seemed haphazard and capricious.

There was one perversely comical moment. The Dodds received a terse RSVP from Röhm's office, stating that "to his great sorrow" he could not attend a dinner at the Dodds' house set for the coming Friday, July 6, "because he will be on vacation to seek a cure for an illness."

"In view of the uncertainty of the situation," Dodd wrote in his diary, "perhaps it was best he did not accept."

ADDING TO THE DAY'S sense of upheaval was a collision that occurred just outside 27a when the embassy chauffeur—a man named Pickford—struck a motorcycle and broke off the rider's leg. A wooden leg.

In the midst of it all, there lingered for Dodd a particularly pressing question: what had happened to Papen, the hero of Marburg, whom Hitler so loathed? Reports held that Edgar Jung, the author of Papen's speech, had been shot and that Papen's press secretary likewise had been killed. In that murderous climate, could Papen himself possibly have survived?

CHAPTER 49

The Dead

At three o'clock on Saturday afternoon, Berlin's foreign correspondents gathered at the Reich chancellery on the Wilhelmstrasse for a press conference to be given by Hermann Göring. One witness was Hans Gisevius, who seemed to be everywhere that day.

Göring arrived late, in uniform, huge and arrogant. The room was hot and smoldered with "unbearable tension," Gisevius wrote. Göring positioned himself at the podium. With great drama he scanned the crowd, and then, with what appeared to be a series of rehearsed gestures, placed his chin in his hand and rolled his eyes, as if what he was about to say was momentous even to him. He spoke, Gisevius recalled, "in the lugubrious tone and flat voice of a practiced funeral orator."

Göring gave a brief account of the "action," which he said was still under way. "For weeks we have been watching; we knew that some of the leaders of the Sturmabteilung [SA] had taken positions very far from the aims and goals of the movement, giving priority to their own interests and ambitions, indulging their unfortunate and perverse tastes." Röhm was under arrest, he said. A "foreign power" also was involved. Everyone in the room presumed he meant France. "The Supreme Leader in Munich and I as his deputy in Berlin have struck with lightning speed without respect for persons."

Göring took questions. One reporter asked about the deaths of Vice-Chancellor Papen's speechwriter, Jung, and his press secretary, Herbert von Bose, and Erich Klausener, a prominent Catholic critic of the regime—what possible connection could they have had to an SA putsch?

"I expanded my task to take in reactionaries also," Göring said, his voice as bland as if he were quoting a telephone book.

And what of General Schleicher?

Göring paused, grinned.

"Ah, yes, you journalists always like a special headline story; well, here it is. General von Schleicher had plotted against the regime. I ordered his arrest. He was foolish enough to resist. He is dead."

Göring walked from the podium.

NO ONE KNEW EXACTLY how many people had lost their lives in the purge. Official Nazi tallies put the total at under one hundred. Foreign Minister Neurath, for example, told Britain's Sir Eric Phipps that there had been "forty-three or forty-six" executions and claimed that all other estimates were "unreliable and exaggerated." Dodd, in a letter to his friend Daniel Roper, wrote that reports coming in from America's consulates in other German cities suggested a total of 284 deaths. "Most of the victims," Dodd wrote, "were in no sense guilty of treason; merely political or religious opposition." Other tallies by American officials put the number far higher. The consul in Brandenburg wrote that an SS officer had told him five hundred had been killed and fifteen thousand arrested and that Rudolf Diels had been targeted for death but was spared at Göring's request. A memorandum from one of Dodd's secretaries of embassy in Berlin also put the number of executions at five hundred and noted that neighbors in the vicinity of the Lichterfelde barracks "could hear the firing squads at work the whole night." Diels later estimated seven hundred deaths; other insiders placed the total at over one thousand. No definitive total exists.

The death of General Schleicher was confirmed—he'd been shot seven times, his body and that of his wife discovered by their sixteen-year-old daughter. Another general, Ferdinand von Bredow, a member of Schleicher's cabinet when he was chancellor, was also shot. Despite these killings, the army continued to stand aside, its loathing for the SA trumping its distaste for the murder of two of its own. Gregor Strasser, a former Nazi leader with past ties to

Schleicher, was having lunch with his family when two Gestapo cars pulled up outside his home and six men came to his door. He was taken away and shot in a cell in the basement prison at Gestapo headquarters. Hitler was the godfather of his twins. A friend of Strasser's, Paul Schulz, a senior SA leader, was taken into a forest and shot. As his would-be executioners went back to their car to get a sheet for his body, he got up and bolted, and survived. It was this escape, apparently, that had triggered Göring's outburst of bloodthirsty rage. Gustav Ritter von Kahr, at seventy-three years of age hardly a threat to Hitler, was killed as well—"hacked to death," according to historian Ian Kershaw—apparently to avenge his role in undermining a Nazi putsch attempt a decade earlier. Karl Ernst, married only two days, had no comprehension of what was occurring as he was placed under arrest in Bremen just before his honeymoon cruise. Hitler had been a guest at his wedding. When Ernst realized he was about to be shot, he cried out, "I am innocent. Long live Germany! *Heil Hitler!*" At least five Jews were shot for the sin of being Jews. And then there were the innumerable, nameless souls executed by firing squad at the Lichterfelde barracks. The mother of one dead Storm Trooper only received official notification of his death six months after the fact, in a curt one-paragraph letter that stated he had been shot in defense of the state and thus no further explanation was needed. The letter ended as did all letters in the new Germany: "Heil Hitler!"

Again there were moments of dark comedy. One target, Gottfried Reinhold Treviranus, a minister under General Schleicher when he was chancellor, was in the middle of a tennis game at the Wannsee Tennis Club when he spotted four SS men outside. Wisely trusting his instincts, he excused himself and ran. He scaled a wall, caught a taxi, and eventually made his way to England.

In central Berlin, the SA man moonlighting as the driver of the Hotel Adlon's catering van found himself stopped by the SS at a checkpoint near the Brandenburg Gate, not far from the hotel. The hapless driver had made the unfortunate decision to wear his brown Storm Trooper shirt under his suit jacket.

The SS officer asked where he was going.

"To the king of Siam," the driver said, and smiled.

The SS man took this as a wisecrack. Enraged by the driver's impudence, he and his associates dragged the Storm Trooper out of the van and forced him to open the rear doors. The cargo space was filled with trays of food.

Still suspicious, the SS officer accused the driver of bringing the food to one of Röhm's orgies.

The driver, no longer smiling, said, "No, it's for the king of Siam."

The SS still believed the driver was merely being insolent. Two SS men climbed onto the van and ordered the driver to continue to the palace where the party supposedly was being held. To their chagrin, they learned that a banquet for the king of Siam was indeed planned and that Göring was one of the expected guests.

And then there was poor Willi Schmid—Wilhelm Eduard Schmid, respected music critic for a Munich newspaper—who was playing his cello at home with his wife and three children nearby when the SS came to the door, hauled him away, and shot him.

The SS had erred. Their intended target was a different Schmid. Or rather, a Schmitt.

Hitler dispatched Rudolf Hess to make a personal apology to the dead critic's wife.

PUTZI HANFSTAENGL, WHOSE RELATIONSHIP with Hitler had grown strained, was rumored to have been on Hitler's list of targets. Providently, he was in America to take part in the twenty-fifth reunion of his class at Harvard. The invitation to attend had caused an outcry in America, and until the last moment Hanfstaengl had offered no indication as to whether he actually would attend. On the night of June 10, 1934, he threw a dinner party, whose timing in retrospect seemed all too convenient given that surely he knew the purge was coming. In midmeal, he stepped from the dining room, disguised himself in a raincoat and sunglasses, and left. He took a night train to Cologne, where he climbed into a mail plane that took him directly to Cherbourg, France, and there he boarded his ship, the *Europa*, bound for New York. He brought five suitcases and three crates containing sculptural busts meant as gifts.

The New York City police department, fearing threats to Hanf-staengl from outraged protesters, sent six young officers aboard to guide him from the ship. They were dressed in Harvard jackets and ties.

On June 30, 1934, the day of the purge, Putzi attended the New-port, Rhode Island, wedding of Ellen Tuck French and John Jacob Astor III, said to be the richest bachelor in America. His father had been lost with the *Titanic*. A crowd of about a thousand people gath-ered outside the church to catch a glimpse of the bride and groom and the arriving guests. One of the first "to cause the crowd to gasp with excitement," wrote a gushing society reporter for the *New York Times*, was Hanfstaengl, "in a top hat, black coat and striped gray trousers."

Hanfstaengl knew nothing about events back home until asked about them by reporters. "I have no comment to make," he said. "I am here to attend the wedding of my friend's daughter." Later, after learning more details, he stated, "My leader, Adolf Hitler, had to act and he acted thus as always. Hitler has proven himself never greater, never more human, than in the last forty-eight hours."

Inwardly, however, Hanfstaengl worried about his own safety and that of his wife and son back in Berlin. He sent a discreet inquiry to Foreign Minister Neurath.

HITLER RETURNED TO BERLIN that evening. Again, Gisevius stood witness. Hitler's plane appeared "against the background of a blood-red sky, a piece of theatricality that no one had staged," Gise-vius wrote. After the plane came to a stop, a small army of men moved forward to greet Hitler, among them Göring and Himmler. Hitler was first to emerge from the aircraft. He wore a brown shirt, dark brown leather jacket, black bow tie, high black boots. He looked pale and tired and had not shaved but otherwise seemed untroubled. "It was clear that the murders of his friends had cost him no effort at all," Gisevius wrote. "He had felt nothing; he had merely acted out his rage."

In a radio address, propaganda chief Goebbels reassured the nation.

"In Germany," he said, "there is now complete peace and order. Public security has been restored. Never was the *Führer* more completely master of the situation. May a favorable destiny bless us so that we can carry our great task to its conclusion with Adolf Hitler!"

Dodd, however, continued to receive reports that indicated the purge was far from ended. There was still no firm news as to what had happened to Röhm and Papen. Waves of gunfire continued to roll from the courtyard at Lichterfelde.

CHAPTER 50

Among the Living

Sunday morning was cool, sunny, and breezy. Dodd was struck by the absence of any visible markers of all that had occurred during the past twenty-four hours. "It was a strange day," he wrote, "with only ordinary news in the papers."

Papen was said to be alive but under house arrest at his apartment along with his family. Dodd hoped to use what little influence he possessed to help keep him alive—if indeed the reports of Papen's continued survival were correct. Rumor held that the vice-chancellor was marked for execution and that it could happen at any time.

Dodd and Martha took the family Buick for a drive to Papen's apartment building. They drove past the entrance very slowly, intending that the SS guards see the car and recognize its provenance.

The pale face of Papen's son appeared at a window, partially hidden by curtains. An SS officer on guard at the building entrance glared as the car passed. It was clear to Martha that the officer had recognized the license plate as belonging to a diplomat.

That afternoon Dodd drove to Papen's home again, but this time he stopped and left a calling card with one of the guards, on which he had written, "I hope we may call on you soon."

Though Dodd disapproved of Papen's political machinations and his past behavior in the United States, he did like the man and had enjoyed sparring with him ever since their dinner confrontation at the Little Press Ball. What motivated Dodd now was revulsion at the idea of men being executed at Hitler's whim without warrant or trial.

Dodd drove back home. Later, Papen's son would tell the Dodds how grateful he and his family had been for the appearance of that simple Buick on their street that lethal afternoon.

REPORTS CONTINUED TO ARRIVE at the Dodds' residence of new arrests and murders. By Sunday night Dodd knew with reasonable certainty that Captain Röhm was dead.

The story, pieced together later, went like this:

At first Hitler was undecided as to whether to execute his old ally, locked in a cell at Stadelheim Prison, but eventually he bowed to pressure from Göring and Himmler. Even then, however, Hitler insisted that Röhm first should have an opportunity to kill himself.

The man assigned the task of offering Röhm this opportunity was Theodor Eicke, commander of Dachau, who drove to the prison on Sunday along with a deputy, Michael Lippert, and another SS man from the camp. The three were led to Röhm's cell.

Eicke gave Röhm a Browning automatic and a fresh edition of the *Völkischer Beobachter* containing an account of what the paper called the "Röhm Putsch," apparently to show Röhm that all was indeed lost.

Eicke left the room. Ten minutes passed with no gunfire. Eicke and Lippert returned to the cell, removed the Browning, then came back with their own weapons drawn. They found Röhm standing before them, shirtless.

Accounts vary as to exactly what happened next. Some report that Eicke and Lippert said nothing and began firing. One account holds that Eicke shouted, "Röhm, make yourself ready," at which point Lippert fired two shots. Yet another account gives Röhm a moment of gallantry, during which he declared, "If I am to be killed, let Adolf do it himself."

The first salvo did not kill Röhm. He lay on the floor moaning, "Mein Führer, mein Führer." A final bullet was fired into his temple.

As a reward, Eicke received a promotion that placed him in charge of all Germany's concentration camps. He exported the draconian regulations he had put in place at Dachau to all the other camps under his command.

That Sunday a grateful Reichswehr made another payment on the deal struck aboard the *Deutschland*. Defense Minister Blomberg in his order of the day for that Sunday, July 1, announced, "The *Führer* with soldierly decision and exemplary courage has himself attacked and crushed the traitors and murderers. The army, as the bearer of arms of the entire people, far removed from the conflicts of domestic politics, will show its gratitude through devotion and loyalty. The good relationship towards the new SA demanded by the *Führer* will be gladly fostered by the Army in the consciousness that the ideals of both are held in common. The state of emergency has come to an end everywhere."

AS THE WEEKEND PROGRESSED, the Dodds learned that a new phrase was making the rounds in Berlin, to be deployed upon encountering a friend or acquaintance on the street, ideally with a sardonic lift of one eyebrow: "Lebst du noch?" Which meant, "Are you still among the living?"

CHAPTER 51

Sympathy's End

Though rumors continued to sketch a blood purge of startling dimension, Ambassador Dodd and his wife chose not to cancel the embassy's Fourth of July celebration, to which they had invited some three hundred guests. If anything, there was more reason now to hold the party, to provide a symbolic demonstration of American freedom and offer a respite from the terror outside. This was to be the first formal occasion since the weekend at which Americans and Germans would encounter each other face to face. The Dodds had invited a number of Martha's friends as well, including Mildred Fish Harnack and her husband, Arvid. Boris apparently did not attend. One guest, Bella Fromm, noted an "electric tension" that pervaded the party. "The diplomats seemed jittery," she wrote. "The Germans were on edge."

Dodd and his wife stood at the entrance to the ballroom to greet each new arrival. Martha saw that outwardly her father was behaving as he always did at such affairs, hiding his boredom with ironic quips and sallies, his expression that of an amused skeptic seemingly on the verge of laughter. Her mother wore a long blue and white dress and greeted guests in her usual quiet manner—all southern grace, with silver hair and a gentle accent—but Martha detected an unusual flush to her mother's cheeks and noted that the nearly black irises of her eyes, always striking, were especially so.

Tables throughout the ballroom and the garden were decorated with bouquets of red, white, and blue flowers and small American flags. An orchestra played American songs quietly. The weather was warm but cloudy. Guests wandered through the house and garden. All in all it was a peaceful and surreal scene, in powerful contrast to the bloodshed of the prior seventy-two hours. For Martha and her brother the juxtaposition was simply too glaring to go unacknowledged, so they made a point of greeting the younger German guests with the question "Lebst du noch?"

"We thought we were being sarcastic, revealing to the Germans some of the fury we felt," she wrote. "No doubt many of them thought the remark bad taste. Some Nazis showed extreme irritation."

Guests arrived bearing fresh news. Now and then a correspondent or embassy staffer pulled Dodd away for a few moments of conversation. One topic, surely, was a law enacted the day before by Hitler's cabinet that made all the murders legal; it justified them as actions taken in "emergency defense of the state." Guests arrived looking pale and shaken, fearing the worst for their friends throughout the city.

Fritz, the butler, brought Martha word that a visitor was waiting for her downstairs. "Der junge Herr von Papen," Fritz said. The young Mr. Papen—the vice-chancellor's son, Franz Jr. Martha was expecting him and had alerted her mother that if he appeared she might have to leave. She touched her mother's arm and left the reception line.

Franz was tall, blond, and slender, with a sharply sculpted face and, Martha recalled, "a certain fine beauty—like that of blonde fox." He was graceful as well. To dance with him, she wrote, "was like living in music itself."

Franz took her arm and briskly led her away from the house. They crossed the street to the Tiergarten, where they strolled awhile, watching for signs of being followed. Finding none, they walked to an outdoor café, took a table, and ordered drinks.

The terror of the last few days showed on Franz's face and in his manner. Anxiety muted his usual easygoing humor.

Though grateful for Ambassador Dodd's appearance outside his family's home, Franz understood that what had really saved his father was his relationship with President Hindenburg. Even that closeness, however, had not kept the SS from terrorizing Papen and his family, as Franz now revealed. On Saturday armed SS men had taken up positions within the family's apartment and at the street entrance. They told the vice-chancellor that two of his staff had been shot and indicated the same end awaited him. The order, they said, would arrive at any moment. The family spent a lonely, terrifying weekend.

Franz and Martha talked awhile longer, then he escorted her back through the park. She returned to the party alone.

LATE ONE AFTERNOON DURING that week, Mrs. Cerruti, wife of the Italian ambassador, happened to look out a window of her residence, which stood across the street from Röhm's house. At that moment, a large car pulled up. Two men got out and went into the house and emerged carrying armloads of Röhm's suits and other clothing. They made several trips.

The scene brought home to her the events of the past weekend in a particularly vivid manner. "The sight of these clothes, now deprived of their owner, was nauseating," she recalled in a memoir. "They were so obviously 'the garments of the hanged' that I had to turn away my head."

She suffered "a regular fit of nerves." She ran upstairs and vowed to take an immediate break from Berlin. She left the next day for Venice.

THE DODDS LEARNED THAT Wilhelm Regendanz, the wealthy banker who had hosted the fateful dinner for Captain Röhm and French ambassador François-Poncet at his Dahlem home, had managed to escape Berlin on the day of the purge and make his way safely to London. He feared now, however, that he could never return. Worse, his wife was still in Berlin and his adult son, Alex, who also had been present at the dinner, had been arrested by the Gestapo. On July 3 Regendanz wrote to Mrs. Dodd to ask if she would go to Dahlem to check on his wife and younger children and "to bring her my heartiest greetings." He wrote, "It seems that I am suspect now, because so many diplomats have been in my house and because I was also a friend of General von Schleicher."

Mrs. Dodd and Martha drove to Dahlem to see Mrs. Regendanz. A servant girl met them at the door, her eyes red. Soon Mrs. Regendanz herself appeared, looking dark and thin, her eyes deeply shadowed and her mannerisms halting and nervous. She knew Martha and Mattie and was perplexed to see them there in her home. She led them inside. After a few moments of conversation, the Dodds told Mrs. Regendanz about the message from her husband. She put her hands to her face and wept softly.

Mrs. Regendanz recounted how her house had been searched and her passport confiscated. "When she spoke of her son," Martha wrote, "her self-control collapsed and she became hysterical with fear." She had no idea where Alex was, whether he was alive or dead.

She pleaded with Martha and her mother to locate Alex and visit him, bring him cigarettes, anything to demonstrate to his captors that he had drawn the attention of the U.S. embassy. The Dodds promised to try. Mrs. Dodd and Mrs. Regendanz agreed that henceforth Mrs. Regendanz would use a code name, Carrie, in any contact with the Dodds or the embassy.

Over the next few days the Dodds spoke with influential friends, diplomats, and friendly government officials about the situation. Whether their intercession helped or not can't be known, but Alex was freed after about a month of incarceration. He left Germany immediately, by night train, and joined his father in London.

Through connections, Mrs. Regendanz managed to acquire another passport and to secure passage out of Germany by air. Once she and her children were also in London, she sent a postcard to Mrs. Dodd: "Arrived safe and sound. Deepest gratitude. Love. Carrie."

IN WASHINGTON, WESTERN EUROPEAN affairs chief Jay Pierrepont Moffat noted a surge of inquiries from American travelers asking whether it was still safe to visit Germany. "We have replied to them," he wrote, "that in all the trouble to date no foreigner has been molested and we see no cause for worry if they mind their own business and keep out of trouble's way."

His mother, for one, had survived the purge unscathed and professed to have found it "quite exciting," Moffat wrote in a later entry.

His sister's home was in the Tiergarten district, where it "was blocked off by soldiers and they had to make quite a detour to get in or out." Nonetheless, mother, daughter, and granddaughter set off by car, with chauffeur, for their previously planned tour of Germany.

What most occupied the attention of the State Department was the outstanding German debt to American creditors. It was a strange juxtaposition. In Germany, there was blood, viscera, and gunfire; at the State Department in Washington, there were white shirts, Hull's red pencils, and mounting frustration with Dodd for failing to press America's case. In a telegram from Berlin dated Friday, July 6, Dodd reported that he had met with Foreign Minister Neurath on the bond issue and that Neurath had said he would do what he could to ensure that interest was paid but that "this would be extremely difficult." When Dodd asked Neurath whether the United States could at least expect the same treatment as other international creditors, Neurath "merely expressed the hope that this might be possible."

The telegram infuriated Secretary Hull and the elders of the Pretty Good Club. "By his own showing," Moffat wrote in his diary, Dodd "put up very little fight and rather let von Neurath walk away with the situation. The Secretary knows that [Dodd] has scant sympathy with our financial interests but even so was pretty fed up with the Dodd telegram."

Hull angrily ordered Moffat to compose a harsh response to Dodd to compel him "not only to take but to create every opportunity to drive home the justice of our complaints."

The result was a cable transmitted at 4:00 p.m. on Saturday, July 7, under Secretary Hull's name that questioned whether Dodd had challenged Germany's failure to pay its bond debt "with the utmost vigor alike from the point of view of logic, equity, and its effect upon the estimated 60,000 mainly innocent holders in this country. . . ."

Moffat wrote, "It was a fairly stiff telegram, one sentence of which the Secretary with his intense kindly nature modified to salve Dodd's feelings." Moffat noted that "the irreverent ones" in the department had begun referring to Dodd as "Ambassador Dud."

During another meeting on the bond situation later that week, Hull continued to express his dissatisfaction with Dodd. Moffat wrote, "The Secretary kept repeating while Dodd was a very fine man in many ways, he certainly had a peculiar slant to his make-up."

That day Moffat attended a garden party at the home of a wealthy friend—the friend with the pool—who had invited as well "the entire State Department." There were exhibition tennis matches and swimming races. Moffat had to leave early, however, for a cruise down the Potomac on a power yacht "fitted out with a luxury that would satisfy the soul of any sybarite."

IN BERLIN, DODD WAS UNMOVED. He thought it pointless to pursue full payment, because Germany simply did not have the money, and there were far more important issues at stake. In a letter to Hull a few weeks later he wrote, "Our people will have to lose their bonds."

EARLY ON THE MORNING of Friday, July 6, Martha went to her father's bedroom to tell him good-bye. She knew he disapproved of her journey to Russia, but as they hugged and kissed he seemed at ease. He urged her to be careful but hoped she would have "an interesting trip."

Her mother and brother took her to Tempelhof Airport; Dodd remained in the city, aware, no doubt, that the Nazi press might try to capitalize on his presence at the airport, waving farewell as his daughter flew off to the hated Soviet Union.

Martha climbed a tall set of steel stairs to the three-engine Junker that would take her on the first leg of her journey. A photographer captured her looking jaunty at the top of the stairs, her hat at a rakish angle. She wore a plain jumper over a polka-dotted blouse and matching scarf. Improbably, given the heat, she carried a long coat draped over her arm and a pair of white gloves.

She claimed later that she had no idea her trip would be of interest to the press or that it would create something of a diplomatic scandal. This hardly seems credible, however. After a year in which she had come to know intimately such intriguers as Rudolf Diels and Putzi Hanfstaengl, she could not have failed to realize that in Hitler's

Germany even the smallest actions possessed exaggerated symbolic power.

On a personal level her departure marked the fact that the last traces of the sympathy she had felt for the strange and noble beings of the Nazi revolution had disappeared, and whether she recognized it or not, her departure, as captured by news photographers and duly registered by embassy officials and Gestapo watchers alike, was a public declaration of her final disillusionment.

She wrote, "I had had enough of blood and terror to last me for the rest of my life."

HER FATHER REACHED a similar moment of transformation. Throughout that first year in Germany, Dodd had been struck again and again by the strange indifference to atrocity that had settled over the nation, the willingness of the populace and of the moderate elements in the government to accept each new oppressive decree, each new act of violence, without protest. It was as if he had entered the dark forest of a fairy tale where all the rules of right and wrong were upended. He wrote to his friend Roper, "I could not have imagined the outbreak against the Jews when everybody was suffering, one way or another, from declining commerce. Nor could one have imagined that such a terroristic performance as that of June 30 would have been permitted in modern times."

Dodd continued to hope that the murders would so outrage the German public that the regime would fall, but as the days passed he saw no evidence of any such outpouring of anger. Even the army had stood by, despite the murder of two of its generals. President Hindenburg sent Hitler a telegram of praise. "From the reports placed before me, I learn that you, by your determined action and gallant personal intervention, have nipped treason in the bud. You have saved the German nation from serious danger. For this I express to you my most profound thanks and sincere appreciation." In another telegram Hindenburg thanked Göring for his "energetic and successful proceeding of the smashing of high treason."

Dodd learned that Göring personally had ordered over seventy-five executions. He was glad when Göring, like Röhm before him, sent his regrets at not being able to attend the dinner party the Dodds had planned for Friday evening, July 6. Dodd wrote, "It was a relief that he did not appear. I don't know what I would have done if he had."

FOR DODD, DIPLOMAT by accident, not demeanor, the whole thing was utterly appalling. He was a scholar and Jeffersonian democrat, a farmer who loved history and the old Germany in which he had studied as a young man. Now there was official murder on a terrifying scale. Dodd's friends and acquaintances, people who had been to his house for dinner and tea, had been shot dead. Nothing in Dodd's past had prepared him for this. It brought to the fore with more acuity than ever his doubts about whether he could achieve anything as ambassador. If he could not, what then was the point of remaining in Berlin, when his great love, his *Old South*, languished on his desk?

Something left him, a vital last element of hope. In his diary entry for July 8, one week after the purge began and just before the one-year anniversary of his arrival in Berlin, he wrote: "My task here is to work for peace and better relations. I do not see how anything can be done so long as Hitler, Göring and Goebbels are the directing heads of the country. Never have I heard or read of three more unfit men in high place. Ought I to resign?"

He vowed never to host Hitler, Göring, or Goebbels at the embassy or his home and resolved further "that I would never again attend an address of the Chancellor or seek an interview for myself except upon official grounds. I have a sense of horror when I look at the man."

CHAPTER 52

Only the Horses

But like seemingly everyone else in Berlin, Dodd wanted to hear what Hitler had to say about the purge. The government announced that Hitler would speak on the evening of Friday, July 13, in an address before the deputies of the Reichstag at their temporary hall, the nearby Kroll opera house. Dodd decided not to attend but to listen over the radio. The prospect of being there in person and listening to Hitler justify mass murder as hundreds of sycophants repeatedly thrust out their arms was too abhorrent.

That Friday afternoon, he and François-Poncet arranged to meet in the Tiergarten, as they had done in the past to avoid eavesdropping. Dodd wanted to find out whether François-Poncet planned to attend the speech but feared that if he visited the French embassy, Gestapo watchers would observe his arrival and conclude that he was conspiring to have the great powers boycott the speech, as indeed he was. Dodd had called on Sir Eric Phipps at the British embassy earlier in the week and learned that Phipps too planned to forgo the speech. Two such visits to major embassies in so short a time would surely draw attention.

The day was cool and sunny, and as a consequence the park was crowded with people, most on foot but quite a few on horseback, moving slowly through shadow. Now and then the air was punctuated by laughter and the barking of dogs and plumed with the ghosts of cigars fading slowly in the stillness. The two ambassadors walked for an hour.

As they prepared to part company, François-Poncet volunteered,

"I shall not attend the address." He then offered an observation that Dodd had never expected to hear from a modern diplomat in one of the great capitals of Europe. "I would not be surprised any time to be shot on the streets of Berlin," he said. "Because of this my wife remains in Paris. The Germans hate us so and their leadership is so crazy."

At eight o'clock that night, in the library at Tiergartenstrasse 27a, Dodd turned on his radio and listened as Hitler took the dais to address the Reichstag. A dozen deputies were absent, murdered in the purge.

The opera house was just a twenty-minute walk across the Tiergarten from where Dodd now sat listening. On his side of the park, all was peaceful and quiet, the evening fragrant with the scent of night flowers. Even over the radio Dodd could hear the frequent risings and *Heilings* of the audience.

"Deputies," Hitler said. "Men of the German Reichstag!"

Hitler detailed what he described as a plot by Captain Röhm to usurp the government, aided by a foreign diplomat whom he did not identify. In ordering the purge, he said, he had acted only in the best interests of Germany, to save the nation from turmoil.

"Only a ferocious and bloody repression could nip the revolt in the bud," he told his audience. He himself had led the attack in Munich, he said, while Göring, with his "steel fist," had done so in Berlin. "If someone asks me why we did not use the regular courts I would reply: at the moment I was responsible for the German nation; consequently, it was I alone who, during those twenty-four hours, was the Supreme Court of Justice of the German People."

Dodd heard the clamor as the audience leapt to its feet, cheering, saluting, and applauding.

Hitler resumed: "I ordered the leaders of the guilty shot. I also ordered the abscesses caused by our internal and external poisons cauterized until the living flesh was burned. I also ordered that any rebel attempting to resist arrest should be killed immediately. The nation must know that its existence cannot be menaced with impunity by anyone, and that whoever lifts his hand against the State shall die of it."

He cited the "foreign diplomat's" meeting with Röhm and other alleged plotters and the diplomat's subsequent declaration that the meeting was "entirely inoffensive." It was a clear allusion to the dinner François-Poncet had attended in May at the home of Wilhelm Regendanz.

"But," Hitler continued, "when three men capable of high treason organize a meeting in Germany with a foreign statesman, a meeting which they themselves characterize as a 'working' meeting, when they send the servants away, and give strict orders that I should not be informed of their meeting, I have those men shot, even if in the course of those secret conversations the only subjects discussed were the weather, old coins and similar objects."

Hitler acknowledged that the cost of his purge "has been high," and then lied to his audience by setting the death toll at seventy-seven. He sought to temper even this count by claiming that two of the victims killed themselves and—laughably, here—that the total included three SS men shot for "mistreating prisoners."

He closed, "I am ready before history to take the responsibility for the twenty-four hours of the bitterest decision of my life, during which fate has again taught me to cling with every thought to the dearest thing we possess—the German people and the German Reich."

The hall resounded with the thunder of applause and massed voices singing the "Horst Wessel Lied." Had Dodd been present, he would have seen two girls give Hitler bouquets of flowers, the girls dressed in the uniform of the Bund Deutscher Mädel, the female branch of the Hitler Youth, and would have seen Göring step briskly to the dais to take Hitler's hand, followed by a surge of officials bent on offering their own congratulations. Göring and Hitler stood close and held the pose for the scores of photographers pressing near. The *Times'* Fred Birchall witnessed it: "They stood face to face on the dais for almost a minute, hand grasping hand, looking into each other's eyes while the flashlights popped."

Dodd turned off his radio. On his side of the park the night was cool and serene. The next day, Saturday, July 14, he sent a coded telegram to Secretary Hull: "NOTHING MORE REPULSIVE THAN TO

WATCH THE COUNTRY OF GOETHE AND BEETHOVEN REVERT TO THE
BARBARISM OF STUART ENGLAND AND BOURBON FRANCE . . ."

Late that afternoon, he devoted two quiet hours to his *Old South*, losing himself in another, more chivalrous age.

PUTZI HANFSTAENGL, ASSURED of his safety by Foreign Minister Neurath, sailed for home. When he arrived at his office he was struck by the somber, dazed aspect of those around him. They behaved, he wrote, "as if they were chloroformed."

HITLER'S PURGE WOULD BECOME KNOWN as "The Night of the Long Knives" and in time would be considered one of the most important episodes in his ascent, the first act in the great tragedy of appeasement. Initially, however, its significance was lost. No government recalled its ambassador or filed a protest; the populace did not rise in revulsion.

The most satisfying reaction from a public official in America came from General Hugh Johnson, administrator of the National Recovery Administration, who by now had become notorious for intemperate speeches on a variety of subjects. (When a general strike had taken place in San Francisco in July led by a longshoreman who had emigrated from Australia, Johnson had called for deportation of all immigrants.) "A few days ago, in Germany, events occurred which shocked the world," Johnson said in public remarks. "I don't know how they affected you, but they made me sick—not figuratively, but physically and very actively sick. The idea that adult, responsible men can be taken from their homes, stood up against a wall, backs to the rifles and shot to death is beyond expression."

The German foreign office protested. Secretary Hull replied that Johnson "was speaking as an individual and not for the State Department or for the Administration."

This lack of reaction arose partly because many in Germany and elsewhere in the world chose to believe Hitler's claim that he had suppressed an imminent rebellion that would have caused far more bloodshed. Evidence soon emerged, however, that showed that in fact Hitler's account was false. Dodd at first seemed inclined to believe a plot really had existed but quickly grew skeptical. One fact seemed most clearly to refute the official line: when the SA's Berlin chief, Karl Ernst, was arrested, he was about to set off on a honeymoon cruise, not exactly the behavior of a man supposedly plotting a coup for that same weekend. Whether Hitler at first believed his own story is unclear. Certainly Göring, Goebbels, and Himmler had done all they could to make him believe it. Britain's Sir Eric Phipps initially accepted the official story; it took him six weeks to realize that no plot had existed. When Phipps met Hitler face-to-face several months later, his thoughts harked back to the purge. "It has not increased his charm or attractiveness," Phipps wrote in his diary. "Whilst I spoke he eyed me hungrily like a tiger. I derived the distinct impression that had my nationality and status been different I should have formed part of his evening meal."

In this appraisal he came closest to grasping the true message of the Röhm purge, which continued to elude the world. The killings demonstrated in what should have been unignorable terms how far Hitler was willing to go to preserve power, yet outsiders chose to misinterpret the violence as merely an internal settling of scores—"a type of gangland bloodbath redolent of Al Capone's St. Valentine's Day massacre," as historian Ian Kershaw put it. "They still thought that in the business of diplomacy they could deal with Hitler as a responsible statesman. The next years would provide a bitter lesson that the Hitler conducting foreign affairs was the same one who had behaved with such savage and cynical brutality at home on 30 June 1934." Rudolf Diels, in his memoir, acknowledged that at first he also missed the point. "I . . . had no idea that this hour of lightning was announcing a thunderstorm, the violence of which would tear down the rotten dams of the European systems and would put the entire world into flames—because this was indeed the meaning of June 30, 1934."

The controlled press, not surprisingly, praised Hitler for his decisive behavior, and among the public his popularity soared. So weary had Germans become of the Storm Troopers' intrusions in their lives that the purge seemed like a godsend. An intelligence report from the exiled Social Democrats found that many Germans were "extolling Hitler for his ruthless determination" and that many in the working class "have also become enslaved to the uncritical deification of Hitler."

Dodd continued to hope for some catalyst to cause the end of the regime and believed the imminent death of Hindenburg—whom Dodd called modern Germany's "single distinguished soul"—might provide it, but again he was to be disappointed. On August 2, three weeks after Hitler's speech, Hindenburg died at his country estate. Hitler moved quickly. Before the day was out he assumed the duties of president as well as chancellor, thereby at last achieving absolute power over Germany. Contending with false humility that the title "president" could only be associated with Hindenburg, who had borne it so long, Hitler proclaimed that henceforth his own official title would be "Führer and Reich Chancellor."

In a confidential letter to Secretary Hull, Dodd forecast "an even more terroristic regime than we have endured since June 30."

Germany accepted the change without protest, to the dismay of Victor Klemperer, the Jewish philologist. He too had hoped the blood purge would at last cause the army to step in and remove Hitler. Nothing happened. And now, this new outrage. "The people hardly notice this complete coup d'etat," he wrote in his diary. "It all takes place in silence, drowned out by hymns to the dead Hindenburg. I would swear that millions upon millions have no idea what a monstrous thing has occurred."

The Munich newspaper *Münchner Neueste Nachrichten* gushed, "Today Hitler is the Whole of Germany," apparently choosing to ignore the fact that just a month earlier its own gentle music critic had been shot dead by mistake.

THE RAINS CAME that weekend, a three-day downpour that drenched the city. With the SA quiescent, its brown uniforms prudently if temporarily closeted, and the nation mourning Hindenburg's death, a rare sense of peace spread over Germany, allowing Dodd a few moments to muse on a subject freighted with irony but dear to that part of him that remained a farmer from Virginia.

In his diary entry for Sunday, August 5, 1934, Dodd remarked upon a trait of the German people that he had observed in his Leipzig days and that had persisted even under Hitler: a love of animals, in particular horses and dogs.

"At a time when nearly every German is afraid to speak a word to any but the closest friends, horses and dogs are so happy that one feels they wish to talk," he wrote. "A woman who may report on a neighbor for disloyalty and jeopardize his life, even cause his death, takes her big kindly-looking dog in the Tiergarten for a walk. She talks to him and coddles him as she sits on a bench and he attends to the requirements of nature."

In Germany, Dodd had noticed, no one ever abused a dog, and as a consequence dogs were never fearful around men and were always plump and obviously well tended. "Only horses seem to be equally happy, never the children or the youth," he wrote. "I often stop as I walk to my office and have a word with a pair of beautiful horses waiting while their wagon is being unloaded. They are so clean and fat and happy that one feels that they are on the point of speaking." He called it "horse happiness" and had noticed the same phenomenon in Nuremberg and Dresden. In part, he knew, this happiness was fostered by German law, which forbade cruelty to animals and punished violators with prison, and here Dodd found deepest irony. "At a time when hundreds of men have been put to death without trial or any sort of evidence of guilt, and when the population literally trembles with fear, animals have rights guaranteed them which men and women cannot think of expecting."

He added, "One might easily wish he were a horse!"

CHAPTER 53

Juliet #2

Boris was right. Martha had packed her itinerary too full and as a consequence found her journey anything but uplifting. Her travels made her cranky and critical, of Boris and of Russia, which struck her as a drab and weary land. Boris was disappointed. "I am very sad to hear that you do not like everything in Russia," he wrote to her on July 11, 1934. "You ought to review it with completely different eyes than America. You should not settle with a superficial glance (such as bad clothes and bad food). Please, dear Miss, look 'inside,' a bit deeper."

What most annoyed Martha, unfairly, was that Boris did not join her on her travels, even though soon after her departure he too had gone to Russia, first to Moscow, and then to a resort in the Caucasus for a vacation. In an August 5 letter from the resort, Boris reminded her, "You are the one who said we do not have to meet each other in Russia." He acknowledged, however, that other obstacles also had intruded, though he was vague as to their precise nature. "I could not spend my vacation together with you. It was not possible for various reasons. The most important reason: I had to stay in Moscow. My stay in Moscow was not very happy, my destiny is unresolved."

He professed to be hurt by her letters. "You should not write such angry letters to me. I did not deserve it. I was already very sad in Moscow after some of your letters, since I felt that you were so far away and unreachable. But after your angry letter I am more than sad. Why did you do that, Martha? What happened? Can you not be 2 months without me?"

Just as she had wielded other lovers to hurt her ex-husband, Bassett, so she hinted to Boris that she might renew her affair with Armand Berard of the French embassy. "Immediately threatening with Armand?" Boris wrote. "I cannot dictate or suggest anything to you. But don't make any stupidities. Stay calm and don't destroy all the good things we both have together."

At some point during her journey, Martha was approached by emissaries of the Soviet NKVD seeking to recruit her as a source of covert information. It is likely that Boris was ordered to stay away from her so as not to interfere with the process, although he also played a role in her recruitment, according to Soviet intelligence records uncovered and made available to scholars by a leading expert on KGB history (and a former KGB agent), Alexander Vassiliev. Boris's superiors felt he was not energetic enough in formalizing Martha's role. They transferred him back to Moscow and then to an embassy post in Bucharest, which he loathed.

Martha, meanwhile, returned to Berlin. She loved Boris, but the two remained separated; she dated other men, including Armand Berard. In autumn 1936, Boris was transferred again, this time to Warsaw. The NKVD assigned another agent, one Comrade Bukhartsev, to take over the effort to recruit Martha. A progress report in NKVD files states: "The entire Dodd family hates National Socialists. Martha has interesting connections that she uses in getting information for her father. She has intimate relations with some of her acquaintances."

Despite their continued separation and emotional battles and Martha's periodic brandishing of Armand and other lovers, her affair with Boris progressed to the point where on March 14, 1937, during a second visit to Moscow, she formally petitioned Stalin for permission to marry. Whether Stalin ever saw or responded to the request isn't known, but the NKVD was ambivalent about their romance. Although Boris's masters professed to have no objection to the marriage, they at times also seemed intent on stripping Boris from the picture in order to allow better focus on Martha. At one point the agency commanded that they stay apart for six months, "in the interests of business."

Boris, as it happened, was more reluctant than Martha ever knew. In a peeved memorandum to his superiors in Moscow dated March 21, 1937, Boris complained, "I don't quite understand why you have focused so much on our wedding. I asked you to point out to her that it is impossible in general and, anyway, won't happen in the next several years. You spoke more optimistically on this issue and ordered a delay of only 6 months or a year." But what would happen then? he asked. "Six months will pass quickly, and who knows? She may produce a bill that neither you nor I is going to pay. Isn't it better to soften slightly the explicitness of your promises if you really gave them to her?"

In the same memorandum he refers to Martha as "Juliet #2," a reference that KGB expert Vassiliev and Allen Weinstein, in their book *The Haunted Wood*, see as indicating that there might have been another woman in his life, a "Juliet #1."

Martha and Boris had a tryst in Warsaw in November 1937, after which Boris sent a report to Moscow. The meeting "went off well," he wrote. "She was in a good mood." She was still intent on marriage and "waits for the fulfillment of our promise despite her parents' warning that nothing would come of it."

But once again Boris revealed a decided lack of interest in actually marrying her. He cautioned: "I think that she shouldn't be left in ignorance with regard to the real situation, for if we deceive her, she may become embittered and lose faith in us."

CHAPTER 54

A Dream of Love

In the months that followed Hitler's final ascent, Dodd's sense of futility deepened, as did a collateral longing to be back on his farm in the soft rise of the Appalachians, among his rich red apples and lazy cows. He wrote, "It is so humiliating to me to shake hands with known and confessed murderers." He became one of the few voices in U.S. government to warn of the true ambitions of Hitler and the dangers of America's isolationist stance. He told Secretary Hull in a letter dated August 30, 1934, "With Germany united as it has never before been, there is feverish arming and drilling of 1,500,000 men, all of whom are taught every day to believe that continental Europe must be subordinated to them." He added, "I think we must abandon our so-called isolation." He wrote to the army chief of staff, Douglas MacArthur, "In my judgment, the German authorities are preparing for a great continental struggle. There is ample evidence. It is only a question of time."

Roosevelt largely shared his view, but most of America seemed more intent than ever on staying out of Europe's squabbles. Dodd marveled at this. He wrote to Roosevelt in April 1935, "If Woodrow Wilson's bones do not turn in the Cathedral grave, then bones never turn in graves. Possibly you can do something, but from reports of Congressional attitudes, I have grave doubts. So many men . . . think absolute isolation a coming paradise."

Dodd resigned himself to what he called "the delicate work of watching and carefully doing nothing."

His sense of moral revulsion caused him to withdraw from active engagement with Hitler's Third Reich. The regime, in turn, recognized that he had become an intractable opponent and sought to isolate him from diplomatic discourse.

Dodd's attitude appalled Phillips, who wrote in his diary, "What in the world is the use of having an ambassador who refuses to speak to the government to which he is accredited?"

GERMANY CONTINUED ITS MARCH toward war and intensified its persecution of Jews, passing a collection of laws under which Jews ceased to be citizens no matter how long their families had lived in Germany or how bravely they had fought for Germany in the Great War. Now on his walks through the Tiergarten Dodd saw that some benches had been painted yellow to indicate they were for Jews. The rest, the most desirable, were reserved for Aryans.

Dodd watched, utterly helpless, as German troops occupied the Rhineland on March 7, 1936, without resistance. He saw Berlin transformed for the Olympics as the Nazis polished the city and removed their anti-Jewish banners, only to intensify their persecution once the foreign crowds were gone. He saw Hitler's stature within Germany grow to that of a god. Women cried as he passed near; souvenir hunters dug up parcels of earth from the ground on which he stepped. At the September 1936 party rally in Nuremberg, which Dodd did not attend, Hitler launched his audience into near hysteria. "That you have found me . . . among so many millions is the miracle of our time!" he cried. "And that I have found you, that is Germany's fortune!"

On September 19, 1936, in a letter marked "Personal and Confidential," Dodd wrote to Secretary Hull of his frustration at watching events unfold with no one daring to intercede. "With armies increasing in size and efficiency every day; with thousands of airplanes ready on a moment's notice to drop bombs and spread poison gas over great cities; and with all other countries, little and great, arming as never before, one can not feel safe anywhere," he wrote. "What mistakes and blunders since 1917, and especially during the past twelve months—and no democratic peoples do anything, economic or moral penalties, to halt the process!"

The idea of resigning gained appeal for Dodd. He wrote to Martha,

"You must not mention to anyone, but I do not see how I can continue in this atmosphere longer than next spring. I can not render my country any service and the stress is too great to be always doing nothing."

Meanwhile, his opponents within the State Department stepped up their campaign to have him removed. His longtime antagonist Sumner Welles took over as undersecretary of state, replacing William Phillips, who in August 1936 became ambassador to Italy. Closer to hand a new antagonist emerged, William C. Bullitt, another of Roosevelt's handpicked men (a Yale grad, however), who moved from his post as ambassador to Russia to lead the U.S. embassy in Paris. In a letter to Roosevelt on December 7, 1936, Bullitt wrote, "Dodd has many admirable and likeable qualities, but he is almost ideally ill equipped for his present job. He hates the Nazis too much to be able to do anything with them or get anything out of them. We need in Berlin someone who can at least be civil to the Nazis and speaks German perfectly."

Dodd's steadfast refusal to attend the Nazi Party rallies continued to rankle his enemies. "Personally, I cannot see why he is so sensitive," Moffat wrote in his diary. Alluding to Dodd's Columbus Day speech in October 1933, Moffat asked, "Why is it worse for him to listen to the Germans inveigh against our form of Government when he chose, at the Chamber of Commerce, to inveigh to a German audience against an autocratic form of government?"

A pattern of leaks persisted, building public pressure for Dodd's removal. In December 1936 columnist Drew Pearson, primary author with Robert S. Allen of a United Features Syndicate column called "Washington Merry-Go-Round," published a harsh assault on Dodd, "attacking me violently as a complete failure here and pretending that the President is of the same opinion," Dodd wrote on December 13. "This is news to me."

Pearson's attack deeply wounded Dodd. He had spent the better part of four years seeking to fulfill Roosevelt's mandate to serve as a model of American values and believed he had done as well as any man could have been expected to do, given the strange, irrational, and brutal nature of Hitler's government. He feared that if he re-

IN THE GARDEN OF BEASTS

signed now, under such a black cloud, he would leave the impression that he had been forced to do so. "My position is difficult, but under such criticism I cannot resign, as I planned, next spring," he wrote in his diary. "To give up my work here under these circumstances would put me in a defensive and positively false position at home." His resignation, he acknowledged, "would at once be recognized as a confession of failure."

He decided to postpone his departure, even though he knew that the time had come to step down. In the meantime he requested another leave in America, to get some rest on his farm and meet with Roosevelt. On July 24, 1937, Dodd and his wife made the long drive to Hamburg, where Dodd boarded the *City of Baltimore* and at 7:00 p.m. began the slow sail down the Elbe to the sea.

LEAVING DODD ABOARD SHIP broke his wife's heart. The next evening, Sunday, she wrote him a letter so that he would receive it upon his arrival. "I thought of you, my dear, all the way back to Berlin and felt very sad and lonely, especially to see you go away feeling so bad and so miserable."

She urged him to relax and try to quell the persistent "nervous headaches" that had plagued him for the last couple of months. "Please, please, for our sakes, if not your own, take better care of yourself and live less strenuously and exacting." If he kept well, she told him, he would still have time to achieve the things he wanted to achieve—and presumably here she meant the completion of his *Old South*.

She worried that all this sorrow and stress, these four years in Berlin, had been partly her fault. "Perhaps I have been too ambitious for you, but it does not mean that I love you any the less," she wrote. "I can't help it—my ambitions for you. It is innate."

But all that was done with, she told him now. "Decide what is best and what you want most, and I shall be content."

Her letter turned grim. She described the drive back to Berlin that night. "We made good time although we passed and met many army trucks—those awful instruments of death and destruction within. I still feel a shudder run through me when I see them and the many other signs of coming catastrophe. Is there no *possible* way to stop men and nations from destroying each other? Horrible!"

This was four and a half years before America's entry into the Second World War.

DODD NEEDED THE RESPITE. His health had indeed begun to trouble him. Ever since arriving in Berlin he had experienced stomach troubles and headaches, but lately these had grown more intense. His headaches sometimes persisted for weeks on end. The pain, he wrote, "spread over the nerve connections between the stomach, shoulders and brain until sleep is almost impossible." His symptoms had worsened to the point where on one of his previous leaves he had consulted a specialist, Dr. Thomas R. Brown, chief of the Division of Digestive Diseases at Johns Hopkins Hospital in Baltimore (who, at a 1934 gastroenterological symposium, noted with dead sobriety that "we must not forget it is essential to study the stool from every angle"). Upon learning that Dodd was at work on an epic history of the South and that completing it was the great goal of his life, Dr. Brown gently recommended that he quit his post in Berlin. He told Dodd, "At sixty-five one must take stock and decide what are the essentials, and lay one's plans to complete the major work, if possible."

By the summer of 1937, Dodd was reporting near continuous headaches and bouts of digestive trouble that in one case caused him to go without food for thirty hours.

Something more serious than the stress of work may have lain at the root of his health troubles, though certainly stress was a contributing factor. George Messersmith, who eventually moved from Vienna to Washington to become an assistant secretary of state, wrote in an unpublished memoir that he believed Dodd had undergone an organic intellectual decline. Dodd's letters rambled and his handwriting degraded to the point where others in the department passed them to Messersmith for "deciphering." Dodd's use of longhand increased as his distrust of his stenographers grew. "It was quite obvious that something had happened to Dodd," Messersmith wrote. "He was suffering from some form of mental deterioration."

The cause of all this, Messersmith believed, was Dodd's inability to adjust to the behavior of Hitler's regime. The violence, the obsessive march toward war, the ruthless treatment of Jews—all of it had made Dodd "tremendously depressed," Messersmith wrote. Dodd could not grasp how these things could be occurring in the Germany he had known and loved as a young scholar in Leipzig.

Messersmith wrote: "I think he was so thoroughly appalled by everything that was happening in Germany and the dangers which it had for the world that he was no longer capable of reasoned thought and judgment."

AFTER A WEEK on his farm, Dodd felt much better. He went to Washington and on Wednesday, August 11, met with Roosevelt. During their hourlong conversation, Roosevelt said he'd like him to stay in Berlin a few months longer. He urged Dodd to do as many lectures as he could while in America and "speak the truth about things," a command that affirmed for Dodd that he still had the president's confidence.

But while Dodd was in America the Pretty Good Club engineered a singular affront. One of the embassy's newest men, Prentiss Gilbert, standing in as acting ambassador—the chargé d'affaires—was advised by the State Department to attend the upcoming Nazi Party rally in Nuremberg. Gilbert did so. He rode in a special train for diplomats whose arrival in Nuremberg was greeted by seventeen military aircraft flying in swastika formation.

Dodd sensed the hand of Undersecretary Sumner Welles. "I have long believed Welles was opposed to me and everything I recommended," Dodd wrote in his diary. One of Dodd's few allies in the State Department, R. Walton Moore, an assistant secretary of state, shared Dodd's distaste for Welles and confirmed his fears: "I have not the slightest doubt that you are correct in locating the influence that has been determining very largely the action of the Department since last May."

Dodd was angry. Staying clear of these congresses was one of the few ways he believed he could signal his, and America's, true feelings about the Hitler regime. He sent a pointed and—he thought—

confidential protest to Secretary Hull. To Dodd's great dismay, even this letter was leaked to the press. On the morning of September 4, 1937, he saw an article on the subject in the *New York Herald Tribune*, which excerpted an entire paragraph from the letter, along with a subsequent telegram.

Dodd's letter incensed Hitler's government. The new German ambassador to America, Hans-Heinrich Dieckhoff, told Secretary of State Hull that while he was not making a formal request for Dodd's removal, he "desired to make it plain that the German Government did not feel that he was *persona grata*."

ON OCTOBER 19, 1937, Dodd had a second meeting with Roosevelt, this at the president's home in Hyde Park—"a marvelous place," Dodd wrote. His son Bill accompanied him. "The President revealed his anxiety about foreign affairs," Dodd wrote in his diary. They discussed the Chinese-Japanese conflict, then in full flare, and the prospects of a major peace conference soon to take place in Brussels aimed at bringing it to an end. "One thing troubled him," Dodd wrote: "Could the United States, England, France and Russia actually co-operate?"

The conversation shifted to Berlin. Dodd asked Roosevelt to keep him in place at least until March 1, 1938, "partly because I did not wish to have the German extremists think their complaints . . . had operated too effectively." He was under the impression that Roosevelt agreed.

Dodd urged the president to choose a fellow history professor, James T. Shotwell of Columbia University, as his replacement. Roosevelt seemed willing to consider the idea. As the conversation came to an end, Roosevelt invited Dodd and Bill to stay for lunch. Roosevelt's mother and other members of the Delano clan joined them. Dodd called it "a delightful occasion."

As he prepared to leave, Roosevelt told him, "Write me personally about things in Europe. I can read your handwriting very well."

In his diary Dodd added: "I promised to write him such confidential letters, but how shall I get them to him unread by spies?"

Dodd sailed for Berlin. His diary entry for Friday, October 29, the day of his arrival, was brief but telling: "In Berlin once more. What can I do?"

He was unaware that in fact Roosevelt had bowed to pressure from both the State Department and the German foreign office and had agreed that Dodd should leave Berlin before the end of the year. Dodd was stunned when on the morning of November 23, 1937, he received a curt telegram from Hull, marked "Strictly Confidential," that stated, "Much as the President regrets any personal inconvenience which may be occasioned to you, he desires me to request that you arrange to leave Berlin if possible by December 15 and in any event not later than Christmas, because of the complications with which you are familiar and which threaten to increase."

Dodd protested, but Hull and Roosevelt stood fast. Dodd booked passage for himself and his wife on the SS *Washington*, to depart on December 29, 1937.

MARTHA SAILED TWO WEEKS earlier, but first she and Boris met in Berlin to say good-bye. To do so, she wrote, he left his post in Warsaw without permission. It was a romantic and heartbreaking interlude, at least for her. She again declared her desire to marry him.

This was their final meeting. Boris wrote to her on April 29, 1938, from Russia. "Until now I have lived with the memory of our last get-together in Berlin. What a pity that it was only 2 nights long. I want to stretch this time to the rest of our lives. You were so nice and kind to me darling. I will never forget that. . . . How was the trip across the ocean? One time we will cross this ocean together and together we will watch the eternal waves and feel our eternal love. I love you. I feel you and dream of you and us. Don't forget me. Yours, Boris."

Back in America, true to her nature if not to Boris, Martha met and promptly fell in love with a new man, Alfred Stern, a New Yorker of left-leaning sensibility. He was a decade older, five foot ten, handsome, and rich, having received a lush settlement upon his earlier divorce from an heiress of the Sears Roebuck empire. They became engaged and in breathtakingly short order they married, on June 16, 1938, though news reports show there was a second ceremony, later, on the farm in Round Hill, Virginia. She wore a black velvet dress with red roses. She would write years later that Stern was the third and last great love of her life.

She told Boris of her marriage in a letter dated July 9, 1938. "You know, honey, that for me, you meant more in my life than anybody else. You also know that, if I am needed, I will be ready to come when called." She added, "I look into the future and see you in Russia again."

By the time her letter arrived in Russia, Boris was dead, executed, one of countless NKVD operatives who fell victim to Stalin's paranoia. Martha learned later that Boris had been accused of collaborating with the Nazis. She dismissed the charge as "insane." She wondered long afterward if her relationship with him, especially that final, unauthorized meeting in Berlin, had played a role in sealing his fate.

She never learned that Boris's last letter, in which he claimed to dream of her, was a fake, written by Boris at the direction of the NKVD shortly before his execution, in order to keep his death from destroying her sympathy for the Soviet cause.

CHAPTER 55

As Darkness Fell

A week before his voyage home, Dodd gave a farewell speech at a luncheon of the American Chamber of Commerce in Berlin, where just over four years earlier he had first kindled Nazi ire with his allusions to ancient dictatorships. The world, he said, "must face the sad fact that in an age when international cooperation should be the keyword, nations are farther apart than ever." He told his audience that the lessons of the Great War had gone unlearned. He praised the German people as "basically democratic and kindly toward each other." And he said, "I doubt whether any Ambassador in Europe properly performs his duties or earns his pay."

He struck a different tone once he arrived in America. On January 13, 1938, at a dinner given in his honor at the Waldorf-Astoria in New York, Dodd declared, "Mankind is in grave danger, but democratic governments seem not to know what to do. If they do nothing, Western civilization, religious, personal and economic freedom are in grave danger." His remarks prompted an immediate protest from Germany, to which Secretary Hull replied that Dodd was now a private citizen and could say what he wished. First, however, there was some debate among State Department officials as to whether the department should also apologize with a statement along the lines of "We always regret anything that might give resentment abroad." This idea was rejected, opposed by none other than Jay Pierrepont Moffat, who wrote in his diary, "I personally felt quite strongly that, much as I disliked and disapproved of Mr. Dodd, he should not be apologized for."

With that speech, Dodd embarked on a campaign to raise the alarm about Hitler and his plans, and to combat the increasing drift in America toward isolationism; later he would be dubbed the Cassandra of American diplomats. He founded the American Council Against Nazi Propaganda and became a member of the American Friends of Spanish Democracy. At a speech in Rochester, New York, on February 21, 1938, before a Jewish congregation, Dodd warned that once Hitler attained control of Austria—an event that appeared imminent—Germany would continue seeking to expand its authority elsewhere, and that Romania, Poland, and Czechoslovakia were at risk. He predicted, moreover, that Hitler would be free to pursue his ambitions without armed resistance from other European democracies, as they would choose concessions over war. "Great Britain," he said, "is terribly exasperated but also terribly desirous of peace."

THE FAMILY DISPERSED, Bill to a teaching job and Martha to Chicago and then New York. Dodd and Mattie retired to the farm at Round Hill, Virginia, but made occasional forays into Washington. On February 26, 1938, just after seeing Dodd off at the train station in Washington for the start of a journey full of lectures, Mattie wrote to Martha in Chicago, "I do wish we were all nearer together so that we could discuss things and spend some time with each other. Our lives are slipping by so fast. Father often speaks of your being with us and what a joy it would be to have you with him and Billy nearby. I do wish he were younger and more vigorous. He is very delicate & his nervous energy depleted."

She was deeply concerned about events in Europe. In another letter to Martha soon afterward she wrote, "The world seems in such a mess now, I don't know what will happen. Too bad that maniac was allowed to go his way so long uncurbed. We may be, sooner or later, involved, God forbid."

Mrs. Dodd did not share her husband's deep love of the Round Hill farm. It was fine for summers and vacations, but not as a full-time residence. She hoped they could secure an apartment in Washington where she could live for a portion of each year, with or without him. In the meantime, she set out to make the farm more habitable. She bought curtains in gold silk, a new General Electric refrigerator, and a new stove. As spring advanced, she grew increasingly unhappy about the lack of progress both in finding the Washington pied-à-terre and in fixing up the farmhouse. She wrote to Martha, "So far I can't get anything done that I want in the house but about 8 or 10 men [are] working on stone fences, beautifying his fields, picking up rocks, hauling, etc. It makes me feel like 'throwing up the sponge' and quitting the whole d— business."

On May 23, 1938, in another letter to her daughter, she wrote, "Wish I did have a home—Washington instead of Chicago. It would be lovely."

Four days later, Mrs. Dodd was dead. On the morning of May 28, 1938, she failed to join Dodd for breakfast, as was her custom. They kept separate bedrooms. He went to check on her. "It was the greatest shock that ever came to me," he wrote. She died of heart failure in her bed, with no advance warning of trouble. "She was only sixty-two years old, and I was sixty-eight," Dodd wrote in his diary. "But there she lay, stone dead, and there was no help for it; and I was so surprised and sad I could hardly decide what to do."

Martha attributed her mother's death to "the strain and terror of life" in Berlin. On the day of the funeral Martha pinned roses to her mother's burial dress and wore matching roses in her own hair. Now, for only the second time, Martha saw tears in her father's eyes.

Suddenly the farm at Round Hill was not so much a place of rest and peace as one of melancholy. Dodd's sorrow and loneliness took a toll on his already fragile health, but still he pressed on and gave lectures around the country, in Texas, Kansas, Wisconsin, Illinois, Maryland, and Ohio, always reprising the same themes—that Hitler and Nazism posed a great risk to the world, that a European war was inevitable, and that once war began the United States would find it impossible to remain aloof. One lecture drew an audience of seven thousand people. In a June 10, 1938, speech in Boston, at the Harvard Club—that den of privilege—Dodd talked of Hitler's hatred of Jews and warned that his true intent was "to kill them all."

Five months later, on November 9 and 10, came Kristallnacht, the

Nazi pogrom that convulsed Germany and at last drove Roosevelt to issue a public condemnation. He told reporters he "could scarcely believe that such a thing could occur in twentieth century civilization."

On November 30, Sigrid Schultz wrote to Dodd from Berlin. "My hunch is that you have lots of chances to say or think 'didn't I say so beforehand?' Not that it is such a great consolation to have been right when the world seems divided between ruthless Vandals and decent people unable to cope with them. We were witnesses when much of the wrecking and looting occurred and yet there are times when you wonder whether what you actually saw was really true— there is a nightmarish quality around the place, even surpassing the oppressiveness of June 30."

A STRANGE EPISODE SIDETRACKED DODD. On December 5, 1938, as he was driving to a speaking engagement in McKinney, Virginia, his car struck a four-year-old black girl named Gloria Grimes. The impact caused significant injury, including an apparent concussion. Dodd did not stop. "It was not my fault," he later explained to a reporter. "The youngster ran into the path of my automobile about thirty feet ahead. I put on the brakes, turned the car and drove on because I thought the child had escaped." He made things worse by seeming to be insensitive when, in a letter to the girl's mother, he added, "Besides, I did not want the newspapers all over the country to publish a story about the accident. You know how newspapers love to exaggerate things of this sort."

He was indicted, but on the day his trial was to begin, March 2, 1939, he changed his plea to guilty. His friend, Judge Moore, sat beside him, as did Martha. The court fined him $250 but did not sentence him to jail, citing his poor health and the fact he had paid $1,100 in medical costs for the child, who by now was, reportedly, nearly recovered. He lost his driving privileges and his right to vote, an especially poignant loss for so ardent a believer in democracy.

Shattered by the accident, disillusioned by his experience as ambassador, and worn down by declining health, Dodd retreated to his farm. His health worsened. He was diagnosed as suffering from a neurological syndrome called bulbar palsy, a slow, progressive paralysis of the muscles of the throat. In July 1939 he was admitted to Mount Sinai Hospital in New York City for minor abdominal surgery, but before the operation took place he contracted bronchial pneumonia, a frequent complication of bulbar palsy. He became gravely ill. As he lay near death, he was taunted from afar by the Nazis.

A front-page article in Goebbels's newspaper *Der Angriff* said Dodd was in a "Jewish clinic." The headline stated: "End of notorious anti-German agitator Dodd."

The writer spat a puerile brand of malice typical of *Der Angriff*. "The 70-year-old man who was one of the strangest diplomats who ever existed is now back among those whom he served for 20 years— the activist war-mongering Jews." The article called Dodd a "small, dry, nervous, pedantic man . . . whose appearance at diplomatic and social functions inevitably called forth yawning boredom."

It took note of Dodd's campaign to warn of Hitler's ambitions. "After returning to the United States, Dodd expressed himself in the most irresponsible and shameless fashion over the German Reich, whose officials had for four years, with almost superhuman generosity, overlooked his and his family's scandalous affairs, faux pas and political indiscretions."

Dodd emerged from the hospital and retired to his farm, where he continued to nurture the hope that he would have time to finish the remaining volumes of his *Old South*. The governor of Virginia restored his right to vote, explaining that at the time of the accident Dodd was "ill and not entirely responsible."

In September 1939, Hitler's armies invaded Poland and sparked war in Europe. On September 18, Dodd wrote to Roosevelt that it could have been avoided if "the democracies in Europe" had simply acted together to stop Hitler, as he always had urged. "If they had co-operated," Dodd wrote, "they would have succeeded. Now it is too late."

By fall, Dodd was confined to bed, able to communicate only with a pad and pencil. He endured this condition for several more months, until early February 1940, when he suffered another round of pneumonia. He died in his bed at his farm on February 9, 1940, at 3:10 p.m., with Martha and Bill Jr. at his side, his life work—his *Old South*—anything but finished. He was buried two days later on the farm, with Carl Sandburg serving as an honorary pallbearer.

Five years later, during the final assault on Berlin, a Russian shell scored a direct hit on a stable at the western end of the Tiergarten. The adjacent Kurfürstendamm, once one of Berlin's prime shopping and entertainment streets, now became a stage for the utterly macabre—horses, those happiest creatures of Nazi Germany, tearing wildly down the street with manes and tails aflame.

HOW DODD'S COUNTRYMEN JUDGED his career as ambassador seemed to depend in large part on which side of the Atlantic they happened to be standing.

To the isolationists, he was needlessly provocative; to his opponents in the State Department, he was a maverick who complained too much and failed to uphold the standards of the Pretty Good Club. Roosevelt, in a letter to Bill Jr., was maddeningly noncommittal. "Knowing his passion for historical truth and his rare ability to illuminate the meanings of history," Roosevelt wrote, "his passing is a real loss to the nation."

To those who knew Dodd in Berlin and who witnessed firsthand the oppression and terror of Hitler's government, he would always be a hero. Sigrid Schultz called Dodd "the best ambassador we had in Germany" and revered his willingness to stand up for American ideals even against the opposition of his own government. She wrote: "Washington failed to give him the support due an ambassador in Nazi Germany, partly because too many of the men in the State Department were passionately fond of the Germans and because too many of the more influential businessmen of our country believed that one 'could do business with Hitler.'" Rabbi Wise wrote in his memoir, *Challenging Years*, "Dodd was years ahead of the State Department in his grasp of the political as well as of the moral implications of Hitlerism and paid the penalty of such understanding by being virtually removed from office for having the decency and the courage alone among ambassadors to decline to attend the annual Nuremberg celebration, which was a glorification of Hitler."

Late in life even Messersmith applauded Dodd's clarity of vision. "I often think that there were very few men who realized what was happening in Germany more thoroughly than he did, and certainly there were very few men who realized the implications for the rest of Europe and for us and for the whole world of what was happening in the country more than he did."

The highest praise came from Thomas Wolfe, who during a visit to Germany in the spring of 1935 engaged in a brief affair with Martha. He wrote to his editor, Maxwell Perkins, that Ambassador Dodd had helped conjure in him "a renewed pride and faith in America and a belief that somehow our great future still remains." The Dodds' house at Tiergartenstrasse 27a, he told Perkins, "has been a free and fearless harbor for people of all opinions, and people who live and walk in terror have been able to draw their breath there without fear, and to speak their minds. This I know to be true, and further, the dry, plain, homely unconcern with which the Ambassador observes all the pomp and glitter and decorations and the tramp of marching men would do your heart good to see."

Dodd's successor was Hugh Wilson, a diplomat of the old-fashioned mode that Dodd long had railed against. It was Wilson, in fact, who had first described the foreign service as "a pretty good club." Wilson's maxim, coined by Talleyrand before him, was not exactly stirring: "Above all, not too much zeal." As ambassador, Wilson sought to emphasize the positive aspects of Nazi Germany and carried on a one-man campaign of appeasement. He promised Germany's new foreign minister, Joachim von Ribbentrop, that if war began in Europe he would do all he could to keep America out. Wilson accused the American press of being "Jewish controlled" and of singing a "hymn of hate while efforts are made over here to build a better future." He praised Hitler as "the man who has pulled his people from moral and economic despair into the state of pride and evident prosperity they now enjoyed." He particularly admired the Nazi "Strength through Joy" program, which provided all German workers with no-expense vacations and other entertainments. Wilson saw it as a powerful tool for helping Germany resist communist inroads and suppressing work-ers' demands for higher wages—money that workers would squander on "idiotic things as a rule." He saw this approach as one that "is going to be beneficial to the world at large."

William Bullitt, in a letter from Paris dated December 7, 1937, praised Roosevelt for choosing Wilson, stating, "I do think that the chances for peace in Europe are increased definitely by your appoint-ment of Hugh to Berlin, and I thank you profoundly."

In the end, of course, neither Dodd's nor Wilson's approach mat-tered very much. As Hitler consolidated his power and cowed his public, only some extreme gesture of American disapproval could have had any effect, perhaps the "forcible intervention" suggested by George Messersmith in September 1933. Such an act, however, would have been politically unthinkable with America succumbing more and more to the fantasy that it could avoid involvement in the squabbles of Europe. "But history," wrote Dodd's friend Claude Bowers, ambassador to Spain and later Chile, "will record that in a period when the forces of tyranny were mobilizing for the extermina-tion of liberty and democracy everywhere, when a mistaken policy of 'appeasement' was stocking the arsenals of despotism, and when in many high social, and some political, circles, fascism was a fad and democracy anathema, he stood foursquare for our democratic way of life, fought the good fight and kept the faith, and when death touched him his flag was flying still."

And indeed one has to wonder: For Goebbels's *Der Angriff* to at-tack Dodd as he lay prostrate in a hospital bed, was he really so in-effectual as his enemies believed? In the end, Dodd proved to be exactly what Roosevelt had wanted, a lone beacon of American freedom and hope in a land of gathering darkness.

The Queer Bird in Exile

The Tiergarten after the Russian offensive,
with the Reichstag building in the background

Martha and Alfred Stern lived in an apartment on Central Park West in New York City and owned an estate in Ridgefield, Connecticut. In 1939 she published a memoir entitled *Through Embassy Eyes*. Germany promptly banned the book, no surprise given some of Martha's observations about the regime's top leaders—for example: "If there were any logic or objectivity in Nazi sterilization laws Dr. Goebbels would have been sterilized quite some time ago." In 1941 she and Bill Jr. published their father's diary. The two also hoped to publish a book-length collection of letters to and from Dodd and asked George Messersmith to let them use several that he had posted to Dodd from Vienna. Messersmith refused. When Martha told him she would publish them anyway, Messersmith, never a fan of hers, got tough. "I told her that if she published my letters, either through an irresponsible or responsible publisher, that I would write a little article about what I knew about her and about certain episodes in her life and that my article would be much more interesting than anything that would be in her book." He added, "That ended the matter."

These were compelling years. The war Dodd had forecast was waged and won. In 1945, at long last, Martha achieved a goal she long had dreamed of: she published a novel. Entitled *Sowing the Wind* and clearly based on the life of one of her past lovers, Ernst Udet, the book described how Nazism seduced and degraded a good-hearted World War I flying ace. That same year, she and her husband adopted a baby and named him Robert.

Martha at last created her own successful salon, which from time to time drew the likes of Paul Robeson, Lillian Hellman, Margaret Bourke-White, and Isamu Noguchi. The talk was bright and good and evoked for Martha those lovely afternoons in the home of her friend Mildred Fish Harnack—although now the recollection of Mildred was bordered in black. Martha had received news about her old friend that suddenly made their last meeting in Berlin seem laced with portent. She recalled how they had chosen a remote table at an out-of-the-way restaurant and how pridefully Mildred had described the "growing effectiveness" of the underground network she and her husband, Arvid, had established. Mildred was not a physically demonstrative woman, but at the close of this lunch she gave Martha a kiss.

By now, however, Martha knew that a few years after that meeting Mildred had been arrested by the Gestapo, along with Arvid and dozens of others in their network. Arvid was tried and condemned to death by hanging; he was executed at Berlin's Plötzensee Prison on December 22, 1942. The executioner used a short rope to ensure slow strangulation. Mildred was forced to watch. At her own trial she was sentenced to six years in prison. Hitler himself ordered a retrial. This time the sentence was death. On February 16, 1943, at 6:00 p.m., she was executed by guillotine. Her last words: "And I have loved Germany so."

FOR A TIME AFTER leaving Berlin, Martha continued her covert flirtation with Soviet intelligence. Her code name was "Liza," though this suggests more drama than surviving records support. Her career as a spy seems to have consisted mainly of talk and possibility, though the prospect of a less vaporous participation certainly intrigued Soviet intelligence officials. A secret cable from Moscow to New York in January 1942 called Martha "a gifted, clever and educated woman" but noted that "she requires constant control over her behavior." One rather more prudish Soviet operative was unimpressed. "She considers herself a Communist and claims to accept the party's program. In reality 'Liza' is a typical representative of

American bohemia, a sexually decayed woman ready to sleep with any handsome man."

Through Martha's efforts, her husband also aligned himself with the KGB—his code name was "Louis." Martha and Stern were very public about their mutual interest in communism and leftist causes, and in 1953 they drew the attention of the House Committee on Un-American Activities, chaired then by Representative Martin Dies, which issued subpoenas to have them testify. They fled to Mexico, but as pressure from federal authorities increased, they moved again, settling ultimately in Prague, where they lived a very noncommunistic lifestyle in a three-story, twelve-room villa attended by servants. They bought a new black Mercedes.

At first, the idea of being an international fugitive appealed to Martha's persistent sense of herself as a woman of danger, but as the years passed, a weariness overtook her. During the couple's first years of exile, their son began exhibiting signs of severe psychic unrest and was diagnosed as schizophrenic. Martha became "obsessed"—her husband's term—with the idea that the commotion of their flight and subsequent travels had caused Robert's illness.

Martha and Stern found Prague an alien place with an unfathomable language. "We can't say we like it here, to be perfectly honest," she wrote to a friend. "Naturally we would prefer to go home but home won't take us yet. . . . It is a life of considerable limitations intellectually and creatively (also we don't speak the language; a great handicap) and we feel isolated and often very lonely." She spent her time housekeeping and gardening: "fruit trees, lilacs, vegetables, flowers, birds, insects . . . only one snake in four years!"

Martha learned during this time that one of her ex-loves, Rudolf Diels, had died, and in a fashion wholly unexpected for a man so adept at survival. After two years in Cologne, he had become regional commissioner in Hannover, only to be fired for exhibiting too much moral scruple. He took a job as director of inland shipping for a civilian company but was later arrested in the vast roundup that followed the July 20, 1944, assassination attempt against Hitler. Diels survived the war and during the Nuremberg trials testified on behalf of the prosecution. Later, he became a senior official in the government of West Germany. His luck ran out on November 18, 1957, during a hunting trip. As he was removing a rifle from his car, the weapon discharged and killed him.

MARTHA GREW DISILLUSIONED with communism as practiced in everyday life. Her disenchantment became outright disgust during the "Prague Spring" of 1968, when she awoke one day to find tanks rumbling past on the street outside her house during the Soviet invasion of Czechoslovakia. "It was," she wrote, "one of the ugliest and most repugnant sights we had ever seen."

She renewed old friendships by mail. She and Max Delbrück launched a spirited correspondence. She addressed him as "Max, my love"; he called her "my dearly beloved Martha." They bantered about their increasing physical imperfections. "I am fine, fine, just fine," he told her, "except for a little heart disease, and a little multiple myeloma." He swore the chemotherapy had caused his hair to grow back.

Other men fared less well in Martha's retroactive appraisal. Prince Louis Ferdinand had become "that ass," and Putzi Hanfstaengl "a real buffoon."

But one great love now appeared to burn just as bright as ever. Martha began writing to Bassett, her former husband—the first of her three great loves—and soon they were corresponding as if they were back in their twenties, parsing their past romance to try to figure out what had gone wrong. Bassett confessed he had destroyed all the love letters she had ever sent him, having realized "that, even with the passage of time, I could never bear to read them, much less would I want anyone else to share them after I've gone."

Martha, however, had kept his. "Such love letters!" she wrote.

"One thing is sure," she told him in a November 1971 letter, when she was sixty-three years old. "Had we stayed together, we would have had a vital, varied and passionate life together. . . . I wonder if you would have remained happy with a woman as unconventional as I am and was, even though we would not have had the complications that came to me later. Still I have had joy with sorrow, productiveness with beauty and shock! I have loved you and Alfred and one other, and still do. So that is the queer bird, still lively, that you once loved and married."

In 1979 a federal court cleared her and Stern of all charges, albeit grudgingly, citing lack of evidence and the deaths of witnesses. They longed to return to America, and considered doing so, but realized another obstacle remained in their path. For all those years in exile they had not paid U.S. taxes. The accumulated debt was now prohibitively high.

They considered moving elsewhere—perhaps England or Switzerland—but another obstacle arose, the most stubborn of all: old age.

By now the years and illness had taken a serious toll on the world of Martha's recollection. Bill Jr. had died in October 1952 of cancer, leaving a wife and two sons. He had spent his years after Berlin moving from job to job, ending as a clerk in the book department of Macy's in San Francisco. Along the way, his own left-leaning sympathies had caused him to run afoul of the Dies Committee, which had declared him "unfit" for employment by any federal agency, this at a time when he was working for the Federal Communications Commission. His death had left Martha the sole survivor of the family. "Bill was a very swell guy, a warm and fine person, who had his share of frustration and suffering—maybe more than his share," Martha wrote in a letter to Bill's first wife, Audrey. "I miss him so terribly and feel empty and alone without him."

Quentin Reynolds died on March 17, 1965, at the not-very-old age of sixty-two. Putzi Hanfstaengl, whose sheer size had seemed to make him invulnerable, died on November 6, 1975, in Munich. He was eighty-eight. Sigrid Schultz, the Dragon from Chicago, died on May 14, 1980, at eighty-seven. And Max Delbrück, presumably with a full head of hair, passed away in March 1981, his exuberance quenched at last. He was seventy-four.

This great withering was very sad and raised powerful questions. In March 1984, when Martha was seventy-five years old and Stern eighty-six, Martha asked a friend, "Where do you think we should die if we could choose? Here or abroad? Would it be easier if the survivor was left here with painful memories? or to get the hell out and go alone to a new place; or is it better to go together and then be bereft and saddened by unrealized dreams and no or few friends in a new environment but still having had a few years to establish some sort of home abroad?"

Martha was the survivor. Stern died in 1986. Martha remained in Prague even though, as she wrote to friends, "Nowhere could be as lonely for me as it is here."

She died in 1990 at the age of eighty-two, not precisely a hero but certainly a woman of principle who never wavered in her belief that she had done the right thing in helping the Soviets against the Nazis at a time when most of the world was disinclined to do anything. She died still dancing on the rim of danger—a queer bird in exile, promising, flirting, remembering—unable after Berlin to settle into her role as hausfrau and needing instead to see herself once again as something grand and bright.

Bassett, old loyal Bassett, outlasted her by another six years. He had forsaken the magnificent copper beech of Larchmont for an apartment on Manhattan's Upper East Side, where he died peacefully at age 102.

CODA

"Table Talk"

Years after the war, a cache of documents came to light that proved to be transcripts of conversations between Hitler and his men, recorded by his deputy Martin Bormann. One of these transcripts concerned a conversation over dinner in October 1941 at Wolfsschanze, or Wolf's Lair, Hitler's redoubt in East Prussia. The subject of Martha Dodd came up.

Hitler, who once had kissed her hand, said, "To think that there was nobody in all this ministry who could get his clutches on the daughter of the former American ambassador, Dodd—and yet she wasn't difficult to approach. That was their job, and it should have been done. In short, the girl should have been subjugated. . . . In the old days when we wanted to lay siege to an industrialist, we attacked him through his children. Old Dodd, who was an imbecile, we'd have got him through his daughter."

One of Hitler's dinner companions asked, "Was she pretty at least?"

Another guest snorted, "Hideous."

"But one must rise above that, my dear fellow," Hitler said. "It's one of the qualifications. Otherwise, I ask you, why should our diplomats be paid? In that case, diplomacy would no longer be a service, but a pleasure. And it might end in marriage!"

SOURCES AND ACKNOWLEDGMENTS

The country club where Dodd's farm stood

What I did not realize as I ventured into those dark days of Hitler's rule was how much the darkness would infiltrate my own soul. I generally pride myself on possessing a journalist's remove, the ability to mourn tragedy and at the same time appreciate its narrative power, but living among Nazis day in, day out proved for me a uniquely trying experience. For a time I kept on my desk a copy of Ian Kershaw's *Hitler, 1889–1936: Hubris*, a work of grand scope that served as my field guide to the politics of the era. On the cover is a photograph of Hitler that became for me so repulsive—apologies to Sir Ian—that I had to keep the book on my desk facedown, as it were, for to start each day with a look at those hate-filled eyes and slack cheeks and that fragment of Brillo that passed for a mustache was far too dispiriting.

There exists a vast oeuvre of historical writing on Hitler and World War II that must be read no matter how small the episode one plans to study. All this reading deepened my spiritual malaise, not because of the sheer volume involved but because of the horrors revealed. It is difficult to fathom the breadth and depth of the landscape of war created by Hitler—the deportations of Jews to extermination camps even after the inevitability of Germany's defeat became obvious to all; the tank battles against Russian forces that took tens of thousands of lives in a matter of days; the reprisal killings for which the Nazis became infamous, where on some sunny afternoon in a village in France a dozen men and women would be whisked from their homes and shops, stood before a wall, and shot. No preamble, no good-byes; just birdsong and blood.

Certain books, Kershaw's *Hubris* foremost among them, proved exceptionally helpful in detailing the broad play of forces and men in the years that preceded World War II. I include here a couple of old but still worthy classics, Alan Bullock's *Hitler: A Study in Tyranny* and William Shirer's *The Rise and Fall of the Third Reich*, as well as the more recent works of Kershaw's doppelgänger in scholarship, Richard J. Evans, whose *The Third Reich in Power: 1933–1939* and *The Third Reich at War: 1939–1945* are massive volumes lush with compelling, if appalling, detail.

A number of books that focused more closely on my particular parcel of ground proved very useful, among them *Resisting Hitler: Mildred Harnack and the Red Orchestra*, by Shareen Blair Brysac; *The Haunted Wood*, by KGB historians Allen Weinstein and Alexander Vassiliev; and *Spies: The Rise and Fall of the KGB in America*, by Vassiliev, John Earl Haynes, and Harvey Klehr.

Of particular, and obvious, value were *Ambassador Dodd's Diary*, edited by Martha and Bill Jr., and Martha's memoir, *Through Embassy Eyes*. Neither work is wholly trustworthy; both must be treated with care and used only in conjunction with other, corroborative sources. Martha's memoir is necessarily her own rendering of the people and events she encountered and as such is indispensable as a window into her thoughts and feelings, but it contains interesting omissions. Nowhere, for example, does she refer by name to Mildred Fish Harnack or to Boris Winogradov, presumably because to have done so in a work published in 1939 would have placed both of them at grave risk. However, documents among Martha's papers in the Library of Congress reveal by triangulation the points in her memoir where both Harnack and Winogradov make appearances. Her papers include her detailed and never-published accounts of her relationships with Boris and Mildred and correspondence from both. Boris wrote his letters in German, salted with English phrases and the occasional "Darling!" For translations of these, I turned to a fellow Seattle resident, Britta Hirsch, who also gamely translated lengthy portions of far more tedious documents, among them an old bill of sale for the house on Tiergartenstrasse and portions of Rudolf Diels's memoir, *Lucifer Ante Portas*.

As for Ambassador Dodd's diary, questions persist as to whether it is truly a diary as conventionally understood or rather a compendium of his writings pieced together in diary form by Martha and Bill. Martha always insisted the diary was real. Robert Dallek, biographer of presidents, wrestled with the question in his 1968 biography of Dodd, titled *Democrat and Diplomat*, and had the benefit of having received a letter from Martha herself in which she described its genesis. "It is absolutely authentic," she told Dallek. "Dodd had a couple of dozen of black shiny medium size notebooks in which he wrote every night he could possibly do so, in his Berlin study before going to bed, and at other times as well." These, she explained, formed the core of the diary, though she and her brother included elements of speeches, letters, and reports that they found appended to the pages within. The initial draft, Martha wrote, was a diary 1,200 pages long, pared down by a professional editor hired by the publisher. Dallek believed the diary to be "generally accurate."

All I can add to the discussion are some little discoveries of my own. In my research at the Library of Congress, I found one leather-bound diary full of entries for the year 1932. At the very least, this testifies to Dodd's inclination to keep such a record. It resides in Box 58. In Dodd's other papers, I found oblique references to a more comprehensive and confidential diary. The most telling such reference appears in a letter dated March 10, 1938, from Mrs. Dodd to Martha, written shortly before the then-retired ambassador made a trip to New York. Mrs. Dodd tells Martha, "He is taking some of his diary for you to look over. Send them back by him as he will need them. Be careful what you quote."

Finally, after having read Martha's memoir, her Udet novel, and her papers, and after reading thousands of pages of Ambassador Dodd's correspondence, telegrams, and reports, I can offer one of those intangible observations that comes only after long exposure to a given body of material, and that is that Dodd's published diary *sounds* like Dodd, *feels* authentic, and expresses sentiments that are in perfect accord with his letters to Roosevelt, Hull, and others.

The National Archives branch in College Park, Maryland—known as National Archives II—proved to have an amazing collection of materials, twenty-seven boxes' worth, relating to the Berlin embassy and consulate, including a count of all the dinnerware in each, down to the number of finger bowls. The Library of Congress, home to the papers of William and Martha Dodd, Cordell Hull, and Wilbur J. Carr, proved as always to be heaven's gift to research. At the University of Delaware in Newark, I examined the papers of George Messersmith, one of the most beautifully archived collections I've ever come across, and had the pleasure while there of staying at the home of great friends Karen Kral and John Sherman and drinking far too much. At Harvard—which rejected my application to its undergraduate college some years ago, surely an oversight, and one that I have forgiven, mostly—I spent several delightful days scouring the papers of William Phillips and Jay Pierrepont Moffat, both Harvard men. The folks at Yale University's Beinecke Rare Book and Manuscript Library were kind enough to raid their collection of Thornton Wilder's papers and provide me with copies of letters sent to him by Martha Dodd. Other archives proved useful as well, especially the oral-history collections at both Columbia University and the New York Public Library.

I tend to distrust online resources but located several that proved extremely helpful, including a digitized collection of letters between Roosevelt and Dodd, courtesy of the Franklin Delano Roosevelt Presidential Library in Hyde Park, New York, and the notebooks of Alexander Vassiliev, the ex-KGB agent turned scholar, who graciously made them accessible to the public through the Web site of the Cold War International History Project at the Woodrow Wilson Center for Scholars in Washington, D.C. Anyone who wishes can also digitally thumb through the so-called Venona Intercepts, communications between Moscow Center and KGB agents in America intercepted and decoded by American intelligence officials, including missives involving Martha Dodd and Alfred Stern. Once one of America's most closely guarded secrets, these materials now reside on the public Web site of the National Security Agency and reveal not only that America was rife with spies but that spying tended to be an excruciatingly mundane pursuit.

One challenge I faced in researching this book was how to gain a sense of the Tiergarten district of prewar Berlin, where Dodd and

Martha spent so much of their time and which was in large part obliterated by Allied bombers and the final Russian assault on the city. I acquired a prewar Baedeker guide, which proved invaluable in helping me locate important landmarks, such as the Romanisches Café at Kurfürstendamm 238 and the Hotel Adlon at Unter den Linden 1. I read as many memoirs of the era as I could, mining them for insights into daily life in Berlin while keeping in mind that memoirs of the Nazi era tend to contain a good deal of self-engineering to make the author seem less complicit in the rise and rule of the Nazi Party than perhaps he or she truly was. The most glaring example of this must surely be Franz von Papen's *Memoirs*, published in 1953, in which he claims that he prepared his Marburg speech "with great care," a contention no one takes seriously. It was as big a surprise to him as it was to his audience.

The memoirlike novels of Christopher Isherwood, namely *The Last of Mr. Norris* and *Goodbye to Berlin*, proved especially useful for their observations about the look and feel of the city in the years immediately preceding Hitler's rise, when Isherwood was himself a resident of Berlin. I took great delight in now and then visiting YouTube.com to search for old film footage of Berlin and found quite a bit, including the 1927 silent film *Berlin: Symphony of a Great City*, which sought to capture one full day of Berlin life. I was especially pleased to find a 1935 propaganda film, *Miracle of Flight*, intended to attract young men to the Luftwaffe, in which Martha's onetime lover Ernst Udet stars as himself and even shows off his Berlin apartment, which looks very much the way Martha described it in her memoir.

I found the State Historical Society of Wisconsin to be a trove of relevant materials that conveyed a sense of the woof and weave of life in Hitler's Berlin. There, in one locale, I found the papers of Sigrid Schultz, Hans V. Kaltenborn, and Louis Lochner. A short and lovely walk away, in the library of the University of Wisconsin, I found as well a supply of materials on the only UW alumna to be guillotined at Hitler's command, Mildred Fish Harnack.

Most important, however, was my experience of Berlin itself. Enough of the city remains to provide a sense of the overall layout of things. Oddly enough the buildings of Göring's Air Ministry survived the war largely intact, as did those of army headquarters, the Bendler Block. What I found most striking was how close everything was to the Dodds' home, with every major government office an easy walk away, including Gestapo headquarters and Hitler's chancellery, neither of which exists today. Where the Dodds' home at Tiergartenstrasse 27a once stood there is now a vacant, overgrown lot surrounded by a chain-link fence. The Bendler Block is visible in the background.

I owe special thanks to Gianna Sommi Panofsky and her husband, Hans, son of Alfred Panofsky, the Dodds' landlord in Berlin. The couple settled in Evanston, Illinois; Hans taught at Northwestern University. Mrs. Panofsky graciously provided me with the original floor plans for the house on Tiergartenstrasse (which a Northwestern journalism graduate student, Ashley Keyser, carefully secured and copied on my behalf). Mrs. Panofsky was a delight to talk to. Sadly, she died in early 2010 of colon cancer.

Above all, I thank my loyal early readers Carrie Dolan and her husband, Ryan Russell; my daughters, Kristen, Lauren, and Erin; and, as always, my wife and secret weapon, Christine Gleason, whose margin notes—complete with crying faces and trailing lines of zzzzzzz's—once again proved indispensable. Thanks to my daughters also for their increasingly astute critiques of my manner of dress. I owe a huge debt to Betty Prashker, my editor of nearly two decades, and to John Glusman, whose deft hand guided this book to publication. Thanks also to Domenica Alioto for taking on tasks she should not have to take on, and Jacob Bronstein, who so ably straddles the boundary between Web and world. An extra huzzah to Penny Simon for her friendship and expertise at getting me to do things I don't want to do; to Tina Constable for her confidence; and to David Black, my longtime agent, wine adviser, and great friend. Finally, a long, long hug to Molly, our lovely, sweet dog, who succumbed to liver cancer at the age of ten as my work on this book neared its end. In her last weeks, however, she did manage to catch a rabbit, something she had sought unsuccessfully to do for years. We miss her every day.

✢ ✢ ✢

WHEN I WAS IN BERLIN a strange thing happened, one of those odd little moments of space-time congruity that always seem to occur when I'm most deeply immersed in researching a book. I stayed at the Ritz-Carlton near the Tiergarten, not because it was a Ritz but because it was a brand-new Ritz offering rooms at compellingly low come-hither rates. That the month was February helped also. On my first morning, too jet-lagged to do anything terribly ambitious, I set out for a walk and headed for the Tiergarten, with the vague idea that I'd walk until I found the Dodds' address, unless I froze to death first. It was an icy, blustery morning, marked by the occasional appearance of flecks of snow falling at oblique angles. As I walked, I came upon a particularly interesting bit of architectural preservation—a large portion of the facade of an old bullet-pocked building standing behind a giant wall of glass. A bridgelike deck spanned the top of this facade and supported several stories of modern luxury apartments. Out of random curiosity, I walked to an informational plaque that identified the facade. It belonged to the Hotel Esplanade, where the Dodds stayed when they first arrived in Berlin. Here as well, also behind glass, was an inside wall of the Esplanade's breakfast room restored to original condition. It was strange to see these architectural artifacts lodged behind glass, like giant, immobile fish, but also revelatory. For an instant I could *see* Dodd and Martha setting off to begin their days, Dodd heading north at a brisk clip to the Tiergarten for his walk to the embassy offices on Bendlerstrasse, Martha rushing south to meet Rudolf Diels at the old art school on Prinz-Albrecht-Strasse before a quiet lunch in some discreet locale.

The following notes are by no means exhaustive. I have been careful always to credit material quoted from other works and to annotate those facts and observations that for one reason or another cry out for attribution, such as Ian Kershaw's revelation—*Hubris*, page 485—that one of Hitler's favorite movies was *King Kong*. As always, for those readers who like reading footnotes—and there are many of you—I have included little stories and facts that did not fit the main narrative but that struck me as too interesting or compelling to omit. For this indulgence, forgive me.

NOTES

The Man Behind the Curtain

3 It was common: For details of the Schachno case, see "Conversation with Goering," unpublished memoir, 5–6; and Messersmith to Hull, July 11, 1933, and July 18, 1933, all in Messersmith Papers. See also cumulative report on assaults against Americans in Phillips to Roosevelt, Aug. 23, 1933, file no. 362.1113 /4 1 /2, State/Decimal.

3 "From the neck down": Messersmith, "Conversation with Goering," unpublished memoir, 6, Messersmith Papers.

4 "From the shoulder blades": Messersmith to Hull, July 11, 1933, Messersmith Papers.

4 "I wish it were": Messersmith to Phillips, June 26, 1933, Messersmith Papers.

5 Inauguration Day in 1933: The Twentieth Amendment, passed in 1933, moved the inauguration date from March 4 to the now familiar January 20, a measure to reduce the amount of time that an outgoing president would be a lame duck.

5 Incredibly, the new ambassador: For more detail than you'll ever need about the shipping of Dodd's car, see Howard Fyfe to Harry A. Havens, July 8, 1933; Herbert C. Hengstler to Dodd, July 10, 1933; and Paul T. Culbertson to Dodd, June 19, 1933, all in Box 40, W. E. Dodd Papers.

PART I: INTO THE WOOD

Chapter 1: Means of Escape

9 The telephone call: Dodd, *Diary*, 3.

9 Dodd also owned: "Farming Implements" and Survey, Box 59, W. E. Dodd Papers.

10 "The fruit is so beautiful": William E. Dodd to Martha Dodd, Oct. 15, 1926, Box 2, Martha Dodd Papers.

10 "sudden surprise": Dodd to Westmoreland Davis, June 22, 1933, Box 40, W. E. Dodd Papers.

10 he pleaded for heat: Dodd to Lester S. Ries, Oct. 31, 1932, Box 39,
W. E. Dodd Papers.
10 "embarrassing": Dodd to Charles E. Merriam, Aug. 27, 1932, Box 39, W. E.
Dodd Papers.
11 "hard men": Bailey, 6.
11 "Monk Dodd": Dallek, 6.
11 Other students indulged: Ibid., 9.
12 "How helpless": "Brief Note," 6, Box 58, W. E. Dodd Papers.
12 "There was too much": Ibid., 7.
12 at Randolph-Macon: Bailey, 35–36; Dallek, 31–32.
12 In October 1912: Dallek, 70; Dodd to Mrs. Dodd, March 26, 1930, Box 2,
Martha Dodd Papers.

In this letter to his wife, composed one fine night while on his farm, Dodd
wrote, "I am sitting by the dining room table in work-a-day clothes, the old-red
sweater and the easy-slippers—a great oak log on the fire and a bed of hot coals
three inches deep, all surrounded by white ashes. The old andirons ('firedogs' of
my boyhood parlance) lean their solid black heads back in contented contempla-
tion of their efficient service—the old red-brick fireplace as dignified as George
Washington and the eighteenth century, when men had time to be dignified."
13 Dodd also discovered: Bailey, 97–99; Dallek, 88–89.
14 More and more he considered: Dodd to William Dodd, Jr., Dec. 9, 1932,
Box 39, W. E. Dodd Papers.
14 "These are posts": Ibid.
14 "As to high diplomacy": Dodd to Mrs. Dodd, March 25, 1933, Box 40,
W. E. Dodd Papers.
15 Hull was tall and silver haired: Messersmith, "Cordell Hull and my
personal relationships with him," 7, unpublished memoir, Messersmith
Papers.

Messersmith writes, "When I heard this strong language from this saintly
looking man and who was in so many ways a saint, I almost fell through the
floor from surprise." See also Graebner, 193; Weil, 76–77, 87; and, of course,
Hull's own *Memoirs*.

One of Hull's memorable aphorisms, directed at Hitler and his allies as war
loomed, was this: "When you're in a pissin' contest with a skunk, make sure
you got plenty of piss." Weil, 77.
15 "After considerable study": Dodd, pocket diary, March 2, 1933, Box 58,
W. E. Dodd Papers.

Chapter 2: That Vacancy in Berlin

16 No one wanted the job: Noakes and Pridham, 180; Rürup, 84–86;
Wheaton, 428; Ladd, 123; Evans, *Power*, 11; Stackelberg and Winkle, 132;
Wise, *Servant*, 177.

17 "It is not only because": Roosevelt, *Personal Letters*, 337–38.

17 Cox said no.: Ibid., 338.

17 Roosevelt set the matter aside: Dallek, 187–89; Flynn, 148.

17 "You know, Jimmy": Warburg, 124.

18 "ROOSEVELT TRIMS PROGRAM": *New York Times*, June 8, 1933.

18 Thus, he now found himself: Dallek, 187.

18 On Wednesday, June 7: Ibid., 189.

19 Polls showed: Herzstein, 77.

19 Secretary Roper believed: Roper, 335.

20 "I want to know": Dodd, *Diary*, 3.

20 Roosevelt gave him two hours: Ibid., 3.

20 His wife, Mattie, understood: Mrs. Dodd to William Dodd Jr., April 19, 1933, Box 1, Martha Dodd Papers.

20 "There is no place": Dodd to Mrs. Dodd, March 25, 1933, Box 40, W. E. Dodd Papers.

21 Even had he been present: Messersmith, "Cordell Hull and My Personal Relationships," 17, unpublished memoir, Messersmith Papers.

Messersmith wrote, "As Secretary of State he should have had really the deciding voice in determining who occupied the principal as well as the secondary posts of chief of mission." Instead, Messersmith wrote, Hull abdicated and gave Roosevelt a free pass. "Some of us always felt that some of the more unfortunate appointments which were made during the time that Mr. Hull was Secretary could have been avoided if Mr. Hull had directly intervened in the matter."

21 "get out of bounds": Hull, *Memoirs*, 182.

21 "Telephone Book Dodd": Flynn, 148. See also Martha Dodd to Flynn, Oct. 17, 1947; *New York Times*, Nov. 2, 1947; and *New York Herald Tribune*, Nov. 9, 1947, all in Box 13, Martha Dodd Papers.

22 "My dear child": Dodd to Martha, Dec. 16, 1928, Box 2, Martha Dodd Papers.

Chapter 3: The Choice

23 "William is a fine teacher": Dodd to Mrs. Dodd, April 20, 1933, Box 2, Martha Dodd Papers.

23 "It would never do": Dodd to Mrs. Dodd and Martha Dodd, April 13, 1933, Box 2, Martha Dodd Papers.

23 Her very first word: "Baby Book," 1908–c. 1916, Box 1, Martha Dodd Papers.

23 In April 1930: *Chicago Daily Tribune*, April 25, 1930.

24 "I want nothing from life": W. L. River to Martha Dodd, c. 1927, Box 8, Martha Dodd Papers.

24 "kisses soft": James Burnham to Martha Dodd, n.d., Box 4, Martha Dodd Papers.

24 "His face is smooth-shaven.": *Cincinnati Times-Star*, n.d., but likely Jan. 13, 1932, Box 8, Martha Dodd Papers.

24 "It was pain and sweetness": Martha to Bassett, Feb. 19, 1976, Box 8, Martha Dodd Papers.

24 "What fun it was": Bassett to Martha, Sept. 19, 1931, Box 8, Martha Dodd Papers.

I love these letters in large part because they are so full of Jimmy Stewart–esque prose. In this letter Bassett deploys the greeting "Honeybuncha mia." His first line reads, "I had the swellest love letter from you this morning." And I, personally, had the swellest time reading all these letters. To quote Bassett again, "Yes, you bet, I have."

25 "Never before or since": Martha to Bassett, Nov. 1 ("more or less," she writes), 1971, Box 8, Martha Dodd Papers.

25 "Either you love me": Bassett to Martha, Feb. 21, 1932, Box 8, Martha Dodd Papers.

By this point, things are getting a little tense. Bassett begins this letter with a more sober "Martha dearest." The "honeybuncha-mia" days are gone.

Three days later (Bassett to Martha, Feb. 24, 1932) he tried again: "Surely you cannot feel bound to go on and marry some one you do not love, merely because of a mistaken promise, when we both know how deeply, irrevocably, we are bound to each other."

He began this letter with the greeting: "Dearest of women." For a return address, he wrote: "The Bank."

Honestly, we men can be so tone deaf.

25 "I desperately loved": Martha to Bassett, Feb. 19, 1976, Box 8, Martha Dodd Papers.

25 It was bad enough: Ibid.

25 "show some nervousness": Ibid.

25 She acknowledged later: Martha to Bassett, Nov. 1, 1976, Box 8, Martha Dodd Papers.

25 "That was IT for me": Ibid.

25 "flirting": Ibid.

26 "I love you past telling": Carl Sandburg to Martha, n.d., Box 63, W. E. Dodd Papers.

26 "I was busy": Martha to Bassett, Nov. 1, 1971, Box 8, Martha Dodd Papers. The greeting on this letter is "My dear Ex."

26 "Do you know really": Martha to Bassett, Feb. 19, 1976, Box 8, Martha Dodd Papers.

26 "I had to choose": Ibid.

Chapter 4: Dread

27 Roosevelt, smiling and cheerful: Dodd, *Diary*, 4–5.

28 "But our people are entitled": Ibid., 5.

28 For Roosevelt, this was treacherous ground: Breitman and Kraut, 18, 92; Wise, *Servant*, 180; Chernow, 388; Urofsky, 271.

28 Even America's Jews: Urofsky, 256; Wise, *Challenging Years*, 238–39; Wise, *Servant*, 226.

29 "If he refuse [sic] to see me": Wise, *Personal Letters*, 221.

29 On the other side: Chernow, 372–73; Leo Wormser to Dodd, Oct. 30, 1933, Box 43, W. E. Dodd Papers.

29 As Ron Chernow wrote: Chernow, 373.

29 In early June 1933: Quoted in Breitman and Kraut, 227.

30 a *Fortune* poll: Ibid., 230.

30 Within the Roosevelt administration: Ibid., 12–15.

30 "my little Jewish friend": Phillips, Diary, April 20, 1935.

30 "The place is infested with Jews": Phillips, Diary, Aug. 10, 1936; Breitman and Kraut, 36–37.

Breitman and Kraut are rather direct in their description of Phillips. They write on page 36: "Phillips hated Jews."

30 "kikes": Gellman, 37.

30 "They are filthy Un-American": Breitman and Kraut, 32.

30 "dust, smoke, dirt, Jews": Gellman, 37.

30 "In all our day's journey": Carr, Diary, Feb. 22, 1934, Carr Papers.

31 "How different from the Jewish atmosphere": Ibid., Feb. 23, 1934.

31 "an anti-Semite and a trickster": Breitman and Kraut, 36.

31 "likely to become a public charge": Wilbur Carr offers a detailed, bloodless discussion of the "LPC clause" and other immigration rules in his memorandum "The Problem of Aliens Seeking Relief from Persecution in Germany," dated April 20, 1933, Carr Papers.

31 "It seems quite preposterous": Wolff, 89.

31 Jewish activists charged: Breitman and Kraut, 15.

31 "an almost insuperable obstacle": Proskauer to Phillips, July 18, 1933, vol. 17, p. 35, *Archives of the Holocaust*.

31 "The consul," Phillips replied: Phillips to Proskauer, Aug. 5, 1933, vol. 17, p. 40, *Archives of the Holocaust*.

The exchange of letters between Phillips and Proskauer, pages 32–46, makes compelling reading, for both what is said and what is not said. On the one side, deploying statistics and dispassionate prose, is Phillips, who, as we have seen, disliked Jews. On the other was Proskauer, a judge, whose careful prose seems clearly to be masking a scream of anguish.

31 One result, according to Proskauer: Dippel, 114; Proskauer to Phillips, July 18, 1933, vol. 17, p. 36, *Archives of the Holocaust*.

Proskauer tells Phillips, "The well-known fact that only a negligible number of U.S. quota visas have been issued in recent years, and are believed to be likely to be issued, other than to relatives of U.S. citizens, has prevented applications being made by German Jews, believed in advance to be futile. . . ."

32 It was an argument: Breitman and Kraut, 14.

32 "The German authorities": Dodd, *Diary*, 5.

32 Dodd insisted: Ibid.

32 "You are quite right": Ibid.

33 Here at the State Department: Dallek, 191; Stiller, 33, 36–37; Kershaw, *Hubris*, 473–74.

33 "Forty-Page George": Stiller, 5.

Jay Pierrepont Moffat, Western European affairs chief, left the following entry in his diary for Oct. 6 and 7, 1934: "Saturday afternoon being cold and rainy, I was sitting home reading through Messersmith's four last personal letters (that does not sound like an afternoon's job but it took nearly two hours). . . ."

34 "has probably ever existed": Messersmith to Hull, May 12, 1933, Messersmith Papers.

34 "Responsibility has already changed": Ibid., 15. See also Messersmith to Hull, June 19, 1933, Messersmith Papers.

In his June 19 dispatch, Messersmith wrote, "The primary leaders have under the sobering influence of responsibility become steadily more moderate in practically all of their views and have in many ways endeavored to translate this moderation into action."

34 "I have tried to point out": Messersmith to Phillips, June 26, 1933, Messersmith Papers.

35 "Pleasing, interesting person": Diary, June 15, 1933, Carr Papers.

35 distaste for Jews: Weil, 41.

35 "He is extremely sure of his opinion": Moffat, Diary, June 15, 1933.

35 Undersecretary Phillips grew up: Phillips, "Reminiscences," 3, 50, 65, 66, 99; Phillips, *Ventures*, 4, 5, 183.

In "Reminiscences," the transcription of an oral history interview, Phillips (on pages 2–3) stated, "The Boston that I grew up in was limited to friends who lived on the Hill and in the Back Bay district. The community was self-centered—we lived surrounded by cousins, uncles and aunts and there was no incentive to discuss national or world affairs. . . . I must say it was a very pleasant place in which to grow up, but it was a very easy and indulgent life. We saw no signs of poverty. . . . We were in fact on a sort of island of well-being. . . ."

35 "They have all felt that they belonged": Weil, 47.

36 "I am sorry": Dodd to John D. Dodd, June 12, 1933, Box 2, Martha Dodd Papers.

36 "this great honor from D.C.": John D. Dodd to Dodd, June 15, 1933, Box 2, Martha Dodd Papers.

36 "A rather sorrowful day": Dodd, *Diary*, 8.

37 Dodd feared: Dallek, 194; Floyd Blair to Jay Pierrepont Moffat, June 28, 1933, Box 40, W. E. Dodd Papers.

37 A letter from a prominent Jewish relief activist: George Gordon Battle to Dodd, July 1, 1933, Box 40, W. E. Dodd Papers. See also telegram, Battle to Dodd, July 1, 1933, Box 40.

37 "There was much talk": Dodd, *Diary*, 9.

37 "For an hour and a half": Ibid.

37 During this meeting: Chernow, 374–75, 388.

37 "I insisted that the government": Dodd, *Diary*, 9.

38 The news was humbling.: Ibid., 10.

38 "the Jews should not be allowed to dominate": Ibid., 10.

38 "The Jews, after winning the war": Crane to Dodd, June 14, 1933, Box 40, W. E. Dodd Papers.

39 Dodd partly embraced Crane's notion: Dodd to Crane, Sept. 16, 1933, Box 40, W. E. Dodd Papers.

39 "Let Hitler have his way.": Dodd, *Diary*, 11.

39 A dozen or so reporters: Ibid., 11.

39 By this point he had begun: Ibid., 7.

39 "a disproportionate amount of sadness": Dodd, *Embassy Eyes*, 17.

Chapter 5: First Night

40 Martha continued to cry: Dodd, *Embassy Eyes*, 17–18.

40 She saw Hitler as "a clown": Ibid., 10.

41 As a student at the University of Chicago: Ibid., 5.

41 "I was slightly anti-Semitic": Ibid., 5.

41 One poll found: Breitman and Kraut, 88.

41 A poll taken decades in the future: Anti-Defamation League, 2009, ADL.org.

41 "an enchantress": Vanden Heuvel, 225.

41 "The personality is all there": Sandburg, Box 63, W. E. Dodd Papers.

41 "give way to every beckoning": Ibid.

41 "find out what this man Hitler": Dodd, *Embassy Eyes*, 16–17.

41 Thornton Wilder also offered: Wilder to Martha, n.d., Box 63, W. E. Dodd Papers.

In one letter, dated Sept. 15, 1933, Wilder wrote, "I can see the plane rides"—here an apparent reference to the airborne courtship of her by Ernst Udet, World War I flying ace and aerial adventurer—"and the tea dances and the movie-stars; and the brisk (soon autumnal) stroll in the most autumnal of all great parks. But I cannot see what you're like when you're alone—or alone just with the family—or alone with the typewriter. Your letters are so vivacious that they deafen my mind's eye to all this other."

He opens his letters to her, variously, with "Dear Marthy," "Dear Handsome," "Dear Marthy-la-Belle."

"We're cusses," he wrote in April 1935, "both of us, preposterous exasperating cusses and were meant to be friends."

42 Martha kept a picture: Brysac, 142.

42 "half a dozen or more": Wise, *Servant*, 191–92.

42 "He was most friendly": Ibid.

42 "One cannot write the whole truth": Ibid.

43 "unfair at many points": Dodd, *Diary*, 241.

43 His daughter, Martha: Dodd, *Embassy Eyes*, 12.

43 He told a friend: Bailey, 150.

43 Dodd had assumed: Dodd, *Embassy Eyes*, 20.

43 Meanwhile, Dodd fielded questions: Ibid., 20; Dodd, *Diary*, 12.

44 He was stiff and arrogant: Dodd, *Embassy Eyes*, 20–21.

44 "very choleric temperament": Messersmith, "Some Observations on the appointment of Dr. William Dodd, as Ambassador to Berlin," unpublished memoir, 8, Messersmith Papers.

44 "clipped, polite, and definitely condescending": Dodd, *Embassy Eyes*, 20.

44 "the like of which": Ibid., 21.

44 Mrs. Dodd—Mattie: Ibid., 21.

45 "a dry, drawling, peppery man": Breitman and Kraut, 40.

45 "I liked Dodd": Messersmith, "Some Observations on the appointment of Dr. William Dodd, as Ambassador to Berlin," unpublished memoir, 3, Messersmith Papers.

45 "a perfect example": Fromm, 121.

46 "looks like a scholar": Ibid., 120.

46 "is clear and capable": Brysac, 141.

46 "a woman who is seriously interested": Ibid.

46 "I was drawn to her immediately": Unpublished memoir, 3, Box 13, Martha Dodd Papers.

46 She found long, straight boulevards: While I ought to footnote every little nugget in this rather long paragraph, frankly the effort would be too tedious and of limited value. So allow me to refer the reader to a couple of sources that provided me with a vivid sense of old Berlin: Ladd, *The Ghosts of Berlin*; Friedrich, *Before the Deluge*; Richie, *Faust's Metropolis*; Gill, *A Dance Between Flames*. For a quirky look at Berlin's night life, see Gordon, *Voluptuous Panic*. Also I urge anyone with a yearning for still more knowledge of Berlin to visit YouTube.com and search for "Symphony of a Great City." You'll be delighted.

47 "The bells on the streetcars": Kaes et al., 560–62.

48 "Oh, I thought it was burned down!": Dodd, *Embassy Eyes*, 22.

48 "Sssh! Young lady": Ibid., 22.

48 Greta Garbo once was a guest: Kreuder, 26.

Kreuder's "cultural history" of the Hotel Esplanade includes a number of photographs of the hotel before and immediately after World War II, and in its current incarnation as an artifact sequestered behind a wall of glass. For more on this, please read my source essay (pp. 367–75).

48 the Imperial Suite: Dodd, *Embassy Eyes*, 22; for specific room numbers, see letter, Hotel Esplanade to George Gordon, July 6, 1933, Box 40, W. E. Dodd Papers.

48 "that there was scarcely space": Dodd, *Embassy Eyes*, 22.

48 "modest quarters": Messersmith, "Some Observations on the appointment of Dr. William Dodd, as Ambassador to Berlin," unpublished memoir, 2, Messersmith Papers.

49 The family settled in: Dodd, *Embassy Eyes*, 22–23.

49 Later that evening: Ibid., 23–24.

50 "In the Tiergarten": Kaes et al., 425.

50 "I am sure this was": Dodd, *Embassy Eyes*, 23.

50 "I felt the press had badly maligned": Ibid., 24.

PART II: HOUSE HUNTING IN THE THIRD REICH

Chapter 6: Seduction

53 "A little pudgy": Dodd, *Embassy Eyes*, 24.

53 "the dragon from Chicago": Schultz, "Dragon," 113.

54 The opening of one such camp: Stackelberg and Winkle, 145.

Regarding "wild" camps, KZs, and such, see Krausnick et al., 400, 410, 419; Richie, 412; Fritzsche, 43; Fest, 115–16; Kershaw, *Hubris*, 462, 464; Deschner, 79. As of July 31, 1933, some 26,789 people were held in protective custody, according to Krausnick et al., 410.

54 "I didn't believe all her stories": Dodd, *Embassy Eyes*, 24.

55 "What a youthful, carefree": de Jonge, 140.

55 Within days she found herself: Dodd, *Embassy Eyes*, 24.

55 "their funny stiff dancing": Ibid., 24.

55 "weren't thieves": Ibid., 25.

56 the *Berliner Schnauze*: Jelavich, 31.

56 "I'm not Jewish": Grunberger, 371; de Jonge, 161; for more on Finck, see Jelavich, 236–41, 248.

56 "The sun shines": Isherwood, *Berlin Stories*, 207.

It cannot be said enough that Germany's seeming normalcy in this period was deeply seductive to outsiders. Angela Schwarz, in her article "British Visitors to National Socialist Germany," writes that "a considerable number of British travellers concluded after a tour through the Third Reich, perhaps even one organized by the authorities, that in Germany everything was as quiet and peaceful as could be." Schwarz, 497.

56 *Gleichschaltung*—meaning "coordination": Orlow, 29; Bullock, 149; Kershaw, *Hubris*, 479; Hughes and Mann, 81; Gill, 238.

Engelmann, 36, offers a slightly different translation: "bringing into line." Orlow, in his *History of the Nazi Party*, notes that the literal translation is "to switch equal," a physics term that "originally denoted the coordination of different types of electrical current." Orlow, 29.

56 "self-coordination": Kershaw, *Hubris*, 481; Gisevius, 96; Gellately, *Gestapo*, 11, 137.

57 Gerda Laufer: Gellately, *Gestapo*, 97.

57 coined by a post office clerk: Crankshaw, 15.

57 One study of Nazi records: Cited in Gellately, *Gestapo*, 146.

57 In October 1933: Gellately, *Gestapo*, 137–38.

57 "we are living at present": Ibid., 139.

There was nothing funny about the Gestapo, but this did not stop Berliners from quietly—very quietly—coining and trading jokes about the agency. Here's one of them: "At the Belgian border crossing, huge numbers of rabbits appear one day and declare that they are political refugees. 'The Gestapo wants to arrest all giraffes as enemies of the state.'—'But you're not giraffes!'—'We know that, but try explaining that to the Gestapo!'" Evans, *Power*, 106.

57 only about 1 percent: Dippel, xviii; Gill, 238.

Kershaw, in his *Popular Opinion and Political Dissent*, presents statistics that show that 70.9 percent of Germany's Jews lived in cities having more than 100,000 inhabitants. In Bavaria, the percentage was 49.5. "One implication of this is obvious," he writes: "the population of large tracts of Bavaria had no, or at best minimal, contact with Jews. For very many, therefore, the Jewish Question could be of no more than abstract significance." Kershaw, *Popular Opinion*, 226–27.

58 some ten thousand émigrés: Dippel, 114.

58 "Hardly anyone thought": Zuckmayer, 320.

58 "It was easy to be reassured": Dippel, 153.

58 The salute, he wrote: Messersmith to Hull, Aug. 8, 1933, Messersmith Papers.

59 "I felt really quite fortunate": Ibid., 4.

59 Dodd threw him a mock salute: Martha to Thornton Wilder, Sept. 25, 1933, Wilder Papers.

59 "You remember our bicycle ride": George Bassett Roberts to Martha, Oct. 22, 1971, Box 8, Martha Dodd Papers.

60 "You had had it": Ibid.

60 "To my charming and lovely ex-wife": George Bassett Roberts to Martha, n.d., Box 8, Martha Dodd Papers.

60 "I'm not at all sure": George Bassett Roberts to Martha, Oct. 22, 1971, Box 8, Martha Dodd Papers.

60 A Harvard graduate: Conradi, 22.

Chapter 7: Hidden Conflict

61 "the most beautiful park": Dodd to R. Walton Moore, March 22, 1936, 124.621/338, State/Decimal.

61 "A photograph of you": Phillips to Dodd, July 31, 1933, Box 42, W. E. Dodd Papers.

62 "rolled in the gutter": Martha to Thornton Wilder, Sept. 25, 1933, Wilder Papers.

62 "Gordon is an industrious career man": Dodd, *Diary*, 16.

62 "come to Germany to rectify the wrongs": Ibid., 13.

62 On his first full day in Berlin: Friedlander, 496.

63 He also learned that staff: Dodd to Hull, July 17, 1933, 124.626/95, State/ Decimal.

63 The consul general now dispatched: For example, Messersmith to Hull, July 15, 1933, 125.1956/221, State/Decimal.

63 In notes for a personnel report: Dodd, Memorandum, 1933, Box 40 (1933-C), W. E. Dodd Papers.

64 "Evangelical Christian": *New York Times*, July 1, 1933.

65 He also recognized: For a summary of the conflict between Hitler and Röhm, see Evans, *Power*, 20–26; Kershaw, *Hubris*, 505–7; and Wheeler-Bennett, *Nemesis*, 307–11.

65 admittedly homosexual: Röhm was outed when his letters to a medical researcher were made public. In one letter he wrote, "I make no secret of my inclinations," and acknowledged that the Nazi Party had needed "to get used to this criminal peculiarity of mine." He also wrote, "Today all women are an abomination to me, particularly those who pursue me with their love." Hancock, 625–29.

65 "adolescents in the great game": Dodd to Newton Baker, Aug. 12, 1933, Box 40, W. E. Dodd Papers.

65 "These men wish to stop all Jewish persecution": Ibid.

66 "his face," she wrote: Dodd, *Embassy Eyes*, 247.

66 "he was trying to train the Nazis": Heineman, 66.

66 "He always believed": Ibid., 82.

66 "most agreeable": Dodd, *Diary*, 13.

66 "Hitler will fall into line": Dodd to Newton Baker, Aug. 12, 1933, Box 40, W. E. Dodd Papers.

67 "It is not unlikely that [Zuckerman]": Messersmith to Hull, Aug. 9, 1933, Messersmith Papers.

67 Messersmith added, "It is interesting to note": Ibid., 4.

67 "It has been a favorite pastime of the SA men": Messersmith to Hull, July 26, 1933, Messersmith Papers.

68 "inaccurate and overdrawn": Messersmith, "Attack on Kaltenborn," unpublished memoir, 2, Messersmith Papers.

68 "was a German by origin": Ibid.

68 "to influence Americans coming to Germany": Messersmith to Hull, Sept. 26, 1933, p. 1, Messersmith Papers.

68 He saw evidence of this: Ibid., 3.

68 "that if Americans in Germany": Ibid., 3.

69 "The fact that Jews are permitted": Ibid., 7–8.

69 "The Americans coming to Germany": Ibid., 15.

Chapter 8: Meeting Putzi

70 She also became a regular: Dodd, *Embassy Eyes*, 100.

70 "Everybody else in the restaurant": Isherwood, *Berlin Stories*, 204.

70 "pretty, vivacious": Shirer, *Berlin Diary*, 34.

70 In this new world: I was struck during my research by the extent to which my key protagonists saved the calling cards they received during their days in Berlin. Martha's cards—scores of them—can be found in Box 1, file 2, of her papers at the Library of Congress. Armand Berard, her much-abused future lover, jotted on one of his cards, "Rang you up in vain / and came in vain." A good friend of Martha's, Elmina Rangabe, wrote, cryptically, "'Be still, my soul, be still; the arms you bear are brittle,'" from A. E. Housman's *A Shropshire Lad*. She crossed out Rangabe to indicate intimacy.

71 "If you have nothing more important to do": Ibid.

71 "a lavish and fairly drunken affair": Dodd, *Embassy Eyes*, 25.

71 "in a sensational manner": Ibid., 25.

71 "supremely awkward-looking": Dalley, 156.

72 "an instinctive dislike": Messersmith, "Dr. Hanfstaengl," unpublished memoir, 1, Messersmith Papers.

72 "He is totally insincere": Messersmith to Jay Pierrepont Moffat, June 13, 1934, Messersmith Papers.

72 "went out of his way to be cordial": Reynolds, 107.

72 "You had to know Putzi": Ibid., 207.

72 At Harvard: Hanfstaengl, 27, 32; Conradi, 20.

72 One story held that Hanfstaengl: Conradi, 21.

72 "Uncle Dolf ": Ibid., 46.

Egon Hanfstaengl told the *Sunday Telegraph* of London (Feb. 27, 2005) that Hitler made an excellent playmate. "I loved him. He was the most imaginative playmate a child could wish for. My favourite game with him was trains. He would go on his hands and knees, and pretend to be a tunnel or a viaduct. I was the steam engine going on the track underneath him. He would then do all the noises of the steam train."

72 "so blatantly proclaiming his charm": Dodd, *Embassy Eyes*, 26.

73 "of almost frightening dimensions": Fromm, 90.

73 "He had a soft, ingratiating manner": Dodd, *Embassy Eyes*, 25–26.

73 "He could exhaust anyone": Ibid., 26

73 "He was a modest little southern history professor": Hanfstaengl, 214.

73 "Papa" Dodd: Conradi, 121.

73 "The best thing about Dodd": Hanfstaengl, 214.

Chapter 9: Death Is Death

74 One of his foremost sources: Mowrer, *Triumph*, 218.

74 Putzi Hanfstaengl tried to undermine: Ibid., 219.

75 "I was inclined to think him Jewish": Dodd, *Embassy Eyes*, 39.

75 "To no purpose": Mowrer, *Triumph*, 224.

75 "almost as vehement": Dodd, *Diary*, 24.

75 Gestapo chief Rudolf Diels felt compelled: Messersmith, "Some observations on my relations with the press," unpublished memoir, 20, Messersmith Papers.

76 "people's righteous indignation": Mowrer, *Triumph*, 225–26.

76 "one of the most difficult conversations": Messersmith, "Some observations on my relations with the press," unpublished memoir, 21, Messersmith Papers.

76 "If you were not being moved": Mowrer, *Journalist's Wife*, 308.

76 "never quite forgave my father": Dodd, *Embassy Eyes*, 39.

76 "perhaps the foremost chemist": Dodd, *Diary*, 17.

77 $C \times t = k$: See "Fritz Haber," JewishVirtualLibrary.org.

77 On a personal level: Stern, 121. Also see "Fritz Haber," NobelPrize.org.

77 "In this profound dejection": Ibid., 53.

77 "trembled from head to foot": Memorandum, Sept. 14, 1933, Box 59, W. E. Dodd Papers.

78 "the saddest story of Jewish persecution": Dodd, *Diary*, 17.

78 "He wished to know the possibilities": Ibid., 17.

78 "You know the quota is already full": Dodd to Isador Lubin, Aug. 5, 1933, Box 41, W. E. Dodd Papers.

78 "The Ambassador appears": D. W. MacCormack to Isador Lubin, Aug. 23, 1935, Box 41, W. E. Dodd Papers.

79 He left for England: Goran, 169, 171.

79 Zyklon B: Stern, 135.

79 "How I wish": Stephen S. Wise to Dodd, July 28, 1933, Box 43,
W. E. Dodd Papers.

79 Dodd "is being lied to": Wise, *Personal Letters*, 223.

79 "the many sources of information": Dodd to Stephen S. Wise, Aug. 1,
1933, Box 43, W. E. Dodd Papers.

80 "tell him the truth": Wise, *Personal Letters*, 224.

80 "I might be recognized": Wise, *Challenging Years*, 254.

81 "Briefly it may be said": Messersmith to Hull, Aug. 24, 1933, Messersmith
Papers.

82 "fundamentally, I believe": Dodd to Roosevelt, Aug. 12, 1933, Box 42,
W. E. Dodd Papers.

Chapter 10: Tiergartenstrasse 27a

83 Though he reviled: Dodd to William Phillips, Nov. 13, 1933, Box 42.

83 "Personally, I would rather": Dodd to Sam D. McReynolds, Jan. 2, 1934,
Box 42, W. E. Dodd Papers.

84 The Dodds found many properties: Dodd, *Embassy Eyes*, 32.

85 "We have one of the best residences": Dodd to Roosevelt, Aug. 12, 1933,
Box 42, W. E. Dodd Papers.

85 Trees and gardens: In the course of my research I had the pleasure of
interviewing Gianna Sommi Panofsky, the daughter-in-law of the Dodds'
landlord, who provided me with detailed plans for the house and photocopies of
several photographs of its exterior. Sadly, she died before I completed this book.

86 "twice the size of an average New York apartment": Dodd, *Embassy Eyes*,
33–34.

86 "entirely done in gold": Ibid., 34.

87 "We are convinced": Dodd to Mrs. Alfred Panofsky, undated letter,
provided by Gianna Sommi Panofsky.

87 "I love going there": Fromm, 215.

87 "second home": Ferdinand, 253.

87 "When the servants were out of sight": Ibid., 253.

88 "If you don't try to be more careful": Ibid., 253.

88 "We love each other": Martha to Thornton Wilder, Sept. 25, 1933, Wilder
Papers.

88 "short, blond, obsequious": Dodd, *Embassy Eyes*, 147.

88 "Now the hegira begins": Carl Sandburg to Martha, n.d., Box 63,
W. E. Dodd Papers.

89 They traveled first by car: Dodd, *Diary*, 22–23; Dodd, *Embassy Eyes*, 27;
Reynolds, 118.

PART III: LUCIFER IN THE GARDEN

Chapter 11: Strange Beings

94 "an American citizen of a fine type": Messersmith to Hull, Aug. 19, 1933,
Messersmith Papers.
94 "very young, very energetic": Messersmith to Hull, Aug. 25, 1933,
Messersmith Papers.
95 "confessions of regret": Dodd, *Diary*, 26–27.
95 "The excitement of the people": Dodd, *Embassy Eyes*, 28.

Details of the episode described on this and following pages may be found
mainly in Martha's memoir, pages 27–32, and in Quentin Reynolds's memoir,
pages 118–21.

Martha's account varies a bit from that of Reynolds. She claimed Reynolds agreed to write the story upon his return to Berlin, rather than cable it
directly from Nuremberg, and that he would leave her and Bill out of the account. Reynolds, in a later memoir, reported that he did omit reference to the
Dodds, but wrote the story while still in Nuremberg and filed it by mail rather
than by cable. Dodd, *Embassy Eyes*, 29; Reynolds, 120.

98 "a short, squat, shaven-headed bully": Kershaw, *Hubris*, 179.
99 Goebbels smiled: One problem with the Nazis' adulation of Aryan
perfection was that none of the regime's most senior leaders fit the tall, blond,
blue-eyed model. Hitler, when not ranting, looked to be a rather prosaic
type, a middle manager of middle age with a strange mustache that evoked
the American comic actor Charlie Chaplin. Göring was hugely overweight,
and increasingly given to odd quirks of narcissistic display, such as painting
his nails and changing his uniform several times a day. Himmler looked
like a practitioner of the field in which he had been employed before being
anointed by Hitler: chicken farming.

Goebbels's appearance posed the greatest challenge, however. He was a
shrunken figure with a crippled foot whose looks bore a startling resemblance
to the grotesquely distorted caricatures that appeared regularly in Nazi hate
literature. A bit of doggerel discreetly made the rounds in Berlin: "Dear God,
make me blind / That I may Goebbels Aryan find." Gallo, 29.

100 "The youth are bright faced": Martha to Thornton Wilder, Dec. 14, 1933,
Wilder Papers.

Many people held similar views, at least early on. I was struck in particular
by the observations of Marsden Hartley, an American painter living in Berlin,
who on Dec. 28, 1933, wrote, "It takes one's breath really to see the young
here all marching and marching of course as usual. One gets the feeling Germany is always marching—but O such health and vigor and physical rightness they possess." Hartley, 11.

100 "I received a non-committal reply": Dodd, *Diary*, 26.
100 "very pleasantly unconventional": Ibid., 25.

Chapter 12: Brutus

103 "It was all over": Dodd, *Diary*, 30–31.
103 "really doing wrong": This quote and other details of the Kaltenborn
episode come from Messersmith, "Attack on Kaltenborn," unpublished
memoir, Messersmith Papers; Kaltenborn's correspondence in his archive at the
Wisconsin Historical Society; and Kaltenborn's memoir, *Fifty Fabulous Years*.
103 "This is no more to be expected": Kaltenborn Papers.
105 "otherwise tried to prevent unfriendly demonstrations": Dodd, *Diary*, 36.
105 "I was trying to find excuses": Dodd, *Embassy Eyes*, 36.
105 "I felt there was something noble:" Ibid., 36–37.
105 "and that the press reports": Ibid., 37.
106 "And when are you coming back": Mowrer, *Triumph*, 226.
106 "And you too, Brutus": Messersmith, "Some observations on my relations
with the press," unpublished memoir, 22, Messersmith Papers.
106 Mowrer "was for a time": Dodd to Walter Lichtenstein, Oct. 26, 1933,
Box 41, W. E. Dodd Papers.
106 "His experiences, however": Ibid.
107 "Nowhere have I had such lovely friends": Reynolds, *Journalist's Wife*, 309.
107 "The protokoll arbiters": Dodd to Hull, Oct. 19, 1933, Box 41, W. E.
Dodd Papers.
107 "So today the show began": Dodd, *Diary*, 33.
107 "Well, if at the last minute": Dodd, *Embassy Eyes*, 236.
108 "You people in the Diplomatic Corps": Dodd to Hull, Feb. 17, 1934
(unsent), Box 44, W. E. Dodd Papers.
108 "We simply cannot stand the pace": Ibid.
108 "Infectious and delightful": Dodd, *Embassy Eyes*, 233.
108 "one of the few men": Ibid., 233.
108 An extraordinary newspaper photograph: A copy of this image can be
found in Dodd, *Embassy Eyes*, opposite page 118.
108 "certainly looked flirtatious": Schultz, "Sigrid Schultz Transcript-Part I,"
10, Box 2, Schultz Papers.
108 "you felt you could be in the same room": Schultz, Catalogue of Memoirs,
transcript fragment, Box 2, Schultz Papers.
108 "I was always rather favorably impressed": Reminiscences of John
Campbell White, Oral History Collection, Columbia University, 87–88.
109 "three times the size": Dodd, *Embassy Eyes*, 221.
109 "To illustrate," he wrote: Dodd to Hull, Oct. 19, 1933, Box 41, W. E.
Dodd Papers.

110 "But," he vowed: Ibid.

110 The embassy's cupboard: Berlin Embassy Post Report (Revision), p. 10, 124.62/162, State/Decimal.

111 "We shall not use silver platters": Dodd to Hull, Oct. 19, 1933, Box. 41, W. E. Dodd Papers.

111 "I can never adapt myself": Dodd to Carl Sandburg, Nov. 21, 1934, Box 45, W. E. Dodd Papers.

111 "with attacks of headaches": Dr. Wilbur E. Post to Dodd, Aug. 30, 1933, Box 42, W. E. Dodd Papers.

112 a *Sonderzug*: Metcalfe, 141.

112 *Knight, Death and the Devil*: Burden, 68.

Chapter 13: My Dark Secret

113 "I suppose I practiced": Dodd, *Embassy Eyes*, 41.

114 She had a brief affair with Putzi: Conradi, 122.

114 "like a butterfly": Vanden Heuvel, 248.

114 "You are the only person": Armand Berard to Martha, n.d., Box 4, Martha Dodd Papers.

114 "Of course I remember": Max Delbrück to Martha, Nov. 15, 1978, Box 4, Martha Dodd Papers.

115 "I often felt like saying something": Messersmith to Jay Pierrepont Moffat, June 13, 1934, Messersmith Papers.

115 "she had behaved so badly": Messersmith, "Goering," unpublished memoir, 5, Messersmith Papers.

115 "That was not a house": Brysac, 157.

116 "created a nervousness": Dodd, *Embassy Eyes*, 52.

116 "the most sinister, scar-torn face": Ibid., 52.

116 "a cruel, broken beauty": Ibid., 53.

116 "Involved affairs with women": Gisevius, 39.

116 "I felt at ease": Ludecke, 654–55.

116 "He took a vicious joy": Dodd, *Embassy Eyes*, 52.

117 "remarkably small": Gellately, *Gestapo*, 44–45.

117 "Most of them were neither crazed": Ibid., 59.

117 "One can evade a danger": Quoted in Gellately, *Gestapo*, 129.

Even within the Gestapo there was fear, according to Hans Gisevius, author of the Gestapo memoir *To the Bitter End*: "For we were living in a den of murderers in which we did not even dare step ten or twenty feet across the hall to wash our hands without telephoning a colleague beforehand and informing him of our intention to embark on so perilous an expedition." His boss advised him always to stay close to the wall and away from the banister when walking up a stairway, on the theory that this made it harder for an assassin above to get a clear shot. "Not for a moment was anyone's life secure." Gisevius, 50–51.

118 "like a mass of inanimate clay": Gallo, 25–26.

118 "They ordered me to take off my pants": Rürup, 92.

118 "The value of the SA": Metcalfe, 133.

118 "the golden death of the Tiergarten": Martha to Thornton Wilder, Nov. 10, 1934, Wilder Papers.

119 a "most indiscreet" young lady: Quoted in Wilbur Carr, Memorandum, June 5, 1933, Box 12, Carr Papers.

119 "he was constantly facing the muzzle of a gun": Dodd, *Embassy Eyes*, 56.

119 "There began to appear before my romantic eyes": Ibid., 53.

Chapter 14: The Death of Boris

120 "He had an unusual mouth": Agnes Knickerbocker, in miscellaneous notes, Box 13, Folder 22, Martha Dodd Papers.

120 In a later unpublished account: Martha left a rich typescript account of her relationship with Boris that includes passages of dialogue and myriad observational details, such as who laughed at what remark, who frowned, and so forth. "Bright Journey into Darkness," Box 14, Martha Dodd Papers.

121 "nigger-Jew jazz": Kater, 15.

125 "seemed totally unintimidated": Quoted in "Bright Journey into Darkness," Box 14, Martha Dodd Papers.

125 "made some ceremony": Agnes Knickerbocker, in miscellaneous notes, Box 13, Folder 22, Martha Dodd Papers.

Chapter 15: The "Jewish Problem"

128 It began amiably enough: My account of Dodd's meeting with Neurath is derived from Dodd's *Diary*, pages 35–37, and from his seven-page Memorandum, Sept. 14, 1933, Box 59, W. E. Dodd Papers.

130 "No doubt can be entertained": Leon Dominian to Hull and to Berlin Embassy, Sept. 15, 1933, 862.113/49 GC, State/Decimal.

131 On one notorious occasion: Messersmith to Hull, July 29, 1933, Messersmith Papers.

Chapter 16: A Secret Request

132 "this disagreeable and difficult business": Dodd to Samuel F. Bemis, Aug. 7, 1933, Box 40, W. E. Dodd Papers.

132 "Herewith I am informing you": Alfred Panofsky to Dodd, Sept. 18, 1933, Box 42, W. E. Dodd Papers.

133 Dodd's first draft: For first and final drafts, see Dodd to Alfred Panofsky, Sept. 20, 1933, Box 41, W. E. Dodd Papers.

133 "There was too much noise": Memorandum, n.d. (c. 1935), Box 47, W. E. Dodd Papers.

134 "happy mix of courage": Klemperer, *Language*, 32, 43, 48, 60.

135 Another attack occurred against an American: Dodd, *Diary*, 44; Messersmith to William Phillips, Oct. 19, 1933, Messersmith Papers.

135 The Ministry of Posts: Miller, 53.

135 "There has been nothing in social history": Messersmith to William Phillips, Sept. 29, 1933, Messersmith Papers.

136 "forcible intervention from the outside": Ibid.

136 "There is nothing here": Dodd to Edward M. House, Oct. 31, 1933, Box 41, W. E. Dodd Papers.

136 "It defeats my history work": Dodd to Jane Addams, Oct. 16, 1933, Box 40, W. E. Dodd Papers.

137 "Please do not refer to others": Dodd to Hull, Oct. 4, 1933, Box 41, W. E. Dodd Papers; Hull to Dodd, Oct. 16, 1933, Box 41, W. E. Dodd Papers.

Chapter 17: Lucifer's Run

138 "harshness and callousness": Diels, 328–31; also, Crankshaw, 51–61.

140 "From his retreat in Bohemia": Quoted in Crankshaw, 56.

141 "very much the German Frau": Brysac, 200.

141 "She was slow to speak": Unpublished Memoir, p. 9 (marked as p. 8), Box 13, Martha Dodd Papers.

141 While abroad he was recruited: Dallin, 236.

142 Arvid had "gone Nazi": Brysac, x.

142 "dove tans, soft blues": Ibid., 111.

142 "to build up a little colony": Martha to Thornton Wilder, Sept. 25, 1933, Wilder Papers.

142 "Martha, you know that I love you": Mildred Fish Harnack to Martha, May 4 (probably 1934), Box 5, Martha Dodd Papers.

142 "I prized these post-cards": Unpublished Memoir, p. 4 (marked as p. 3), Box 13, Martha Dodd Papers.

143 "the kind of person": Martha to Thornton Wilder, Dec. 14, 1933, Wilder Papers.

143 "And there I sit on the sofa": Quoted in Brysac, 419.

144 "the astonishment": Ibid., 146.

144 "the capital's jeunesse dorée": Ibid., 154.

Chapter 18: Warning from a Friend

145 "to hear amusing conversation": Dodd, *Embassy Eyes*, 86.

146 her birthday party: In her memoir, Martha makes reference to parties on pages 43–45 and 65–66. They appear to be the same party. The late Philip

Metcalfe, in his book *1933*, likewise links these references and states with certainty that they apply to her birthday party. He had the benefit of having corresponded with Martha Dodd well before her death in 1990. Metcalfe, 195–96.

146 "young, heel-clicking, courteous": Dodd, *Embassy Eyes*, 44.

147 "That is not the sort of music": Ibid., 67. The "Horst Wessel Song" was indeed a point of sensitivity for hard-core Nazis. One bandleader who dared to lead a jazz rendition of the song was compelled to flee Germany. Kater, 23.

148 "to continue to persuade": Dodd to Leo Wormser, Sept. 26, 1933, Box 43, W. E. Dodd Papers.

148 "It was because I had seen so much injustice": Dodd to Jane Addams, Oct. 16, 1933, Box 40, W. E. Dodd Papers.

148 "the President told me": Dodd to William Phillips, Oct. 14, 1933, Box 42, W. E. Dodd Papers.

148 "In times of great stress": For the text of Dodd's speech, see enclosure in Dodd to Roosevelt, Oct. 13, 1933, Roosevelt Correspondence.

149 Schacht "applauded extravagantly": Ibid.

149 "When the thing was over": Dodd to Hull, Oct. 19, 1933, Box 41, W. E. Dodd Papers.

150 "Silent, but anxious Germany": Ibid.

150 "I enjoyed all these nicely disguised hints": Fromm, 132.

150 "The situation is very difficult": Metcalfe, 164–65.

150 "My interpretation of this": Dodd to Roosevelt, Oct. 14, 1933, Box 42, W. E. Dodd Papers. (Note: A handwritten version of this letter in Roosevelt's correspondence bears the date Oct. 13, 1933. It seems clear that the typed version, dated Oct. 14, is the final and correctly dated copy.)

150 "to constitute a serious affront": Dodd to Hull, Oct. 13, 1933, 362.1113/13, State/Decimal.

151 "as a sort of rebuke for my speech": Dodd, *Diary*, 47.

151 "that some embarrassing interpretations": Dodd to Roosevelt, Oct. 14, 1933, Box 42, W. E. Dodd Papers.

151 "in the hope that you": Dodd to Phillips, Oct. 14, 1933, Box 42, W. E. Dodd Papers.

151 "the schoolmaster lecturing his pupils": Moffat, Diary, Oct. 12, 1933.

151 "that I was in doubt whether any words": William Phillips to Dodd, Nov. 27, 1933, Box 42, W. E. Dodd Papers.

152 "It was delightful to hear the President": Edward M. House to Dodd, Oct. 21, 1933, Box 41, W. E. Dodd Papers.

152 "It was not the address of a thinker": Dodd, *Diary*, 48.

153 "That the allies at this time": Shirer, *Rise*, 211.

Chapter 19: Matchmaker

154 There had been talk of numerous liaisons: For details on Hitler's love life, see Kershaw, *Hubris*, 284–85, 351–55.
154 his "clammy possessiveness": Ibid., 354.
154 "Believe me," she said: Ibid., 187.
154 "Hitler needs a woman": Conradi, 121.

PART IV: HOW THE SKELETON ACHES

Chapter 20: The Führer's Kiss

157 "neat and erect": Dodd, *Diary*, 49.
157 "Chauffeureska": Kershaw, *Hubris*, 485.
157 *King Kong* was a favorite: Ibid., 485.
157 "Hitler looked like a suburban hairdresser": Hanfstaengl, 22.
158 First Dodd raised the subject: Dodd, *Diary*, 49.
159 "Perhaps I was too frank": Dodd to Roosevelt, Oct. 28, 1933, Box 42, W. E. Dodd Papers.
159 "The total effect of the interview": Dodd to Hull, Oct. 17, 1933, 362.1113/19 GC, State/Decimal.
159 "The Chancellor's assurances": Messersmith to William Phillips, Oct. 19, 1933 (pp. 12–13), Messersmith Papers.
160 "appointed to change the history of Europe": Dodd, *Embassy Eyes*, 63–65.
161 "that Hitler was not an unattractive man": Ibid., 65.
162 "I was a little angry": Ibid., 65.
162 "By promoting me": Diels to Himmler, Oct. 10, 1933, vol. 11, p. 142, *Archives of the Holocaust*.

Chapter 21: The Trouble with George

163 "For the first time, therefore": Henry P. Leverich, "The Prussian Ministry of Justice Presents a Draft for a New German Penal Code," Dec. 21, 1933, GRC 862.0441/5, State/Decimal.
164 "to permit killing incurables": Dodd, Memorandum, Oct. 26, 1933, 862.0441/3, State/Decimal.
164 "could remember neither the name": Enclosed with Dodd to Hull, Nov. 13, 1933, GRC 362.1113 Kaltenborn, H.V./5, State Decimal.
164 "Wealthy staff people": Dodd to Hull, Oct. 19, 1933, Box 41, W. E. Dodd Papers.
165 "It would seem that in view": D. A. Salmon to William Phillips, Nov. 1, 1933, enclosed in Phillips to Dodd, Nov. 4, 1933, Box 42, W. E. Dodd Papers.

165 "the extravagance in the telegraphic business": William Phillips to Dodd, Nov. 4, 1933, Box 42, W. E. Dodd Papers.

165 "Do not think that Mr. Salmon's comparison": Dodd to William Phillips, Nov. 17, 1933, Box 42, W. E. Dodd Papers.

165 "another curious hangover": Dodd to Hull, Sept. 6, 1933, Box 41, W. E. Dodd Papers.

166 "His office is important": Ibid.

166 He had fallen, apparently: Stiller, 40.

166 "They seem to believe": Messersmith to William Phillips, Oct. 28, 1933 (pp. 6, 9–10), Messersmith Papers.

167 "Rosenberg administration": Breitman and Kraut, 225.

167 "has many sources of information": Dodd to William Phillips, Nov. 15, 1933, Box 42, W. E. Dodd Papers.

167 "I must add that he has been": Ibid.

168 "without the slightest injury": Dodd to William Phillips, Nov. 17, 1933, Box 42, W. E. Dodd Papers.

168 "It occurs to me," Dodd told Phillips: Dodd to William Phillips, Nov. 15, 1933, Box 42, W. E. Dodd Papers.

168 "The letters and dispatches": William Phillips to Dodd, Nov. 27, 1933, Box 42, W. E. Dodd Papers.

168 On Sunday, Oct. 29: Dodd, *Diary*, 53.

Chapter 22: The Witness Wore Jackboots

169 "I walked in, my heart in my throat": Dodd, *Embassy Eyes*, 59–60.

170 "a yawning abyss of boredom": Tobias, 211.

   Hans Gisevius, page 29, comments on the slow pace as well: "Slowly, like a heavy, viscous liquid, the stream of witnesses and experts flowed by. . . . The trial proved unexpectedly boring. . . ."

170 "looked wiry, tough, indifferent": Dodd, *Embassy Eyes*, 58.

171 "the hind end of an elephant": Bullitt, 233.

171 "Everyone jumped up as if electrified": Tobias, 223.

171 "With one hand he gestured wildly": Gisevius, 32.

172 "especially anxious to have me present": Dodd, *Embassy Eyes*, 62.

172 "A botch," Göring had acknowledged: Holborn, 143.

172 "thus preventing the apprehension": Tobias, 226.

173 "a brilliant, attractive, dark man": Dodd, *Embassy Eyes*, 60.

173 "For the world had been told": Tobias, 228.

Chapter 23: Boris Dies Again

174 "Boris, stop it": Martha Dodd, "Bright Journey into Darkness," Box 14, Martha Dodd Papers. Martha tells the story of Boris and the roadside shrine in pages 15–16.

Chapter 24: Getting Out the Vote

175 "On an eleventh of November": Shirer, *Rise*, 211.

175 "Show tomorrow your firm national unity": Ibid., 211–12.

176 Every German could find a reason: Messersmith to Hull, "Some Observations on the election of Nov. 12, 1933," p. 3, enclosed in Messersmith to Dodd, Nov. 18, 1933, Box 42, W. E. Dodd Papers.

Ian Kershaw, in *Hubris*, quotes a portion of the ballot: "Do you, German man, and you, German woman, approve this policy of your Reich government, and are you ready to declare it to be the expression of your own view and your own will, and solemnly to give it your allegiance?" Kershaw, *Hubris*, 495.

176 One report held that patients: Messersmith to Hull, "Some Observations on the election of Nov. 12, 1933," p. 5, enclosed in Messersmith to Dodd, Nov. 18, 1933, Box 42, W. E. Dodd Papers.

176 "extravagant propaganda": Klemperer, *Witness*, 41.

176 "In order to bring about clarity": Messersmith to Hull, "Some Observations on the election of Nov. 12, 1933," p. 7, enclosed in Messersmith to Dodd, Nov. 18, 1933, Box 42, W. E. Dodd Papers.

176 Some 45.1 million Germans: Messersmith to Hull, "Some Observations on the election of Nov. 12, 1933," p. 2, enclosed in Messersmith to Dodd, Nov. 18, 1933, Box 42, W. E. Dodd Papers.

176 "historically unique acknowledgment": Ibid., 2.

177 "The election here is a farce": Dodd to Roosevelt, Oct. 28, 1933, Box 42, W. E. Dodd Papers.

177 Nothing indicated this more clearly: Shirer, *Rise*, 212.

177 "I am glad you have been frank": Roosevelt to Dodd, Nov. 13, 1933, Box 42, W. E. Dodd Papers.

178 "that certain reactionary papers": Dodd, *Diary*, 58.

Chapter 25: The Secret Boris

179 "I wanted to love him only lightly": Martha Dodd, "Bright Journey into Darkness," 23, Box 14, Martha Dodd Papers.

179 "You always see the bad things": Ibid., 29.

180 "I love you.": Ibid., 29.

180 "I could not bear to think of the future": Ibid., 21.

180 "Martha!" he wrote: Boris to Martha, Spring 1934, Box 10, Martha Dodd Papers.

180 A bleak day: Details of this encounter between Martha and Boris come from her unpublished memoir, "Bright Journey into Darkness," 21–26, Box 14, Martha Dodd Papers.

Chapter 26: The Little Press Ball

184 "It is always easier to pump a man": Schultz, "Winter of 1933–1934," 4, Personal Writings, Box 29, Schultz Papers.

185 "painfully crowded": Schultz, "1934," 2, Personal Writings, Box 34, Schultz Papers.

185 "without any display of orders": Fromm, 137.

186 "Gravedigger of the Weimar Republic": Ibid., 321.

186 "I have Hindenburg's confidence": Gellately, Gestapo, 1.

186 "Not until they had riveted": Wheeler-Bennett, Nemesis, 293.

187 "When he arrived he was as suave": Schultz, "1934," 3, Personal Writings, Box 34, Schultz Papers.

At diplomatic functions, Papen would often sidle up to George Messersmith's wife and try to pry from her bits and pieces of intelligence about political matters, such as American attitudes toward Germany. She learned to parry these probes by talking about her pastime of collecting porcelain. Papen "never made any progress," Messersmith wrote, "because she always returned to porcelain." Messersmith, "Conversations with Von Papen in Vienna," unpublished memoir, 7, Messersmith Papers.

188 "The louder the motor": Fromm, 136.

189 "Why should you worry?": Ibid., 136–37.

190 Göring had claimed: Messersmith, "When I arrived in Berlin . . . ," unpublished memoir, 7, Messersmith Papers.

190 "sit and calmly tell you": Messersmith to William Phillips, Sept. 29, 1933, (p. 6; see also, pp. 4–5), Messersmith Papers.

190 "I can tell you that": Schultz, "Winter of 1933–1934," 7, Personal Writings, Box 29, Schultz Papers; Schultz, "1934," 4, Personal Writings, Box 34, Schultz Papers.

191 "brutal and ruthless": Fromm, 137, 304.

191 Rumors of suicides were common: Goeschel, 100.

191 "I can't live any more": Fromm, 138.

192 "We all had a really good time": Louis Lochner to Betty Lochner, Dec. 26, 1933, Round Robin Letters, Box 6, Lochner Papers.

192 "The dinner was a bore": Dodd, Diary, 59.

192 "From that day on": Schultz, "Winter of 1933–1934," 7, Personal Writings, Box 29, Schultz Papers.

192 "Bellachen, we are all so shocked": Fromm, 138–39.

Chapter 27: O Tannenbaum

194 "Berlin is a skeleton": Isherwood, *Berlin Stories,* 186.

194 The SA monopolized the sale of Christmas trees: Gilbert L. MacMaster to Clarence E. Pickett, Feb. 12, 1934, vol. 2, p. 49, *Archives of the Holocaust.*

195 "persons who had a grudge against him": Details on the Wollstein incident can be found in Raymond H. Geist to Hull, Dec. 15, 1933, GRC 362.1121 Wollstein, Erwin/1, State/Decimal.

196 Martha assigned herself the task: Martha describes this tree-trimming episode in her unpublished memoir, "Bright Journey into Darkness," 14–17, Box 14, Martha Dodd Papers.

197 "Have you lost even your literary interest": Martha to Thornton Wilder, Dec. 14, 1933, Wilder Papers.

199 "On one occasion the hilarity was so great": Wilbur Carr took careful notes on his conversation with Raymond Geist, and reported them in a "Strictly Confidential" memorandum dated June 5, 1935, Box 12, Carr Papers.

199 "There appears to be a spare typewriter": John Campbell White to Jay Pierrepont Moffat, Nov. 17, 1933, White Papers.

199 "a curious individual": Jay Pierrepont Moffat to John Campbell White, March 31, 1934, White Papers.

200 "Permanent retirement from the post": Dodd to William Phillips, Dec. 4, 1933, Box 42, W. E. Dodd Papers.

200 "I cannot imagine who gave the *Tribune*": William Phillips to Dodd, Dec. 22, 1933, Box 42, W. E. Dodd Papers.

200 "an inside glimpse of conditions": Phillips, Diary, Dec. 20, 1933.

200 "We went over it from all angles": Moffat, Diary, Dec. 14, 1933.

200 "much concerned at letters": Moffat, Diary, Feb. 13, 1934.

201"Our mutual friend G.S.M.": George Gordon to Dodd, Jan. 22, 1934, Box 44, W. E. Dodd Papers.

201 Lochner told Dodd: Details of Lochner's plot to save Dimitrov come from Metcalfe, 232–34; Dodd, *Diary,* 65–66; Conradi, 136–38.

203 "high treason, insurrectionary arson": Tobias, 268.

203 "We were sitting together drinking our coffee": Lochner, Dec. 26, 1933, Round Robin Letters, Box 6, Lochner Papers.

204 Diels's precise motives cannot be known: Wheaton, 430.

Though he found the camps repellent, Diels was not being entirely altruistic. He recognized that an amnesty would have great political value, burnishing Hitler's image both inside and outside Germany. But clearly he also knew that an amnesty would be an affront to Himmler, whose SS ran the camps, and that on that score alone the idea would appeal to Göring. Hitler and Göring approved the idea, but insisted that Dachau be exempted, and limited the number of prisoners to be included. They gave Diels authority to decide who would be freed. Göring announced the decree, and said that a total of five thousand prisoners would be released. In fact, the amnesty was not so wide-ranging as Göring's announcement suggested. A number of camps outside Prussia also were exempted, and the overall total of prisoners released was lower than what Göring had promised. Moreover, plans existed to expand the capacity of the camps in Prussia alone by as many as eight thousand additional prisoners. Crankshaw, 45–47; Wheaton, 429–30.

204 "The Secret Police Chief did": Dodd, *Diary*, 67.

204 "One might think," he wrote: Ibid., 66.

PART V: DISQUIET

Chapter 28: January 1934

209 "Thank you for telling me": Tobias, 284.

209 "Herr Hitler seemed to feel a genuine sympathy": Phipps, 40.

210 "Hitler is improving definitely": Martha to Thornton Wilder, Dec. 14, 1933, Wilder Papers.

210 The official tally of unemployed workers: Fritzsche, 57; Miller, 66–67, 136.

210 Within the Reich Ministry of the Interior: Krausnick et al., 419.

One more sign of normalcy was the way the government dealt with an attack against an American that occurred on Jan. 15, 1934. On that cold, rain-soaked Monday a U.S. citizen named Max Schussler, working in Berlin as a landlord, stumbled into the consulate on Bellevuestrasse "bleeding profusely," according to an account by Raymond Geist, who was serving as acting consul general while Messersmith was in America. Schussler was Jewish. The next morning, after consultation with Dodd, Geist went to Gestapo headquarters and lodged a protest directly with Rudolf Diels. Within forty-eight hours the assailant was arrested, convicted, and sentenced to seven months in prison. What's more, news of the arrest and punishment received broad play over radio and in newspapers. Geist reported to Washington, "It is very gratifying to see how promptly the German authorities acted. . . . I believe that these attacks will now definitely cease." He was wrong, as time would show, but for the moment at least there seemed to be a new effort by the government to win America's goodwill.

There was an unwholesome element to Geist's final conversation with Diels. The Gestapo chief complained that Schussler and certain other abused Americans were "not altogether a desirable lot," as Geist recalled Diels's remarks. The innuendo was clear, and Geist's temper spiked. "I told him," he wrote, "that we would never consider any other fact than that a man was an American citizen, and that the question of race or origin was entirely beside the point, and that any American citizen was entitled to the full protection of the American Government." Geist to Hull, Jan. 16, 1934, FP 362.1113 Schussler, Max/1, State/Decimal; Geist to Hull, Jan. 18, 1934, 362.1113 Schussler, Max/8 GC, State/Decimal.

210 "More atrocity reports": Gilbert L. MacMaster to Clarence E. Pickett, Feb. 12, 1934, vol. 2, pp. 58–59, *Archives of the Holocaust.*

Deschner, in his biography of Reinhard Heydrich, writes that in these early days, "Jews were not imprisoned in Dachau by virture of their being Jews but because of their having been politically active opponents of National Socialism, or communists, or journalists hostile to NS or 'reactionaries.'" Deschner, 79.

211 "Tolerance means weakness": Noakes and Pridham, 284–86.

212 "Any pity whatsoever for 'enemies of the State'": Krausnick et al., 433.

212 "Outwardly Berlin presented": Memorandum, David Schweitzer to Bernhard Kahn, March 5, 1934, vol. 10, pp. 20–30, *Archives of the Holocaust.*

212 Some ten thousand Jews: Dippel, 114; Breitman and Kraut, 25.

213 "Before the end of 1933": Testimony of Raymond Geist, Nazi Conspiracy and Aggression, vol. 4, Document No. 1759-PS, Avalon Project, Yale University Law School.

Germany's supposedly secret effort to rearm itself in contravention of the Treaty of Versailles was, to Berliners, no secret at all, as became evident in the rise of a popular joke. It went like this:

A man complains to a friend that he doesn't have the money to buy a carriage for his new baby. The friend happens to work in a carriage factory and offers to sneak out enough parts to allow the new father to build one on his own. When the two men see each other again, the new father is still carrying his baby.

His friend the factory worker is perplexed, and asks the new father why he's not using his newly built baby carriage.

"Well, you see," the father replies, "I know I'm very dense and don't understand much about mechanics, but I've put that thing together three times and each time it turns out to be a machine gun!" Wheeler-Bennett, *Nemesis*, 336.

214 "Any one motoring out in the country": John Campbell White to Jay Pierrepont Moffat, Nov. 27, 1933, Carr Papers.

214 "You must know that I am grateful": Gallo, 7–8; Gisevius, 171. Gallo and Gisevius present two slightly different translations of Hitler's greeting. I chose Gallo's, but for no particular reason.

214 Soon afterward, however, Hitler ordered: Diels, 385–89; Diels, Affidavit, in Stackelberg and Winkle, 133–34; Wheaton, 439; Metcalfe, 235–36.

215 "I am confident," he wrote: Kershaw, *Myth*, 63.

215 Röhm, the *Hausherr*, or host: Seating chart, Feb. 23, 1934, "Invitations," Box 1, Martha Dodd Papers.

Chapter 29: Sniping

216 "to read a whole series of letters": Moffat, Diary, Dec. 26, 1933.

216 the number of Jews on his staff: Dodd to William Phillips, Dec. 14, 1933, Box 42, W. E. Dodd Papers. Dodd wrote this letter longhand, and added a note at the top, "For you alone."

216 "righteous aloofness": Dodd to William Phillips, Dec. 14, 1933, Box 42, W. E. Dodd Papers. This letter, with the same date as the letter in the preceding citation, is nonetheless markedly different in content and form. It is typed, and marked "Personal and Confidential."

216 "As usual," Moffat wrote: Moffat, Diary, Dec. 26, 1933.

217 "I hope it will not be difficult for you": William Phillips to Dodd, Jan. 3, 1934, Box 45, W. E. Dodd Papers.

217 "I confess I am at a loss": Ibid.

217 "would limit a little the favoritisms": Dodd to Roosevelt, Jan. 3, 1934, Box 45, W. E. Dodd Papers.

Chapter 30: Premonition

218 Early in January, Boris arranged a date: Once again I have relied heavily on Martha's unpublished recollections about Boris, "Bright Journey into Darkness." And once again, this memoir provides invaluable detail. When I say Boris smiled as he opened the door to his room at the embassy, it is because Martha says he smiled at that moment. Whether her recollections are truly accurate, who can say? But she was there, and I am more than happy to rely on her testimony. Box 14, Martha Dodd Papers.

218 if your goal was seduction: MacDonogh, 31.

Chapter 31: Night Terrors

223 "How is Uncle Adolf?": Memorandum, David Schweitzer to Bernhard Kahn, March 5, 1934, vol. 10, pp. 20–30, *Archives of the Holocaust*. See also Grunberger, 27.

223 One German dreamed that an SA man: Peukert, 237.

223 "Here was an entire nation": Brysac, 186.

223 "constant fear of arrest": Johnson and Reuband, 288, 355, 360.

224 Some 32 percent recalled telling anti-Nazi jokes: Ibid., 357.

224 "whisper almost inaudibly": 277. Martha does not refer to Mildred by name in this passage—in fact she never does so in her memoir, for fear of exposing Mildred and her nascent resistance group to danger—but many of Martha's references in *Through Embassy Eyes*, when triangulated with other material from her papers in the Library of Congress, clearly are to Mildred. Dodd, *Embassy Eyes*, 277.

224 One day he invited her to his office: Ibid., 53.

224 "a sinister smile crossed his lips": Ibid., 55.

225 He filled a cardboard box with cotton: Ibid., 55.

225 "the German glance": Evans, *Power*, 105; Grunberger, 338.

225 Whenever he appeared: Dodd, *Embassy Eyes*, 56, 145, 147, 274, 278.
Also, see "Bright Journey into Darkness," Box 14, Martha Dodd Papers.

225 "There is no way on earth": Dodd, *Embassy Eyes*, 277.

226 "As time went on, and the horror increased": Ibid., 368.

226 rudimentary codes: Ibid., 276.

226 Her friend Mildred used a code for letters home: Brysac, 130.
   Another example: In *Beyond Tears*, Irmgard Litten writes of the tribu-
lations of her son, Hans, at the hands of the Gestapo, and tells how she
deployed a code in which "the first letter of the fourth word of each sentence
would serve as a key to the message." Litten, 60.

226 "It seems absolutely unbelievable": Peter Olden to Dodd, Jan. 30, 1934,
Box 45, W. E. Dodd Papers.

226 "to find out the contents of confidential reports": Raymond Geist to Hull,
March 8, 1934, 125.1953/655, State/Decimal.

227 "I shall be walking at 11:30": Dodd, *Diary*, 63.

227 "Could we meet tomorrow morning": Sir Eric Phipps to Dodd, May 25,
1935, Box 47, W. E. Dodd Papers.

227 Despite the toll: Nonetheless, Messersmith claimed in his unpublished
memoir that "on two occasions I was almost run over by a Gestapo car or an
SS or SA car." Both incidents occurred as he tried crossing the street to the
Esplanade Hotel; both involved powerful cars speeding from a narrow alley.
He believed the drivers had been waiting for him. Messersmith, "Additional
paragraph to memorandum on attempts on my life," unpublished memoir,
Messersmith Papers.

227 "If I had been with people who had been brave": Dodd, *Embassy Eyes*, 54.

228 "bordered on the hysterical": Ibid., 54.

228 "I often felt such terror": Ibid., 54.

Chapter 32: Storm Warning

229 "more living space for our surplus population": Kershaw, *Hubris*, 504–5;
Gallo, 81–82.

230 "That was a new Versailles Treaty": Gallo, 83.

230 "We'll have to let the thing ripen": Kershaw, *Hubris*, 505. Kershaw quotes
Röhm as also saying, "What the ridiculous corporal declared doesn't apply
to us. Hitler has no loyalty and has at least to be sent on leave. If not with,
then we'll manage the thing without Hitler." Also see Gallo, 83, for a slightly
different translation.

Chapter 33: "Memorandum of a Conversation with Hitler"

232 "I stated that I was sorry": Hull, Memorandum, Feb. 29, 1934, State/
Foreign. For a full account of the mock trial, see Anthes.

On May 17, 1934, a counter-rally took place in Madison Square Garden
that drew twenty thousand "Nazi friends," as the *New York Times* put it in a
front-page story the next day. The meeting was organized by a group called
Friends of the New Germany, with the stated purpose of opposing "the un-
constitutional Jewish boycott" of Germany.

232 "do something to prevent this trial": John Hickerson, Memorandum,
March 1, 1934, State/Foreign.

232 "that if the circumstances were reversed": Ibid.

232 "I replied," Hickerson wrote: Ibid.

232 the speakers "were not in the slightest": Hull, Memorandum, March 2,
1934, State/Foreign.

232 "noticed and resented": Dodd, *Diary*, 86.

233 "malicious demonstration": Memorandum, "The German Foreign Office
to the American Embassy," enclosed with Dodd to Hull, March 8, 1934,
State/Foreign.

233 "nobody could suppress a private or public meeting": Dodd, *Diary*, 87.

233 "I reminded the Minister": Dodd to Hull, March 6, 1934, State/Foreign.

233 "an extraordinary impression": Ibid.

233 "that nothing which was to be said": William Phillips, Memorandum,
March 7, 1934, State/Foreign.

233 Here too Phillips demurred: Ibid.

234 "take the matter under consideration": Ibid.

234 The trial took place as planned: *New York Times*, March 8, 1934.

234 "We declare that the Hitler government": Ibid.

234 "no comment other than to re-emphasize": Hull to Dodd, March 8, 1934,
State/Foreign.

234 First Dodd asked Hitler: My account of Dodd's meeting with Hitler
draws its details mainly from Dodd's *Diary*, pages 88–91, and his six-page
"Memorandum of a Conversation with Chancellor Hitler," Box 59, W. E.
Dodd Papers.

238 On March 12 an official: Dodd to Roosevelt, Aug. 15, 1934, Box 45,
W. E. Dodd Papers; Dallek, 227.

238 "Dodd made no impression": Hanfstaengl, 214.

238 "Ambassador Dodd, quite without instruction": Moffat, Diary, March 7,
1934.

239 "I do not think it a disgrace": Dodd, *Diary*, 92.

239 "such offensive and insulting acts": Hull, Memorandum, March 13, 1934,
State/Foreign.

239 "I stated further that I trusted": Ibid.

239 "was not feeling as cool as the snow": Hull, Memorandum, March 23, 1934, State/Foreign. This is one of the few official memoranda from these early days of America's relationship with Nazi Germany that makes one want to stand up and cheer—cheer, that is, in a manner as understated and oblique as Hull's prose. Alas, it was only a brief matchbook flare on behalf of liberty.

Undersecretary William Phillips was present for this meeting and was startled by the "violent language" Luther unleashed. "The Secretary," Phillips wrote in his diary, "was very calm and caustic in his replies and I am not sure that Doctor Luther got the underlying tone of coolness." Phillips added that if it had been up to him he would have told Luther to leave and come back "after he had cooled down." Phillips, Diary, March 23, 1934.

240 "tone of asperity": Hull to John Campbell White, March 30, 1934, State/Foreign.

241 "to communicate to the Government of the German Reich": Quoted in Spear, 216.

241 "in an embarrassing position": R. Walton Moore, Memorandum, Jan. 19, 1934, State/Foreign.

241 "exerted his influence": Spear, 216.

Chapter 34: Diels, Afraid

242 "on all sides of the fence at once": Metcalfe, 201.

242 "We didn't take too seriously what he said": Dodd, *Embassy Eyes*, 134.

243 "You are sick?": Diels, 283. Also quoted in Metcalfe, 236.

243 Once again Diels left the country: Metcalfe, 237; Dodd, *Embassy Eyes*, 134.

243 "a pathetic passive-looking creature": Dodd, *Embassy Eyes*, 134.

244 "I was young and reckless enough": Ibid., 136.

244 "like a frightened rabbit": Ibid., 135.

244 "In some ways the danger": Ibid., 135–36.

Chapter 35: Confronting the Club

245 "on a short leave": *New York Times*, March 24, 1934; Dodd to "family," April 5, 1934, Box 61, W. E. Dodd Papers.

245 "handsome limousine": Dodd, *Diary*, 93.

246 "duty, readiness for sacrifice": Hitler to Roosevelt, reproduced in Hull to John Campbell White, March 28, 1934, State/Foreign.

246 "strange message": Phillips, Diary, March 27, 1934.

246 "to prevent our falling into the Hitler trap": Moffat, Diary, March 24–25, 1934.

246 "who have freely and gladly made heroic efforts": Roosevelt to Hitler, reproduced in Hull to John Campbell White, March 28, 1934, State/Foreign.

246 "We sought to sidestep the impression": Phillips, Diary, March 27, 1934.

246 "there might easily be a little civil war": Dodd to Mrs. Dodd, March 28, 1934, Box 44, W. E. Dodd Papers.

247 "to quiet things if possible": Ibid. Also, see Dodd, *Diary*, 95; Dallek, 228.

247 "Louis XIV and Victoria style": Dodd, *Diary*, 94; Dallek, 231.

247 "house with a hundred rooms": It was this mansion that became the new location of the Cosmos Club, after Welles sold it to the club in 1953. Gellman, 106–7, 395.

248 Indeed, his lecture: R. Walton Moore to Dodd, May 23, 1934, Box 45, W. E. Dodd Papers.

Moore compliments Dodd on his presentation to the group, known as the Personnel Board, but adds, with a good deal of understatement, "I am not at all certain that some of the members of the Board were pleased to hear it."

248 had begun to express real hostility: For example, see Moffat, Diary, Dec. 16, 1933; Phillips, Diary, June 25, 1934.

248 "He is . . . by no means a clear thinker.": Moffat, Diary, March 17, 1934.

248 "Their chief protector": Dodd to Mrs. Dodd, March 28, 1934, Box 44, W. E. Dodd Papers.

Chapter 36: Saving Diels

249 "obviously in a greatly perturbed situation": Messersmith, "Goering," unpublished memoir, 3–8, Messersmith Papers.

251 A photograph of the moment: This photograph is one of many in a unique exhibit in Berlin that tracks the growth of the Gestapo and of Nazi terror in a block-long outdoor, and partly subterranean, display erected along the excavated wall of what once was the basement and so-called house prison of Gestapo headquarters. Certain locations in the world seem to concentrate darkness: the same wall once served as the foundation for a segment of the Berlin Wall.

251 "The infliction of physical punishment": Quoted in Richie, 997; Metcalfe, 240.

252 In mid-April, Hitler flew to the naval port: Evans, *Power*, 29; Shirer, *Rise*, 214–15; Wheeler-Bennett, *Nemesis*, 311–13.

252 "Look at those people over there": Gallo, 35.

253 "Reactionaries, bourgeois conformists": Ibid., 37.

253 Two days later, however, a government announcement: Ibid., 88–89; Kershaw, *Hubris*, 509.

253 "the Man with the Iron Heart": Deschner, 61, 62, 65, 66; Evans, *Power*, 53–54; Fest, 98–101.

253 "I could very well venture combat": Gisevius, 137.

253 Toward the end of April the government: Kershaw, *Hubris*, 743; Wheeler-Bennett, 312. Wheeler-Bennett cites a government "communique" issued April 27, 1934, but Kershaw notes that he provides no source to substantiate its existence.

Chapter 37: Watchers

254 "Tell Boris Winogradov": Haynes et al, 432; Weinstein and Vassiliev, 51.
    Both books present the NKVD message, though the translations vary slightly. I use the Haynes version, which is also the version that can be found online at Vassiliev, Notebooks, White Notebook #2, p. 13, March 28, 1934.

Chapter 38: Humbugged

255 A troubling incident: Dodd to Hull, April 17, 1934, Box 44, W. E. Dodd Papers.
255 "It is my opinion," Dodd wrote: Ibid.
256 Dodd only learned of its existence: Dodd to R. Walton Moore, June 8, 1934, Box 44, W. E. Dodd Papers.
256 Entitled "Their Excellencies": "Their Excellencies," 115–16.
257 "reveals a strange and even unpatriotic attitude": Dodd to William Phillips, June 4, 1934, Box 45, W. E. Dodd Papers.
257 "With regard to that article in *Fortune*": William Phillips to Dodd, July 6, 1934, Box 45, W. E. Dodd Papers.
257 "Once there," he wrote to Martha: Dodd to Martha, April 24, 1934, Box 62, W. E. Dodd Papers. He opens the letter, "Dear 'Little' Martha."
257 "how they and their friends had calmed their fellows": Dodd, *Diary*, 95.
258 "THEREFORE HOPE YOU CAN BRING NEW CAR": Mrs. Dodd to Dodd, via John Campbell White, April 19, 1934, Box 44, W. E. Dodd Papers.
258 "I fear Mueller was driving carelessly": Dodd to Martha, April 25, 1934, Box 62, W. E. Dodd Papers.
258 "ridiculously simple for an Ambassador": Dodd, *Diary*, 108.
258 "This was a beautiful day": Ibid., 98.
259 "the syphilis of all European peoples": Dodd to Roosevelt, Aug. 15, 1934, Box 45, W. E. Dodd Papers.
259 "all the animosities of the preceding winter": Ibid.
    Dodd expresses a similar dismay at being embarrassed in a letter to Edward M. House, May 23, 1934, Box 44, W. E. Dodd Papers. He writes: "You recall what we did to ease off the excitement in Chicago, and you remember perhaps my advice to leading Jews that it would be well to let up a little in the boycott if the Germans gave evidence of a conciliatory attitude." He closes, "I am frank to say that it has embarrassed me a good deal."
259 "I was delighted to be home": Dodd, *Diary*, 100.

PART VI: BERLIN AT DUSK

Chapter 39: Dangerous Dining

263 The post of ambassador to Austria: Phillips, Diary, March 16, 1934; Stiller, 54–55.

264 While Dodd was in America: Louis Lochner to Betty Lochner, May 29, 1934, Round Robin Letters, Box 6, Lochner Papers; "List of Persons Invited," Box 59, W. E. Dodd Papers.

264 "I wonder why we were asked today": Fromm, 162–64.

266 The host was a wealthy banker: I pieced together the story of the Regendanz dinner from the following accounts: Evans, *Power*, 26; François-Poncet, 139–40; Phipps, 66–67; Wilhelm Regendanz to Attorney General Brendel of Gestapo, July 2, 1934, Box 45, W. E. Dodd Papers.

Herman Ullstein, of the great German publishing dynasty, tells a darkly amusing story about another meal, this at a fancy restaurant in Potsdam. A man was dining in a group that included an attractive, dark-haired woman. A Nazi from a neighboring table, having concluded the woman was Jewish, asked the group to leave the restaurant. The seated man smiled and asked, "Do you mind if we finish our dinner first?"

Fifteen minutes later, the group was still eating and having a grand time, which caused the Nazi to return and demand that they leave at once.

The seated man calmly gave the Nazi his card, which identified him as "François-Poncet, *Ambassadeur de France*." Ullstein, 287–88.

267 On Thursday, May 24, Dodd walked: Dodd, *Diary*, 101–2.

Chapter 40: A Writer's Retreat

269 One of the most important moments in her education: My account of Martha's day at Carwitz is based on the following sources: Dodd, *Embassy Eyes*, 83–85; Martha Dodd, unpublished memoir, 2–3, Box 13, Martha Dodd Papers; Hans Fallada to Martha Dodd, June 8, 1934, and June 18, 1934, Box 5, Martha Dodd Papers; Williams, xvii, 126, 142, 150, 152–55, 176–78, 185–88, 194, 209; Schueler, 14, 66; Brysac, 148–50; Metcalfe, 193–95. Also see Turner, "Fallada," throughout.

After this episode, Martha and Fallada had a brief exchange of letters. She sent him a short story of hers. He sent her a photograph, one of many he had taken that day at Carwitz—"unfortunately the only picture I took which turned out nicely." Of her story, he wrote, "I wish that you will soon find the necessary quiet time and inner peace to work intensively—it's worthwhile, I can tell from this little example." Martha in turn sent along a collection of Boris's photographs, and told Fallada she hoped one day to visit him again, which seemed to come as a relief to Fallada—"so," he wrote back, "you did enjoy yourselves."

She never returned to Carwitz. As the years advanced, she heard little of Fallada or his work, and believed "he must have surrendered completely both his craft and his dignity." Fallada to Martha, June 8 and June 18, 1934, Box 5, Martha Dodd Papers; Martha Dodd, unpublished memoir, 2, Box 13, Martha Dodd Papers.

269 his pseudonym, Hans Fallada: Ditzen built his pseudonym from the names of two characters from *Grimm's Fairy Tales*, Hans, from "Lucky Hans," and Fallada from "The Goose Girl," in which a horse named Falada (spelled with one *l* in the fable) proves able to detect truth even after being beheaded. Williams, xi.

270 "inner emigration": Ritchie, 112.

273 "It may be superstitious belief": Ibid., 115.

274 "By the spring of 1934," she wrote: Dodd, *Embassy Eyes*, 131–33.

274 "The prospect of a cessation": Dodd to Hull, June 18, 1934 (No. 935), State/Foreign.

275 In May, he reported, the Nazi Party: Ibid.

275 Germany's Aryan population: Dodd to Hull, June 18, 1934 (No. 932), State/Foreign.

275 "Germany looks dry for the first time": Dodd, *Diary*, 105.

276 "the great heat": Moffat, Diary, May 20, 1934.

Chapter 41: Trouble at the Neighbor's

277 "tense and electric": Dodd, *Embassy Eyes*, 134.

277 The change was obvious: Gallo, 122.

Chapter 42: Hermann's Toys

278 Sunday, June 10, 1934: My account of this creepily charming episode is derived from the following sources: Cerruti, 178–80; Dodd, *Diary*, 108–9; Phipps, 56–58. I also examined Göring's own portfolio of photographs of Carinhall, Lot 3810, in the photographic archives of the Library of Congress.

280 "rather attached to her": Dodd, *Embassy Eyes*, 220.

Chapter 43: A Pygmy Speaks

283 The names of two former chancellors: Wheeler-Bennett, *Nemesis*, 315–17.

283 "Everywhere I go men talk of resistance": Dodd to Hull, June 16, 1934, Box 44, W. E. Dodd Papers.

284 "The speech took months of preparation": Evans, *Power*, 29–30; Jones,

167–73; Gallo, 137–40; Kershaw, *Hubris*, 509–10, 744 n. 57; Shirer, *Rise*, 218–19.

284 "I am told," he began: For text, see Noakes and Pridham, 209–10; and Papen, 307. Also see Jones, 172; Gallo, 139–40; Kershaw, *Hubris*, 509. In his memoir, published in 1953, Papen states, "I prepared my speech with great care. . . ." This claim has been widely discounted. Papen, 307.

285 "The thunder of applause": Gallo, 141.

285 "It is difficult to describe the joy": Wheeler-Bennett, *Titan*, 459.

285 "All these little dwarfs": Gallo, 143–44; Shirer, *Rise*, 219. Also see Kershaw, *Hubris*, 510.

285 "If they should at any time": Kershaw, *Hubris*, 510.

286 "were snatched from the hands of the guests": Dodd to Hull, June 26, 1934, State/Foreign. For other details of the government's reaction, see Evans, *Power*, 29–30; Jones, 172–74; Kershaw, *Hubris*, 510–11; Shirer, *Rise*, 218; Wheeler-Bennett, *Titan*, 460, and *Nemesis*, 319.

286 "There was something in the sultry air": Gisevius, 128.

286 Someone threw a hand-grenade fuse: Ibid., 129.

286 "There was so much whispering": Ibid., 129.

287 "Everywhere uncertainty, ferment": Klemperer, *Witness*, 71. Klemperer looked to the weather to fuel his hopes that Hitler would be deposed. He wrote in his diary, "'Beautiful weather' = heat + lack of rain, abnormal lack of rain, such as has been causing havoc for three months now. A weapon against Hitler!" *Witness*, 72.

287 "There is now great excitement": Dodd, *Diary*, 114; Dodd, Memorandum, June 18, 1934, Box 59, W. E. Dodd Papers.

287 "I spoke at Marburg": Gallo, 152.

287 He promised to remove the propaganda: Evans, *Power*, 30; Kershaw, *Hubris*, 510.

288 "It was with cold calculation": Gisevius, 131.

288 The next day, June 21, 1934: Evans, *Power*, 30; Kershaw, *Hubris*, 510–11; Wheeler-Bennett, *Nemesis*, 320.

289 "who after the Marburg speech": Dodd, *Diary*, 114.

289 "The week closes quietly": Ibid., 115.

Chapter 44: The Message in the Bathroom

290 "He was entirely calm and fatalistic": Wheeler-Bennett, *Titan*, 462.

290 "Woe to him who breaks faith": Wheaton, 443.

290 On the medicine chest: Jones, 173.

291 "beautiful Rhineland summer day": Diels, 419.

Chapter 45: Mrs. Cerruti's Distress

292 "During the last five days": Dodd, *Diary*, 115–16.

292 "the situation was much as it was in Paris": Ibid., 116.

292 "by the example of his magnetism": Martha Dodd, "Bright Journey into Darkness," 18, 21, Box 14, Martha Dodd Papers.

293 Under Stalin, peasants had been forced: Riasanovsky, 551, 556. A personal note here: While I was an undergraduate at the University of Pennsylvania, I took two wonderful courses from Riasanovsky's brother, Alexander, who on one noteworthy evening taught me and my roommates how to drink vodka Russian-style. It was his delightful lecture style, however, that had the greater influence, and drove me to spend most of my time at Penn studying Russian history, literature, and language.

293 Tour No. 9, the Volga-Caucasus-Crimea tour: "Detailed Schedule of Tour No. 9 for Miss Martha Dodd," Box 62, W. E. Dodd Papers.

293 "Martha!" he wrote, indulging his passion: Boris to Martha, June 7, 1934, Box 10, Martha Dodd Papers.

294 "I never plotted the overthrow": Martha to Agnes Knickerbocker, July 16, 1969, Box 13, Martha Dodd Papers.

294 "It was the hottest day": Cerruti, 153.

295 "seemed self-confident": Dodd, *Embassy Eyes*, 140.

295 "You and Dr. Goebbels": Dodd, *Diary*, 116.

295 "She sat by my father": Dodd, *Embassy Eyes*, 141.

295 "Mr. Ambassador, something terrible": Ibid., 141.

295 She found this astonishing: Cerruti, 153, 157.

295 "Temperature 101 and ½ in the shade today": Moffat, Diary, June 29, 1934.

295 The three men undressed and climbed in: Ibid.

296 "Presumably the Ambassador has been complaining": Phillips, Diary, June 15, 1934.

296 "well and in extremely high spirits": Moffat, Diary, July 17, 1934.

Chapter 46: Friday Night

297 That Friday evening, July 29, 1934: For this chapter I relied on the following sources: Birchall, 203; Evans, *Power*, 31–32; Gallo, 33, 38, 106; Kershaw, *Hubris*, 511–15. For a lengthy excerpt of Kempka's account, see Noakes and Pridham, 212–14.

PART VII: WHEN EVERYTHING CHANGED

Chapter 47: "Shoot, Shoot!"

303 "strolled serenely through the streets": Adlon, 207.

Hedda Adlon, wife of the Adlon's proprietor, liked driving about town in her white Mercedes, and was said to keep twenty-eight Pekinese dogs. De Jonge, 132.

304 "It was a beautiful serene blue day": Dodd, *Embassy Eyes*, 141.

304 "Röhm," Hitler barked: Various and varying accounts of this episode appear in the literature. I relied on Kershaw, *Hubris*, 514; Noakes and Pridham, 213–14; and Strasser, 250.

305 "It is never safe to despise a telephone call": Birchall, 193.

305 "dead tired—[could] weep": Schultz, Daily Logs, July 5, 1934, Box 32, Schultz Papers.

305 One of the most alarming rumors: Birchall, 198.

305 At the Hotel Hanselbauer, Röhm got dressed: Noakes and Pridham, 213.

306 "You have been condemned to death": Kershaw, *Hubris*, 514.

307 "As I followed Daluege": Gisevius, 150.

308 He looked troubled: Dodd, *Diary*, 117.

Chapter 48: Guns in the Park

309 "our heads giddy": Dodd, *Embassy Eyes*, 142.

311 "to his great sorrow": Office of Der Stabschef der S.-A. to Dodd, June 29, 1934, Box 45, W. E. Dodd Papers.

311 "In view of the uncertainty of the situation": Dodd, *Diary*, 117.

311 A wooden leg: German Office of Foreign Affairs to Dodd, May 28, 1935, Box 47, W. E. Dodd Papers.

Chapter 49: The Dead

313 "unbearable tension": Quoted in Gallo, 257.

313 "For weeks we have been watching": Birchall, 205–7; Gallo, 257.

314 No one knew exactly how many people lost their lives: I constructed this paragraph and the one following from an array of sources: Hugh Corby Fox, Memorandum, July 2, 1934, Box 45, W. E. Dodd Papers; H. C. Flack, Confidential Memorandum, July 7, 1934, Box 45, W. E. Dodd Papers; Wheeler-Bennett, *Nemesis*, 323; Gallo, 256, 258; Rürup, 53, 223; Kershaw, *Hubris*, 515; Evans, *Power*, 34–36; Strasser, 252, 263; Gisevius, 153; Birchall, 20; Metcalfe, 269.

315 One target, Gottfried Reinhold Treviranus: Gallo, 255; Martha offers a slightly different account in her memoir: *Embassy Eyes*, 155.

315 "To the king of Siam": Adlon, 207–9.

316 poor Willi Schmid: Shirer, *Rise*, 224n. See also Birchall, 207; Evans, *Power*, 36; Kershaw, *Hubris*, 515.

316 Providently, he was in America: Casey, 340; Conradi, 143, 144, 148, 151, 157, 159, 163, 167–68; *New York Times*, July 1, 1934.

317 "against the background of a blood-red sky": Gisevius, 160.

317 In a radio address propaganda chief Goebbels: Birchall, 205.

Chapter 50: Among the Living

319 "It was a strange day": Dodd, *Diary*, 117.

That Sunday, the Jewish newspaper *Bayerische Israelitische Gemeinde-zeitung*, still in operation—it would continue until 1937—published caution-ary advice for its readers, urging them, according to one historian's account, "to show more reserve, tact and dignity and to behave impeccably in public places so as not to offend."

That Sunday afternoon, Hitler held a tea party at his chancellery for members of his cabinet, various ministers, and their families. Children were invited. Hitler at one point walked to a window overlooking the street. A crowd gathered below roared its approval.

The ever-present Hans Gisevius was there as well. Hitler spotted him and raised his hand in greeting. Gisevius wrote, "It occurred to me that if he could read my innermost thoughts, he would have me shot." Dippel, 150; Gallo, 269; Kershaw, *Hubris*, 516; Gisevius quoted in Gallo, 270.

319 They drove past the entrance very slowly: Dodd, *Embassy Eyes*, 142–43.

320 The story, pieced together later: Evans, *Power*, 33; Kershaw, *Hubris*, 176, 516.

320 Accounts vary: Evans, *Power*, 33; Kershaw, *Hubris*, 516; Gallo, 270; Shirer, *Rise*, 221; Noakes and Pridham, 215.

After Röhm's murder, Hitler claimed that the SA chief's homosexual prac-tices had come as a complete surprise to him. A new joke promptly made the rounds in Berlin: "What will he do when he finally finds out about Goebbels's club foot?"

Another joke began circulating at about the same time: "It is only now that we can realize the full significance of Röhm's recent address to Nazi youth, 'Out of every Hitler Youth, a Storm Trooper will Emerge.'" Grun-berger, 332, 335.

320 As a reward: Wheaton, 452.

321 "The *Führer* with soldierly decision": Noakes and Pridham, 216; see slightly different version in Wheeler-Bennett, *Nemesis*, 325.

321 "Lebst du noch?": Dodd, *Embassy Eyes*, 151.

Chapter 51: Sympathy's End

322 "The diplomats seemed jittery": Fromm, 171–72. Fromm claimed that after the purge she briefly took to carrying a revolver, but then threw it into a canal. Dippel, 150.

322 Dodd and his wife stood at the entrance: Dodd, *Embassy Eyes*, 157.

323 "Der junge Herr von Papen": Ibid., 158.

323 "a certain fine beauty": Ibid., 157.

324 "The sight of these clothes": Cerruti, 157.

324 "to bring her my heartiest greetings": Wilhelm Regendanz to Mrs. Dodd, July 3, 1934, Box 45, W. E. Dodd Papers.

325 "When she spoke of her son": Dodd, *Embassy Eyes*, 163–65.

325 "Arrived safe and sound": Ibid., 165.

325 "We have replied to them": Moffat, Diary, July 5, 1934.

325 "quite exciting": Moffat, Diary, July 17, 1934.

326 "this would be extremely difficult": Dodd to Hull, July 6, 1934, State/Foreign.

326 "By his own showing": Moffat, Diary, July 7–8, 1934.

326 Hull angrily ordered Moffat: Ibid.

326 "with the utmost vigor": Hull to Dodd, July 7, 1934, State/Foreign.

326 "It was a fairly stiff telegram": Moffat, Diary, July 7–8, 1934.

326 "Ambassador Dud": Moffat, Diary, July 5, 1934.

327 "The Secretary kept repeating": Moffat, Diary, July 11, 1934.

327 "the entire State Department": Ibid.

327 "Our people will have to lose their bonds": Dodd to Hull, Aug. 2, 1934, vol. 37, Reel 11, Hull Papers.

327 "an interesting trip": Dodd, *Embassy Eyes*, 170.

327 A photographer captured her looking jaunty: Ibid., opposite 198.

328 "I had had enough of blood and terror": Ibid., 169.

328 "I could not have imagined the outbreak against the Jews": Dodd to Daniel C. Roper, Aug. 14, 1934, Box 45, W. E. Dodd Papers.

328 "From the reports placed before me": Wheeler-Bennett, *Nemesis*, 325–26.

328 "energetic and successful proceeding": Ibid., 326n1.

329 "it was a relief that he did not appear.": Dodd, *Diary*, 121.

329 "My task here is to work for peace": Ibid., 123.

329 He vowed never to host: Ibid., 126.

Chapter 52: Only the Horses

331 "I shall not attend the address": Dodd, *Diary*, 127.

Sir Eric Phipps, in his own diary, wrote, "So long as the Reichstag merely serves as a convenient platform for the glorification of crime and for attacks on foreign heads of mission in Berlin, I propose to leave vacant the seat which in normal circumstances The King's representative might be glad occasionally to occupy." Phipps, 68.

331 "Deputies," Hitler said: A translation of Hitler's speech appears in Gallo, 298–307. Most accounts agree that Hitler claimed only seventy-seven people had been killed, though at least one (Evans, *Power*, 39) states that Hitler put the number at seventy-four. See also Birchall, 209.

332 Had Dodd been present: Birchall, 209.

332 "They stood face to face on the dais": Ibid.

332 "NOTHING MORE REPULSIVE": Dodd to Hull, July 14, 1934, Box 44, W. E. Dodd Papers.

In Washington, Jay Pierrepont Moffat was able to listen to Hitler's speech over the radio. "It struck me as full of banalities and by far the weakest speech he has thus far made," Moffat wrote in his diary entry for July 13, 1934. "The transmission was extraordinarily clear. He has a curious rasping voice which at moments of excitement rose almost to a shriek. He gave no proof of the conspiracy and his remarks with regard to the outside world were distinctly weak." Moffat, Diary, July 13, 1934.

333 "as if they were chloroformed": Quoted in Conradi, 168.

333 "A few days ago in Germany": Quoted in Hull to Roosevelt, July 13, 1934, State/Foreign.

334 Dodd at first seemed inclined to believe: For the evolution of Dodd's thinking, see Dodd to Hull, July 2, 1934; Dodd to Hull, July 5, 1934; Dodd to Hull, July 6, 1934; and Dodd to Hull, July 7, 1934, all in State/Foreign.

334 Britain's Sir Eric Phipps initially accepted the official story: Phipps, 14, 61.

334 "It has not increased his charm": Ibid., 76.

334 "a type of gangland bloodbath": Kershaw, *Hubris*, 522.

334 "I . . . had no idea that this hour of lightning": Diels, 382.

335 An intelligence report from the exiled Social Democrats: Kershaw, *Myth*, 87.

335 "an even more terroristic regime": Dodd to Hull, Aug. 2, 1934, Box 44, W. E. Dodd Papers.

335 "The people hardly noticed this complete coup d'etat": Klemperer, *Witness*, 80.

335 "Today Hitler is the Whole of Germany": Kershaw, *Myth*, 68.

336 "At a time when nearly every German": Dodd, *Diary*, 140–41.

Chapter 53: Juliet #2

337 "I am very sad": Boris to Martha, July 11, 1934, Box 10, Martha Dodd Papers. Also see, Boris to Martha, "late July-1934," and Boris to Martha, "early Aug. 1934," both also in Box 10.

337 "You are the one": Boris to Martha, Aug. 5, 1934, Box 10, Martha Dodd Papers.

338 Martha was approached by emissaries: Weinstein and Vassiliev, 52.

338 "The entire Dodd family": Ibid., 52; Vassiliev, Notebooks, White Notebook #2, 25.

338 she formally petitioned Stalin: Weinstein and Vassiliev, 55; Vassiliev, Notebooks, White Notebook #2, 37, March 14, 1937.

338 "in the interests of business": Weinstein and Vassiliev, 58. A slightly different translation appears at Vassiliev, Notebooks, White Notebook #2, 33.

339 "I don't quite understand": Weinstein and Vassiliev, 58; Vassiliev, Notebooks, White Notebook #2, 45, March 21, 1937.

339 "Juliet #2": Weinstein and Vassiliev, 58–59; Vassiliev, Notebooks, White Notebook #2, 45, March 21, 1937.

339 The meeting "went off well": Weinstein and Vassiliev, 59; Vassiliev, Notebooks, White Notebook #2, 51, Nov. 12, 1937. Here the translation reads: "The meeting with 'Liza' was successful. She was in a good mood. . . ."

Chapter 54: A Dream of Love

340 "It is so humiliating to me": Dodd, *Diary*, 276.

340 "With Germany united": Dodd to Hull, Aug. 30, 1934, Box 44, W. E. Dodd Papers.

340 "In my judgment, the German authorities": Dodd to Gen. Douglas MacArthur, Aug. 27, 1934, Box 44, W. E. Dodd Papers.

340 "If Woodrow Wilson's bones": Dallek, 279.

340 "the delicate work of watching": Dodd, *Diary*, 216.

341 "What in the world is the use": Phillips, Diary, n.d., 1219.

341 "That you have found me": Kershaw, *Myth*, 82.

341 "With armies increasing in size": Dodd to Hull, Sept. 19, 1936, Box 49, W. E. Dodd Papers.

342 "You must not mention to anyone": Dodd to Martha, Oct. 28, 1936, Box 62, W. E. Dodd Papers.

342 "Dodd has many admirable and likeable qualities": William C. Bullitt to Roosevelt, Dec. 7, 1936, in Bullitt, 194–95.

342 "Personally, I cannot see": Moffat, Diary, Aug. 27, 1934.

342 "attacking me violently": Dodd, *Diary*, 371.

343 "My position is difficult": Ibid., 372.

343 "I thought of you, my dear": Mrs. Dodd to Dodd, July 25, 1937, Box 62, W. E. Dodd Papers.

344 "spread over the nerve connections": Dodd, *Diary*, 334.

344 "at sixty-five one must take stock": Dr. Thomas R. Brown to Dodd, March 7, 1935, Box 46, W. E. Dodd Papers.

344 "It was quite obvious that something had happened": Messersmith, "Visits to Berlin," unpublished memoir, 10, Messersmith Papers.

345 "I think he was so thoroughly appalled": Ibid., 10.

345 "speak the truth about things": Dodd, *Diary*, 426.

345 "I have long believed Welles was opposed to me": Ibid., 427.

345 "I have not the slightest doubt": R. Walton Moore to Dodd, Dec. 14, 1937, Box 52, W. E. Dodd Papers.

346 "desired to make it plain": Dallek, 313.

346 Hyde Park—"a marvelous place": Dodd, *Diary*, 428–29.

347 "In Berlin once more.": Dodd, *Diary*, 430.

347 "Much as the President regrets any personal inconvenience": Hull to Dodd, Nov. 23, 1937, Box 51, W. E. Dodd Papers.

347 "Until now I have lived with the memory": Boris to Martha, April 29, 1938, Box 10, W. E. Dodd Papers.

347 They became engaged: *Chicago Daily Tribune*, Sept. 5, 1938; *New York Times*, Sept. 5, 1938; Weinstein and Vassiliev, 61; Vassiliev, Notebooks, White Notebook #2, 56, July 9, 1938,

348 "You know, honey": Weinstein and Vassiliev, 61; Vassiliev, Notebooks, White Notebook #2, 56, July 9, 1938. In Weinstein and Vassiliev, the translation reads "honey"; in the notebooks, "darling."

348 She never learned that Boris's last letter: Weinstein and Vassiliev, 61–62.

Chapter 55: As Darkness Fell

349 "must face the sad fact": *New York Times*, Dec. 23, 1937.

349 "Mankind is in grave danger": *New York Times*, Jan. 14, 1938.

349 "I personally felt quite strongly": Moffat, Diary, Jan. 14, 1938.

350 "Great Britain," he said: *New York Times*, Feb. 22, 1938.

350 "I do wish we were all nearer together": Mrs. Dodd to Martha, Feb. 26, 1938, Box 63, Martha Dodd Papers.

351 "So far I can't get anything done": Mrs. Dodd to Martha, April 26, 1938, Box 1, Martha Dodd Papers.

351 "Wish I did have a home": Mrs. Dodd to Martha, May 23, 1938, Box 1, Martha Dodd Papers.

351 "It was the greatest shock": Dodd, *Diary*, 446.

351 "the strain and terror of life": Dodd, *Embassy Eyes*, 370.

351 "to kill them all": Bailey, 192, 194.

352 "could scarcely believe": Breitman and Kraut, 230.

352 "My hunch is that you have lots of chances": Sigrid Schultz to Dodd, Nov. 30, 1938, Box 56, W. E. Dodd Papers.

352 "It was not my fault": For details on this episode, see *New York Times*, Dec. 9 and Dec. 10, 1938; March 3 and May 7, 1939; Bailey, 195–96; Dallek, 332.

353 A front-page article: United Press, "Dodd Is Attacked . . .", n.d., Box 2, Martha Dodd Papers.

353 "ill and not entirely responsible": Bailey, 199.

353 "If they had co-operated": Dallek, 332.

353 By fall, Dodd was confined: Bailey, 199–200; *New York Times*, Feb. 10, 1940.

354 He was buried: Martha later had Dodd's body moved to Rock Creek Cemetery in Washington, D.C., Dec. 6, 1946, Section L., Lot 37, Site 4. One lovely spring afternoon, accompanied by one of my daughters, I visited the Stoneleigh Golf and Country Club, which is part of a development that includes large faux-colonial houses on outsized parcels of land an hour or so west of Washington, D.C. Though the golf course (18 holes, par 72) is necessarily closely manicured, I nonetheless got a sense of how compelling this terrain must have been for Dodd, especially during his first visit home from Berlin when the farm's soft hills must have been deeply soothing. His old barn is still there and a few stretches of ancient stone fence, but now instead of pigs the barn shelters masses of suckling golf carts. Dodd took a dim view of golf and golfers, especially those members of his Berlin staff who were continually skipping work to play a few rounds at their Wannsee club. It is a good thing Martha moved his body, because his ghost surely would have proved a daunting hazard, blocking putts and hurling balls far off into the adjacent swales and roughs.

354 Five years later: Ryan, 418.

At war's end the remains of the Tiergarten came under further assault, this time by the starving populace, who cut the shattered trees and stumps into firewood and turned portions of the park into a vegetable garden. In 1947, Berlin's mayor described the devastation of the park as "the most painful wound inflicted on our city by the war." Daum and Mauch, 205.

354 "Knowing his passion": *New York Times*, Feb. 11, 1940.

354 "the best ambassador": Schultz, "Sigrid Schultz on Ambassador Dodd," January 1956, Box 2, Schultz Papers.

354 "Dodd was years ahead": Wise, *Challenging*, 234.

355 "I often think": Messersmith, "Some Observations on the appointment of Dr. William Dodd, as Ambassador to Berlin," 11, unpublished memoir, Messersmith Papers.

355 "a renewed pride and faith": Thomas Wolfe to Maxwell E. Perkins, May 23, 1935, Wolfe, *Selected Letters*, 228.

355 "Above all, not too much zeal": Brysac, 224.

355 "Jewish controlled": Stiller, 129; Weil, 60.

355 "the man who pulled his people": Stiller, 129.

356 "idiotic things as a rule": Weil, 60–61.

Ultimately even Roosevelt was taken aback by Wilson's attitude, as George Messersmith learned during a conversation he had with the president. By this time, Messersmith had been posted to Washington as assistant secretary of state. In a personal memorandum dated Feb. 1, 1938, Messersmith summarized the president's remarks. "He"—Roosevelt—"said he was much surprised that Wilson had indicated that he thought we ought to lay less stress on the democracies and democratic principles." To which Messersmith replied, "There were some things concerning human psychology, and particularly German, that were a strange country to Wilson." The president, he noted, was "somewhat disturbed concerning Wilson's ideas." Messersmith, Memorandum, Feb. 1, 1938, Messersmith Papers.

356 "I do think the chances": William C. Bullitt to Roosevelt, Dec. 7, 1937, Bullitt, 242.

356 "But history," wrote Dodd's friend: *New York Times*, March 2, 1941.

EPILOGUE: THE QUEER BIRD IN EXILE

359 "If there were any logic": Dodd, *Embassy Eyes*, 228.

359 "I told her that if she published my letters": Messersmith, "Goering," unpublished memoir, 7–8, Messersmith Papers.

360 Martha at last created her own successful salon: Vanden Heuvel, 248.

360 "growing effectiveness": Martha Dodd, unpublished memoir, 4, Box 13, Martha Dodd Papers.

At its peak, the network included an operator in Hitler's wire room and a senior officer in the Luftwaffe; Arvid Harnack became an adviser to Hitler's economics minister.

360 By now, however, Martha knew: Falk Harnack, "Notes on the Execution of Dr. Arvid Harnack," Box 13, Martha Dodd Papers; Axel von Harnack, "Arvid and Mildred Harnack," translation of article in *Die Gegenwart*, Jan. 1947, 15–18, in Box 13, Martha Dodd Papers; Falk Harnack, "2nd visit to the *Reichssicherheitshauptamt*," Box 13, Martha Dodd Papers. Also see Rürup, 163.

The network got wind of Germany's surprise invasion of the Soviet Union and tried to notify Stalin. Upon receiving this information, Stalin told its bearer, "You can send your 'source' from the German air force staff to his much fucked mother! This is not a 'source' but a disinformer." Brysac, 277.

360 "And I have loved Germany so": Falk Harnack to Martha, Dec. 29, 1947, Box 13, Martha Dodd Papers. Arvid, in a closing letter to "my beloved ones," wrote, "I should have liked to have seen you all again, but that is unfortunately not possible." n.d., Box 13, Martha Dodd Papers.

360 "a gifted, clever and educated woman": Weinstein and Vassiliev, 51, 62.

360 "She considers herself a Communist": Ibid., 62; Vassiliev, Notebooks, White Notebook #2, 61.

361 Through Martha's efforts: Haynes et al., 440; Weinstein and Vassiliev, 70–71; Alfred Stern to Max Delbrück, Nov. 23, 1970, Box 4, Martha Dodd Papers; Vanden Heuvel, 223, 252.

When toilets broke the Sterns called the Czech foreign minister to effect repairs; they owned paintings by Cézanne, Monet, and Renoir. Vanden Heuvel, 252.

361 They bought a new black Mercedes.: Martha to "David," Feb. 28, 1958, Box 1, Martha Dodd Papers.

361 Martha became "obsessed": Alfred Stern to Max Delbrück, Nov. 23, 1970, Box 4, Martha Dodd Papers.

361 "We can't say we like it here": Martha to Audrey Fuss, July 25, 1975, Box 5, Martha Dodd Papers.

361 After two years in Cologne: Metcalfe, 288.

362 "It was," she wrote, "one of the ugliest": Martha Dodd, "Chapter 30, August 1968," unpublished memoir, 5, Box 12, Martha Dodd Papers.

362 "Max, my love": Martha to Delbrück, April 27, 1979, Box 4, Martha Dodd Papers; Delbrück to Martha, Nov. 15, 1978, Box 4, Martha Dodd Papers.

362 "that ass": Martha to Sigrid Schultz, April 25, 1970, Box 13, Martha Dodd Papers.

362 "a real buffoon": Martha to Philip Metcalfe, April 16, 1982, Box 7, Martha Dodd Papers.

362 Bassett confessed he had destroyed: George Bassett Roberts to Martha, Nov. 23, 1971, Box 8, Martha Dodd Papers.

362 "Such love letters!": Martha to George Bassett Roberts, Feb. 19, 1976, Box 8, Martha Dodd Papers.

362 "One thing is sure": Martha to George Bassett Roberts, Nov. 1, "more or less," 1971, Box 8, Martha Dodd Papers.

363 In 1979 a federal court: *New York Times*, March 23 and March 26, 1979.

363 Bill Jr. had died: *New York Times*, Oct. 19, 1952, and April 22, 1943.

363 "Bill was a very swell guy": Martha to Audrey Fuss, Oct. 31, 1952, Box 1, Martha Dodd Papers.

363 "Where do you think we should die": Martha to Letitia Ratner, March 9, 1984, Box 8, Martha Dodd Papers.

364 "Nowhere could be as lonely": Martha to Van and Jennie Kaufman, March 6, 1989, Martha Dodd Papers.

364 He had forsaken the magnificent copper beech: *New York Times*, Sept. 4, 1996.

CODA: "TABLE TALK"

365 Years after the war, a cache of documents: Hitler, 102. Hitler's off-the-cuff remarks, though passed along with inevitable modifications, provide a chilling and compelling glimpse into his mind.

Epigraph

449 Isherwood, *Visit*, 308.

BIBLIOGRAPHY

ARCHIVAL SOURCES

Carr, Wilbur J. Papers. Library of Congress Manuscript Division. Washington, D.C.

Dodd, Martha. Papers. Library of Congress Manuscript Division. Washington, D.C.

Dodd, William E. Papers. Library of Congress Manuscript Division. Washington, D.C.

Harnack, Mildred Fish. Papers. University of Wisconsin Library. Madison, Wisc.

Hull, Cordell. Papers. Library of Congress Manuscript Division. Washington, D.C.

Kaltenborn, H. V. Papers. Wisconsin Historical Society. Madison, Wisc.

Lochner, Louis P. Papers. Wisconsin Historical Society. Madison, Wisc.

Messersmith, George S. Papers. Special Collections, University of Delaware. Newark, Del.

Moffat, Jay Pierrepont. Diaries. Houghton Library. Harvard University. Cambridge, Mass.

Phillips, William. Diaries. Houghton Library. Harvard University. Cambridge, Mass.

Roosevelt, Franklin D. William E. Dodd Correspondence. Franklin Delano Roosevelt Library. Hyde Park, N.Y. Correspondence online. (Roosevelt Correspondence)

Schultz, Sigrid. Papers. Wisconsin Historical Society. Madison, Wisc.

U.S. Department of State Decimal Files. National Archives and Records Administration. College Park, Md. (State/Decimal)

U.S. Department of State. *Foreign Relations of the United States, 1933 and 1934.* Digital Collection. University of Wisconsin. (State/Foreign)

Vassiliev, Alexander. The Vassiliev Notebooks. Cold War International History Project. Woodrow Wilson International Center for Scholars. Washington, D.C.

Venona Intercepts. National Security Agency.

White, John C. Papers. Library of Congress Manuscript Division. Washington, D.C.

Wilder, Thornton. Papers. Beinecke Rare Book and Manuscript Library. Yale University. New Haven, Conn.

BOOKS AND PERIODICALS

Adlon, Hedda. *Hotel Adlon: The Life and Death of a Great Hotel.* London: Barrie Books, 1958.

American Jewish Congress. *Hitlerism and the American Jewish Congress.* New York: American Jewish Congress, 1934.

Andersen, Hartvig. *The Dark City.* London: Cresset Press, 1954.

Andreas-Friedrich, Ruth. *Berlin Underground: 1938–1945.* Translated by Barrows Mussey. New York: Paragon House, 1989.

"Angora: Pictorial Records of an SS Experiment." *Wisconsin Magazine of History* 50, no. 4 (Summer 1967): 392–413.

Anhalt, Diana. *A Gathering of Fugitives: American Political Expatriates in Mexico 1948–1965.* Santa Maria, Calif.: Archer Books, 2001.

Anthes, Louis. "Publicly Deliberative Drama: The 1934 Mock Trial of Adolf Hitler for 'Crimes Against Civilization.'" *American Journal of Legal History* 42, no. 4 (October 1998): 391–410.

Archives of the Holocaust. Vol. 1: American Friends Service Committee, Philadelphia, part 1, 1932–1939. Edited by Jack Sutters. New York: Garland Publishing, 1990.

———. Vol. 2: Berlin Document Center, part 1. Edited by Henry Friedlander and Sybil Milton. New York: Garland Publishing, 1992.

———. Vol. 2: Berlin Document Center, part 2. Edited by Henry Friedlander and Sybil Milton. New York: Garland Publishing, 1992.

———. Vol. 3: Central Zionist Archives, Jerusalem, 1933–1939. Edited by Francis R. Nicosia. New York: Garland Publishing, 1990.

———. Vol. 7: Columbia University Library, New York: The James G. McDonald Papers. Edited by Karen J. Greenberg. New York: Garland Publishing, 1990.

———. Vol. 10: American Jewish Joint Distribution Committee, New York, part 1. Edited by Sybil Milton and Frederick D. Bogin. New York: Garland Publishing, 1995.

———. Vol. 17: American Jewish Committee, New York. Edited by Frederick D. Bogin. New York: Garland Publishing, 1993.

Augustine, Dolores L. "The Business Elites of Hamburg and Berlin." *Central European History* 24, no. 2 (1991): 132–46.

Baedeker, Karl. *Berlin and Its Environs.* Leipzig: Karl Baedeker, 1910.

————. *Northern Germany*. Leipzig: Karl Baedeker, 1925.

Bailey, Fred Arthur. *William Edward Dodd: The South's Yeoman Scholar*. Charlottesville: University Press of Virginia, 1997.

Baird, Jay W. "Horst Wessel, and the Myth of Resurrection and Return." *Journal of Contemporary History* 17, no. 4 (October 1982): 633–50.

Bankier, David. *The Germans and the Final Solution*. Oxford, U.K.: Blackwell, 1992.

Bendiner, Robert. *The Riddle of the State Department*. New York: Farrar & Rinehart, 1942.

Benson, Robert L. "The Venona Story." Center for Cryptologic History. Washington, D.C.: National Security Agency, n.d.

Berard, Armand. *Un Ambassadeur se Souvient: Au Temps du Danger Allemand*. Paris: Plon, 1976.

Bielenberg, Christabel. *The Past Is Myself*. London: Chatto & Windus, 1968.

Birchall, Frederick T. *The Storm Breaks: A Panorama of Europe and the Forces That Have Wrecked Its Peace*. New York: Viking, 1940.

Bredohl, Thomas M. "Some Thoughts on the Political Opinions of Hans Fallada: A Response to Ellis Shookman." *German Studies Review* 15, no. 3 (October 1992): 525–45.

Breitman, Richard, and Alan M. Kraut. *American Refugee Policy and European Jewry, 1933–1945*. Bloomington: Indiana University Press, 1987.

Brenner, David. "Out of the Ghetto and into the Tiergarten: Redefining the Jewish Parvenu and His Origins in Ost und West." *German Quarterly* 66, no. 2 (Spring, 1993): 176–94.

Brownell, Will, and Richard N. Billings. *So Close to Greatness: A Biography of William C. Bullitt*. New York: Macmillan, 1987.

Brysac, Shareen Blair. *Resisting Hitler: Mildred Harnack and the Red Orchestra*. New York: Oxford University Press, 2000.

Bullitt, William C. *For the President: Personal and Secret*. Edited by Orville H. Bullitt. New York: Houghton Mifflin, 1972.

Bullock, Alan. *Hitler: A Study in Tyranny*. 1962. New York: HarperCollins, 1991 (reprint).

Burden, Hamilton T. *The Nuremberg Party Rallies: 1923–39*. New York: Frederick A. Praeger, 1967.

Burke, Bernard V. *Ambassador Frederic Sackett and the Collapse of the Weimar Republic, 1930–1933*. New York: Cambridge University Press, 1994.

Casey, Steven. "Franklin D. Roosevelt, Ernst 'Putzi' Hanfstaengl and the 'S-Project,' June 1942–June 1944." *Journal of Contemporary History* 35, no. 3 (2000): 339–59.

Cerruti, Elisabetta. *Ambassador's Wife*. New York: Macmillan, 1953.

Chapman, Cynthia C. "Psychobiographical Study of the Life of Sigrid Schultz."

Ph.D. diss., Florida Institute of Technology, 1991. (In Schultz Papers, Wisconsin Historical Society.)

Chernow, Ron. *The Warburgs*. New York: Random House, 1993.

Clyman, Rhea. "The Story That Stopped Hitler." In *How I Got That Story*. Edited by David Brown and W. Richard Bruner. Overseas Press Club of America. New York: Dutton, 1967.

Cockburn, Claud. *In Time of Trouble*. London: Rupert Hart-Davis, 1956.

Conradi, Peter. *Hitler's Piano Player: The Rise and Fall of Ernst Hanfstaengl, Confidant of Hitler, Ally of FDR*. New York: Carroll and Graf, 2004.

Craig, Gordon A., and Felix Gilbert, eds. *The Diplomats, 1919–1939*. Princeton, N.J.: Princeton University Press, 1953.

Crankshaw, Edward. *Gestapo: Instrument of Tyranny*. New York: Viking, 1956.

Dallek, Robert. *Democrat and Diplomat: The Life of William E. Dodd*. New York: Oxford University Press, 1968.

Dalley, Jan. *Diana Mosley*. New York: Knopf, 2000.

Dallin, David J. *Soviet Espionage*. New Haven, Conn.: Yale University Press, 1955.

Daum, Andreas W., and Christof Mauch, eds. *Berlin-Washington, 1800–2000: Capital Cities, Cultural Representation, and National Identities*. Cambridge, U.K.: Cambridge University Press, 2005.

"Death of Auntie Voss." *Time*, April 9, 1934.

de Jonge, Alex. *The Weimar Chronicle: Prelude to Hitler*. New York: Paddington, 1978.

Deschner, Gunther. *Heydrich: The Pursuit of Total Power*. 1977. London: Orbis, 1981 (reprint).

Diels, Rudolf. *Lucifer Ante Portas*. Munich: Deutsche Verlags-Anstalt, 1950.

Dimitroff, Georgi. *Dimitroff's Letters from Prison*. London: Victor Gollancz, 1935.

Dippel, John V. H. *Bound Upon a Wheel of Fire: Why So Many German Jews Made the Tragic Decision to Remain in Nazi Germany*. New York: Basic Books, 1996.

Divine, Robert. "Franklin D. Roosevelt and Collective Security, 1933." *The Mississippi Valley Historical Review* 48, no. 1 (June 1961): 42–59.

Dodd, Christopher J., and Lary Bloom. *Letters from Nuremberg: My Father's Narrative of a Quest for Justice*. New York: Crown Publishing, 2007.

Dodd, Martha. *Through Embassy Eyes*. New York: Harcourt, Brace, 1939.

———. *Sowing the Wind*. New York: Harcourt, Brace, 1945.

Dodd, William E. *Ambassador Dodd's Diary*. Edited by William E. Dodd Jr. and Martha Dodd. New York: Harcourt, Brace, 1941.

Engelmann, Bernt. *In Hitler's Germany: Daily Life in the Third Reich*. Translated by Krishna Winston. New York: Pantheon, 1986.

Evans, Richard J. *The Third Reich in Power 1933–1939*. New York: Penguin, 2005.

———. *The Third Reich at War 1939–1945*. London: Allen Lane / Penguin, 2008.

Feingold, Henry L. *The Politics of Rescue: The Roosevelt Administration and the Holocaust, 1938–1945*. New Brunswick, N.J.: Rutgers University Press, 1970.

Ferdinand, Prince Louis. *The Rebel Prince: Memoirs of Prince Louis Ferdinand of Prussia*. Chicago: Henry Regnery, 1952.

Fest, Joachim C. *The Face of the Third Reich*. New York: Pantheon, 1970.

Flynn, Edward J. *You're the Boss*. New York: Viking Press, 1947.

François-Poncet, Andre. *The Fateful Years: Memoirs of a French Ambassador in Berlin, 1931–38*. Translated by Jacques Le Clercq. London: Victor Gollancz, 1949.

Friedlander, Henry. "Step by Step: The Expansion of Murder, 1939–1941." *German Studies Review* 17, no. 3 (October 1994): 495–507.

Friedrich, Otto. *Before the Deluge: A Portrait of Berlin in the 1920's*. New York: Harper & Row, 1972.

Fritzsche, Peter. *Life and Death in the Third Reich*. Cambridge, Mass.: Harvard University Press/Belknap Press, 2008.

Fromm, Bella. *Blood and Banquets: A Berlin Social Diary*. New York: Harper, 1942.

Fuller, Helga. *Don't Lose Your Head: Coming of Age in Berlin, Germany 1933–1945*. Seattle: Peanut Butter Publishing, 2002.

Gallo, Max. *The Night of Long Knives*. Translated by Lily Emmet. New York: Harper and Row, 1972.

Gay, Peter. *My German Question: Growing Up in Nazi Berlin*. New Haven, Conn.: Yale University Press, 1998.

Gellately, Robert. "The Gestapo and German Society: Political Denunciation in the Gestapo Case Files." *Journal of Modern History* 60, no. 4 (December 1988): 654–94.

———. *The Gestapo and German Society: Enforcing Racial Policy, 1933–1945*. Oxford, U.K.: Clarendon Press, 1990.

Gellman, Irwin F. *Secret Affairs: Franklin Roosevelt, Cordell Hull, and Sumner Welles*. Baltimore: Johns Hopkins University Press, 1995.

"Germany: Head into Basket." *Time*, January 22, 1934.

Gilbert, G. M. *Nuremberg Diary*. New York: Farrar, Straus, 1947.

Gill, Anton. *A Dance Between Flames: Berlin Between the Wars*. London: John Murray, 1993.

Gisevius, Hans Bernd. *To the Bitter End*. New York: Houghton Mifflin, 1947.

Glass, Derek, Dietmar Rosler, and John J. White. *Berlin: Literary Images of a City*. Berlin: Erich Schmidt Verlag, 1989.

Goebel, Rolf J. "Berlin's Architectural Citations: Reconstruction, Simulation, and the Problem of Historical Authenticity." *PMLA* 118, no. 5 (October 2003): 1268–89.

Goeschel, Christian. *Suicide in Nazi Germany.* Oxford, U.K.: Oxford University Press, 2009.

Goldensohn, Leon. *The Nuremberg Interviews.* Edited by Robert Gellately. New York: Alfred A. Knopf, 2004.

Goran, Morris. *The Story of Fritz Haber.* Norman: University of Oklahoma Press, 1967.

Gordon, Mel. *Voluptuous Panic: The Erotic World of Weimar Berlin.* Los Angeles: Feral House, 2006.

Graebner, Norman A. *An Uncertain Tradition: American Secretaries of State in the Twentieth Century.* New York: McGraw-Hill, 1961.

Graf, Christoph. "The Genesis of the Gestapo." *Journal of Contemporary History* 22, no. 3 (July 1987): 419–35.

Graves, Robert, and Alan Hodge. *The Long Week End: A Social History of Great Britain 1918–1939.* New York: Macmillan, 1941.

Grey-Turner, Elston. "Pages from a Diary." *British Medical Journal* 281, no. 6256 (December 20–27, 1980): 1692–95.

Grimm, Jacob, and Wilhelm Grimm. *Grimm's Fairy Tales.* 1912. New York: Barnes and Noble, 2003 (reprint).

Grunberger, Richard. *A Social History of the Third Reich.* London: Weidenfeld and Nicolson, 1971.

Guerin, Daniel. *The Brown Plague.* Translated by Robert Schwartzwald. Durham, N.C.: Duke University Press, 1994.

Hamilton, Gerald. *Mr. Norris and I: An Autobiographical Sketch.* London: Allan Wingate, 1956.

Hammond, Mason. "The War and Art Treasures in Germany." *College Art Journal* 5, no. 3 (March 1946): 205–18.

Hancock, Eleanor. "Only the Real, the True, the Masculine Held Its Value: Ernst Röhm, Masculinity, and Male Homosexuality." *Journal of the History of Sexuality* 8, no. 4 (April 1998): 616–41.

Hanfstaengl, Ernst. *Unheard Witness.* Philadelphia: Lippincott, 1957.

Hartley, Marsden, et al. "Letters from Germany, 1933–1938." *Archives of American Art Journal* 25, nos. 1–2 (1985): 3–28.

Haynes, John Earl, Harvey Klehr, and Alexander Vassiliev. *Spies: The Rise and Fall of the KGB in America.* New Haven, Conn.: Yale University Press, 2009.

———. *Venona: Decoding Soviet Espionage in America.* New Haven, Conn.: Yale University Press, 1999.

Heineman, John L. *Hitler's First Foreign Minister: Constantin Freiherr von Neurath, Diplomat and Statesman.* Berkeley: University of California Press, 1979.

Herzstein, Robert Edwin. *Roosevelt and Hitler*. New York: Paragon House, 1989.

Hitler, Adolf. *Hitler's Table Talk, 1941–1944*. Translated by Norman Cameron and R. H. Stevens. London: Weidenfeld & Nicholson, 1953.

Holborn, Hajo, ed. *Republic to Reich: The Making of the Nazi Revolution*. Translated by Ralph Manheim. New York: Pantheon, 1972.

Hughes, Matthew, and Chris Mann. *Inside Hitler's Germany: Life Under the Third Reich*. Dulles, Va.: Brassey's Inc., 2000.

Hull, Cordell. *The Memoirs of Cordell Hull*. Vol. 1. New York: Macmillan, 1948.

Ickes, Harold L. *The Secret Diary of Harold L. Ickes: The First Thousand Days, 1933–1936*. New York: Simon and Schuster, 1953.

Isherwood, Christopher. *The Berlin Stories*. 1935. New York: New Directions Publishing, 1954 (reprint).

———. *Down There on a Visit*. New York: Simon and Schuster, 1962.

Jaskot, Paul B. "Anti-Semitic Policy in Albert Speer's Plans for the Rebuilding of Berlin." *Art Bulletin* 78, no. 4 (December 1996): 622–32.

Jelavich, Peter. *Berlin Cabaret*. Cambridge, Mass.: Harvard University Press, 1993.

Johnson, Eric A., and Karl-Heinz Reuband. *What We Knew: Terror, Mass Murder, and Everyday Life in Nazi Germany*. New York: Basic Books, 2005.

Jonas, Manfred. "Pro-Axis Sentiment and American Isolationism." *Historian* 29, no. 2 (February 1967): 221–37.

Jones, Larry Eugene. "Edgar Julius Jung: The Conservative Revolution in Theory and Practice." *Central European History* 21, no. 2 (June 1988): 142–74.

Kaes, Anton, Martin Jay, and Edward Dimendberg, eds. *The Weimar Republic Sourcebook*. Berkeley: University of California Press, 1994.

Kaltenborn, H. V. *Fifty Fabulous Years*. New York: G. P. Putnam's Sons, 1950.

Kater, Michael H. "Forbidden Fruit? Jazz in the Third Reich." *American Historical Review* 94, no. 1 (February 1989): 11–43.

Kent, Madeleine. *I Married a German*. New York: Harper and Brothers, 1939.

Kershaw, Ian. *Hitler: 1889–1936: Hubris*. New York: W. W. Norton, 1998.

———. *The 'Hitler Myth': Image and Reality in the Third Reich*. Oxford, U.K.: Clarendon Press, 1987.

———. *Popular Opinion and Political Dissent in the Third Reich: Bavaria 1933–1945*. Oxford, U.K.: Clarendon Press, 1983.

Kessler, Harry. *Berlin in Lights: The Diaries of Count Harry Kessler (1918–1937)*. Translated and edited by Charles Kessler. 1961. New York: Grove Press, 1999 (reprint).

Kessler, Lauren. *Clever Girl: Elizabeth Bentley, the Spy Who Ushered in the McCarthy Era*. New York: HarperCollins, 2003.

Klemperer, Victor. *I Will Bear Witness: A Diary of the Nazi Years, 1933–1941*. Translated by Martin Chalmers. New York: Random House, 1998.

————. *The Language of the Third Reich: LTI—Lingua Tertii Imperii.* Translated by Martin Brady. 1957. London: Athlone Press, 2000 (reprint).

Koehl, Robert Lewis. *The Black Corps: The Structure and Power Struggles of the Nazi SS.* Madison: University of Wisconsin Press, 1983.

Koeves, Tibor. *Satan in Top Hat: The Biography of Franz von Papen.* New York: Alliance, 1941.

Krausnick, Helmut, Hans Buchheim, Martin Broszat, and Hans-Adolf Jacobsen. *Anatomy of the SS State.* Translated by Richard Barry, Marian Jackson, and Dorothy Long. New York: Walker and Co., 1968.

Kraut, Alan M., Richard Breitman, and Thomas W. Imhoof. "The State Department, the Labor Department, and German Jewish Immigration, 1930–1940." *Journal of American Ethnic History* 3, no. 2 (Spring 1984): 5–38.

Kreuder, Friedemann. "Hotel Esplanade: The Cultural History of a Berlin Location." *PAJ: A Journal of Performance and Art* 22, no. 2 (May 2000): 22–38.

Lachmund, Jens. "Exploring the City of Rubble: Botanical Fieldwork in Bombed Cities in Germany after World War II." *Osiris* 2nd Series, vol. 18 (2003): 234–54.

Ladd, Brian. *The Ghosts of Berlin.* Chicago: University of Chicago Press, 1997.

Langer, William L. and S. Everett Gleason. *The Challenge to Isolation, 1937–1940.* New York: Harper and Brothers, 1952.

Le Tissier, Tony. *Race for the Reichstag: The 1945 Battle for Berlin.* London: Frank Cass, 1999.

Lipstadt, Deborah E. *Beyond Belief: The American Press and the Coming of the Holocaust 1933–1945.* New York: Free Press, 1986.

Litten, Irmgard. *Beyond Tears.* New York: Alliance, 1940.

Lochner, Louis P. "Round Robins from Berlin." *Wisconsin Magazine of History* 50, no. 4 (Summer 1967): 291–336.

Ludecke, Kurt. *I Knew Hitler.* New York: C. Scribner's Sons, 1938.

MacDonogh, Giles. "Otto Horcher, Caterer to the Third Reich." *Gastronomica* 7, no. 1 (Winter 2007): 31–38.

Magi, Aldo P. "Thomas Wolfe and Mildred Harnack-Fish: The 1935 Berlin Interview." *Thomas Wolfe Review* 27, nos. 1 and 2 (2003): 100–114.

Mali, Joseph. "The Reconciliation of Myth: Benjamin's Homage to Bachofen." *Journal of the History of Ideas* 60, no. 1 (January 1999): 165–87.

Mann, Klaus. *The Turning Point: The Autobiography of Klaus Mann.* 1942. London: Otto Wolff, 1984 (reprint).

Mann, Thomas. *Diaries 1918–1939.* Translated by Richard and Clara Winston. New York: Harry N. Abrams, 1982.

Manvell, Roger, and Heinrich Fraenkel. *Dr. Goebbels: His Life and Death.* New York: Simon and Schuster, 1960.

McDonough, Frank. "The *Times*, Norman Ebbut and the Nazis, 1927–37." *Journal of Contemporary History* 27, no. 3 (July 1992): 407–24.

Merkl, Peter H. *The Making of a Stormtrooper*. Princeton, N.J.: Princeton University Press, 1980.

Messersmith, George. "Present Status of the Anti-Semitic Movement in German." Sept. 21, 1933. German Historical Institute. http://germanhistory docs.ghi-dc.org/.

Metcalfe, Philip. *1933*. Sag Harbor, N.Y.: Permanent Press, 1988.

Miller, Douglas. *Via Diplomatic Pouch*. New York: Didier, 1944.

Milton, Sybil. "The Context of the Holocaust." *German Studies Review* 13, no. 2 (May 1990): 269–83.

Mowrer, Edgar Ansel. *Germany Puts the Clock Back*. New York: William Morrow, 1939.

———. *Triumph and Turmoil: A Personal History of Our Time*. New York: Weybright and Talley, 1968.

Mowrer, Lilian T. *Journalist's Wife*. New York: William Morrow, 1937.

Myers, Denys P., and Charles F. Ransom. "Reorganization of the State Department." *American Journal of International Law* 31, no. 4 (October 1937): 713–20.

Nabokov, Vladimir. *Speak Memory*. 1947. New York: Vintage, 1989 (reprint).

Noakes, Jeremy, and Geoffrey Pridham. *Documents on Nazism, 1919–1945*. New York: Viking, 1975.

Norden, Peter. *Madam Kitty: A True Story*. Translated by J. Maxwell Brownjohn. London: Abelard-Schuman, 1973.

Nowell, Elizabeth. *Thomas Wolfe: A Biography*. Garden City, N.Y.: Doubleday, 1960.

Offner, Arnold A. *American Appeasement: United States Foreign Policy and Germany, 1933–1938*. Cambridge, Mass.: Harvard University Press, 1969.

Orlow, Dietrich. *The History of the Nazi Party: 1933–1945*. Pittsburgh: University of Pittsburgh Press, 1973.

Owings, Alison. *Frauen: German Women Recall the Third Reich*. New Brunswick, N.J.: Rutgers University Press, 1993.

Papen, Franz von. *Memoirs*. Translated by Brian Connell. New York: E. P. Dutton, 1953.

Peukert, Detlev J. K. *Inside Nazi Germany*. Translated by Richard Deveson. New Haven, Conn.: Yale University Press, 1987.

Phillips, William. "The Reminiscences of William Phillips." Oral History Collection. New York: Columbia University, 1952.

———. *Ventures in Diplomacy*. Portland, Maine: privately printed, 1952.

Phipps, Sir Eric. *Our Man in Berlin: The Diary of Sir Eric Phipps, 1933–1937*. Edited by Gaynor Johnson. Hampshire, U.K.: Palgrave Macmillan, 2008.

Pundeff, Marin. "Dimitrov at Leipzig: Was There a Deal?" *Slavic Review* 45, no. 3 (Autumn 1986): 545–49.

Reynolds, Quentin. *By Quentin Reynolds*. New York: McGraw-Hill, 1963.

Riasanovsky, Nicholas V. *A History of Russia*. 2nd ed. New York: Oxford University Press, 1969.

Richie, Alexandra. *Faust's Metropolis: A History of Berlin*. New York: Carroll and Graf, 1998.

Ritchie, J. M. *German Literature Under National Socialism*. Totowa, N.J.: Barnes and Noble, 1983.

Roosevelt, Franklin Delano. *F.D.R.: His Personal Letters*. Vol. 1, 1928–1945. New York: Duell, Sloan and Pearce, 1950.

Roper, Daniel C. *Fifty Years of Public Life*. New York: Greenwood Press, 1968.

Roth, Joseph. *What I Saw: Reports from Berlin 1920–1933*. Translated by Michael Hofmann. 1996. New York: W. W. Norton, 2003 (reprint).

Rürup, Reinhard, ed. *Topography of Terror: Gestapo, SS and Reichssicherheitshauptamt on the "Prinz-Albrecht-Terrain," A Documentation*. Translated by Werner T. Angress. Berlin: Verlag Willmuth Arenhovel, 1996.

Ryan, Cornelius. *The Last Battle*. New York: Simon and Schuster, 1966.

Schacht, Hjalmar. *My First Seventy-Six Years*. Translated by Diana Pyke. London: Allan Wingate, 1955.

Schleunes, Karl A. *The Twisted Road to Auschwitz: Nazi Policy Toward German Jews, 1933–1939*. Urbana: University of Illinois Press, 1970.

Schueler, H. J. *Hans Fallada: Humanist and Social Critic*. Paris: Mouton, 1970.

Schultz, Sigrid. "Hermann Goering's 'Dragon from Chicago.'" In *How I Got That Story*. Edited by David Brown and W. Richard Bruner. Overseas Press Club of America. New York: Dutton, 1967.

———. Oral History Interview. William E. Wiener Oral History Library. American Jewish Committee. New York Public Library, 1974.

Schwarz, Angela. "British Visitors to National Socialist Germany: In a Familiar or in a Foreign Country?" *Journal of Contemporary History* 28, no. 3 (July 1993): 487–509.

Shafir, Shlomo. "George S. Messersmith: An Anti-Nazi Diplomat's View of the German-Jewish Crisis." *Jewish Social Studies* 35, no. 1 (January 1973): 32–41.

Sherwood, Robert E. *Roosevelt and Hopkins*. New York: Harper and Brothers, 1950.

Shirer, William L. *Berlin Diary*. 1941. New York: Black Dog & Leventhal, 2004 (reprint).

———. *The Rise and Fall of the Third Reich*. 1959. New York: Simon and Schuster, 1990 (reprint).

———. *Twentieth Century Journey: A Memoir of a Life and the Times*. Vol. 2, *"The Nightmare Years, 1930–1940."* New York: Little, Brown, 1984.

Spear, Sheldon. "The United States and the Persecution of the Jews in Germany, 1933–1939." *Jewish Social Studies* 30, no. 4 (October 1968): 216.

Spender, Stephen. *World Within World*. New York: Harcourt, Brace, 1951.

Stackelberg, Roderick, and Sally A. Winkle. *The Nazi Germany Sourcebook*. London: Routledge, 2002.

Stern, Fritz. *Einstein's German World*. Princeton, N.J.: Princeton University Press, 1999.

Stiller, Jesse H. *George S. Messersmith: Diplomat of Democracy*. Chapel Hill: University of North Carolina Press, 1987.

Strasser, Otto, and Michael Stern. *Flight from Terror*. New York: Robert M. McBride, 1943.

Stowell, Ellery C. "A Square Deal for the Foreign Service." *American Journal of International Law* 28, no. 2 (April 1934): 340–42.

Swett, Pamela E. *Neighbors and Enemies: The Culture of Radicalism in Berlin, 1929–1933*. Cambridge, U.K.: Cambridge University Press, 2004.

"Their Excellencies, Our Ambassadors." *Fortune Magazine*, April 1934, pp. 108–22.

Tobias, Fritz. *The Reichstag Fire: Legend and Truth*. Translated by Arnold J. Pomerans. London: Secker and Warburg, 1963.

Turnbull, Andrew. *Thomas Wolfe*. New York: Charles Scribner's Sons, 1967.

Turner, Henry Ashby, Jr. "Fallada for Historians." *German Studies Review* 26, no. 3 (October 2003): 477–92.

———. "Two Dubious Third Reich Diaries." *Central European History* 33, no. 3 (2000): 415–22.

Ullstein, Herman. *The Rise and Fall of the House of Ullstein*. New York: Simon and Schuster, 1943.

Urofsky, Melvin I. *A Voice That Spoke for Justice*. Albany: State University of New York Press, 1982.

U.S. Department of Justice, Federal Bureau of Investigation. Venona File. Washington, D.C.

U.S. Department of State. *Peace and War: United States Foreign Policy, 1931–1941*. Washington, D.C.: U.S. Government Printing Office, 1943.

Vanden Heuvel, Katrina. "Grand Illusions." *Vanity Fair* 54, no. 9 (September 1991): 220–56.

Waln, Nora. *Reaching for the Stars*. New York: Little, Brown, 1939.

Warburg, James P. *The Long Road Home*. Garden City, N.Y.: Doubleday, 1964.

Weil, Martin. *A Pretty Good Club: The Founding Fathers of the U.S. Foreign Service*. New York: W. W. Norton, 1978.

Weinberg, Gerhard L. *The Foreign Policy of Hitler's Germany: Diplomatic Revolution in Europe 1933–36*. Chicago: University of Chicago Press, 1970.

Weinstein, Allen, and Alexander Vassiliev. *The Haunted Wood: Soviet Espionage in America—the Stalin Era.* New York: Random House, 1999.

Weiss, Stuart L. "American Foreign Policy and Presidential Power: The Neutrality Act of 1935." *Journal of Politics* 30, no. 3 (August 1968): 672–95.

Weitz, Eric D. *Weimar Germany.* Princeton, N.J.: Princeton University Press, 2007.

Wheaton, Eliot Barculo. *Prelude to Calamity: The Nazi Revolution 1933–35.* Garden City, N.Y.: Doubleday, 1968.

Wheeler-Bennett, John W. *The Nemesis of Power: The German Army in Politics 1918–1945.* London: Macmillan, 1953.

———. *Wooden Titan: Hindenburg in Twenty Years of Germany History 1914–1934.* New York: William Morrow, 1936.

White, John Campbell. "The Reminiscences of John Campbell White." Oral History Collection. Columbia University, n.d.

Williams, Jenny. *More Lives than One: A Biography of Hans Fallada.* London: Libris, 1998.

Wise, Stephen. *Challenging Years.* New York: G. P. Putnam's, 1949.

———. *The Personal Letters of Stephen Wise.* Edited by Justine Wise Polier and James Waterman Wise. Boston: Beacon Press, 1956.

———. *Stephen S. Wise: Servant of the People.* Edited by Carl Hermann Voss. Jewish Publication Society of America, 1970.

Wolfe, Thomas. *The Letters of Thomas Wolfe to His Mother.* Edited by C. Hugh Holman and Sue Fields Ross. 1943. New York: Charles Scribner's Sons, 1968 (reprint).

———. *The Notebooks of Thomas Wolfe.* Edited by Richard S. Kennedy and Paschal Reeves. Vol. 2. Chapel Hill: University of North Carolina Press, 1970.

———. *Selected Letters of Thomas Wolfe.* Edited by Elizabeth Nowel and Daniel George. London: Heinemann, 1958.

Wolff, Marion Freyer. *The Shrinking Circle: Memories of Nazi Berlin, 1933–1939.* New York: UAHC Press, 1989.

Wrench, Evelyn. *I Loved Germany.* London: Michael Joseph, 1940.

Zuckmayer, Carl. *A Part of Myself.* Translated by Richard and Clara Winston. New York: Harcourt Brace Jovanovich, 1970.

Zweig, Stefan. *The World of Yesterday.* 1943. London: Cassell, 1953 (reprint).

PHOTO CREDITS

INDEX

I walked across the snowy plain of the Tiergarten—a smashed statue here, a newly planted sapling there; the Brandenburger Tor, with its red flag flapping against the blue winter sky; and on the horizon, the great ribs of a gutted railway station, like the skeleton of a whale. In the morning light it was all as raw and frank as the voice of history which tells you not to fool yourself; this can happen to any city, to anyone, to you.

—Christopher Isherwood,
Down There on a Visit

ABOUT THE AUTHOR

ERIK LARSON is the author of *The Devil in the White City*, *Thunderstruck*, *Isaac's Storm*, and other works of nonfiction. He has written for a variety of national magazines and is a former staff writer for the *Wall Street Journal* and *Time*. He lives in Seattle with his wife, three daughters, and an old British sports car named Mrs. Peel.